CW01649260

Leica R

COMPENDIUM

Leica R

COMPENDIUM

Handbook of the Leica R System

by Jonathan Eastland

Jonathan Eastland

HOVE BOOKS

Leica R Compendium
Handbook of the Leica R System
Jonathan Eastland
First English Edition May 1995

British Library Cataloguing-in-Publication Data

A catalogue record for this book is available from the British Library

ISBN 1 897802 07 2

Copyright © 1995 by Hove Collectors Books and Jonathan Eastland

The right of Jonathan Eastland to be identified as the author of this work has been asserted by him in accordance with the Copyright, Designs and Patents Act 1988.

Front and back covers photographed by the author

Editor: *Dennis Laney*

Design and typesetting: *Facing Pages*
Tel: 01273 881572 Fax: 01273 881750

Printed in Wales by *Macdermott & Chant Ltd., Welshpool*

All enquiries to the Publishers:

Hove Books
34 Church Road, Hove
East Sussex BN3 2GJ, England

except for:

U.K. Book Trade to:

Fountain Press Ltd.
2 Gladstone Road
Kingston-upon-Thames
Surrey, KT1 3HD

U.S.A. to:

The Saunders Group
21 Jet View Drive
Rochester, N.Y. 14624-4996
Fax: (716)328-5078

Canada to:

Amplis Foto Inc.
22 Telson Road
Markham, Ontario L3R 1ES
Fax: (416)477-2502

All rights reserved. No part of this book may be reproduced, translated, stored in a retrieval system, or transmitted in any form or by any means, electronic, mechanical, photocopying, recording or otherwise, without prior permission in writing from the publishers.

This publication has not been sponsored in any way by Leica Camera GmbH. Information and data in this book is correct to the best of the author's and publisher's knowledge. Because use of this information is beyond the author's and publisher's control, all liability is disclaimed.

Acknowledgements

In endeavouring to ascertain the difference between fact and fiction with regard to many aspects of the Leicaflex and Leica R systems, it has been necessary to call upon a wealth of knowledge more expert than my own outside the perimeters of already published data.

My ignorance of certain details and what must have seemed to some an insatiable curiousity regarding the marque, has been tolerated, fed and watered by many people who have freely given their time and attention to my demands in a way that has made assembling this volume all the more enjoyable. H.G. von Zydowitz and Nicole Rubbe at Leica GmbH in Solms must be singled out for their enthusiasm in responding to my often numerous and detailed questions. Likewise, Alan Clark in the service department of Leica Camera UK Ltd, has been a fount of knowledge, ready and willing to put me straight whenever I have called. Thanks are also due to Uli Hintner, Peter Melder, Philip Bass, Janet Hills and Brenda Baker at Leica Camera UK Ltd., for their enthusiasm and support of this and other projects as well as for the loan of equipment and photographs whenever it and they were required.

Obtaining new photographs of equipment has not always been easy but I am indebted to Jonathan Harris of Fieldgrass & Gale, London, for supplying the illustrations of rare items and to Michael Pritchard of Christie's for supplying the photograph of R6 number 1750000. My thanks also to Paul Williams, Arthur Crick and Chris Dewhurst for allowing me to raid their extensive stocks at Hove and to Robin Bisiker for modelling it. A special word of thanks to Marc Thelisson at Angénieux of Saint Heand in France for suppling the drawings of Pierre Angénieux's masterpiece, the 45-90mm, f/2.8 zoom.

Inevitably, immediate family and friends have been forced to endure the dominant theme of any and every discussion centred on photography. Frequent sacrifices have been made in the name of Leica! Their interest and unselfish support has been a great encouragement, along with the many letters received from Leicaphiles around the world demanding to know when this volume would be finished. To one and all, thank you, merci, gracias, danke!

My Publisher joins me in thanking Leica Camera GmbH for the use of their registered trademarks.

ABSORBAN®	REPROVIT®
ELMAR®	SUMMARIT®
ELMARIT®	SUMMAR®
LEICA®	SUMMARON®
LEICAFLEX®	SUMMICRON®
LEICAMETER®	SUMMILUX®
MILAR®	TELEVIT®
NOCTILUX®	TELYT®
PHOTAR®	VISOFLEX®

PHOTOGRAPHY

Leica R single lens reflex cameras and Leica M rangefinder cameras fitted with the Visoflex mirror box and objectives were used to make the pictorial photographs for this book. The cameras used were Leica R4s MOD2, Leica R6, Leica M6 and Leica M4P. A Novoflex rapid focus unit fitted with Novflexar 400mm, f/5.6 with Leica R-mount and Visoflex mount was also used. Many of these photographs were originally exposed using colour negative or colour reversal emulsions: where they appear in this volume as black-and-white reproductions, the conversion was made at the scanning stage from the original prints or transparencies prior to film positives being produced. Uncredited product photographs are from the publisher's archives, in most cases previously supplied by Ernst Leitz Wetzlar or Leica Camera GmbH. Except where otherwise credited, all other photographs in this work are the copyright and property of Jonathan Eastland.

Contents

Introduction

A greater part of my working life has been spent making photographs in an environment which, even in its calmest moments, has wreaked havoc on most of my cameras. Those which have escaped destruction by sea water and salt air corrosion have been specially made for the task. From time to time people have suggested various devices which could be employed to protect equipment, including of course custom made waterproof casings. However, the great thing about modern single lens reflex cameras is their versatility; once such a camera is enveloped in polythene or bolted into an underwater housing, that advantage is lost.

Some years ago, I was assigned to cover what eventually turned out to be the longest running sports event ever. The 1986 America's Cup regatta held in the Indian Ocean off Perth was sailed virtually every day for almost five months. For those of us working to produce pictures for the world's newspapers, the event proved to be a testing environment for different marques of photographic equipment. Only one photographer, as far as I know, used Leica cameras.

Roger Garwood's Leica R4's were often subjected to the worst weather imaginable. Shortly after my arrival in Australia, he and I shared a powerful 45ft raceboat tender and headed out off Perth to shoot a practice race. It was blustery; a large Indian Ocean swell soon had the launch slamming into every crest as we chased our quarry. Shooting from the flybridge was a little like being the wrong side of a waterfall. In next to no time, everything was wringing wet. Only on rare occasions during the assignment did we enjoy the idyllic conditions seen on picture post cards.

As the weeks went by, photographers adjusted to the weather conditions. There were many write-offs and many, many, niggling faults in need of repair. The service centres of two other well known marques were never without a back log of equipment in need of a total strip-down. As far as I know, Garwood's Leicas continued to function faultlessly to the end.

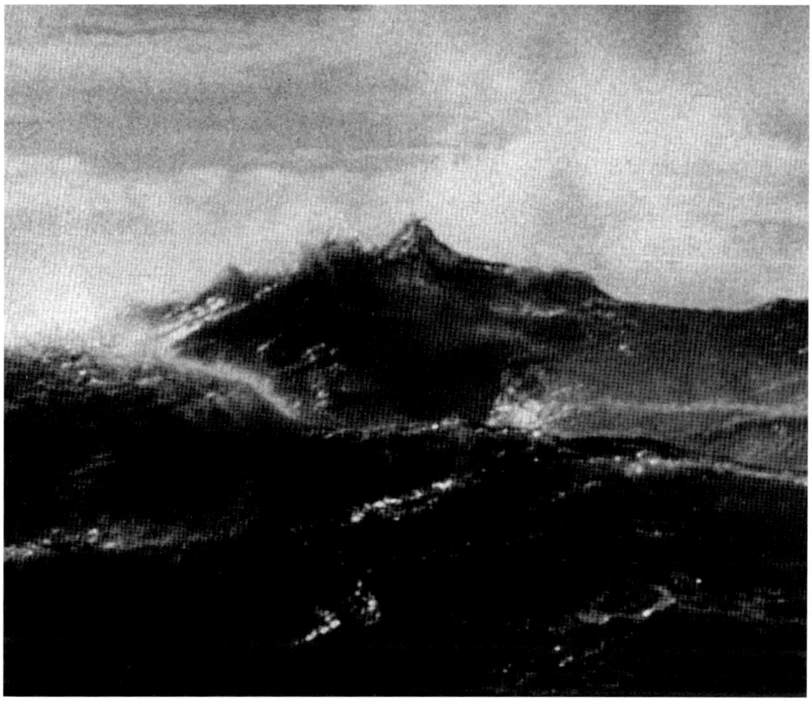

Fig. 1. Gale, Bay of Biscay.

Reliability is a function of painstaking attention to design detail, the choice of raw materials for construction and manufacturing practice. In the case of Leica R-type cameras, as well as earlier Leicaflex cameras, none of these criteria are in doubt. The public relations machine of Leica Camera GmbH has, in its inexorable grinding, furnished all those who would like to know, of virtually every aspect of camera and lens manufacture. In parts of this book, the *aficionado* and the novice may also discover lesser known facts regarding the manufacturer's attitude toward design and build quality.

Aside from such minutia as the finish on machine screws and the accuracy with which they are countersunk into a bottom plate, one of the most striking aspects concerns the silky smooth operating features of the shutter and instant return mirror. The demands on engineering quality of this aspect can be traced back through the line of SLRs to the very first Leicaflex which appeared more than thirty five years ago.

The shutter of earlier cameras was a horizontal cloth focal plane type, more complex than the type found in the M-series rangefinder cameras. Four winding drums instead of three, two for each blind, and a complicated braking system were employed. The Leicaflex SL2 became so expensive to build that it was said at one time the camera actually cost more to manufacture than it could be sold for.

With the introduction of the R3 camera, a completely new vertical-run, metal-bladed shutter, designed by E.Leitz and manufactured by Copal of Japan, made its debut. As well as increasing the electronic flash synchronising speed, the new shutter/mirror operation heightened the sense of 'smoothness' associated with Leicaflexes. The latest R7 camera uses an electronically controlled stepless shutter made by Seikosha. The mechanical R6.2 and its predecessor, the R6, are fitted with a shutter designed and built by Leica. The operating 'feel' between the two models is virtually indistinguishable. It is nevertheless, a particular 'feel', difficult to describe in words, but one which has some significance for the connoisseur of fine equipment.

One facet with which this 'feel' is closely associated has to do with vibration absorption. In the Leica R-models, the instant return mirror damping and shutter braking mechanism effectively reduce vibration to a level where, in experienced hands, it is perfectly possible to make hand-held, shake-free exposures at shutter speeds as low as 1/8th second with certain lenses. This is made possible by the shutter design which opens downwards as the mirror is raised. Any residual vibration of the first curtain is absorbed by the camera mass through to the body of the user. The second curtain is closed milliseconds before the mirror returns to its normal position.

In an age when virtually every other 35mm SLR manufacturer has concentrated its efforts almost exclusively in the direction of auto focus, Leica Camera GmbH remains dedicated to a philosophy of camera design and operation which permits total user control. This is not just a superficial nod in the direction of nostalgia. Leica R-type cameras offer a level of electronic mode operation and metering sophistication of unmatched accuracy. But it was not this way in the beginning.

It could be said that the year 1959 became a turning point for 35mm photography. It was then that the Japanese company Nippon Kogaku K.K. introduced the Nikon F single lens reflex camera and lens system which would, in a very short time, justifiably become established as the professional photographer's standard tool. Indeed, even today and in spite of the fact that Nikon were slow to match some of the electronic focus advances made by other companies in the 1980's, the marque still maintains its number one slot.

Ernst Leitz, then based in Wetzlar, had long since recognized the limitations of their world famous rangefinder camera for certain applications. In 1933 the company developed an accessory reflex mirror box - PLOOT - which permitted the use of medium and long telephoto lenses and focusing bellows. It was originally offered with a flip-up mirror and swing-in magnifier, together with a 200mm, f/4.5 Telyt lens. PLOOT was refined and became VISOFLEX I (OZYXO) in 1952, refined again in 1958 with the MkII and followed by the Mk IIa and Mk III versions.

The PLOOT reflex mirror box was developed and built to such a level of sophistication in respect of what could be achieved photographically, that some experts have suggested the accolade of first single lens reflex camera was wrongly awarded to the Kine Exakta of 1935, or latterly, to the Russian 35mm Sportcamera manufactured by Gomz the previous year. The Leica camera of this period was both a sophisticated rangefinder and reflex camera which could alternate between modes almost as quickly as lenses could be changed - a true 'system' camera. Once in a while, when I can be fairly certain I will not need a complete R-camera outfit on assignment, I pack my Visoflex with its additional lenses. For very long-lens work, its bright, finely ground glass screen is still the equal of the most modern reflex cameras.

The VISOFLEX, however, was not to everyone's liking. As early as 1954, when the first of the M-series rangefinder cameras - the M3 - was launched, it was clear to some that the days of the rangefinder camera might be numbered. Rumblings from the Far East would soon be transformed into an explosion of volcanic dimension.

Walther Benser was for many years a roving ambassador for Leitz. His speciality, involved, complex, audio-visual slide shows and lectures were designed to promote the company's products. He recalled an occasion when the subject of reflex cameras was virtually taboo at Wetzlar. Walther had returned to Wetzlar after a highly successful lecture tour of the United States, visiting some 58 cities during 1955 and'56. The reason for his visit to the factory on this occasion was to report the findings of his tour to the then head of Leitz, Ludwig Leitz, an avid rangefinder enthusiast.

"I began to tell him how Leitz of New York had suggested to me that there was a great demand in America for a Leica reflex camera. Ludwig stopped me before I could explain in any detail. He simply said, 'I will not hear any word about the flex camera' and with that he ended our meeting."

In the main, Leitz company philosophy then viewed the encroaching hoards of Japanese reflex imports with some scepticism, believing that serious photographers would remain loyal to the rangefinder concept. This was indeed to prove true in some respects at a much later date, when in 1976 Leitz made the decision to briefly discontinue rangefinder production. That production of the M4-2 camera was begun at all two years later was largely due to worldwide pressure from enthusiastic amateur photographers and professional photojournalists.

Establishing exactly when a decision was made to proceed with R & D on Leica's first SLR has been virtually impossible. Advocates of the 'flex' like Wilhelm Albert, who was head of the photo design department, must have had some persuasive arguments, because by 1958 preliminary work on an outline specification had begun. A year later, a numberless prototype Leicaflex complete with selenium meter was completed. However, in the same year, the photographer and explorer Wilfred Thesiger exchanged his Leica II rangefinder model for a Leicaflex and three lenses, a Summicron 50mm, and two Elmarits, a 35mm and a 90mm which he took with him on his travels to the Northern Territories of Kenya in 1960. Leitz had a policy at this time of handing out numberless models to well known photographers for field testing. Thesiger was already very well known for his exploits in some of the world's worst environments. Leitz would not have given this man the only prototype to use on an expedition which both parties knew would extend over several years.

But several prototypes of the Leicaflex were built around this time, including at least one model with a removable pentaprism. There was apparently some doubt as to whether a production model with interchangeable heads would be successful, partly because the problem of excluding dust could not be resolved, and partly because it was thought more important the camera should incorporate some form of through-the-lens metering.

Nikon had found a way to incorporate both features in the Nikon F tional Fresenel lens. But the camera lacked a true TTL meter. Instead, a CdS type measuring a relatively narrow angle of view through its collecting lens was mounted on the front face of the pentaprism housing.

Leitz certainly had the know-how, even at this early stage, to produce a reflex camera which would at least be the equal of the best Japanese models. That they did not take advantage of their technological

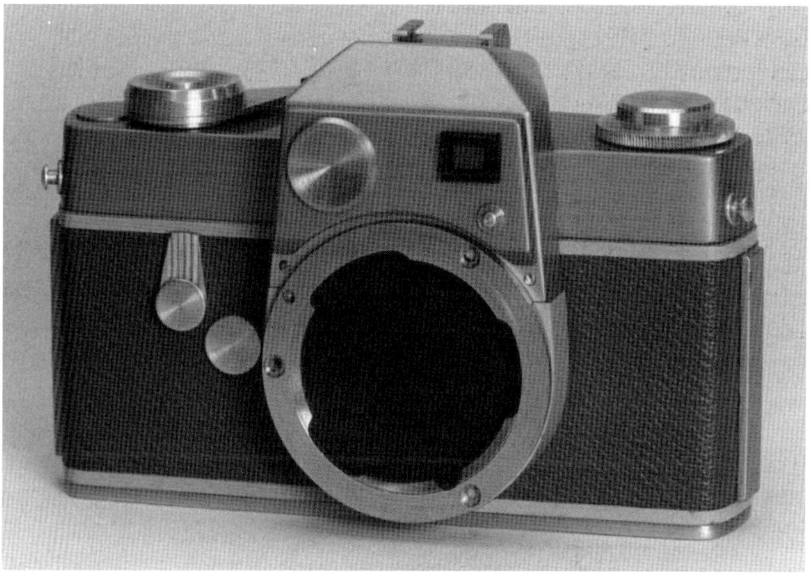

Fig. 2. An early prototype of the Leicaflex, probably dating from 1957/8. The lens mount flange has only 3 retaining screws and the locking bayonet pin position is visible at 10 o'clock. The strap lugs are interesting and suggest a special strap security system in the planning. *Leica Camera GmbH Archive*

camera by 1965, the year the first Leicaflex was launched. The Nikon was already well into its sixth year of production and both the earlier selenium and CdS external metering heads had been replaced by a device which measured light from the focusing screen. Beautifully built as it was, the first Leicaflex was already more or less obsolete before it was launched. The final design featured a fixed pentaprism which incorporated the brightest viewing system then available. It used a prism with a convex underside acting as a collecting lens instead of the conven- position in the field might seem odd, but company philosophy dictated from the top was firmly at variance with those in other departments.

Ludwig Lietz, one of the three sons of Ernst Leitz II, had joined the company in 1925. By the outbreak of the war in 1939 he had become responsible for research and development. Indeed, it was largely due to Ludwig's enormous talent for the marriage of aesthetics and engineering which produced the Leica M3 as well as many other postwar products. His executive position and stance toward the rangefinder camera caused a split on the issue of whether or not the company should invest the huge sums necessary in the R & D of a reflex camera. One has to remember that at this time in the 1950's, the second world war had not long ended.

Japanese industry benefitted hugely from allied financial assistance immediately after the war. Companies there tended to imitate western designs rather than innovate. Nikon for example, who until this time were engaged solely in lens manufacture, copied the Zeiss Contax rangefinder camera, incorporating its best features along with some of those of the Leica camera. Success for both the name of the company and its products was assured in very short order - compared with the length of time it had taken Leitz to establish its reputation - by the advent of the Korean war.

Two famous photojournalists of the time, David Douglas Duncan and Horace Bristol, both working for *Life* magazine and *en route* to Korea through Japan, discovered almost by accident that Nikon had produced a number of very high quality objectives. The two were permitted to visit the factory and purchase sets of lenses for use with their screw thread Leicas. When Duncan eventually returned to the United States, he had the Nikkor lenses tested by the Eastern Optical Co. *Life* magazine purchased entire outfits of Nikkor lenses on the strength of Duncan's work and the tests. The story was related by Jacob Deschin writing in the *New York Times* of 10th December 1950 and almost overnight Nikon became a household word in photographic circles.

Still struggling to re-establish their prewar position of eminence, the Leica image was dealt a serious body blow by the story in the USA. The introduction of the M3 in 1954 did much to redress the situation. The design was well ahead of its time and well over a quarter million cameras were produced during its ten year life, more than any other model in the Leica range. However, almost 60% of the total was manufactured in the first five years from launch. There was no doubt of the M3's popularity amongst serious amateurs and photojournalists, but the wider market eluded Leitz in spite of substantial advertising promotions and the introduction of subsequent rangefinder models. Production figures declined gradually over the next six years as sales were gradually hit harder and harder by the effects of aggressive Japanese marketing techniques in Europe and the U.S.

By 1958, The German camera industry, a pre-war giant in global export terms, was already experiencing a recession. The postwar economic miracle, or 'Wirtschaftswunder', while impressive, was no match for the rapid expansion of Japan's photographic industry. By 1962, American imports of Japanese equipment had grown appreciably, outstripping Germany by 25%. An association of thirteen West German photographic manufacturers, of which Leitz was one, called Camera Industries of West Germany, seemed pathetically ineffectual against the might of the JCIA (Japanese Camera Industries Association) which, with a membership of some forty five manufacturers, represented the bulk of the country's industry. This association was launched with an ambitious programme of joint marketing, publicity and servicing for Japanese camera exports. It was not successful in every endeavour, particularly the latter; nonetheless, its effect was devastating and the rest as they say, is history.

The Leicaflex evolved slowly into a superlative machine as the SL2, but the winds of change had been blowing through the company for several years before production of that model ceased. In 1970, Leitz signed an agreement for technological co-operation with the Minolta Camera Co. The Leica CL compact rangefinder camera, designed by Leitz and built by Minolta, which appeared in 1973, was one of the first products of that marriage and proved highly successful during its short three-year life.

A number of Minolta objectives, remanufactured in Osaka to Leitz specification, were also produced to boost the range for the Leicaflex camera. In 1976 however, Leitz made their most dramatic move by unveiling a completely new single lens reflex camera which bore no resemblance to earlier models. It was in fact, a Minolta XE-1 camera body on which the top plate and a number of other minor features had been changed.

The R3 became the first of a long line of Leica R-type cameras, manufactured at first in 1976 in Wetzlar and then at the new Portugeuse factory facility at Villa Nova de Famalicao, largely from Minolta supplied parts. It proved to be a highly successful model, offering an improved range of features over the SL2 at a more affordable price. This camera also heralded the introduction of a range of single-cam lenses. Earlier Leicaflex types could be converted at moderate cost by service centres around the world. Compatability was maintained.

Four years later, Leitz launched the Leica R4. This was another Minolta based product and is the one on which all subsequent models of the R-camera have been based. Some enthusiasts were not well pleased at this continuing collaboration, but it was undoubtedly a major contribution to the financial survival of the company. The market place for Leica cameras was simply not large enough to justify or sustain the equally large investments in R & D necessary for self development. By taking an existing product and improving its specification in terms of features and build quality, funds for R & D into new objectives, which is what the company was justly famous for, could be maintained.

It is difficult to see how much further the Leica Camera Group can now go in refining existing models. Both the R7 and R6.2 represent state-of-the-art electronic exposure systems which enable the user to tackle virtually any photographic task with ease. A wide range of superb quality lenses, including a number of 'exotic' wide-aperture telephotos, motor drives and close-up accessories, projectors and enlarging equipment, complement these camera models.

In discussions I have had with Berndt Heinrichs at Leica, it is apparent that the company's intention is to pursue the philosophy of manufacturing equipment demanded by enthusiasts interested in upholding the traditional values of photography. Loosely translated, this means that for the present time at least, R & D will be concentrated on making minor improvements to the existing line-up of SLR models while exploring ways of expanding the range of accessories and lenses.

Some of these aims have been more than adequately met, especially in the realm of objectives. The Leica R-lens system now offers a varied and exciting range of focal lengths to meet almost every conceivable application. For example, four models of the 180mm focal length ranging in maximum aperture from f/2 to f/4. A superb range of exotic longer telephoto objectives exists to meet the requirements of the most demanding sports and wildlife photographers. The reproductive quality of these objectives is unmatched in the opinion of many professionals.

The current R7 represents the leading edge of electronic technology in a manually operated camera. The only areas which would benefit from improvement in my view concern those associated with electronic flash operation. Leica are aware of the problem – a relatively low flash synchronization speed - which cannot be solved without a major modification to the size of the camera body, or by employing a different shutter.

Leica Camera GmbH offer convincing arguments regarding the design of some R-camera accessories which I have often questioned over a period of time. One of these concerns the optional motor drive unit and grip. The Motor Drive-R is a robust piece of equipment manufactured for Leica by Eumig in Austria. I have used an R-drive for several years now and have grown to appreciate its precision and reliability. I remodelled the hand grip to suit my own operating techniques.

Leica maintain the advantage of such an add-on accessory is that it permits an option of use. They have a point and there have been many times when I have left the drive off the camera. On the other hand, applications for which a motor drive is often deemed essential, especially by professionals, would seem to demand a unit built into the camera. Modern miniature motors and improved small cell power sources have been well proven in other marques over more than a decade and it seems somewhat baffling that Leica have not taken advantage of this technology to offer a fully integrated motor driven camera body so far.

In a way, company arguments for not exploring this avenue seem at variance with an earlier concern regarding the ingress of foreign matter with interchangeable viewfinders on the Leicaflex. One of the plagues of accessory drives has always been the ingress of moisture

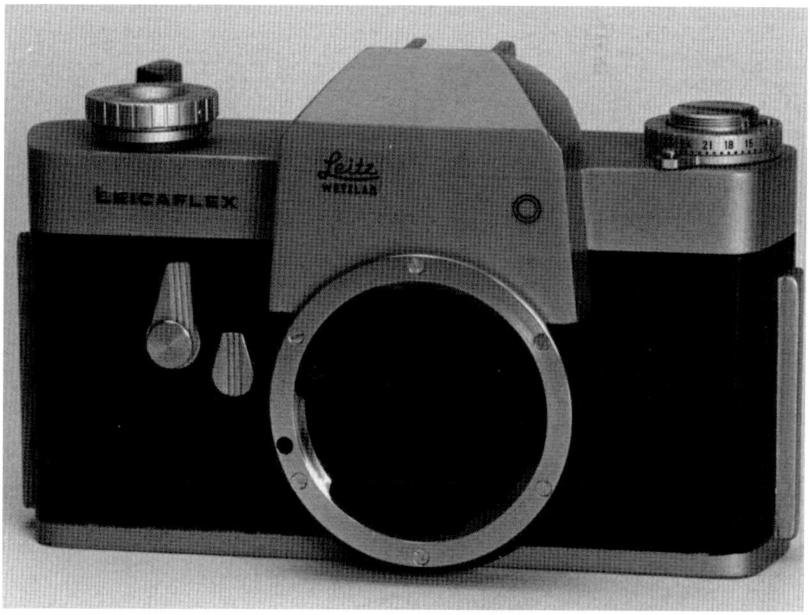

Fig. 3. A later prototype with finished furniture on what appears to be a roughly machined block of aluminium. The lens flange now has six retaining screws and the bayonet locking position has been changed. The problem of what type of light meter to use was obviously still causing some problems at this stage. The pentaprism housing is also more pointed. *Leica Camera GmbH Archive*

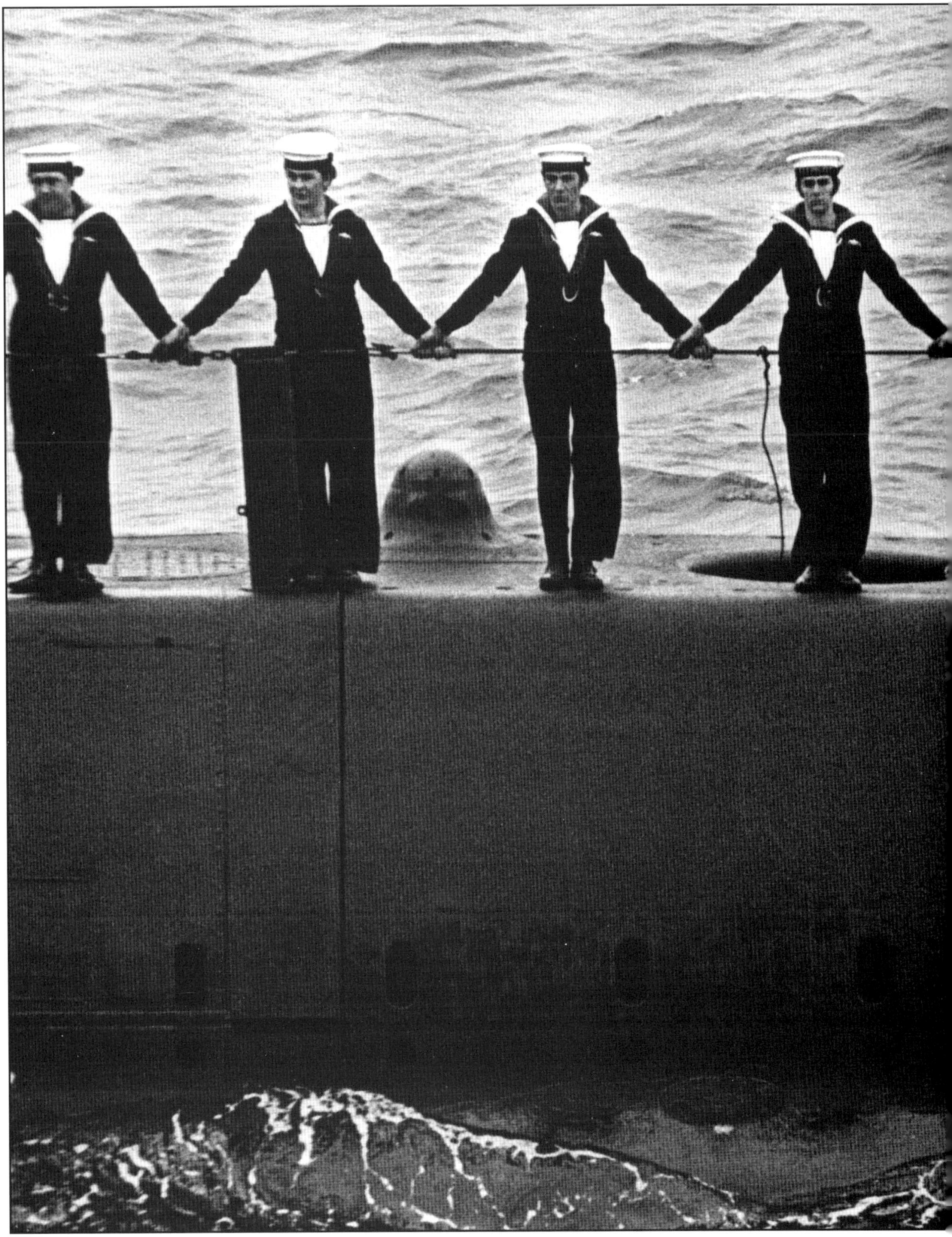

Submariners, Spithead Review. Ceremonial events present great opportunities for the Leica photographer.

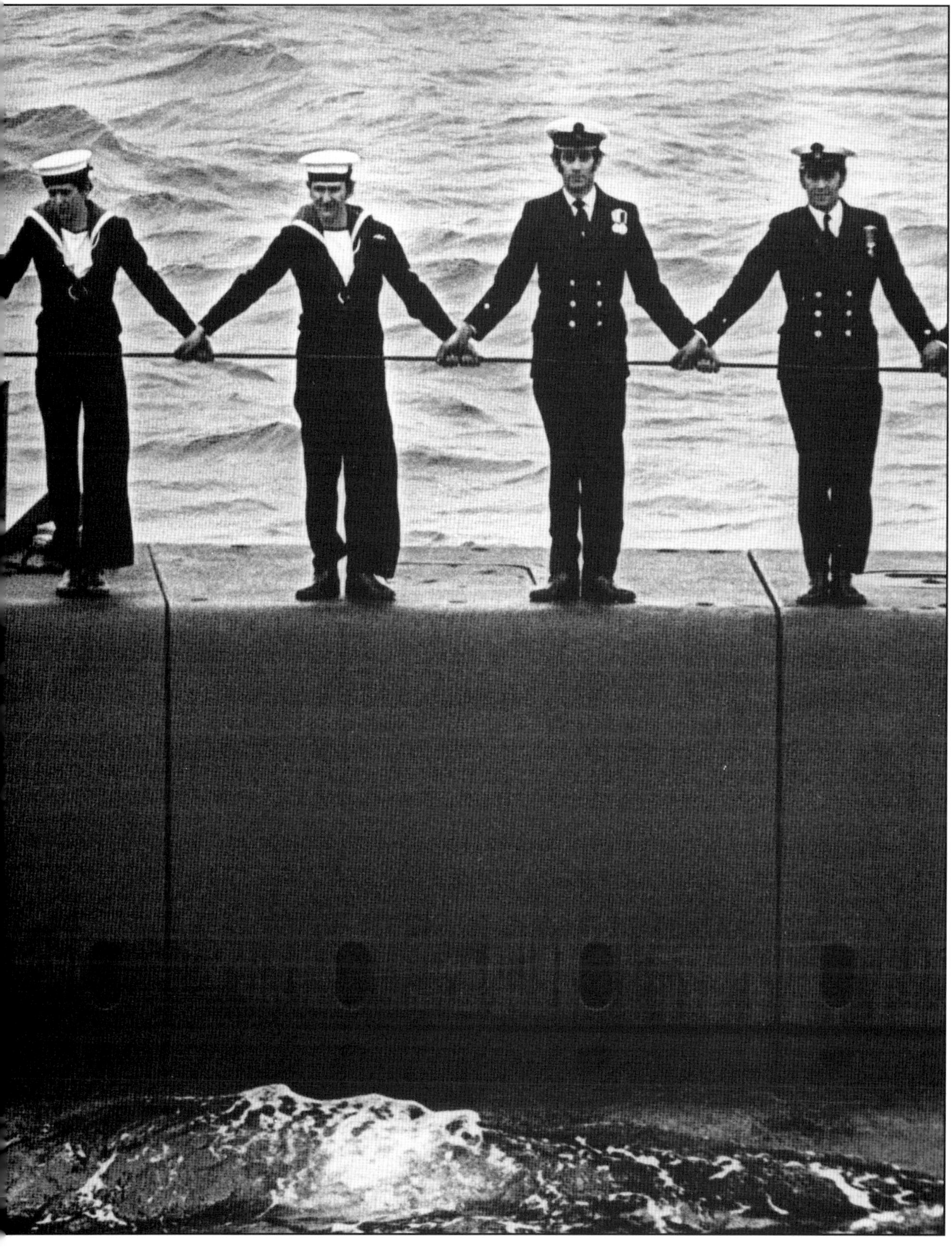

– in my specialist field a nightmare, but equally damaging for other photographers engaged in less demanding environments. Rain, snow, mud and sand can all play havoc with electrical connections.

Ideas concerning digital focus technology, first explored by Leitz in 1976 when the company exhibited a device employing LED's linked to a contrast control sensor, have been discussed as a possible addition to R-type cameras. Such a device might be useful in combination with medium to long telephoto lenses in low-light situations. One could hazard a guess as to the ulterior motives, if any, behind such a move. Could Leica possibly be thinking the unthinkable?

Hard-line traditionalists might baulk at the prospect of a Leica-R autofocus camera. My opinion is that sooner or later the company will be forced to look at this aspect with the seriousness which it deserves. From an economic point of view, sooner rather than later might ensure longevity in the face of continuing Far-Eastern bombardment. Proof that the technology exists and works is no longer needed. Evidence of just how successful and useful it can be is apparent to all discerning users of modern photography.

The Leica Camera Group are in the enviable position of being able to take advantage of their unique position, that of marrying modern 35mm reflex technology to superior optical glass. It is the latter to which so many photographers, amateur and professional, have ultimately turned because they want a recognisably superior product. The possibility that Leica will introduce a full blown autofocus SLR in the short term however, seems unlikely.

At the present time, R & D on a new improved R-model is well advanced. Leica is not currently exploring the possibility of a technological deal with Minolta on autofocus SLR cameras, so one must assume that any new R-model based on the existing chassis will only feature improved electronics for flash exposure, as well as focus confirmation features mentioned earlier. Faster flash synchronization speeds using the existing chassis will only be possible when an entirely new, faster running shutter is developed. The alternative would be to employ an existing shutter design in a deeper chassis.

For the time being at least, it is likely that Leica will continue to make minor improvements to their SLR range while endeavouring to expand their niche market. For the past few years, there seems to have been more emphasis on the expansion of the lens range; this is likely to continue with the introduction of new focal lengths as well as remodelled older types.

The recently introduced 28mm, f/2.8 Elmarit-R is a good example of the kind of forward thinking Leica have developed over the years. Even without the optical improvements to this objective, the redesigned mount incorporating a permanent lens hood would have been modification enough.

The current range of R-type lenses are described in detail in chapter 2. I have limited the information regarding some of the first Leicaflex objectives, although all the basic details pertaining to each model can be found in the Appendix tables. Modification to three-cam standard is no longer possible with all objectives, but this does not necessarily make them obsolete. Many of the first versions of current optics are, in my view, outstanding performers, easily capable of reproduction to exhibition size without noticeable deterioration in image quality.

The fact that these run-of-the-mill objectives are now quite dated also makes them more affordable. As newer models are released from the factory, so dealers' shelves begin to bulge with used stock. One of my all-time favourites is the 35mm, f/2 Summicron-R introduced for the Leicaflex SL in 1970. It is a rather heavy lens, weighing more than 500 grams, of nine-element construction with a distinctive large front element. The lens was recomputed to six elements in 1976, but this version lacks the subtlety of colour rendition apparent with the first version when photographing high contrast subjects.

In years to come, these older lenses will almost certainly increase in value as secondhand stocks now in mint condition diminish. The passing of time is a great leveller in this respect; items which are in daily use soon acquire a patina which reflects their history. A certain scarcity of those remaining in fine condition is bound to push the price up; so right now may be a good time for investment.

The 'flex' and 'R' cameras, lenses and accessories have only recently begun to acquire the collectable status bestowed on Leica rangefinder cameras for decades. Comparatively small numbers of individuals are engaged in searching out the rare and unusual. Models of R-type SLR's produced in small quantities are likely to have a lower value than a rangefinder of comparable age which has been produced in larger quantities. Specially engraved commemorative editions produced by Leitz and Leica, which celebrate certain company anniversaries, have so far maintained a higher premium than specially engraved models commissioned by third parties to mark some other event.

The dedicated collector of Leica SLR equipment will find much to inform and amuse in a number of other works, some of which are listed in the Bibliography at the back of this book. Photographers coming to the Leica R-system for the first time will find some of these other titles a useful aid when searching out older lenses, although it should be pointed out that some anomalies exist relative to certain aspects.

For some years now, Leica Camera GmbH have maintained a policy of not issuing yearly production figures of cameras and lenses, or their relevant serial numbers. One suspects that after the break-up of Ernst Leitz and the formation of Leica Camera GmbH, certain production tasks once undertaken traditionally at Leitz were no longer considered necessary or viable. Even in the case of Leitz, some of the figures produced associated with lens production for example, do not appear to be consistent when related to certain distinguishing marks and production dates. One example I have found is a 250mm, f/4 Telyt-R, manufactured in 1972 at the Midland, Ontario factory. This is a first version of this objective which should have a minimum focusing distance, according to one book, of 5m; on the other hand, another book states that the minimum focusing distance is 4.5m, and also gives a different date relating to when a second, recomputed version featured a closer focus distance engraved on the barrel. My particular example, however, besides a third cam, has a distance scale on which the minimum focus of 4m is clearly engraved - a detail which, if one is to believe the historical data published to date, could not have occurred prior to 1976 or 1978, according to which book you read.

The likelihood of this lens being factory released in the year of serial number allocation seems remote, though not impossible. A more likely explanation is that a batch of early front element retaining rings, with serial numbers already engraved, were used to complete manufacture of a later batch of Leitz modified objectives which may then have quietly been released on to dealers' shelves prior to, or just after official acknowledgement of the modifications.

As with some Leica rangefinder objectives, there are a number of first version reflex objectives which subsequently underwent minor design changes which were not publicly notified. The 135mm, f/2.8 Elmarit-R is another example of optical redesign which retained its original 1964 mount.

Minor detail changes such as these lend an added fascination to the hobby of Leica collecting. Of particular interest to specialists are the exceedingly rare items of which perhaps only one or two examples are known to exist outside of Leica's own museum collection. Small quantities of some early Leicaflex objectives were produced in silver chrome; their scarcity is reflected in the high prices asked by dealers, but that does not mean they cannot be found at more reasonable prices. An acquaintance who visited one recent English camera collectors' fair found a silver chrome 50mm hiding under its own reversed lens hood. It's owner, unaware of its origins, let it go for lunch money. Equally fascinating from a miniature engineering point of view are early complex objectives which, despite relatively small runs, are, for the moment at least, moderately priced. The Angénieux 45-90mm zoom is a fabulous example of 1960's cinematographic design adapted for still camera use. At best, only 2000 of these objectives were made by the French firm over a period of 13 years, but Angénieux readily admit today they have no accurate production figures and the likelihood is that far less than this number were actually produced.

I am sure one of the reasons photographers get 'hooked' into the Leica R-system has to do with the quality of the product. Non-users also voice the opinion that this 'quality' is overrated and that the new price of equipment bears no relation to the quality of the final image. I once used the same argument myself; having been privileged to own, use and review many different types of camera over a number of years. There is an element of truth in this when other perspectives are considered. There is, however, an overwhelming body of evidence to suggest that Leitz and Leica objectives have for long produced a superior quality image of neutral colour rendition across the whole range of lenses, in both the reflex and rangefinder systems, so that it is almost impossible to tell results from one system or the other apart. This and a number of other factors regarding reliability, longevity, metering accuracy, smoothness of operation of all components and the particular 'feel' of Leica equipment, which perhaps encourages a more measured approach to expressive photography, are ultimately what persuades some photographers to change horses and others to begin with the one system that has created a legend of unequalled dimension.

Jonathan Eastland,
Plerin, France, 1995.

CHAPTER 1

Leica Reflex Camera Models 1965-1995

Immediately following the second world war, the Leitz factory at Wetzlar hastened to restart production of the rangefinder cameras. All effort was concentrated in this direction, as well as to designing a radical new model which was to culminate with the launch of the M3 in 1954. The man in charge of camera development and design at this time, Willi Stein, had in his assistant Wilhelm Wiesner, a colleague of strong convictions and foresight.

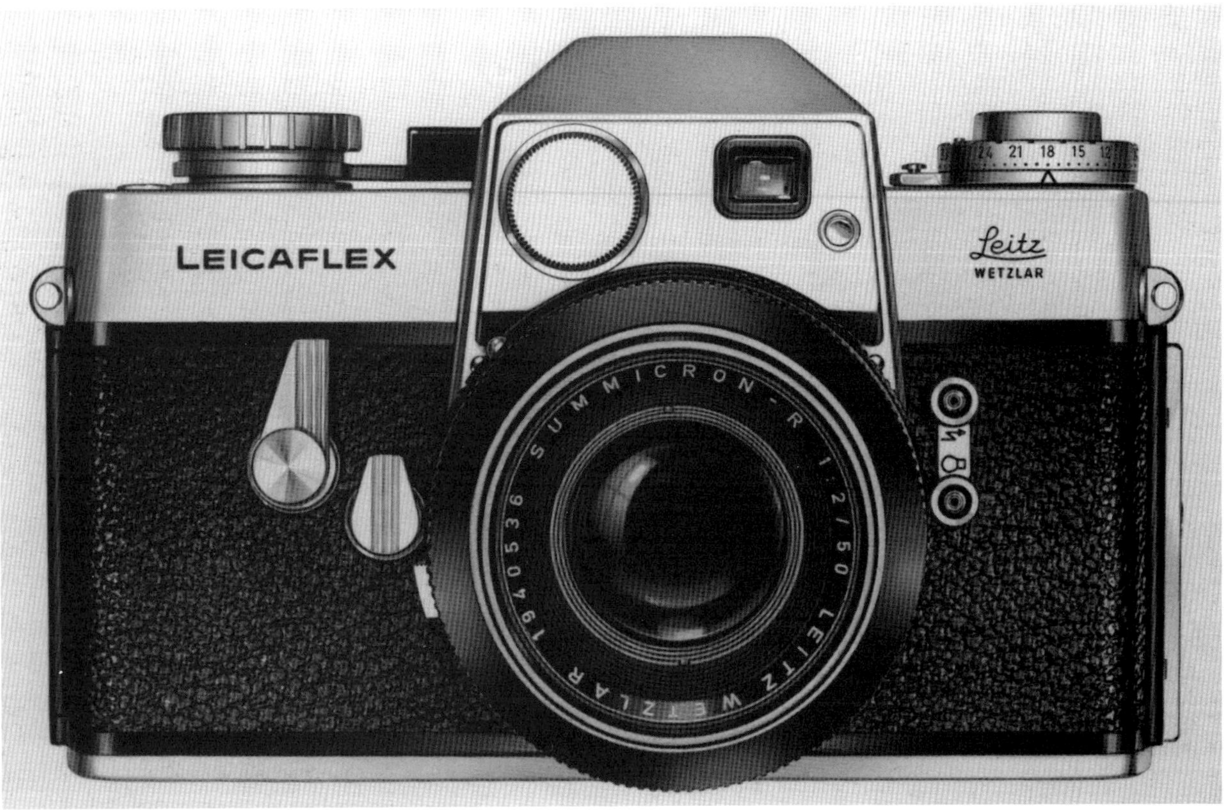

Fig. 6. The first Leicaflex, superbly airbrushed in this Ernst Leitz product photo and still one of the finest of single lens reflex cameras. Immensely durable and amazingly quiet in operation. *Leica Camera GmbH Archive*

While the Leitz hierarchy seemingly turned a blind-eye to developments in the Far East, a group of younger designers within the firm, including Karl Cloes and Paul Naumann, had begun work on a single lens reflex camera as early as 1952. Progress was painfully slow, exacerbated in part by the reluctance of executives to allocate funds to the project and also by the thorough investigation necessary into existing patents for 35mm single lens reflex design.

When it became obvious that the company would have to follow the reflex trend, especially after Walther Benser's successful United States lecture tours of 1955 and '56, Wiesner was put in charge of the design project team. He used Naumann's basic concept, drawn up in 1958, as the starting point. Features from these early drawings, including the pie-crust shaped exposure counter, were ultimately retained in most of the prototype cameras built from 1958 onwards, although Wiesner's later designs lodged in December 1965 oddly omitted the counter.

Ludwig Leitz was still unconvinced of the importance of the 'flex' camera to the continuing good

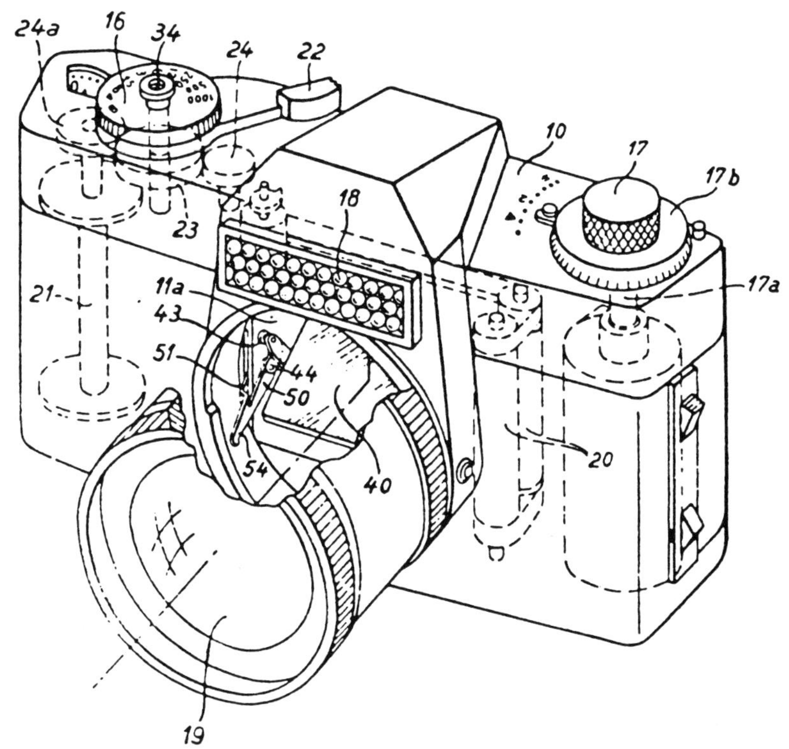

Fig. 4. In this 1958 drawing of the Leicaflex by Paul Naumann, only three curtain drums are shown. The specification was increased to four. Otherwise the sketch has many similarities to the final production models, but without the selenium cell. *Leica Camera GmbH Patent dept.*

health of the company; in particular his main concern centred on the feasibility of designing retrofocus standard and wide-angle objectives which could easily be focused using Fresnel type screens. In the majority of foreign single lens reflex cameras, focusing screens utilised groundglass with a finely etched Fresnel pattern. The quality varied from one marque to another and Leitz were anxious to ensure their first SLR maintained superior viewing facilities.

Leitz designers accomplished this by using a large viewfinder prism under which was a single light-gathering condenser lens. The focusing screen, an optical flat placed under the condenser, incorporated a central circular area of approximately 50 sq.mm containing more than 13,000 micro-prisms for rapid, accurate focusing, while the surrounding full-field prism was etched with an ultra-fine groundglass effect for overall sharpness control. Screen brightness

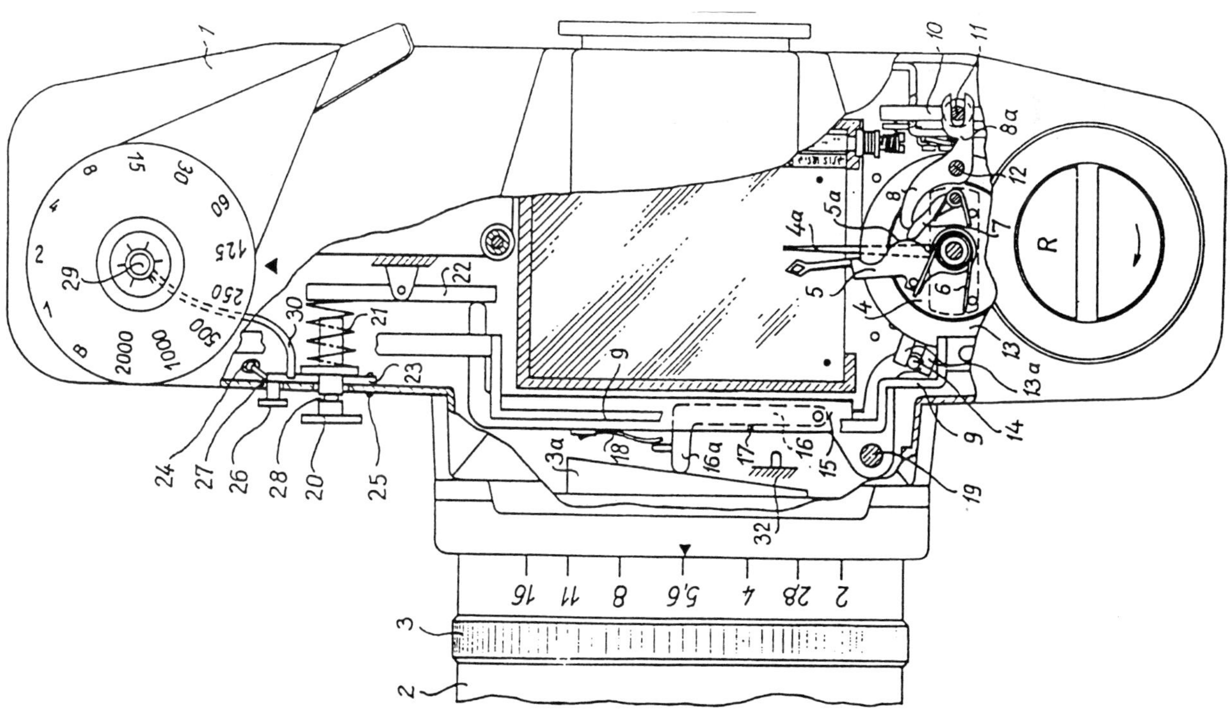

Fig. 5. This is one of Willi Wisesner's drawings for the Leicaflex showing a built-in light meter and automatic diaphragm control. Patent No. 1,295,360 filed on 22nd December 1965. *Leica Camera GmbH Patent dept.*

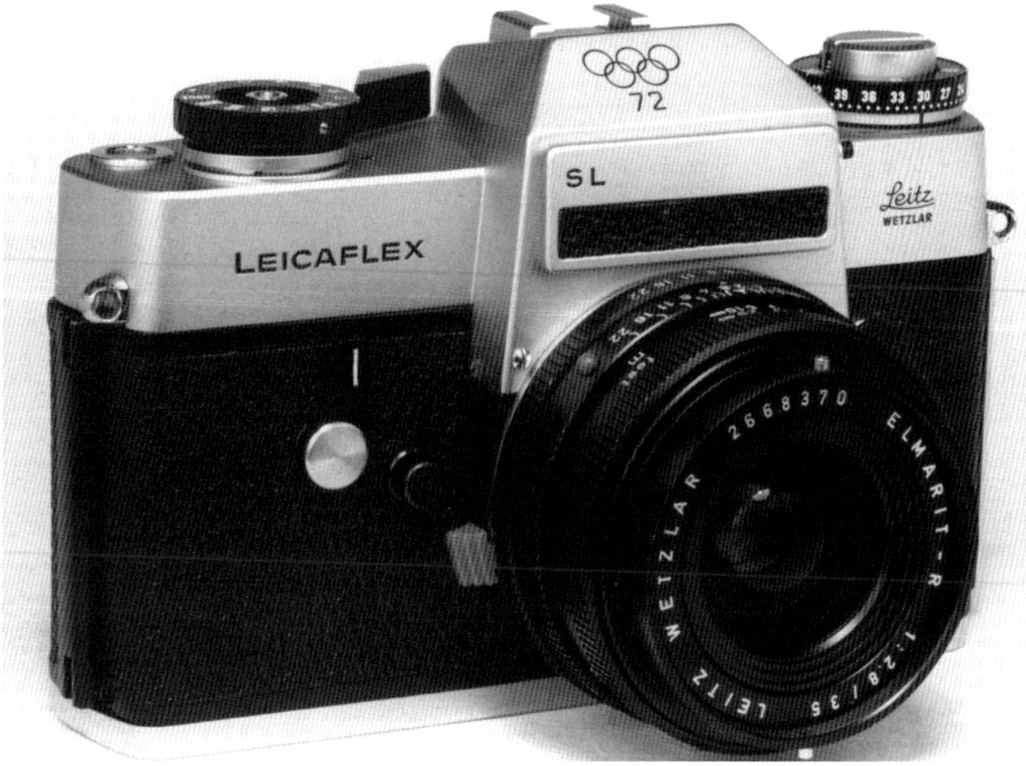

Fig. 7. The TTL metering Leicaflex SL with Olympic logo from 1972. Most silver chrome SL's had black anodised furniture (shutter speed dial, film speed set ring.) and the lens lock release catch was changed to a ridged red plastic type. *Fieldgrass & Gale/Jonathan Harris*

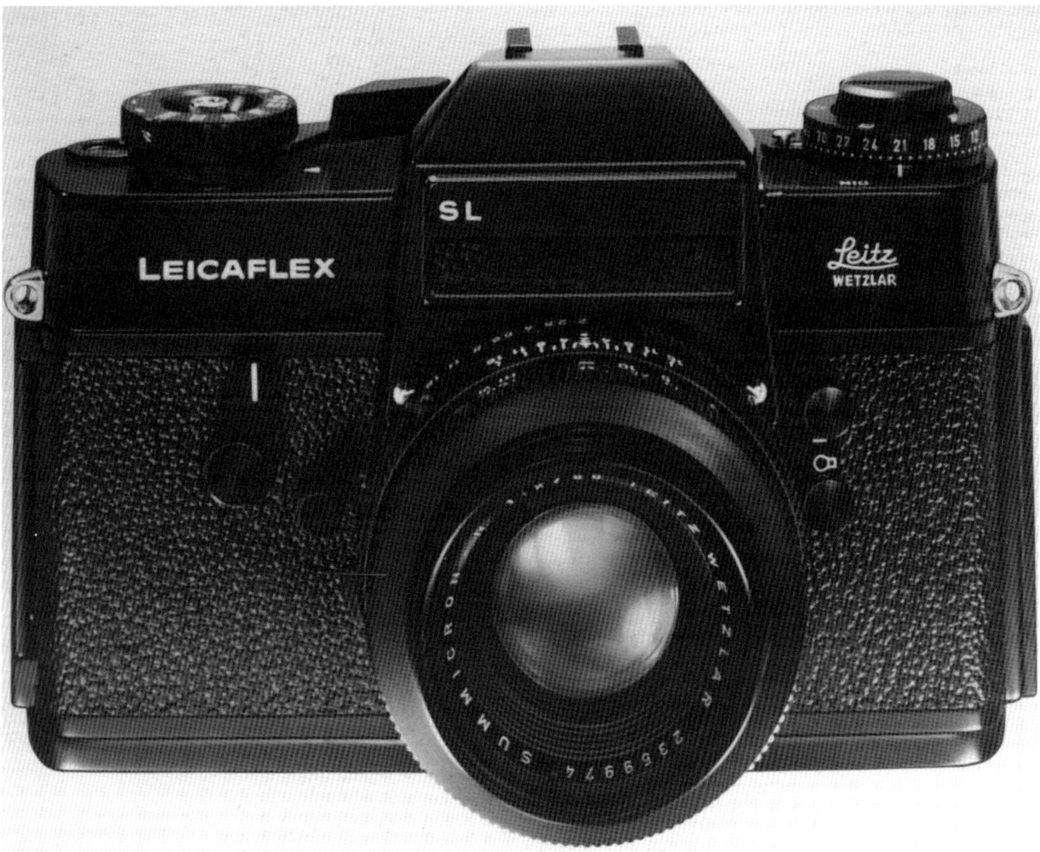

Fig. 8. Leicaflex SL finished in black enamel. *Leica Camera GmbH Archive*

in the first Leicaflex was excellent; in its time brighter than both the Pentax Spotmatic and the Nikon F, its main competitors. The Leicaflex SL viewing screen was even further improved. A large pentaprism was used for this model which allowed Leitz designers to give the underside a convex shape. In effect, the pentaprism acted as the light gathering device, improving brightness still further by eliminating the separate condenser used in the original Leicaflex.

Another problem revolved around the question of whether the exposure meter should be a true through-the-lens type. A number of patents already existed; one by August Abel for selective light metering was dated August 1939. A later version by Willi Goldberg for a similar system in a reflex camera using mirrors was lodged in 1960. Two years later, the Broschkes System employed a measuring cell on the front face of an SLR viewing pentaprism. The majority of prototype Leicaflex SLR's featured a selenium type exposure meter, the light gathering window of which was housed on the front face of the pentaprism. The vexed question of exposure metering seems to have remained unresolved right up to the point of public launch of the Leicaflex, by which time the metering system had advanced only to a narrow angle cadmium sulphide cell mounted above the lens.

The meter coverage approximated the field of view of a 90mm objective. Operation was straightforward enough, utilising a combination of shutter speed and f/stop with a match needle system visible in the viewfinder. The meter appears to have been a modification of the Leicameter-MR type developed for the M3 camera. When the Leicaflex was first launched, only four objectives were available for the camera

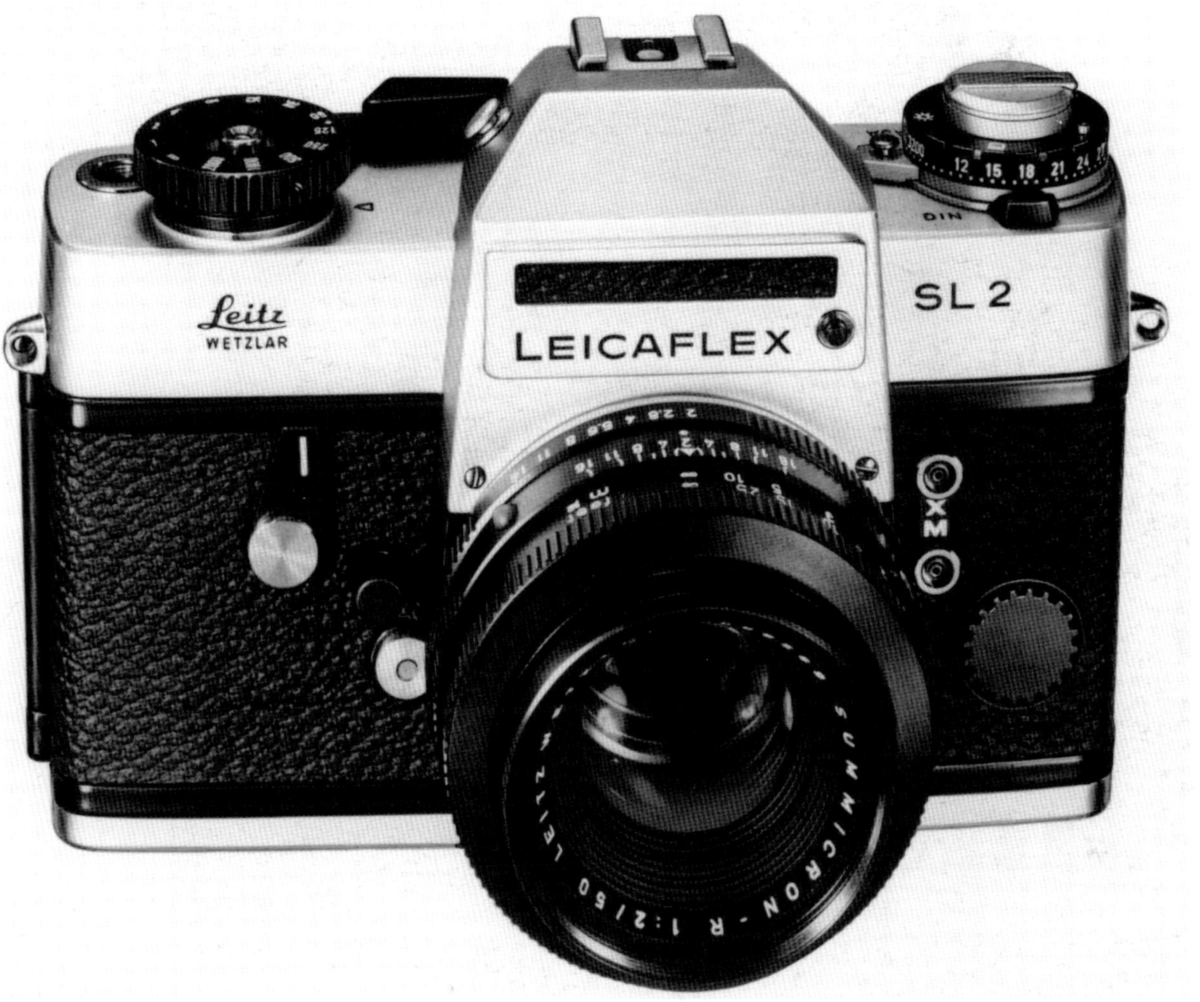

Fig. 9. Silver chrome version of the Leicaflex SL2. The lens lock release catch has been changed from the SL type, back to that used on the Leica M rangefinder cameras; battery location has moved to lower right and a safety catch has been fitted to the rewind lever back opening release.
Leica Camera GmbH Archive

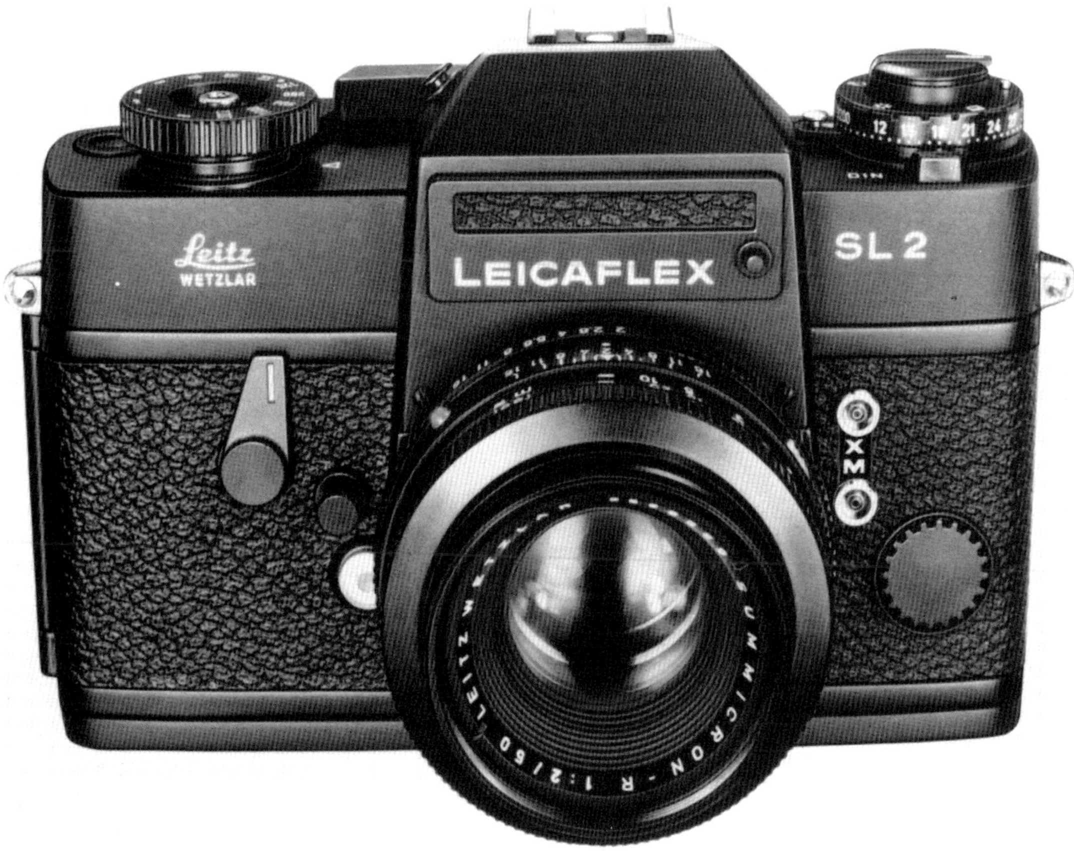

Fig. 10. Standard Leicaflex SL2 in black chrome.

with a focal length spread from 35mm to 135mm, so the meter, with its 27° angle of field, was ideally suited to cover most general subjects. More sophisticated metering of close-up subjects using focusing bellows was not possible with any degree of accuracy.

TTL or not, the Leicaflex Standard, as it later became known, was an advanced example of camera design and engineering. Great attention had been paid to improving the focal plane shutter mechanism employed in the rangefinder cameras. The Leicaflex featured a maximum shutter speed of 1/2000th second and a flash synchronization speed of 1/100th second, both speeds virtually unheard of in the most modern of foreign SLR's then infiltrating the U.S. market, where in 1966 some 3,000 Leicaflex cameras were sold.

Wiesner and his team had virtually ensured success for the camera, in spite of the metering problem, by incorporating a unique mirror damping and shutter braking system into the Leicaflex which gave it a special operating 'feel'. The user was immediately convinced of the possibility of making shake-free exposures at very slow shutter speeds without the aid of a tripod or other support. This is an aspect of Leica engineering which has remained with all the reflex cameras through to the present-day R6.2 and R7.

Ludwig Leitz' insistence that any metering system incorporated into the 'flex' camera should be capable of measuring only the important parts of the picture led to the development of a selective through-the-lens meter. Such a meter had already been perfected and incorporated in the large-format microscope camera device called 'Orthomat' by Dr.Helmuth Frenk, a scientist working in the Leitz instrument division, The new meter featured in the Leicaflex SL launched in 1968. It was the world's first single lens reflex with selective through-the-lens metering. Of the light reflected from the object, 20% was deflected to a CdS photoresistor, housed in the base of the mirror box, by a slightly cylindrical deflecting mirror which collected the light through a pellicle section of the main viewing mirror. The design of the system was so accurate that no extraneous light could affect measurement before or during exposure. As the shutter was released, the main viewing mirror rose and as it did so, the secondary mirror folded flat against the main mirror. Additional baffles prevented unwanted light from affecting the exposure reading.

The acceptance angle of the exposure meter coincided exactly with the central micro-prism focus measuring field of the SL with a diameter of 7mm. This measurement corresponded to ⅙th of the diagonal length of the image field. Irrespective of the focal length of the lens in use, the area covered was large enough to give anaccurate 'integrated' reading of the object area and at the same time narrow enough to facilitate the isolation of important pictorial features. In effect, Leitz developed their own 'spot' meter. The system has endured through to the present camera models where it co-exists with the large-field integrated exposure measurement method.

The TTL exposure system of the Leicaflex SL firmly established Leitz as a major player in the single lens reflex market. New lenses and a range of accessories were added to the system. With the exception of the 400mm and 560mm pre-set aperture objectives, all other focal lengths featured fully automatic iris diaphragms which permitted exposure measurement to be made at maximum aperture. Initially, lenses were indexed to the original Leicaflex camera meter by means of a single cam. The Leicaflex SL required a second cam with which new objectives were factory supplied to enable maximum aperture metering; older ones had to be modified. Later cameras, from the R3 onward, required a third cam.

The differences can easily be seen from the accompanying photographs. Objectives issued since the introduction of the R3 are also only fitted with a single R-type cam; early examples are engraved accordingly on the base of the lens barrel. Some single cam objectives and most two-cam types can still be modified to three cam by Leica service centres at moderate cost.

More than 70,000 Leicaflex SL's had been dispatched from the factory in Wetzlar by the time the Leicaflex SL2 was introduced in 1974. This camera is still regarded by some enthusiasts today as the pinnacle of SLR achievement by Leitz. The camera featured improved metering sensitivity, shutter speed and aperture scale data incorporated in the viewfinder, illuminated viewfinder for low-light operation, improved focusing screen with a central 3mm split image rangefinder, a redesigned mirror and flash hotshoe. Several other aspects of the SL were also redesigned. A year after its launch the Leicaflex SL2 MOT – a special motorized version of which only a little more than a thousand were made – was launched.

The SL2 was certainly the finest of all the Leicaflex cameras but it was also a costly enterprise for the company at a time when the flood of imports from Japan offered many similar features at a much lower

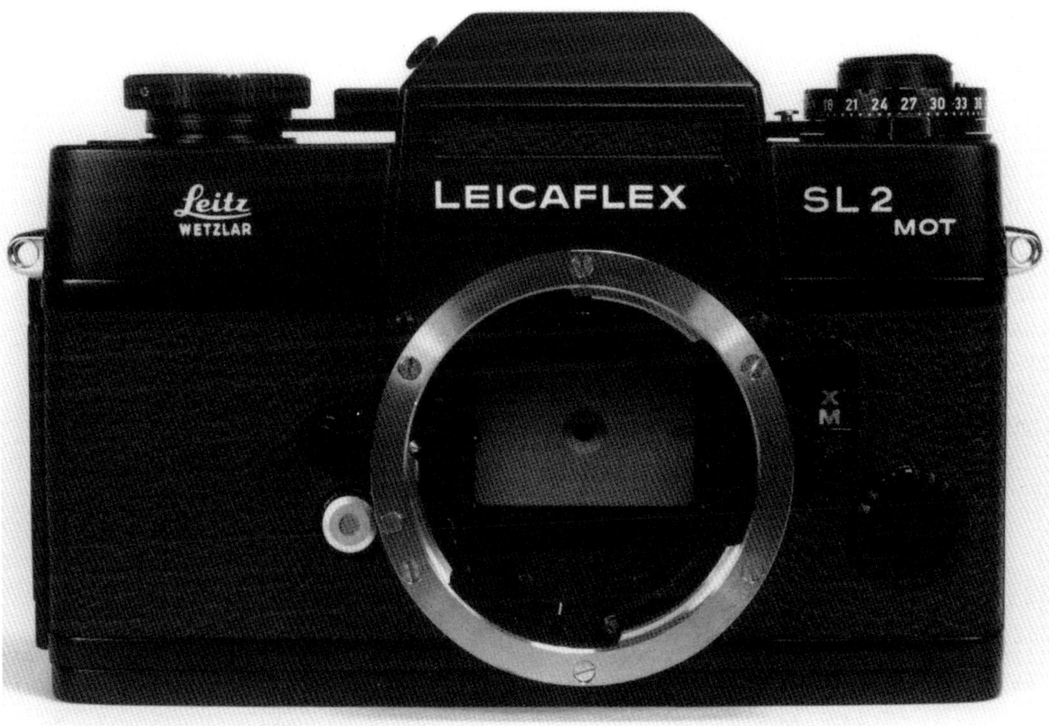

Fig. 11. Leicaflex SL2 MOT in black chrome. A superb example of a rare beast, still claimed by some to be the best example of Leitz single lens reflex craftsmanship. Photojournalists who want the toughest mechanical SLR made need look no further. *Fieldgrass & Gale/Jonathan Harris*

retail cost. Certain Leitz dealers have maintained that to recover production costs and make a profit on the camera, Leitz needed to sell one camera body and one and half standard lenses. Consequently, the SL2 only remained in production for two years, being superseded in 1976 by the Leica R3.

Examples of all three Leicaflex models can still be found on the used market at prices which reflect their cosmetic and mechanical condition. They are all perfectly usable cameras, lacking some of the features of the more modern all-electronic R-types, but nonetheless suitable for virtually all types of photography. In particular, the central micro-prism focusing device on these cameras was one of the finest ever devised for a single lens reflex. The slightest out-of-focus object displays a clear flickering effect which makes these models ideally suited for use with lenses in the focal length range 35mm to 180mm where rapid and accurate focus can be easily accomplished.

Only one problem is likely to present itself for Leicaflex users in the years ahead. The PX 625 mercury battery used to power the CdS meter in all three models was banned in some states of the U.S.A. following a Senate ruling in 1994; an EEC ruling preventing the sale of these batteries followed and, although existing stocks are still good in Europe, they will eventually disappear from retailers' shelves.

At the time of writing, a number of reports in the photographic press following announcement of the ban implied that cameras using the PX 625 will become obsolete when existing stocks of the batteries run out. It may be of some interest to Leicaphiles with Leicaflex cameras (as well as to owners of the Leica M5 and CL) that Leica Camera GmbH in Solms are aware of the problem facing owners if a suitable replacement power source cannot be found. Like a number of other manufacturers whose earlier models relied on this battery for meter power, Leica are investigating the possibility of a factory modification service to the models affected which will enable more modern power sources to be used. I hasten to emphasise that until an announcement is made officially by Leica Camera GmbH concerning whether modification of the battery compartment and meter circuitry is possible or not, the reader should not construe from what I have written here that a service already exists for this purpose. It does not.

Regrettably there is no exact replacement for this type of power cell. Its main advantage for designers in the 60's and 70's was that the use of mercury oxide provided a natural voltage stabiliser, obviating the need for additional meter circuitry. Silver oxide batteries of the same voltage can be used as an alternative, but there is no guarantee of exposure meter accuracy for more than a few months at a time. Kodak have produced an alkaline battery which is almost identical in size and shape, but its potential is different from the mercury oxide type. It is called a 625 battery, but its voltage is 1.5 not 1.3 and the use of it in Leicaflex and Leica M5/CL cameras would almost certainly provide the user with incorrect meter readings of up to between ½ and 1 full stop different from those obtained using the correct power cell.

It is still perfectly practicable to use these older models with most objectives in conjunction with a hand-held meter, or, in the event a more modern R-type is also used alongside a Leicaflex, to transfer meter readings from the R-type. Both amateur and professional enthusiasts may have the time to explore these methods and come to some happy compromise when the sheer joy of being able to use these older models is a priority. In general, however, this is not an efficient way to concentrate on the art of picture making and while occasionally some reference is made in the following pages to certain aspects of Leicaflex use, the main thrust of this work concerns the R-cameras.

A New Era for Leica Reflex Design

In 1971, Leitz signed a technology development agreement with the Minolta Camera Co Ltd of Osaka in Japan. This was a logical move for the German company enabling it to expand the lens range for the Leicaflex quickly by buying in certain Minolta made products, badged and cosmetically finished to Leitz specification. A new compact rangefinder camera, the Leica CL (Leitz-Minolta CL in Japan) supplied with three special lenses and launched in 1973 was one of the early successes of co-operation between the two companies.

Minolta had long been established as one of the more advanced Japanese camera manufacturers, producing a number of sophisticated single lens reflex models incorporating integrated circuit electronics. Additionally, the company was then, and is today, one of the few in Japan producing its own optical glass.

There is some confusion as to who exactly was responsible for designing the Leica R3 camera which was launched with much fanfare at Photokina in 1976 as the eventual successor to the Leicaflex SL2. Leitz were perhaps not unnaturally keen to play down the Far Eastern connection and this may be one of the reasons why the public relations department of the time made little, if any, reference to the facts.

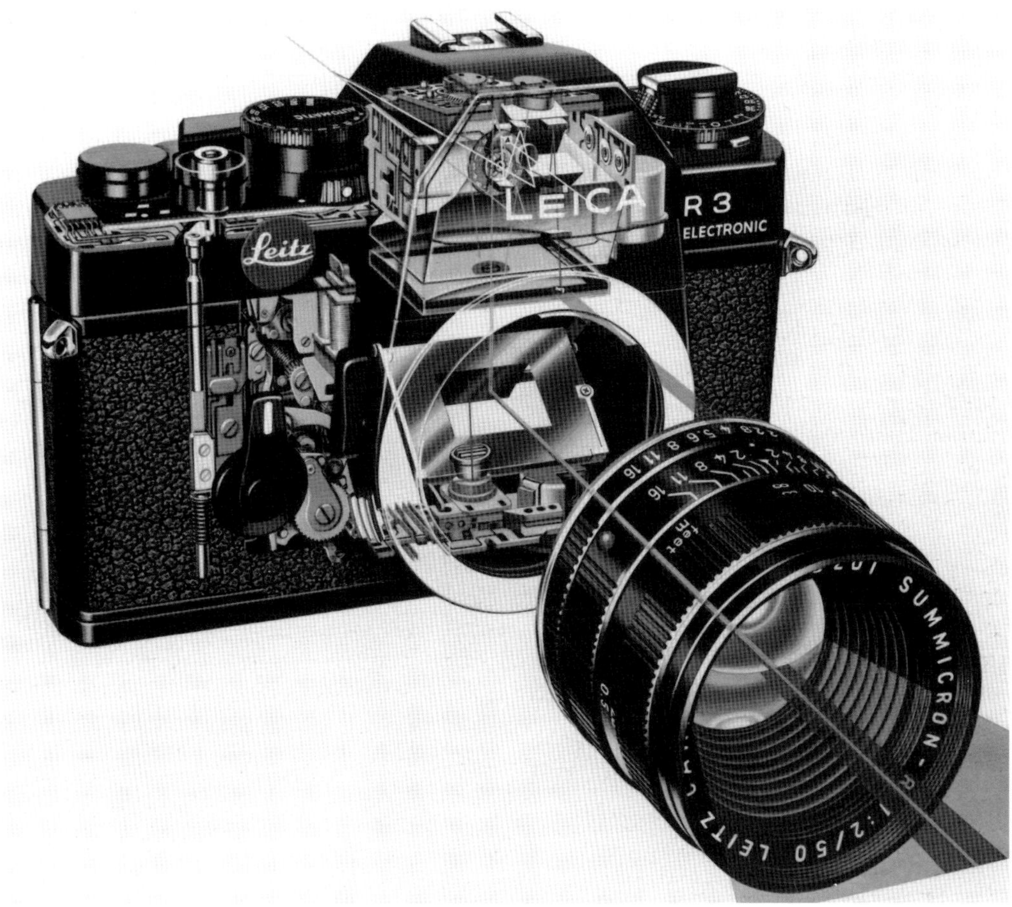

Fig. 12. A new era of Leica reflex design. The Leica R3, the first of the R-type cameras was a development of the Minolta Camera Company's XE-1 SLR, incorporating many new Leitz patented features, including the famous CLS vertical travel shutter and 'selective' TTL light metering. *Leica Camera GmbH Archive*

These were that the Leica R3, with one or two minor cosmetic and several component changes, was a Minolta based camera. In almost every aspect the Leica R3 SLR was a Minolta XE-1 which was developed in the early 1970's and launched on to the Japanese market in 1974. It is possible of course that the original concept for this camera came from Leitz who may well have been working on a successor to the SL2 but lacked the funds necessary for development. The agreement with Minolta would almost certainly have provided the necessary vehicle in this regard, affording the Leitz design team a year or so for market evaluation and modification to German standards. This scenario is more the result of wishful thinking than fact; there are too many similarities between the XE-1 and earlier generations of Minolta SLR cameras over which Leitz had no influence. In any event, it is well known that the metal bladed, vertical-traverse roller shutter was a Leitz design – the Leitz rotary shutter or LSV – developed and manufactured by The Copal Company Ltd of Japan with huge success some years before the advent of the R3.

Copal's own mechanical metal bladed vertical focal plane shutter had already been well proven in reflex cameras; Nikon's Nikkormat is a good example of the type. It was a similar blade system which was incorporated into the Leitz rotary shutter mechanism facilitating earlier series production than would have been otherwise possible. The smooth operation of the CLS shutter compared with the more conventional cloth focal plane types was an outstanding feature of both the Minolta XE-1 and the Leica R3. The Copal-Leitz Shutter is electronically operated, providing a range of stepless speeds from 4 secs to $^1/_{1000}$th second when either camera is set to automatic exposure mode, in steps when the mode is set to manual and with mechanical back-up speeds of $^1/_{90}$th, X (= electronic flash synchronization) and B. One other advantage of this type of shutter over conventional horizontal, cloth/metal focal plane types, was its compact size, permitting an overall saving in body size and weight. The Leica R3 when fitted with the 50mm Summicron f/2 lens, weighed some 20 grams less than a Leicaflex SL.

Leitz modified the metering system of the XE-1. This employed a pair of CdS cells mounted in the pentaprism and measured the whole image field. Leitz incorporated a third CdS cell in the base of the mirror box which measured only the central portion of the field. Thus they were able to continue the 'selective' light metering policy adopted for the Leicaflex SL and SL2. The addition of a switch at the base of the shutter speed dial also enabled the user to change from selective to integrated full-field, or centre-weighted exposure measurement in a fraction of a second.

The viewing mirror of the R3 was another modification adapted from the SL camera, multicoated with 17 layers for maximum reflectivity and driven by a rotary cam which helped to suppress vibration. Both these Leitz innovations (patented) maintained the 'feel' factor of earlier models and the viewfinder brightness.

A number of other useful features appeared on the R3, two of which were subsequently adopted into future models. A film cassette viewing window was fitted to the swing-open back, and a special film transport and loading system developed for the XE-1 was retained. It was one of those quirky systems which takes a little time to adjust to if more conventional loading techniques have been the order of the day, but is virtually 100% secure in terms of film loading accuracy. The multiple exposure lever sited beneath the film transport and shutter cocking lever, with automatic return after exposure, was not retained in future cameras, being replaced instead with the film rewind sprocket release button in the base of the camera.

Apart from design changes to the top plate and pentaprism cover, changes in the body lens mount to permit mounting of the R-type objectives and the provision of a depth-of-field preview lever above the lens lock/release lever, the R3 was the same as the XE-1 in all other respects. For Leitz, the addition of this camera to the range provided a much needed financial boost for the company. The R3 was cheaper to manufacture, and virtually the whole production, except for 2,000, was concentrated in the new factory in Portugal. The retail price of the R3 was also considerably lower than for the top of the line SL2, with which it co-existed for a short

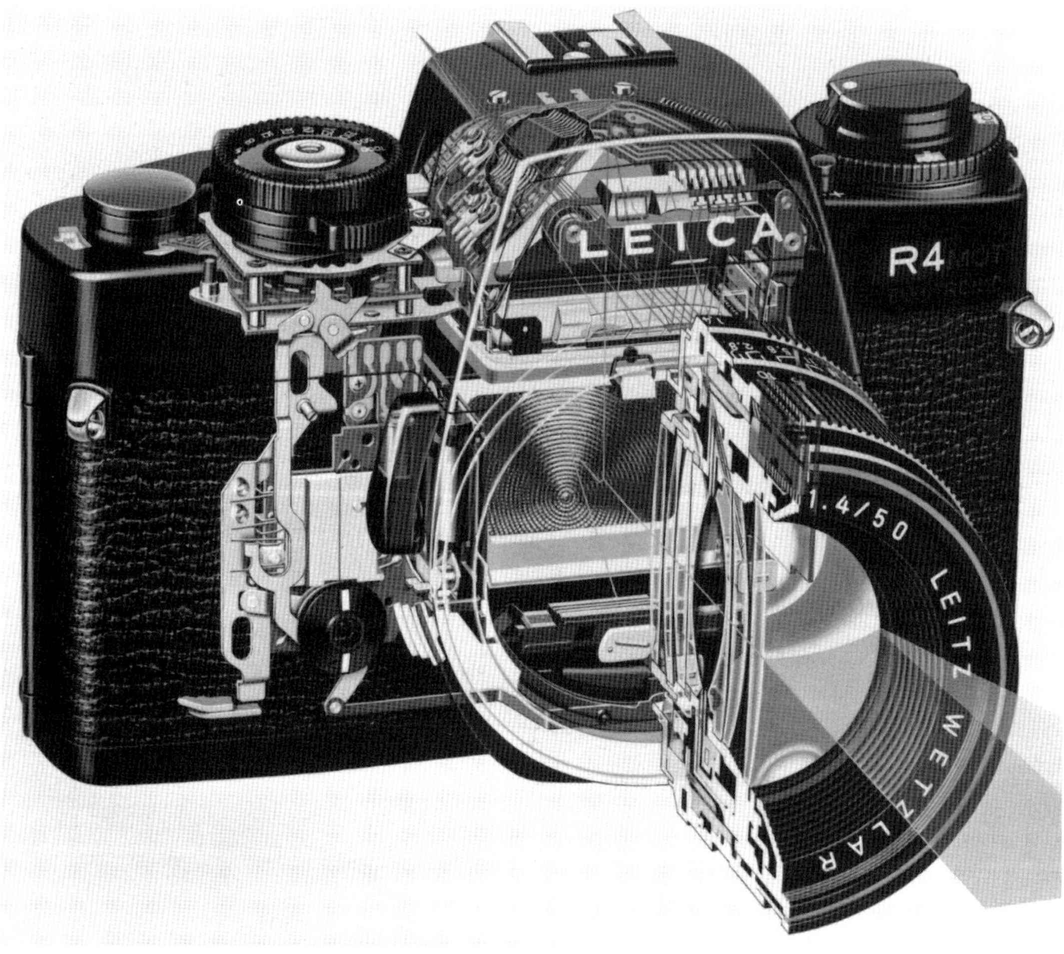

Fig. 13. The R4 MOT Electronic was modelled on Minolta's XD-7, but apart from the back and inner chassis, was essentially a Leitz camera featuring advanced electronic exposure programs linked to the (then) new Seiko shutter which is clearly seen in Fig 14. *Leica Camera GmbH Archive*

period, and this encouraged a broader customer base.

Some 70,000 R3 cameras were produced during a relatively short three year period. Over the years it has proved to be one of the most durable and reliable of the early R-type cameras and many are still in daily use around the world. One of its attractions I think, is its basic simplicity of operation combined with a very accurate metering specification. In the automatic aperture priority mode, the stepless shutter can take care of the majority of lighting situations, using either centre-weighted full-field or selective measurement. A feature of the camera permits storage of the metered exposure by depressing the shutter button to the first pressure, allowing certain pictorial elements to be accurately measured before composition is finalised. Another popular feature of the camera is the top plate mounted double exposure device, permitting any number of exposures to be made on a single frame, even while the camera is tripod mounted.

Third Generation Concepts and the Future

Compared to the SL, the Leica R3 was a compact single lens reflex. Compared to Yoshihsa Maitani's Olympus OM 1 however, it was, like the majority of contemporary 35mm reflex cameras, a leviathan. The OM cameras took the photographic world by storm and 'compact' became a byword in the vocabulary of camera designers. All the major players in the field struggled to compete, producing hybrid models which maintained many features of earlier cameras, while saving size and weight in slimmed down body constructions.

Whereas Olympus had begun from scratch by designing a whole compact camera system, other manufacturers were forced to maintain existing lines of lenses and work new body designs around them. Advances in electronic circuits and the use of miniature computerised central processing units to handle exposure metering programs also enabled engineers to reduce sizes further, but they still could not

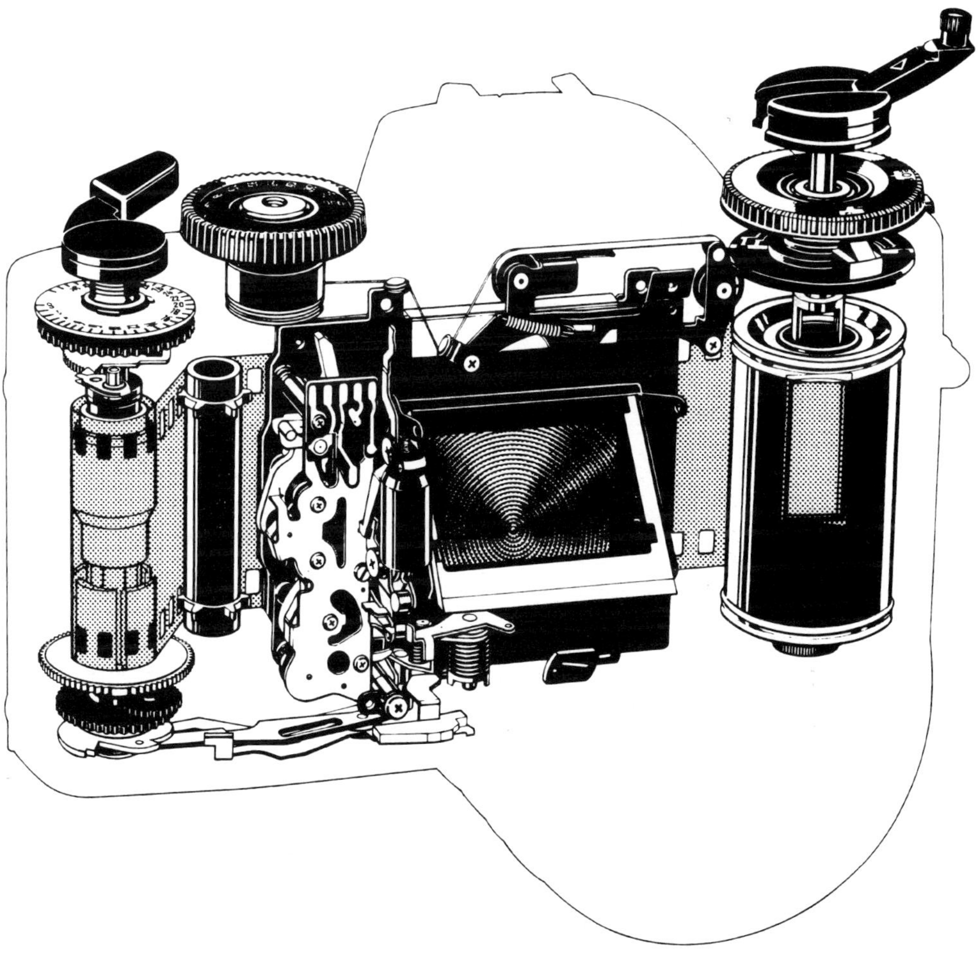

Fig. 14. The guts of the Leica R4 showing the sophisticated control mechanism for the Seiko shutter and damping unit for the reflex mirror.

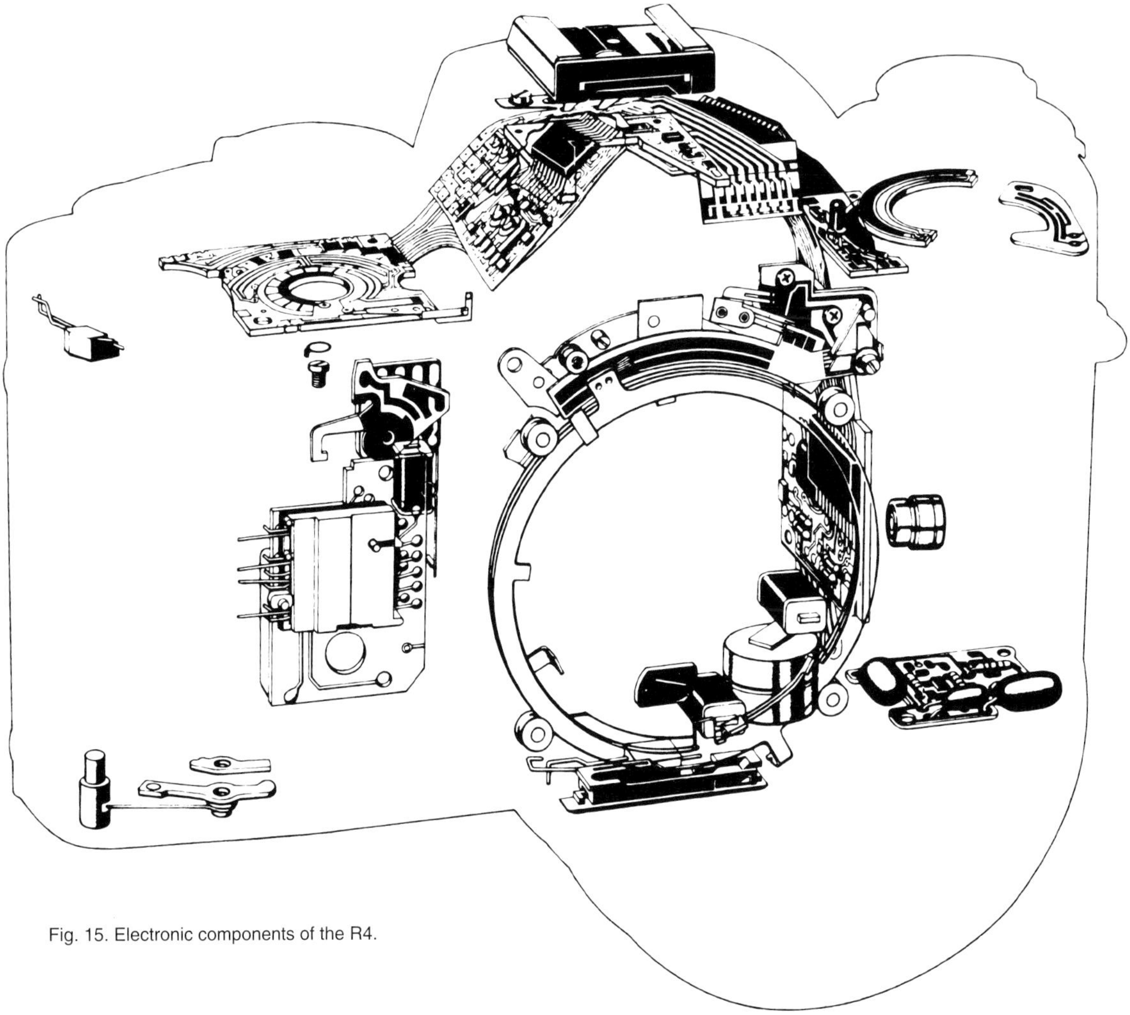

Fig. 15. Electronic components of the R4.

match Maitani's feat of genuine creativity.

Various schools of thought at the time debated the miniaturization issue, some professionals arguing vociferously that a 35mm single lens reflex camera needed both bulk and weight to remain efficient. The additional mass helped to absorb mirror flop vibration and thus reduce the possibility of blurred pictures. This of course, was all just so much nonsense, for although extra mass can certainly help to dampen vibration, the perfect mirror braking system can do far more to eliminate the problem.

Leitz were undoubtedly working closely with Minolta on the next generation of that company's SLR's through the remainder of the decade. When the R4 MOT Electronic camera was introduced in 1980 it was immediately apparent to Leica cognoscenti that a very similar camera already existed in the Minolta line-up. Indeed, the Minolta XD-7 bore many of the R4's features. Importantly, the two cameras shared the same inner chassis design; the R4 however received a completely reshaped exterior. The film transport system first used in the R3 camera was retained and the R4 also used the same swing-open removable back of the XD-7. But that is about as far as the two cameras went in sharing the same specification.

Leitz developed and produced the mirror housing, including a new mirror and satellite mirror for exposure metering, as well as its braking system which was adopted from the R3. This time Leitz used, in addition to its well proven selective metering control, its own centre-weighted large-field measuring system. The whole of the top plate design, location, type, style and placement of the various controls were all to German specification, even though one or two appear in Minolta literature of the time to bear a striking resemblance to those on the Leica R4. Leitz developed its own flash synchronization system and film speed control as well as the electrical controls for the Eumig-produced motor winder and motor drive units.

Like the R3, the R4 also employed a stepless speed electronic metal-bladed, vertical traverse roller shutter, but it was not the CLS version. Instead, a shutter developed and manufactured by the Seikosha Company of Osaka, a subsidiary of the famous watchmakers Hattori Seiko Co Ltd of Japan, was used. All subsequent electronic models of the R-camera have also been fitted with the Seiko shutter. The two R6 models, being entirely mechanical, employ a metal bladed vertical shutter designed and built by Leica Camera GmbH at their factory in Solms.

The main features of the R4 MOT ELECTRONIC – later R4 – centred on the new compact design. Relative to the R3, the R4 had a certain familiarity in style but it was in fact a radically different camera with controls positioned in such a way that even a gloved hand would have little difficulty operating them.

The outer body is contoured slightly on the front right hand face and features neatly rounded ends which are angled outward. The back of the camera is actually longer than its front face measurement, so it has the appearance of being small. This is quite deceptive. When fitted with a standard Summicron 50mm, f/2 lens, the camera has the feel of a heavyweight, but because of its relatively small size, compared to the R3, it nestles comfortably in the hands, with all operating controls falling precisely where you would expect to find them.

Many modifications have been made to this camera over the past fourteen years, but fundamentally it has remained the same. Only the current R7 received a noticeable design change with the body height being extended a few millimetres to permit additional electronics to be fitted in the base. This has had a secondary benefit to the user in providing extra protection for the contents with a deeper walled base plate as well as minutely improved handling.

Over the years, Leitz technicians and designers have striven to improve many features of the camera while keeping abreast of most electronic advances. In particular, the main developments have been in the exposure metering system and flash control. The R4 MOT was (in 1980) a highly specified SLR in this respect, offering the user continued access to 'selective' metering as well as full-field measurement in a variety of modes, thus;

1. Automatic aperture priority with selective spot measurement
2. Automatic aperture priority with full-field measurement
3. Automatic shutter priority with full-field measurement
4. Automatic program mode with full-field measurement
5. Manual shutter and/or aperture selection with selective spot measurement

Changing from one mode to another is accomplished in a fraction of a second by activating a lever control switch at the base of the shutter speed dial. This can be done while the camera is at eye level, even during the process of making a photograph if necessary, because the viewfinder provides visual confirmation by means of simple red LED's of the mode selected.

In the R3 camera it had been necessary to install a third CdS photoresistor in the base of the mirror box for selective metering. In the R4 MOT, Leitz developed a completely new system using a single silicon photodiode, which had a faster light-to-dark reaction time, in combination with a 4.5mm, f/1 adjustable converging lens which was mechanically moved in and out of position as the mode lever switch was operated.

This was accomplished by a series of lever arms linked to the switch at the base of the shutter speed dial. In the selective 'spot' mode, the lens was positioned in front of the silicon photodiode. Light passing through the semi-silvered main viewing mirror was bounced to the lens via a Leitz patented Fresnel-type reflector comprising 1345 micro mirrors. The metering lens brought the light rays to convergence into the narrow angle required for effective 'spot' measurement. When the mode switch was turned to the full-field measuring position, the tiny focusing lens was moved out of the diode light path.

Later models of the R-camera have maintained the same light measuring system but with improvements to light sensitivity as well as some expansion of mode options. The R4 MOT permitted automatic flash control using the appropriate dedicated electronic flash units, but as demands on flash photography by users increased, new facilities for controlling exposure were incorporated into the system.

The R5 camera launched in 1986 was the first Leica SLR to offer through-the-lens electronic flash exposure control. Using the special 'System Camera Adaption 300' (SCA300) modules fitted to independent electronic flash units such as those manufactured by Metz and Vivitar, the camera electronics automatically switched to a flash synchronization speed of 1/100th second when the flash was ready to fire. During exposure, light reflected from the film was measured by a secondary silicon photodiode sited next to the main metering silicon diode in the base of the mirror box. In effect, this secondary diode provided for a full-field flash measurement. As soon as sufficient light for

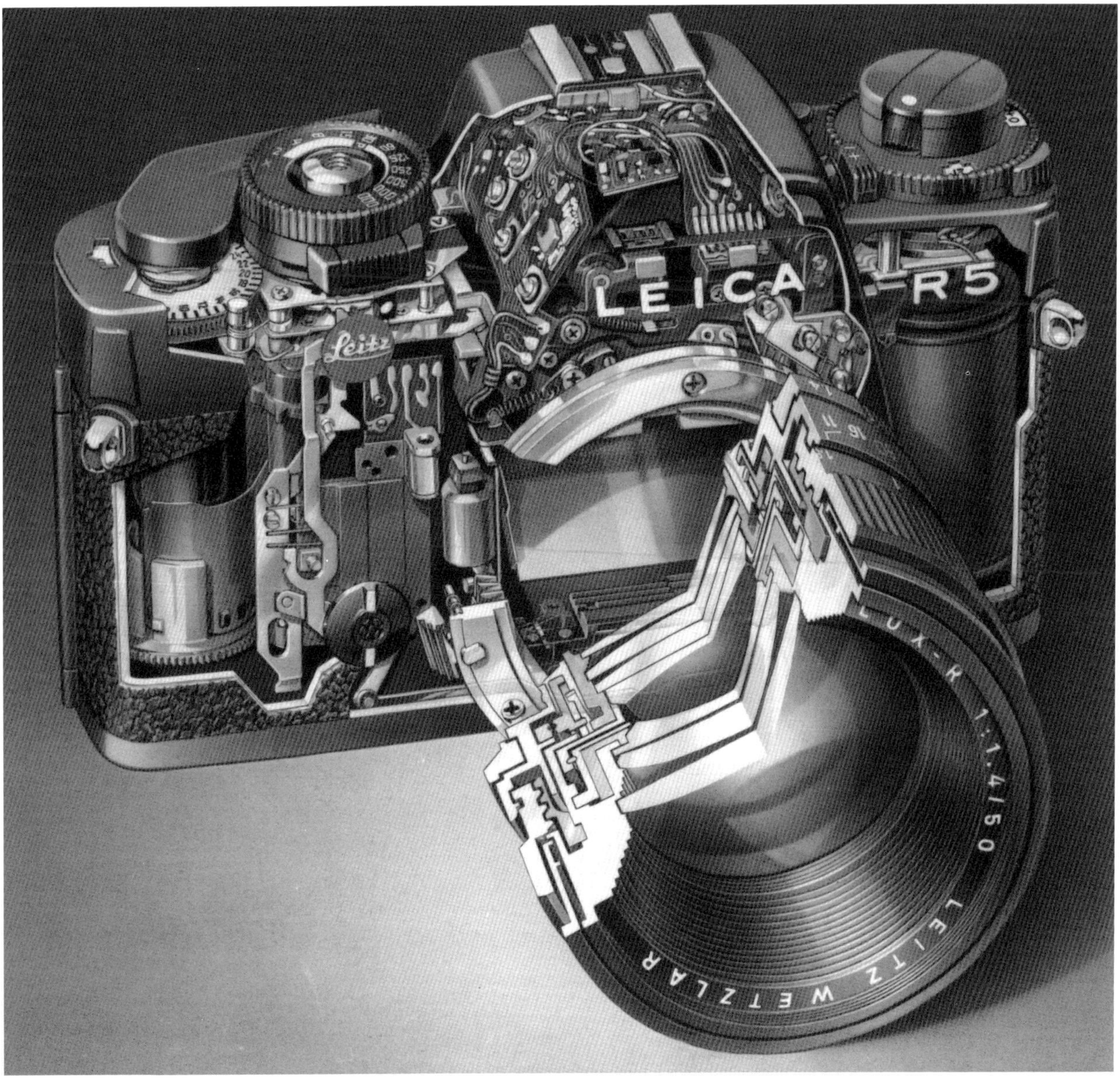

correct exposure had reached the film, electronic circuitry interrupted the flash power and the light was cut off. The viewfinder of the R5 offered the user visual indication of both 'flash-ready' and 'correct exposure' by means of intermittent flashing LED's.

The R6.2, as well as its predecessor, the R6, and the electronic R-E camera incorporate TTL flash control. With the launch of the R7 in 1992, flash control had almost reached perfection. Using this camera, it is possible to use electronic flash as a primary light source or as a fill-in to ambient light. When the camera is set to Automatic Program mode, the camera integral computer takes over, controlling flash intensity in harmony with the ambient light conditions. In other modes, it is possible to control the output intensity of electronic flash using selective or full-field metering.

Many other aspects of functional design have been improved on the models launched since the R4. These include such items as the shutter speed setting dial which has been increased in height to make it more convenient in use. The shutter speed range has been increased and the R7 now features DX film coding. The film transport and wind-on lever from the R4S-MOD 2 (MOD-P in USA) was encased in a tough polycarbonate plastic. A special camera back fitted with a contoured thumbgrip was also introduced, and older models could have this useful accessory retro-fitted at Leica service cen-

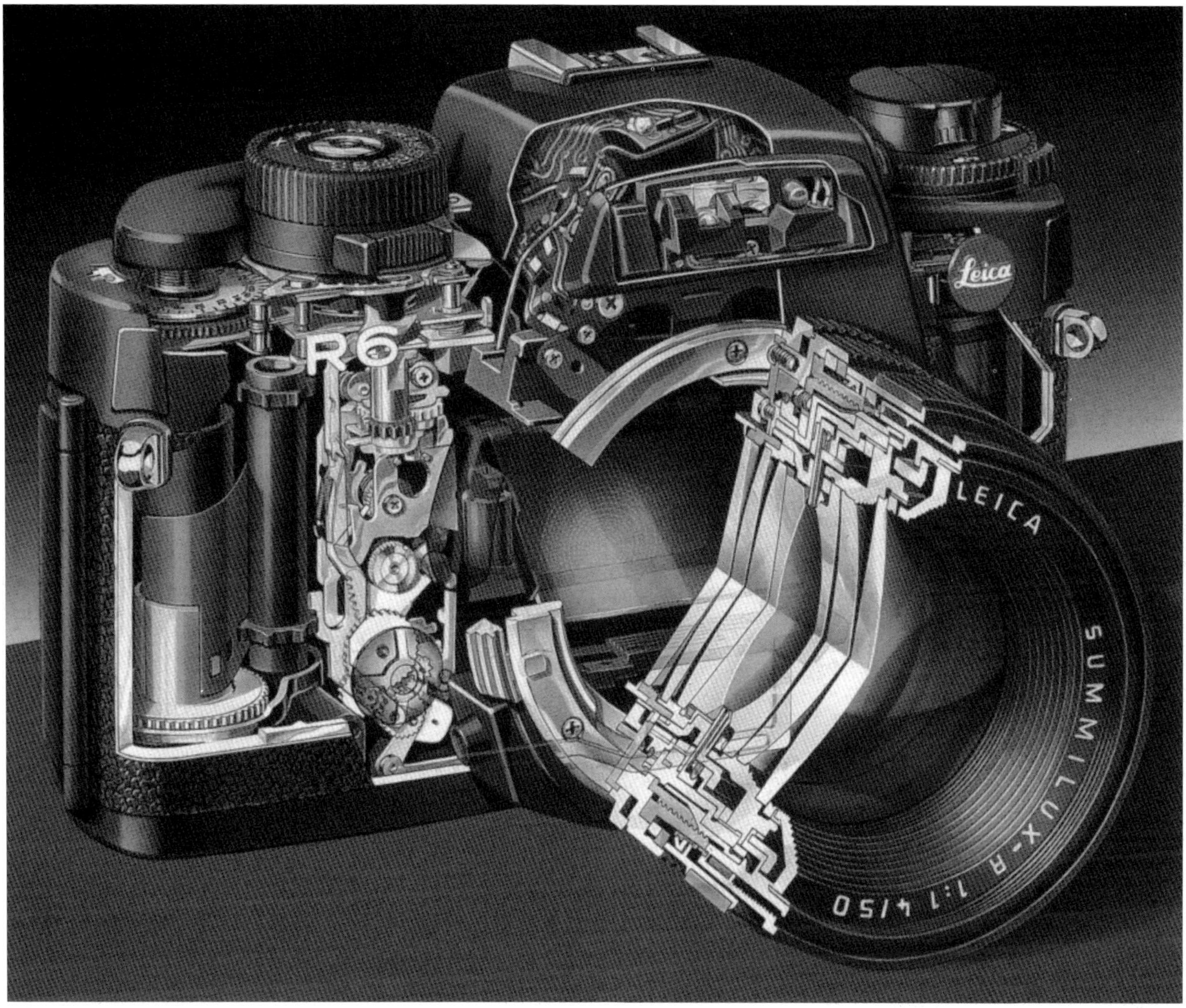

Figs. 16 & 17. Leica R5 (left) and Leica R6 (right). Highly detailed artist's cut-aways clearly illustrate the differences between the all-electronic Leica R5 camera and the all-mechanical Leica R6 (right), the first mechanical Leica single lens reflex since the last of the Leitz Leicaflexes. The R5 uses the stepless Seiko shutter, while the R6 and its later brother, the R6.2 use shutters designed and built by Leica at Solms. *Leica Camera GmbH*

tres. Modifications have been made to the eye-piece outer frame as well as to the ocular itself. Built-in dioptre adjustment is possible. Strap anti-rub inserts were added at an early stage in the development of the camera.

In spite of the advent of auto-focus, there is still a healthy demand amongst specialists and enthusiasts for the manually operated single lens reflex camera. Leica Camera GmbH have so far resisted the temptation to change their policy of providing equipment for the traditional market even though they almost certainly have access to the new technology. By concentrating their efforts toward developing what is probably the finest 35mm traditional single lens reflex camera, both newcomers to and veteran users of the Leica R-system are assured of some continuity well into the future. Equally important to these photographers is the fact that all models of Leica SLR's can still be properly serviced and repaired when the need arises by fully trained Leica experts – a situation which does not exist with most older models of other marques.

My remarks in the introduction concerning auto focus notwithstanding, R & D at Solms is presently engaged in finding yet more ways to improve the current R-models, the R6.2 and the R7. One function being researched is digital focus confirmation which could certainly be of some use to photographers operating in low-light conditions as well as in sports and wildlife photography. The real problem with this idea is not that it doesn't have a practical use, but whether it would appeal to the majority for every-day general shooting. Considering the already

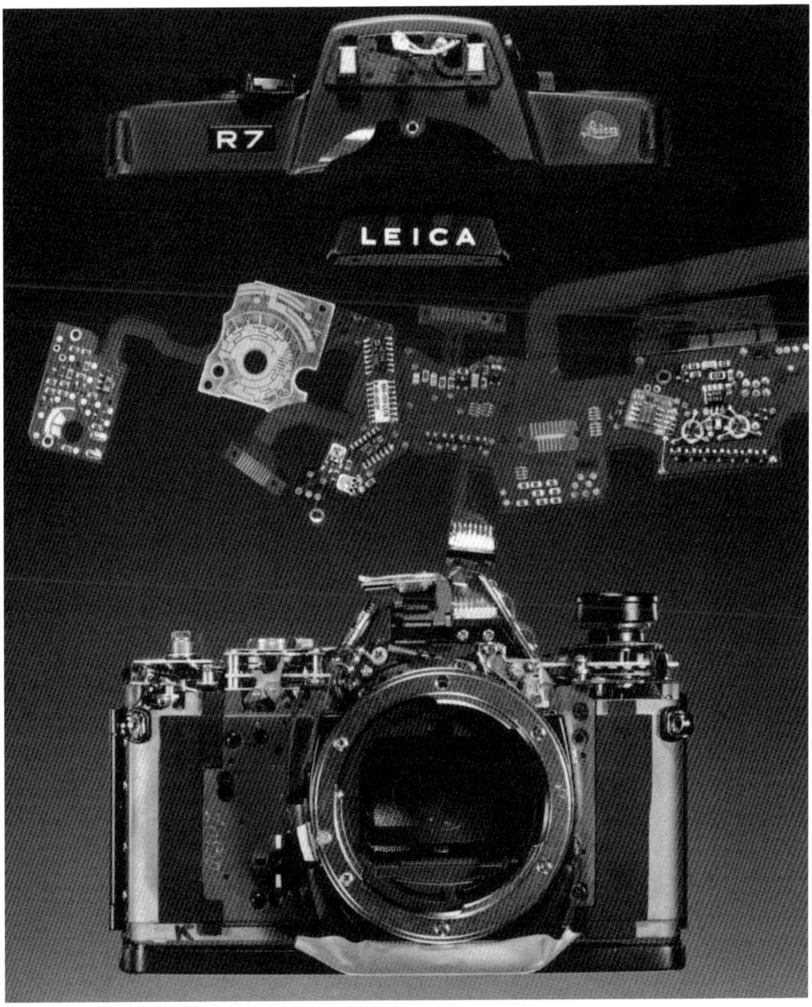

Fig. 18. This picture clearly shows the extensive pcb film circuitry and various microchips which have to be fitted into the Leica R7. Also clearly visible is the two-part inner and outer chassis.
Leica Camera GmbH

superb clarity of the R-type focusing system, it is difficult to see how DFC would provide an all-round benefit. The other question must lie in the way in which such a function is displayed in the viewfinder, which at the present time is nearing its limit of capacity in the information it can carry.

One problem which seems to have beset Leica designers is that of electronic flash exposure technology. Almost all other marques feature systems which are more sophisticated than can be found in the current Leica-R models. In particular, one feature which press and sports photographers find so useful, that of high speed shutter synchronization, is lacking. This is an aspect which Leica engineers are currently endeavouring to resolve, but they have been constrained by the height of the inner camera chassis which does not currently permit the fitting of a shutter mechanism whose vertical traverse speed is fast enough to enable synchronization speeds to be increased.

This problem is only likely to be resolved when the present design is radically reconfigured. Obtaining information as to the possible future look of a Leica R single lens reflex has proved virtually impossible – such secrets are closely guarded. However, it is my opinion that future models will be taller and will in all probability incorporate integral film transport, shutter arming and rewind motors in a single modular construction. Such a design would permit a more sophisticated shutter mechanism to be installed. The next logical step would be to install an automatic film loading system while maintaining the manual film advance and rewind found in present models. The current system is certainly secure, but it suffers from being inherently slow in operation and I know from personal experience that under certain circumstances, film reloading can sometimes become an infuriating test of dexterity.

Fig. 19. A Leica R6.2 being assembled in one of the special bays at the Solms factory in Germany. Apart from the CNC machining of the chassis and some furniture, each camera is hand-built and thoroughly tested by each assembler, and then re-tested before being packed for dispatch.
Leica Camera GmbH

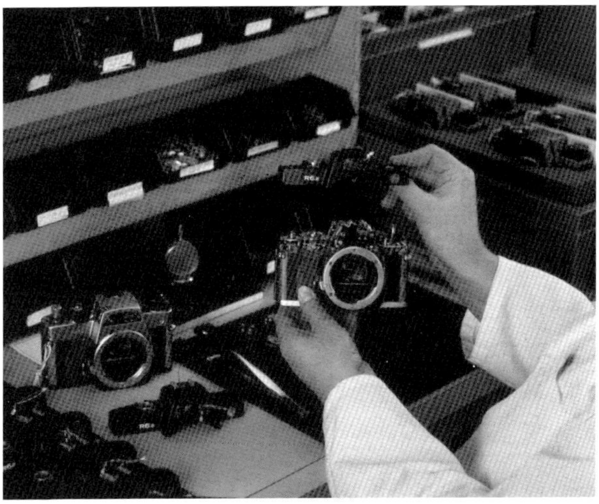

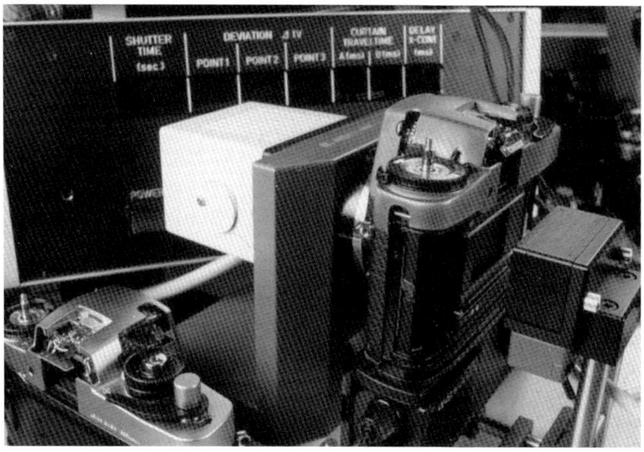

Fig. 20. The 100,000 shutter firing test. A Leica R camera body on test set up on the special shutter testing rig at Solms. It is connected to a Leica Motor Drive-R unit with special power adapter. *Leica Akademie*

But these are thoughts for the future and they are mine and not Leica's. After several years of working with all models in the Leica R-range I have to confess to being hooked on their ease of operation and to the accuracy of metering – even between models manufactured a decade apart I have not yet experienced a noticeable difference in respect of the latter. Perhaps above all else, it is the smoothness of shutter and mirror operation which gives such a feeling of user satisfaction, a phenomenon I have not experienced in any other type of 35mm SLR in more than 30 years of photography.

Today's Leica R-cameras are pre-assembled at the Leica Aparelhos Opticos de Precisao S.A. factory at Vila Nova de Famalicao in Portugal where about 500 highly trained staff are employed. Final assembly and quality control is carried out at Solms in Germany where cameras are produced in small batches and each one is thoroughly inspected before it is allowed to be packed and despatched to the worldwide sales network.

Leicaflex and Leica-R Models – Technical Specifications.

LEICAFLEX (Standard)

Year introduced: Pre-production models 1964, officially launched 1965, production ceased 1968.

Construction: Die-cast aluminium body, brass top and bottom plates.

Lens mount: Leicaflex R-type bayonet, single cam.

Shutter: Mechanical horizontal cloth focal plane type. Release located in centre of shutter speed dial.

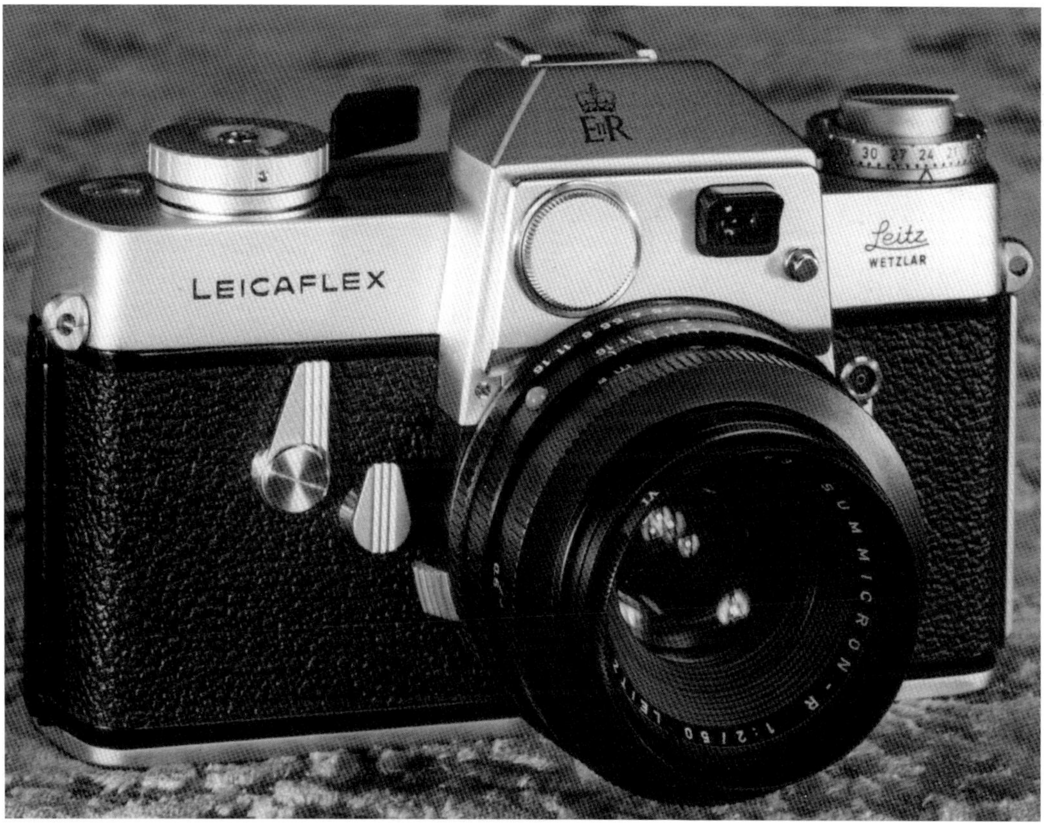

Fig. 21. A very special Leicaflex with pie-crust counter presented to H.M. Queen Elizabeth II. *Ernst Leitz GmbH Wetzlar Werkfoto/Leica Camera GmbH*

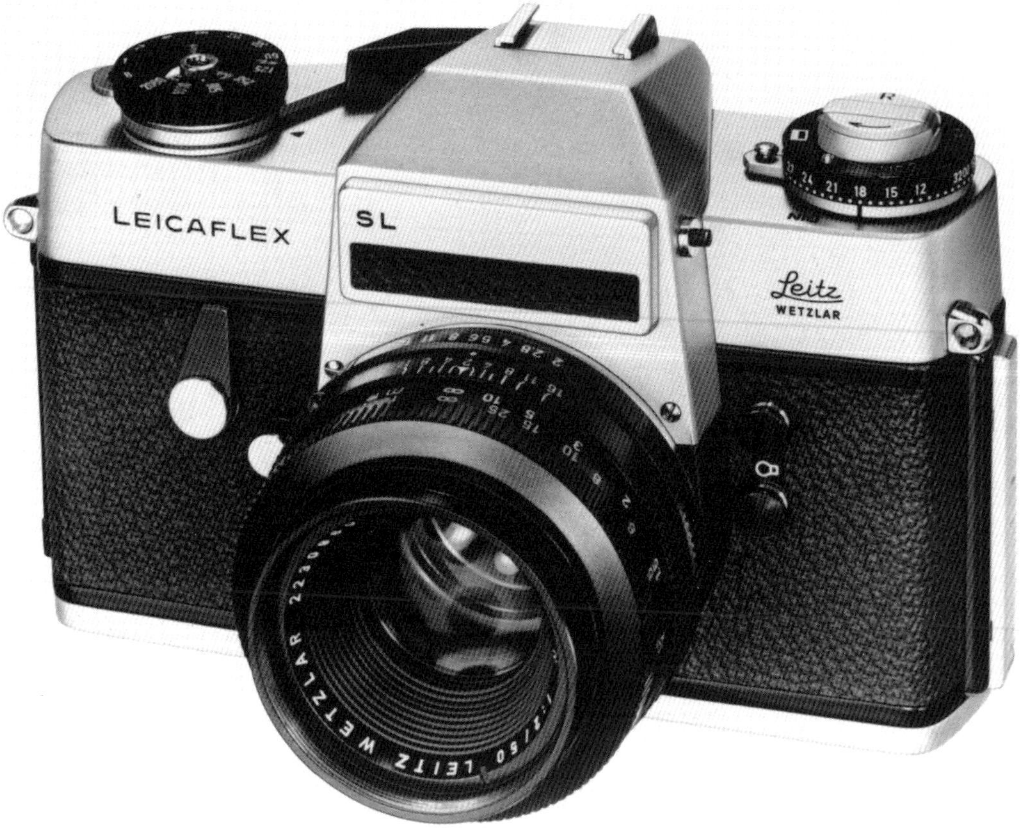

Fig. 22. Standard Leicaflex SL without the white marker on the self-timer in this Leitz factory production picture.

Shutter speeds: 1 second to 1/2000th second in 13 click-stop settings, B, 1, 1/2, 1/4, 1/8th, 1/15th, 1/30th, 1/60th, 1/125th, 1/250th, 1/500th, 1/1000th, 1/2000th. X = Electronic flash synchronization 1/100th second. M-synchronization (FP type flashbulbs) from 1/60th to 1/250th second.

Exposure measurement: utilising a single CdS cell mounted on front pentaprism face measures an angle of 27° approximating field of view of 90mm lens. Sensitivity range 6.3 to 50,000 apostilb; film speed range 8:6500 ISO (10:39 DIN)

Exposure modes: Semi-automatic, match needle coupled to lens diaphragm, shutter speed dial and film ISO setting disc.

Viewfinder: eye-level pentaprism type displays shutter speed range outside of image area at base, central focusing microprism, match needle exposure measuring device at right hand side with indicators for over and under exposure.

Focus: Special pentaprism with etched convex underside providing bright full-field viewing. Central circle 50mm sq. with more than 13,000 microprisms ensures high degree of focus accuracy.

Other features: Self timer, delay apx. 8 seconds. Depth of field preview. PC socket, twin 3mm, for 'X' and 'M' synchronization. Mirror-up facility (camera fitted with similar mirror operation to that found on Visoflex IIa and III for rangefinder cameras; three positions provided facility for 1, instant return mirror; 2, mirror locked up before exposure with return to normal viewing position after exposure; 3, mirror lock-up before and after exposure). Multiple exposure.

Film transport by single-stroke lever wind.

Power source: Single PX-type mercury oxide button cell.

Size: Length 149mm, height 94mm, depth 56mm.

Variations: Most obvious variation between early models concerns exposure frame counter which is pie-crust shaped on Mk I version and circular under magnifying lens with chromed retaining ring on Mk II. No meter switch-off on Mk I version. Mk II version switch activated by film advance lever, 'off' when lever flush with camera body. Initial models finished in anodised (electroplated) silver chrome sold with matching Summicron-R 50mm, f/2. lens. (see also under lens specification, Chapter 2.) Standard production offered with black chrome lenses. Small quantity later produced in black enamel paint finish. Ten motorised works evaluation models produced, 8 in chrome, 2 in black enamel.

LEICAFLEX SL

Year introduced: 1968, production ceased 1974.

Construction: Die-cast aluminium body, brass top and bottom plates.

Lens mount: Leicaflex R-type bayonet. New type red plastic lens release/lock catch fitted. SL production lenses fitted with two cams. Earlier single cam models required modification.

Shutter: Mechanical horizontal-run cloth focal plane type.

Shutter speeds: As Leicaflex Standard above.

Exposure measurement: True through-the-lens measuring system covering 'selective' field of 8°; uses single CdS photo-resistor mounted in base of mirror box.

Exposure modes: Manually adjusted match needle linked to shutter speed, lens diaphragm and film ISO speed setting. Shutter speed range visible at base of viewfinder outside picture area. Over/under exposure indicators above and below match needle at right hand side.

Viewfinder: As Leicaflex Standard, but fitted with ancillary light with sprung push switch located at top right of lens mount housing.

Focus: As Leicaflex Standard.

Other features: Self timer. Depth of field preview. PC socket as Leicaflex Standard. Mirror-up facility, but no third position mirror-up after exposure position as on Leicaflex Standard. Multiple exposure. Single-stroke lever-wind advance, special Leitz film take-up spool for rapid film loading.

Power source: Single PX mercury oxide button type.

Size: as Leicaflex Standard.

Variations: Camera available in black or silver chrome. Most silver chrome SL models fitted with black chrome shutter speed setting and film speed ISO dials. 1000 Leicaflex SL's issued in 1972 to commemorate the Munich Olympic Games. These cameras had special serial numbers engraved on the front face of the pentaprism next to the five-ring Olympic symbol and '72' to mark the year. 200 extra cameras were also made to meet the strong demand for this special edition but none were given special serial numbers. A Leicaflex SL fitted with a plain groundglass screen and central circle to mark metering area could be specially ordered from the factory. The finish was black enamel. Several interchangeable viewing system Leicaflex SL's were made and supplied with optional waist-level finders. These were works evaluation models not released to the public.

LEICALEX SL MOT

Year introduced: 1972, production ceased 1974.

Construction: As Leicaflex Standard, fitted with special motordrive shaft; all electrical contacts, film advance drive connector and positioning lug

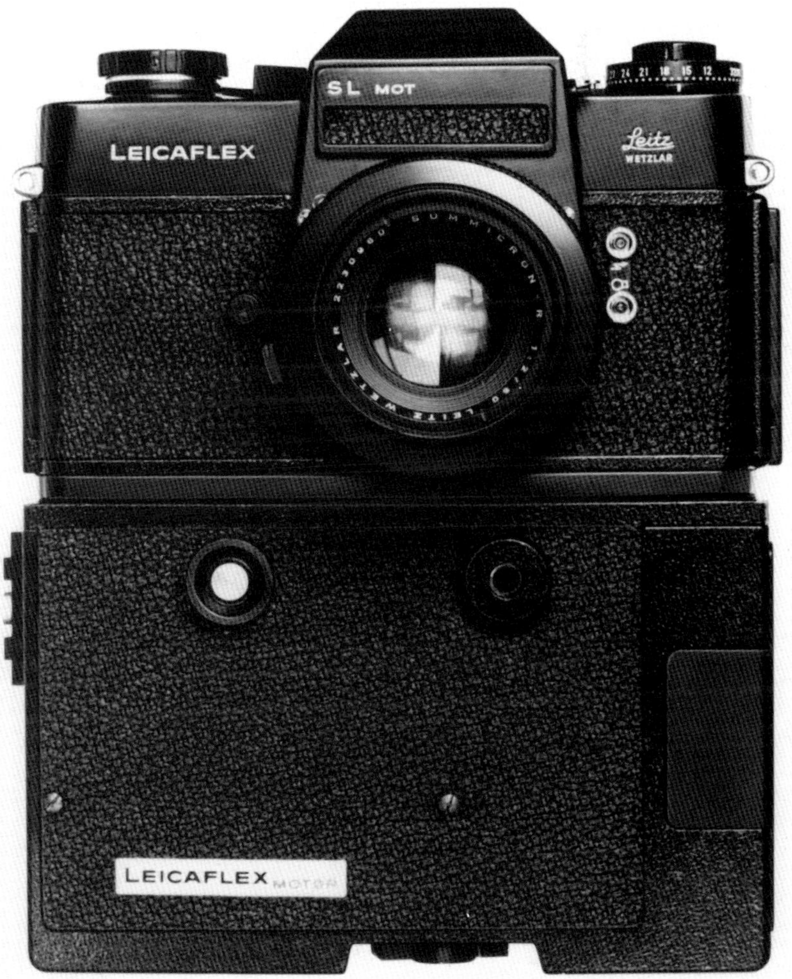

Fig. 23. Black enamel Leicaflex SL MOT rigged to the motor drive unit. Note the right hand side rear door catch difference between this model and the later SL2 MOT (see Fig. 145.) *Leica Camera GmbH*

slots on camera baseplate to obviate removal of motor while reloading film.

Specification: as Leicaflex SL, except:-

Other features: No self timer. Depth of field preview. PC socket as Leicaflex SL. Mirror-up facility as Leicaflex SL. Multiple exposure. Single stroke lever wind.

Motor drive: Separate unit (14 077). Leicaflex Motor (manufactured 1971-1977) for continuous exposures at between 3 – 4 fps and single shot, manufactured by Balda to Leitz design. Early models with serial Nos. below 2600 not fitted with single shot facility. Comprised of massive cast aluminium housing for motor, gearing and battery pack which required 10 x AA size alkaline batteries or special rechargeable NiCd pack. Various accessories simultaneously marketed; handgrip for motor permitted easy firing via electro mechanical shutter release on motor front just beneath camera baseplate (14 181), spare battery housing (14 147), 2.5 meter (8ft 4ins) remote power supply cable with button switch (14 176), Remote release with additional built-in frame counter (14177) required 5 meter (17ft) or 25 meter (83ft) extension cable (14 178 or 14 179 respectively). A twin cable release for radio remote operation (14 180) connected to camera and motor via 14 177.

Camera power source: as Leicaflex SL.

Size: as Leicaflex SL.

Variations: Finished in anodised black chrome. About 1080 SL MOT cameras were produced starting with serial No. 1336991.

LEICALEX SL2

Year introduced: 1974, production ceased 1976.

Specification: This camera was an updated version of the Leicaflex SL. Technical specification was the same as for that model with the following exceptions:-

Construction: As Leicaflex SL but thinner; back was less rounded.

Lens mount: As Leicaflex SL, but lens release/lock device changed from serrated catch to button type similar to that used on M-type rangefinder cameras.

Exposure measurement: As Leicaflex SL, but sensitivity range increased.

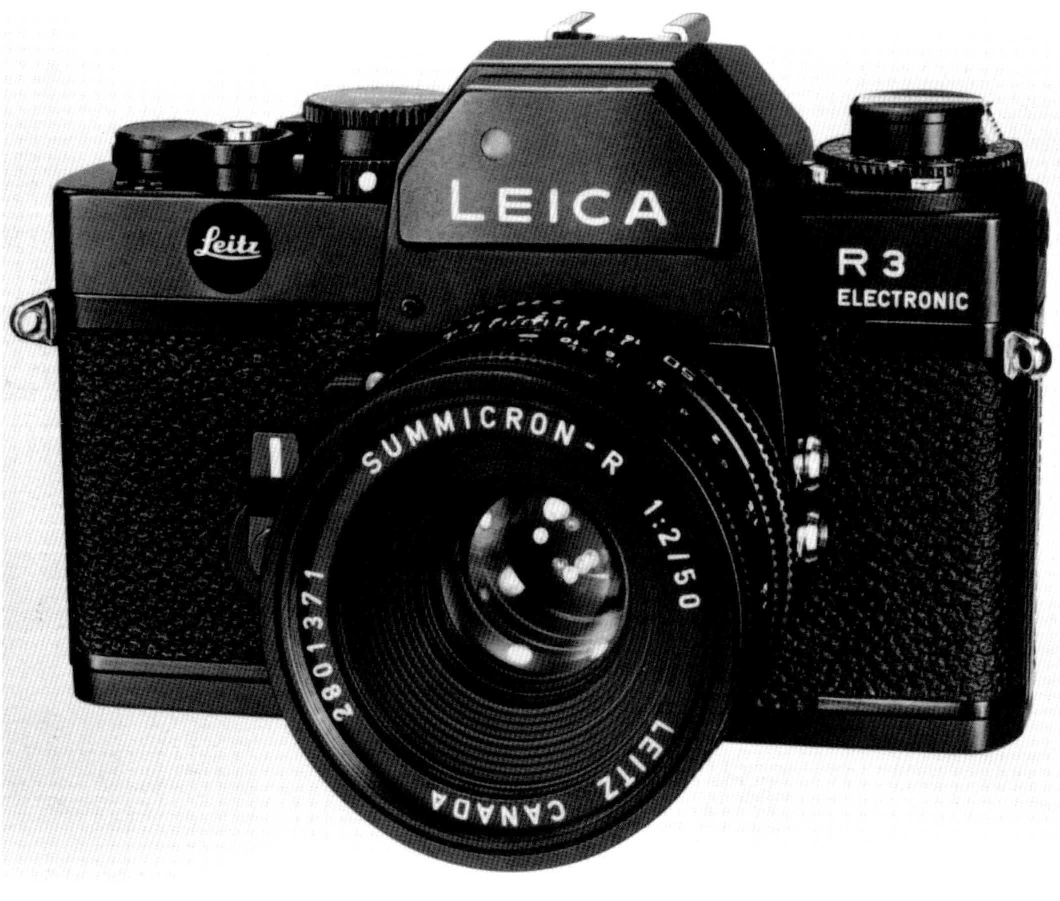

Fig. 24. The Leica R3 Electronic was modelled on the Minolta XE-1 camera.

Viewfinder: As Leicaflex SL, but aperture scale added to shutter speed scale. Ancillary illumination provided by depressing sprung push button switch on front face of pentaprism housing next to camera name. Battery for this item served as back-up power in event of meter battery failure.

Focus: As Leicaflex SL, 3mm central split image rangefinder added.

Other features: Camera back fitted with safety lock under film speed ISO setting dial, once activated, film rewind lever was pulled up to open back. PC socket as Leicaflex SL, plus additional hot-shoe on pentaprism housing top. Mirror-up facility. Mirror also redesigned to permit fitting of extreme wide-angle objectives (see also Chapter 2.). Multiple exposure.

Variations: Camera available in silver or black chrome. 1750 units issued in 1975 to mark 50th Leica anniversary. These were mainly finished in black chrome. Some silver chrome examples exist. Cameras are engraved on the pentaprism housing with the figure '50' surrounded by oak leaf cluster with the word 'Jahre' beneath. Approximately 75 pre-production models were made for factory evaluation and field testing in 1974.

LEICALEX SL2 MOT

Year introduced: 1975, production ceased 1975.

Essentially the same as the Leicaflex SL2 but built to accept the Leicaflex Motor. Approximately 1020 examples of this camera were made in 1975, the year of its introduction.

Variations: Only available in black chrome. No delayed action. Camera accepted the SL Leicaflex Motor and the SL2 Motor is interchangeable between both models. The Leicaflex SL2 MOT camera ceased production in 1976 (none are believed to have been made after 1975) but the product was still listed in Leitz 1980 catalogues.

LEICA R3 Electronic

Year introduced: 1976, production ceased 1979.

Construction: Die-cast body, brass top and bottom plate.

Lens mount: Leica R-type, single cam. Older 2-cam Leicaflex objectives fitted with third cam. Early (Leicaflex) single cam required modification to 3-cam.

Shutter: Copal-Leitz (CLS) electronically controlled, vertical traverse, metal bladed roller type.

Shutter speeds: Automatic mode; steplessly variable between $\frac{1}{1000}$th second and 4 seconds. In manual mode; $\frac{1}{1000}$th, $\frac{1}{500}$th, $\frac{1}{250}$th, $\frac{1}{125}$th, $\frac{1}{60}$th, $\frac{1}{30}$th, $\frac{1}{15}$th, $\frac{1}{8}$th, $\frac{1}{4}$, $\frac{1}{2}$, 1, 2 & 4 seconds. Bulb = brief time. X = electronic flash synchronization at $\frac{1}{60}$th second. Mechanical speeds. X & B usable without batteries.

Exposure measurement: 3 x CdS photo-resistor type providing full-field, integrated (centre weighted) measurement. Dual photo-resistor in mirror box base provides facility for 'selective' exposure measurement. Light to this cell is reflected by a secondary mirror hinged to the rear of the main viewing mirror.

Exposure modes: Automatic aperture priority in combination with full-field integrated or selective measurement operated by electronic switchover. Manual operation permitting shutter speed/aperture combination using selective or full-field exposure measurement. Automatic exposure reading memory lock by depressing shutter release button to 'first pressure'.

Viewfinder: In some respects a radical departure from the Leicaflex

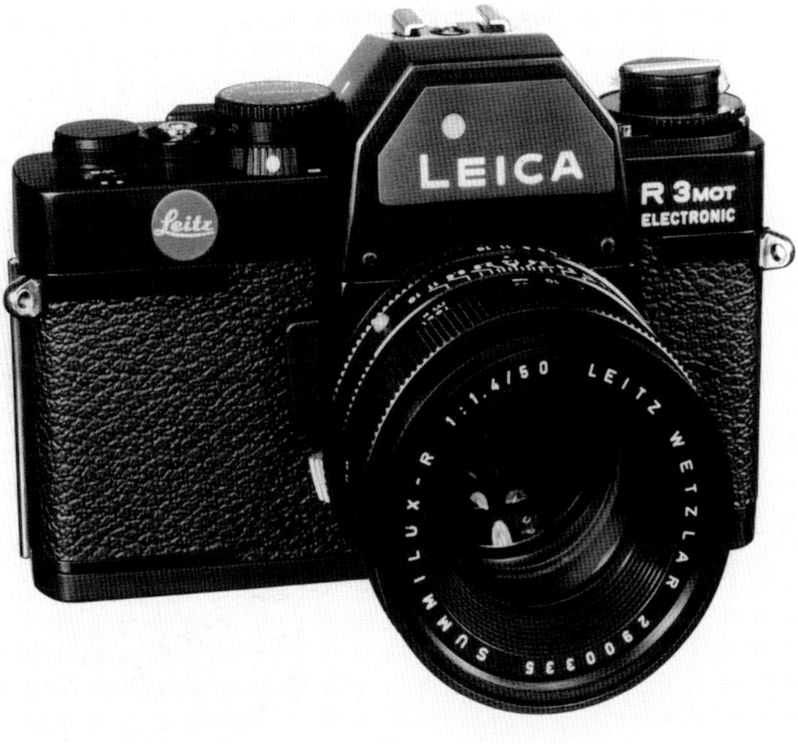

Fig. 25. The Leica R3 MOT Electronic has no self-timer lever.

SL2, while retaining its central split-image rangefinder and course micro-prism collar, which also indicates the limit of 'selective' exposure metering. The visual data display was imported from the Minolta XE-1. To the right a window displays the range of stepless shutter speeds from 45 to 1/1000 sec., while at the top a small window shows the aperture set on the lens and next to it the working mode of the camera.

Focus: Central split-image horizontal rangefinder; outer coarse micro-prism collar, fine microprism outer field simulates groundglass with enhanced image brightness.

Other features: Self timer, delayed action from between 6 to 10 seconds. Depth of field preview, lever at right hand side of lens mount. PC socket, provision for X & M synchronization in addition to X synchronized hot-shoe. No mirror-up facility. Multiple exposure, lever on top plate under film advance lever provides for infinite multiple exposures, automatically resets to prevent accidental double exposure. Film transport by rapid lever wind in single 115° stroke.

Motor winder: separate unit, extra compact with provision for up to 2 frames per second for R3 MOT Electronic only (see below).

Camera power source: 2 x 1.55 volt silver-oxide cells. On/off switch provided on back of top plate next to exposure counter.

Size: 148mm x 96.5mm x 64.6mm (5.8 x 3.8 x 2.4 inches).

Weight: 780 grams (27.5 ozs.)

Variations: The R3 was introduced at Photokina in 1976. The first 2000 cameras were made at Wetzlar and are inscribed 'made in Germany'. Remainder inscribed 'made in Portugal'. Majority finished in black chrome, 4,250 in silver. 100 Wetzlar made examples in silver chrome. Early versions had yellow tinted mirror which locked in half-way position when battery power failed. 5000 safari green R3 kits comprising body, standard Summicron-R 50mm f/2, or Summilux-R 50mm f/1.4, Elmarit-R 28mm f/2.8 and Elmar-R 180mm f/4 with Leitz Trinovid 10x22C binoculars were produced and allocated a special serial No. found on the rear of the pentaprism above the eyepiece. Special versions with a gold plated 'C' surrounding a crown badge were sold as in-flight souvenirs on the Concorde aircraft. 1,000 special 24-carat gold-plated R3's with black reptile skin covering and mahogany presentation case issued in 1979 to mark 100th anniversary of the birth of Oskar Barnack. The Leica inventor's signature appeared on the front face of the pentaprism together with the dates 1879-1979.

LEICA R3 MOT Electronic

Year introduced: Late 1978, production ceased 1979.

Specification: as above, except:-

Exposure measurement: same as for R3, except metering mode now displayed in the viewfinder.

Other features: As for R3, except delayed action function was deleted from R3 MOT Electronic cameras which were manufactured in Wetzlar with strengthened winding gears.

Motor winder: Special separate compact motor winder manufactured by Eumig in Austria permitted drive frequency of up to two frames per second. This hybrid winder was fitted with an elctro-mechanical vertical shutter release button. A special handgrip was offered as an optional extra.

Variations: R3 models could be converted to R3 MOT Electronic specification by Leitz service centres for a short period. A limited edition of 100 R3 MOT cameras were manufactured in 1979 and offered for sale to members of the Leica Historical Society of America to mark its 10th anniversary. The logo 'LHSA' and the dates 1968-1978 were engraved on the pentaprism.

LEICA R4 MOT Electronic and LEICA R4

Year introduced: 1980, production ceased 1986.

Construction: Die-cast aluminium inner chassis and outer thick walled body. 0.8mm top and bottom plates die-cast zinc and brass respectively.

Lens mount: Leica R-type single cam. Earlier Leicaflex single cam and 2-cam lenses required conversion to 3-cam for fully automatic operation. Conversion service still available for most objectives of this type. Early R-type lenses engraved on bottom of barrel, 'For Leica R only'.

Shutter: Electronically operated vertical traverse, metal bladed roller type, manufactured by Seikosha Co Ltd of Japan.

Shutter speeds: In automatic modes, shutter set steplessly from 8 seconds to 1/1000th second. In manual mode, shutter speeds set as marked on setting dial; 100 (mechanical back-up), B, X = 1/100th sec, 1 sec, 1/2, 1/4, 1/8, 1/15th, 1/30th, 1/60th, 1/125th, 1/250th, 1/500th, 1/1000th second.

Exposure measurement: Single silicon photo diode sited at base of mirror box measures full field, with integrated centre weighted readings via light transferred through semi-transparent main viewing mirror to special Leitz designed hinged Fresnel type secondary mirror containing 1345 'micromirrors'. A 4.5mm f/1 converging condenser lens is moved into position over the silicon diode for 'selective' spot exposure metering by a series of levers acti-

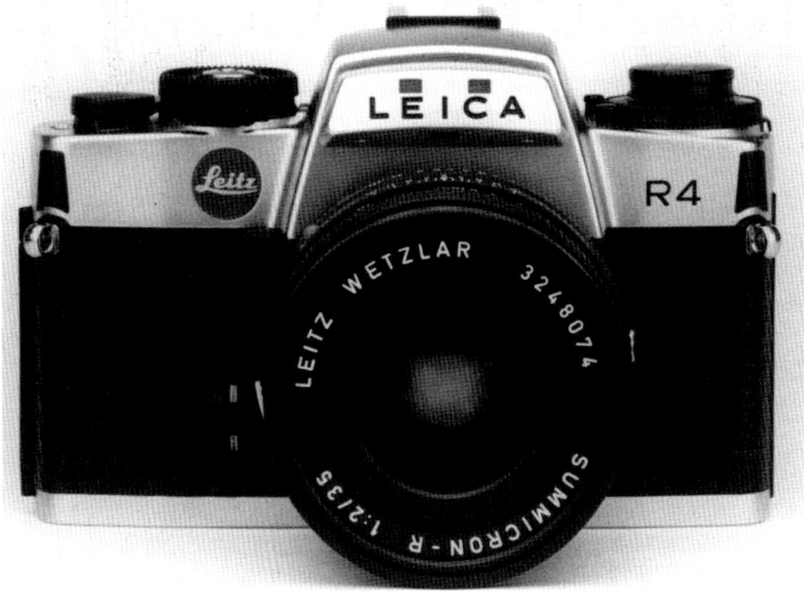

Fig. 26. Standard production, but scarce silver chrome Leica R4 with anti-rub inserts and later Wetzlar Summicron 35mm, f/2. Only about 8,000 were finished in silver.
Fieldgrass & Gale/Jonathan Harris

vated by switch beneath shutter speed setting dial.

Exposure modes: With 'selective' spot measurement; Automatic aperture priority, manual shutter/aperture setting. With full-field measurement; automatic aperture priority, automatic shutter priority, automatic program.

Viewfinder: Built-in pentaprism, image corresponds to 92% of film area; magnification apx; 0.85x with 50mm objective fitted. Shutter speeds displayed at right of screen out of frame, vertical travel red LED indicates speed selected in auto, aperture set shown at base. Red LED's indicate exposure mode set to bottom left.

Focus: universal focus screen, full-field finely etched groundglass effect, central 3mm split-wedge rangefinder surrounded by 7mm diameter coarse micro-prism collar, perimeter of which also signifies outer limit of 'selective' spot measurement area. Four other screens available.

Other features: Self timer, electro-magnetic type with 8-second delay, red LED visible in pentaprism front top flashes with increasing frequency as time decreases; depth of field preview. PC socket, also hot shoe. No mirror-up facility. Multiple exposure, by depressing film rewind clutch release on camera base. Single lever advance with 130° throw, Leica film loading spool as for R3.

Motor winder: optional extra.

Motor drive; optional extra.

Camera power source 2x silver oxide button cells or 1x 3 volt lithium battery.

Size: length 138.5mm, height 88.1mm, depth 60mm.

Weight: 620 grams.

Variations: The name 'R4 MOT Electronic' was deleted and replaced with the simplified 'R4' following pressure from a German consumer association who complained the original name implied the camera was fitted with an integral motor drive and therefore was misleading to the public. The change came after approximately 25,000 units had been manufactured. 1000 gold plated R4's with a body covering of brown water-snake skin were offered for sale in 1984. 600 camera sets including the Vario-Elmar-R 70-200mm f/4.5 zoom lens and a series of photographs depicting the 1936 Olympics by Lother Rubelt were inscribed 'Jessie Owens Golden Anniversary 1936-1986', together with similarly inscribed camera body and lens caps were offered by E. Leitz Inc., Rockleigh, USA to commemorate the 50th anniversary of the athlete's performance at the Berlin Olympics in 1936. Later models of the R4 camera were factory fitted with black plastic anti-rub strap inserts and after serial No. 1,600,000, numbers were engraved on the back-side lip of the base plate instead of on the bottom.

LEICA R4s

Year introduced: 1983, production ceased 1985.

The R4s was a simplified version of the R4 which offered aperture priority with 'selective' and full-field measurement and manual setting of shutter and/or aperture in 'selective' mode only, otherwise it was identical to the latter. It was available in a black chrome finish and 19,000 cameras were produced.

LEICA R4s MOD 2 – MOD P

Year introduced: 1986, production ceased 1988.

The R4s was produced by Leitz following demands from enthusiastic professionals and amateur photographers who claimed the aperture priority system of exposure measurement was the most useful mode of the five offered on the R4. The R4s MOD 2 (R4s MOD P in the USA), was a second generation R4s with further minor improvements. These

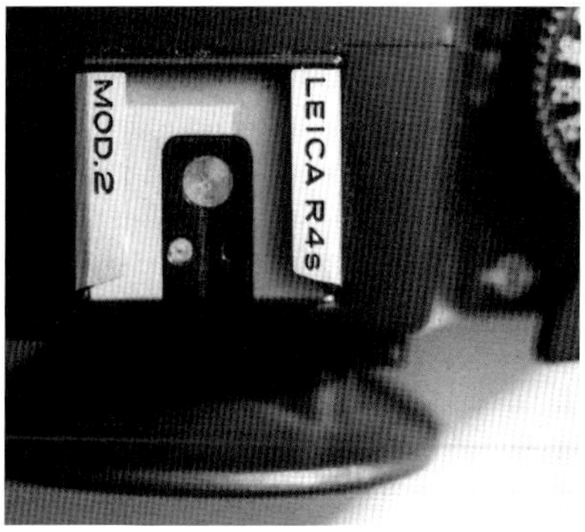

Fig. 28. There are few differences between the Leica R4s and the Leica R4s MOD 2 (MOD P in USA). This is the main one, engraved on the flanges of the accessory shoe.

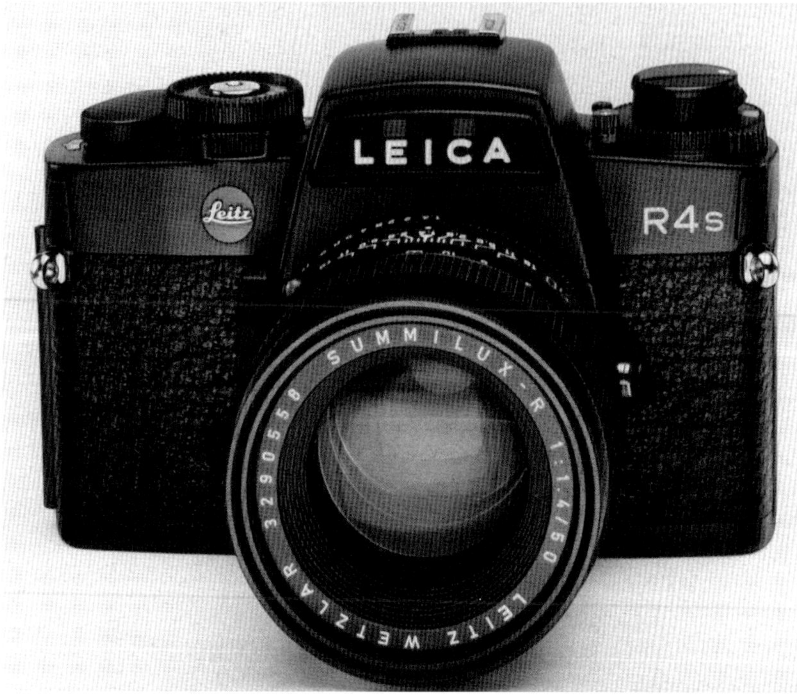

Fig. 27. The Leica R4s was an electronically simplified version of the R4 with aperture priority program only, linked to 'selective' or centre-weighted metering and manual override. *Leica Camera GmbH*

included the film advance lever which was totally encased in a tough plastic moulding, new design rapid exposure measurement method changeover switch beneath shutter dial. In Aperture priority mode, metered exposure measurement could be held while depressing the central portion of the changeover switch, a useful facility when reframing was required; viewfinder display of shutter speed dial setting when in manual mode; eyepiece ocular frame for fitting 'spring-lock' rubber eye-cup or dioptre correction lenses and sliding exposure compensation switch instead of the previous button type. Camera also featured the new high profile shutter speed setting dial and rewind knob. Compensation adjustments could be made in ⅓rd stop increments. All other specification details were the same as for the R4s. The camera retained the 'R4s' designation of its predecessor on the right hand side of the camera, but the model number and name was engraved on both flanges of the pentaprism hot shoe. All of the 6,931 unit production was finished in black chrome.

Although less highly specified than the original R4 camera, the R4s MOD 2 was probably the most ergonomic and functional of the three R4 models; certainly a desirable piece of equipment for the photo-journalist and travel specialist. This model commands a premium price on the used market because of its rarity and the special engraving. Even so, it is an ideal 'introductory' camera for the budget conscious just entering the Leica reflex fraternity.

LEICA R5

Year introduced: January 1987, production ceased 1992.

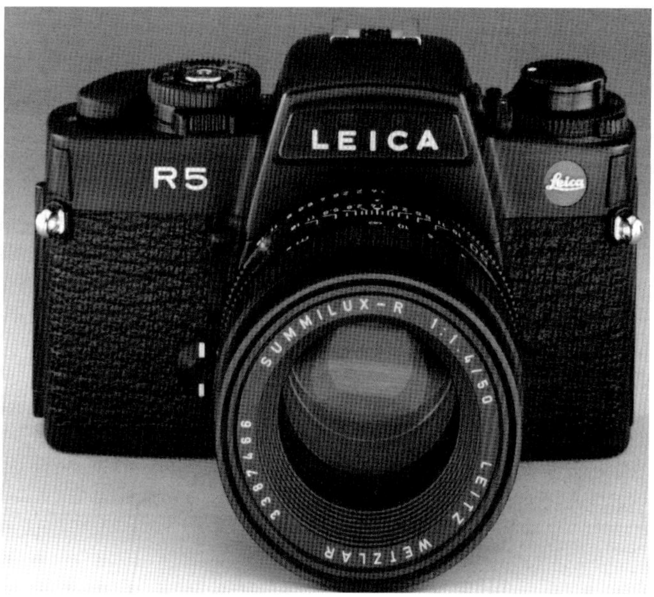

Fig. 29. Leica R5, the first R-model to incorporate TTL flash control. *Leica Camera GmbH*

Construction: Modular die-cast aluminium inner chassis and outer shell. 1.0mm-thick die-cast zinc top plate, 0.8mm-thick brass bottom plate.

Lens mount: Leica R-type bayonet.

Shutter: Electronically controlled vertical traverse, metal bladed roller type.

Shutter speeds: With automatic electronic programs, steplessly variable from 15 seconds to 1/2000th second. In manual mode, shutter set in full indicated values from ½ second to 1/2000th second. Mechanical shutter speeds, 1/100th sec indicated by orange '100' marker on shutter speed dial; 'B' for brief time. Electronic flash synchronization = X = 1/100th second (mechanical).

Exposure measurement: Single silicon photo diode in mirror box base measures full field with integrated centre-weighted metering; switchable converging lens over diode provides for 'selective' spot metering measurement.

Exposure modes: Aperture priority with selective metering, aperture priority with full-field exposure measurement, shutter priority with full-field measurement, variable mode (Program) with full-field measurement, manual selection of shutter/aperture combination with selective metering.

Viewfinder: Built-in pentaprism with 5 interchangeable viewing screens indicating 92% of film area (23 x 34.6mm), magnification 0.8x with 0 dioptre ocular using 50mm objective. User dioptre adjustment possible. Display indicates program mode, exposure metering method, shutter and aperture speed selected; measured exposure holding indicator. Flash ready LED and flash correct/incorrect TTL exposure indicated by intermittent flashing LED's. Shutter speed/aperture set disappears when flash is used.

Focus: With standard screen; central split image horizontal rangefinder surrounded by 7mm coarse microprism collar (also indicates 'selective' spot metering area), finely etched groundglass effect screen for full-field focus control.

Other features: Self timer, approx 9 seconds indicated by flashing red LED on pentaprism front. Depth of field preview, sited above lens lock/release catch. PC socket, for X/M sited on left side pentaprism housing. No mirror-up facility. Multiple exposure, using film rewind release button on camera base. Single stroke lever advance (130°). Standard Leica R-type film take-up as described in text.

Motor winder: Optional, up to 2 fps. Front electro-mechanical release in addition to camera operation. Optional hand-grip available with electro-magnetic operating switch.

Motor drive: Optional, up to 4 fps, switchable to 2 fps and single frame operation. Front electro-mechanical release for vertical shooting in addition to camera release. Optional hand-grip available with electro-magnetic shutter release.

Camera power source: 2x silver oxide button cells or one lithium cell. Camera has built-in battery tester on top plate.

Size: height 89.1mm, length 138.5mm, depth 62.2mm.

Weight: 625 grams.

Variations: Red 'Leitz' roundel badge replaced with word 'Leica' when company named changed in 1988. Production moved from Portugal to Solms in 1990. Camera available in black or silver chrome. German version factory fitted with rear thumb grip from 1992.

LEICA R6

Year introduced: 1987, Production ceased 1992.

Construction: Die-cast aluminium inner chassis and outer body shell, 1.0mm-thick die-cast zinc top plate, 0.8mm-thick brass bottom plate.

Lens mount: Leica R-type bayonet.

Shutter: Mechanical, Leica patent vertical traverse, metal bladed roller type.

Shutter speeds: 1 second to 1/1000th second in values as set by click-stop circular shutter dial. X = 1/100th second for electronic flash synchronization.

Exposure measurement: Single silicon photo diode in base of mirror box for full-field, integrated centre-weighted measurement. Adjustable converging condenser lens moved over silicon diode by exposure mode selection switch at base of shutter speed dial connected to levers provides for 'selective' spot measurement at full aperture with R-type objectives incorporating full automatic diaphragm, at working aperture with preset aperture objectives and accessories. Secondary silicon photo diode installed adjacent to main one used for TTL flash exposure measurement. Exposure compensation device to +/- 2 stops for use with electronic flash TTL sited on ISO film speed setting ring with lock device. Meter range: Selective; EV +1 to +19 (ISO 100,DIN 21). Full Field Integrated; EV -1 to +19 (ISO 100, DIN 21). Film speed settings possible from ISO 12, DIN 12, to ISO 3200, DIN 36.

Exposure modes: User switchable 'selective' spot indicated in viewfinder by red 'o', full-field, integrated centre-weighted measurement indicated by red ⚡. Exposure changeover switch cuts power supply to meter in 'off' position.

Viewfinder: Built-in pentaprism. Dial-in user dioptre correction facility from +2 to -2 dioptres. Eyepiece shutter. Field of view, 92% of film frame size (34.6mm x 23mm). Magnification 0.8x at 0-dioptre with

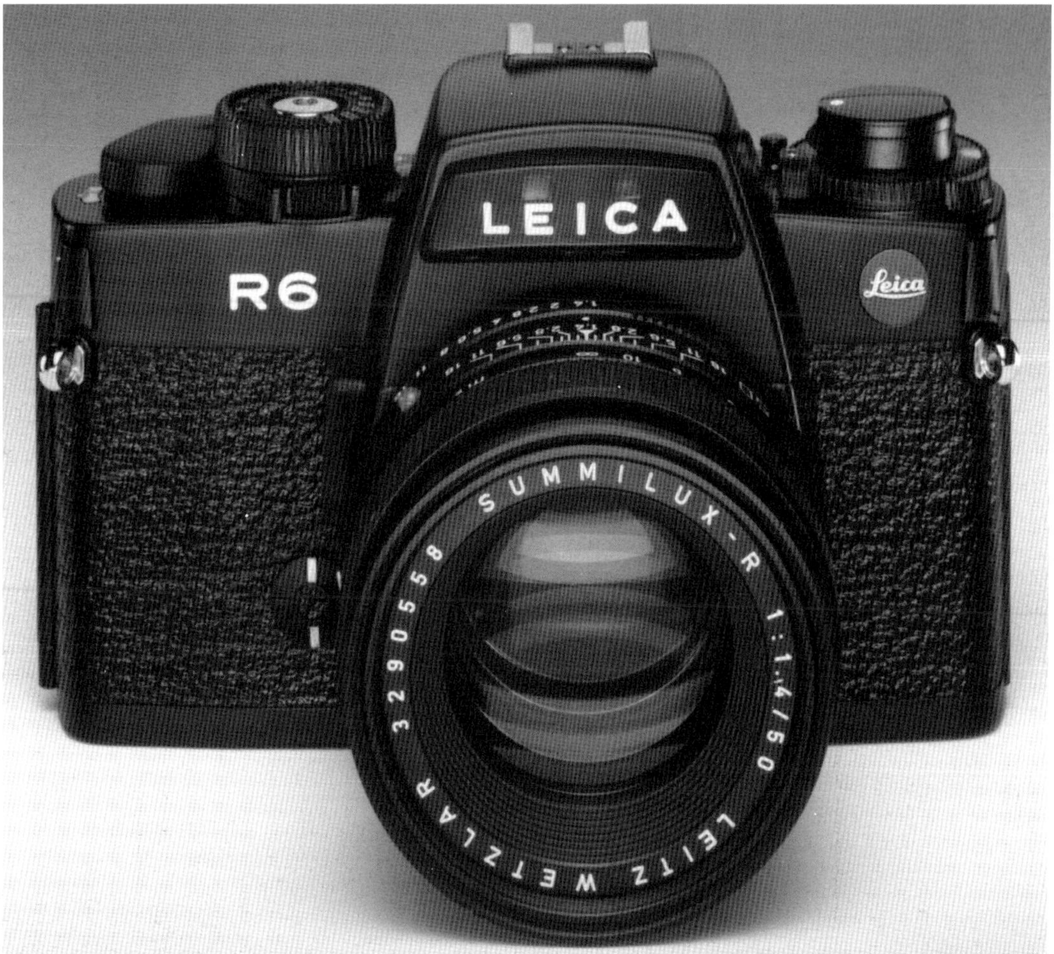

Fig. 30. Leica R6, the first all-mechanical camera since the Leicaflex SL2. Note the higher shutter speed setting dial. Silver chrome versions rare. *Leica Camera GmbH*

50mm objective. Data display includes exposure measurement mode selected, shutter/aperture setting and correct exposure balance. Electronic flash-ready symbol and correct/incorrect TTL flash exposure by intermittent flashing LED symbol. Low-light warning with over- and underexposure override. Ancillary viewfinder light manually activated by switch at lower left of lens mount base.

Focus: Central split-image horizontal rangefinder surrounded by 7mm diameter coarse micro-prism collar which also indicates extent and area covered by 'selective' spot exposure measurement. High contrast fine groundglass effect for remainder of screen permits accurate full-field focus. 5 user interchangeable focusing screens available.

Other features: Self timer, delay time about 9 seconds, activated by electro magnetic switch next to lens lock/release catch, can be stopped while red LED on front of camera pentaprism is blinking and reset for further extension.

Depth of field preview, above lens lock/release catch.

Standard PC X socket on left hand side of pentaprism. Dedicated hot shoe for 'X' synchronization using SCA 351 or 551 adapter with compatible electronic flash units, no flash-ready light. Viewfinder safety features indicated by display operating mode, i.e. shutter speed incorrectly set. Mirror-up facility; with cable release inserted in special socket sited immediately below lens lock/release catch, squeezing cable release raises mirror and closes lens diaphragm; exposure made by firing shutter in normal way after which mirror returns to normal viewing position and lens diaphragm fully opened.

Multiple exposure by depressing film rewind button located in base of camera. Single throw lever wind (130°). Film loading as per Leica-R method described intext.

Motor winder: Optional, maximum 2 fps fitted with electro-mechanical switch for vertical shooting. Powered by 6x rechargeable NiCad or 6x alkaline batteries. Camera shutter release used for normal landscape operation. Optional handgrip with electro-magnetic shutter release.

Motor drive; Optional, up to 4 fps maximum, also 2 fps and single fps modes selected by switch on front face of drive unit. This robust unit is manufactured by Eumig in Austria. Front face fitted with electro-mechanical switch for convenient vertical user operation. Requires 10x rechargeable NiCad or 10x alkaline High Power batteries for maximum efficiency. Power sufficient for exposure of approx 150x 36 exposure films at 20° C. Power supply from drive unit used to power camera meter when attached, thus saving camera supply.

Camera power source: 2x silver oxide button cells or one lithium battery. Battery test button on left hand side of top plate with red LED indicator. Sufficient power for approx 70 films of 36 exposure using 12 second exposure duration.

Size: height 89.1mm, length 138.5mm, depth 32.2mm.

Weight: 625 grams.

Variations: The R6 was the first all-mechanical single lens reflex camera to be launched by Leica since the demise of the Leicaflex SL2. It was warmly welcomed by enthusiasts and professionals alike. Only available with a black chrome finish at first, silver chrome versions are scarce, commanding high prices for mint condition examples on the used market. In 1989, a special commemorative version of the camera, serial no. 1,750,000 was manufactured complete with Summilux 50mm f/1/4 lens in polished platinum plate and covered with Karung leather. A platinum plate on the rear of the camera was engraved '150 Jahre Photographie 1989. 75 Jahre Leica Photographie. Leica'. The camera left the factory in a lined mahogany box with platinum catch and a plaque engraved as the back of the camera and was sold at Christies in London on November 9th, 1989 for the princely sum of £26,400, the proceeds being donated to the World Wild Life Fund.

Advertised on release as a camera for the dedicated professional it is indeed a superb instrument, giving its user a real sense of confidence and satisfaction. Combined with the Leica Motor Drive-R, it makes a durable and highly reliable all round package for the specialist engaged in environmentally tough assignments.

LEICA R-E

Year introduced: 1990, production ceased July 1994.

Construction: Die-cast aluminium inner chassis and outer bodyshell. 1.0mm thick zinc top plate and 0.8mm thick brass bottom plate.

Lens mount: Leica R-type bayonet.

Shutter: Electronically controlled vertical travel, metal bladed roller type manufactured by Seikosha Co Ltd. Japan.

Shutter speeds: In automatic program modes, from 15 seconds to 1/2000th second.

Exposure measurement: Single silicon photo diode in base of mirror box controls 'selective' spot or full-field, integrated centre-weighted exposure measurement activated by switch at base of shutter speed dial as for R5.

Exposure modes: This camera was launched as a simplified version of the R5 and offered Manual or Aperture priority modes with 'selective' or full-field, integrated centre-weighted exposure measurement.

Viewfinder: As R5.

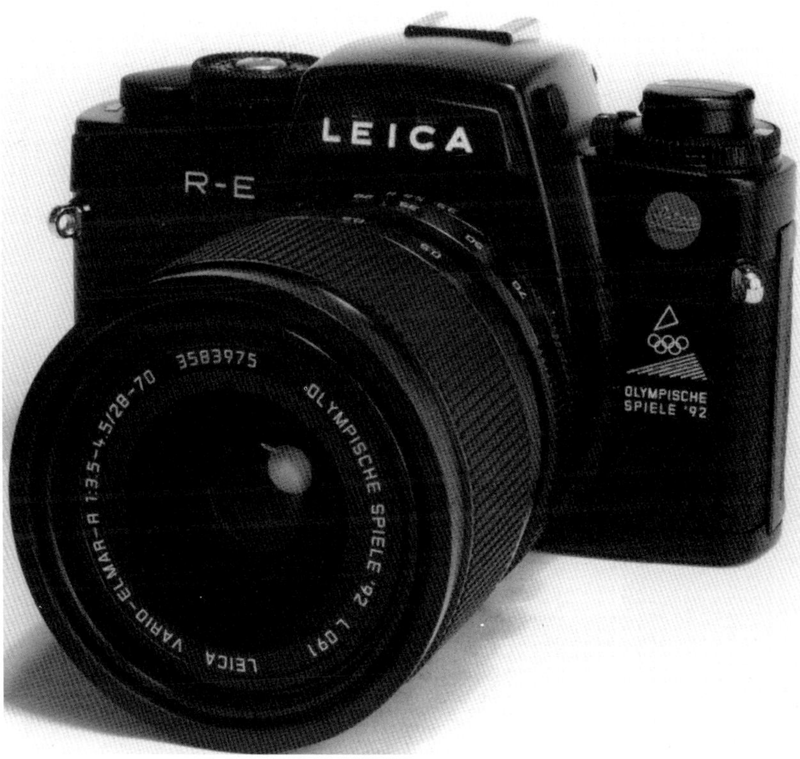

Fig. 31. 'Leica Olympia Set'. Commemorative version of the Leica RE issued in 1992 with Vario-Elmar-R 28-70mm, f/3.5-4.5 lens. 5,000 pieces were made in batches of 500 with special serial numbers prefixed by a letter of the word LEICA followed by a three-digit number engraved on the base plate and lens front rim. This camera was made at Solms and could be bought complete in 1992 for US$ 2,360. *Fieldgrass & Gale/Jonathan Harris*

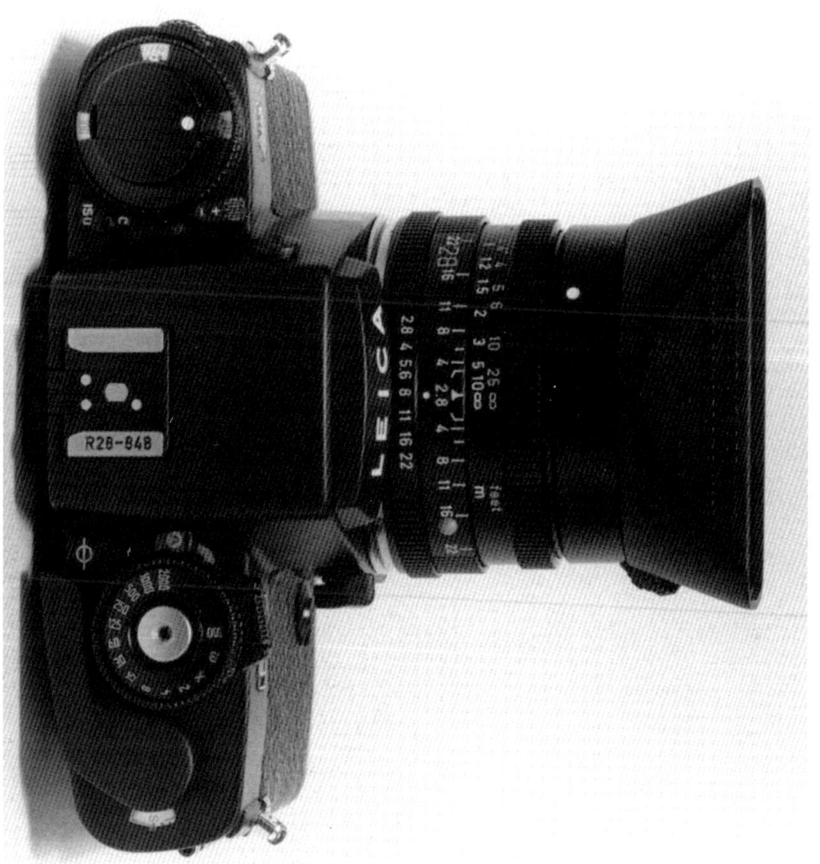

Fig. 32. Neither of the Leica RE limited edition cameras receive a mention in the Leica Pocket Book (LPG); only the standard version of this simplified R5 gets a grudging entry along with a lowly R1 rarity guide. Why this should be so is a little baffling since the camera is far more sophisticated than its earlier R4s counterpart. One suspects Leicaphiles 'downgraded' the RE because of its links with the Sigma made zoom (see Chapter 2) and the body model badge which does nothing for aesthetic appeal. These cosmetic observations aside, the R-E is a tough Leica, built to the same exacting standards as all other models (see spec.). The version illustrated here was called the Leica-R28, and was issued in limited quantities with a serial number matched Elmarit-R 28mm, f/2.8 lens, an ideal combination for the photojournalist.
Fieldgrass & Gale/Jonathan Harris

Focus: As R5

Other features: Self timer; as R5. Depth of field preview. PC socket; as R5. No mirror-up facility. Multiple exposure; as R5. Film transport; as R5.

Motor winder: Optional as R5.

Motor drive: Optional as R5.

Camera power source: 2x silver oxide button cells or lithium battery.

Size: As R5.

Variations: The camera was available only in black chrome finish. A special commemorative edition was launched in 1992 with a badge fitted to the right hand side of the body as viewed from the front with the inscription 'OLYMPIC SPIELE 1992' and was offered as a kit with the specially engraved Vario-Elmar-R 28mm-70mm, f/3/5-4.5 zoom lens which featured the same wording around the front lens retaining ring, together with a special serial number which was also engraved on the base plate of the camera. 5,000 camera outfits in batches of 500 incorporating one letter of the name 'Leica' prefixing the special number, were officially offered by the dealer Foto-Hobby GmbH of Frankfurt, Germany and retailed at a cost of DM3,770 or US$2,360 without tax.

LEICA R6.2

Year introduced: 1992, current model.

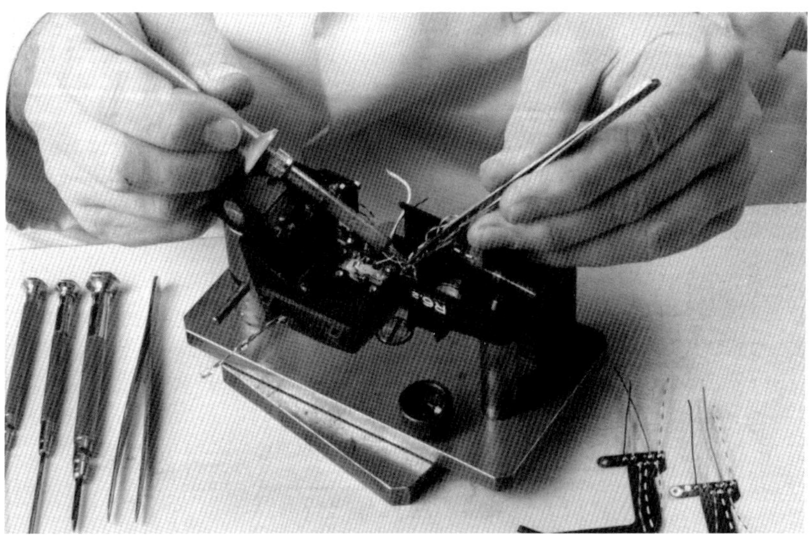

Fig. 33. Flash control and viewfinder wiring being hand soldered into the top cover plate of a Leica R6.2. Note the special support jig incorporates a finger rest for the assembler.
Leica Camera GmbH

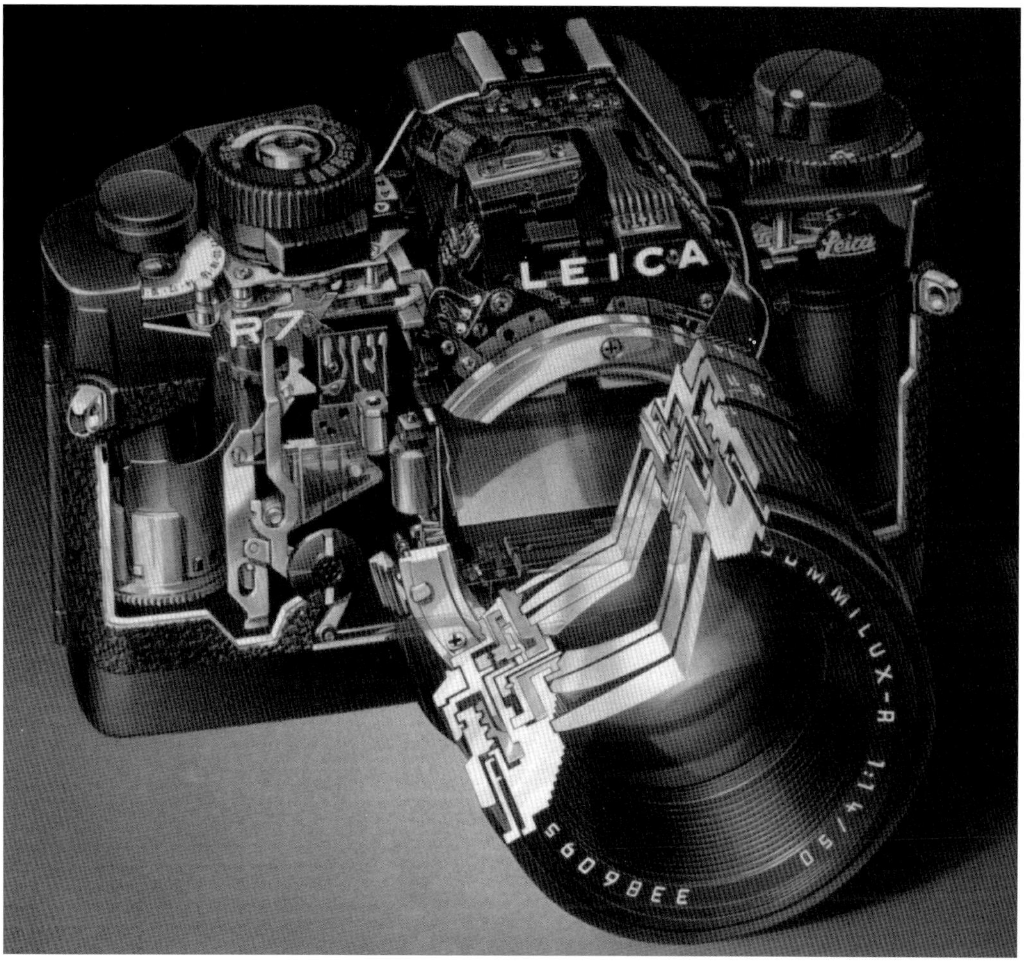

Fig. 34. Cutaway view of the Leica R7 which shows clearly the improved electronic system used in this model. Compare with Fig16. *Leica Camera GmbH*

This model is essentially the same as the R6 but is fitted with improved lightweight shutter blades for greater efficiency, improved mechanical governors for greater shutter speed accuracy and has a one step faster shutter speed, 1/2000th second installed. The film exposure counter is relocated in front of the film advance lever and returns to the circular magnifier window type for easier reading. Metering sensitivity is also increased, providing a truly superb instrument for the 'purist'.

LEICA R7

Year introduced: 9/1992, current model.

Construction: Die-cast aluminium inner chassis and outer bodyshell. 1.0mm thick die-cast zinc top plate, 0.8mm thick brass high walled base plate.

Lens mount: Leica R-type bayonet.

Shutter: Electronically controlled vertical traverse, metal bladed roller type.

Shutter speeds: In automatic programs, continuously stepless from 16 seconds to 1/2000th second. In manual and shutter priority modes, from 4 seconds to 1/2000th second in half values. Mechanically controlled speeds; 100⚡ = 1/100th second = 'X' electronic flash synchronization + 'B' for brief time. B setting also controlled electronically when Leica Motor Drive-R is fitted. Shutter speed setting dial is new 6.5 mm high type.

Exposure measurement: 'Selective' spot and Full Field, integrated centre-weighted through-the-lens metering by single silicon photodiode incorporated in mirror box base. Converging condenser lens moved over silicon photodiode for 'selective' spot measurement as R4, R5 etc. Exposure meter measures at maximum lens aperture with fully automated diaphragm Leica R-type objectives as well as certain focal lengths manufactured by Angénieux S.A. of France (see Chapter 2). Metering at working aperture with pre-set aperture objectives. Meter measures approximately 4.5% of 35mm format in 'Selective' spot mode. Exposure compensation device on top left hand of camera seen from rear adjustable +/- 3 stops in half stop

CHAPTER 2

Leica Reflex Lenses 1965-1995

In committing the company to expensive research, design and tooling for the Leicaflex camera, Leitz also had to design and develop the new objectives for the camera. This was no small undertaking for a firm which, though it had carved out a tiny niche for itself since 1925 with the rangefinder camera and had built a substantial body of research data pertaining to optical glass, was now about to enter a market in which customers expected a larger lens range.

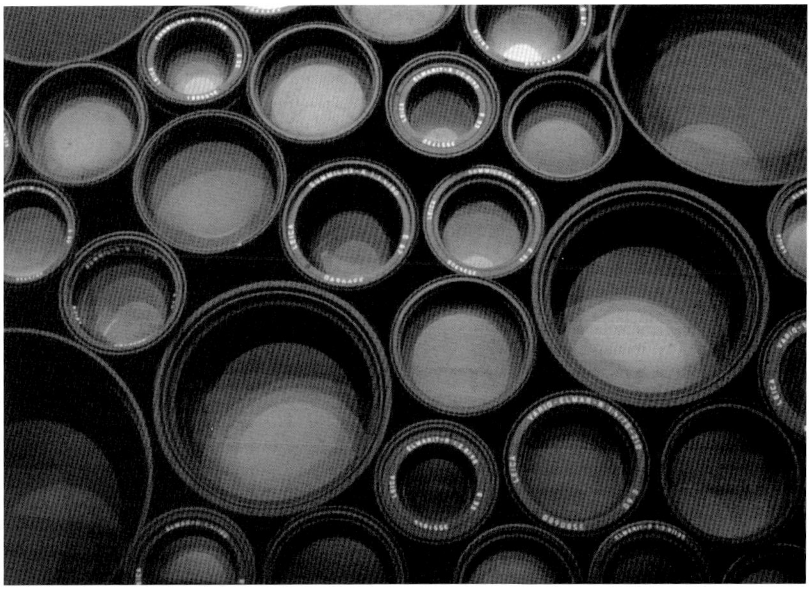

Leica Akademie

From the beginning in 1965, only four focal lengths were offered with the Leicaflex; 35mm, 50mm, 90mm and 135mm. The Super-Angulon-R 21mm, f/3.4, which was similar in optical configuration to its rangefinder counterpart, became available in the same year. Other focal length objectives (from the 65mm Elmar to 400mm Telyt) which already existed for the rangefinder for use with the Visoflex mirror box housing, could be used with the 'flex' camera with a special adaptor, but these were aperture pre-set and had limited applications. It seemed at first as if Leitz had actually bitten off more than they could chew and for a while at least, they circumscribed the demands of many by placing heavy emphasis on the benefits of the existing range while lauding the special benefits of the 'flex' camera for close-up and macro photography using normal rangefinder lenses.

The problem at Leitz at this time was not so much a lack of enthusiasm for expanding the Leicaflex system as fast as possible, but a lack of cash. Although the rangefinder continued to sell quite well, development of new models and lenses in that department was also taking place. In the first year of release, more than 11,000 objectives of all types were sold in America, as well as several thousand Leicaflex Standard cameras, but this was nothing like enough to keep development going fast enough; consequently, no additions to the range were made until after three years five new lenses were added to the system. Of these, at least one (the new f/4, 21mm Super Angulon) was made by Schneider for Leitz.

Leitz had previously bought in some lenses, to their own specification, from Schneider for the Leica rangefinder camera, so it was no accident that this policy continued. Indeed, Leitz and later Leica GmbH, expanded the practice of buying-in and subcontracting the manufacture of certain objectives. This policy applied especially to objectives that were beyond the company's development budget and thus could not be produced in-house quickly enough to satisfy market demand, as well as to several 'off-the-shelf' designs which met the stringent Leitz/Leica optical standards. Of the latter, the Vario-Elmar-R 80-200mm, f/4.5 zoom and later models of this same lens are good examples; it is in fact a Minolta designed and made lens. Only the outer barrel, lens mount, automatic diaphragm coupling levers and cosmetic appearance are to Leitz specification. A shorter zoom lens, the lightweight Vario-Elmar-R 28-70mm f/3.4-4.5, is manufactured by the Sigma Corporation of Japan and is identical in optical design to that company's own version of this lens.

In another example which exhibits all the outward signs of superior Leica manufacturing

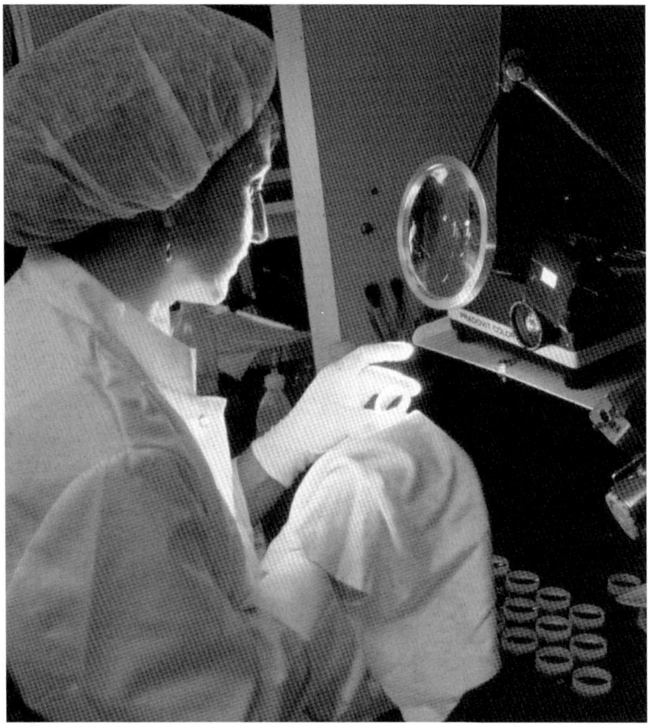

Fig. 39. Inspecting lens elements for flaws before anti-reflection coatings are applied. *Leica Camera GmbH*

quality, we can look to the Super-Elmar-R 15mm, f/3.5. This beautiful piece of glass is, in another world, the Distagon T* f/3.5, 15mm manufactured by Carl Zeiss of Oberkochen. The same lens is available to fit the Contax RTS camera as well as the Rollei 3003 series cameras. The optical construction of this lens in all three versions is identical, however Leica doubtless specified that their own special thin-film coating formula be used to maintain the typical Leica colour rendition peculiar to all other objectives in the Leica R-lens range. While the mount, barrel and fine black chrome finish of this lens in the Leica version exhibit the familiar high quality one expects, it is the lens coating which gives this particular bought-in objective the edge over the other two, and is one of the reasons its retail cost is that much higher.

The relatively high retail cost of Leica objectives is often a lively point of discussion with some photographers, especially those new to the system, or those 'thinking about' jumping the fence. It is perhaps worth noting some of the reasons for this, in particular with reference to those objectives which are marketed by Leica but not manufactured by them.

In the world of Leica rangefinder cameras and lenses, it has always been accepted that Leitz (and now Leica) glass offers the photographer the means to obtain a superior quality image. For many years after World War II, Leitz maintained an optical research laboratory (sold in 1989 to Corning Glass of the USA). This laboratory was responsible for formulating many of the special glasses and the thin-film lens coatings used in both Leitz and Leica designed objectives.

No other company in the world has access to the formulae used to produce objectives which exhibit the very particular Leica image quality. It is not only that overall sharpness, resolution, delineation and the differentiation of tones and colours is superior in the eyes of experienced Leica users, but additionally, this quality can be easily held when making very big enlargements straight from an original negative or transparency. These differences are also apparent when transparencies are projected onto large screens using Leica projectors and lenses.

In the normal course of producing machine made colour negative enprints, or even when enlarging black-and-white negatives to say 10 x 8 ins size, the outstanding optical qualities of Leica optical glass may not be readily apparent when prints are viewed from the normal distance of 12 inches (30 cms) with unaided eyesight. But these are not standard print sizes for many enthusiastic Leica users who frequently enlarge to 12 x 14 ins or 16 x 20 ins or larger, and it is only when you begin to work at these sizes with the 35mm format that the real differences between marques begin to show.

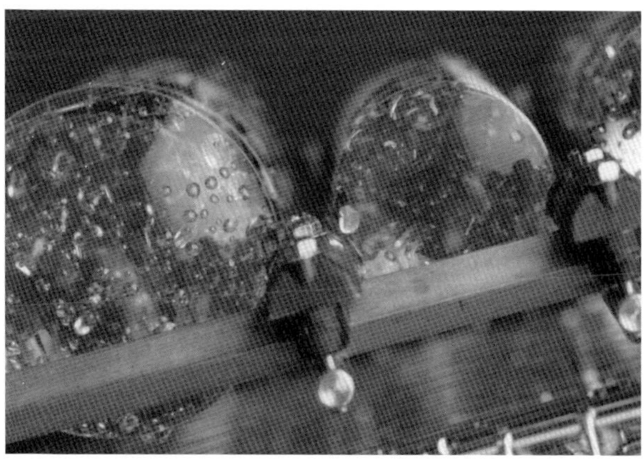

Fig. 40. Lens elements emerging from an ultrasonic cleaning tank prior to anti-reflection coating. *Leica Akademie*

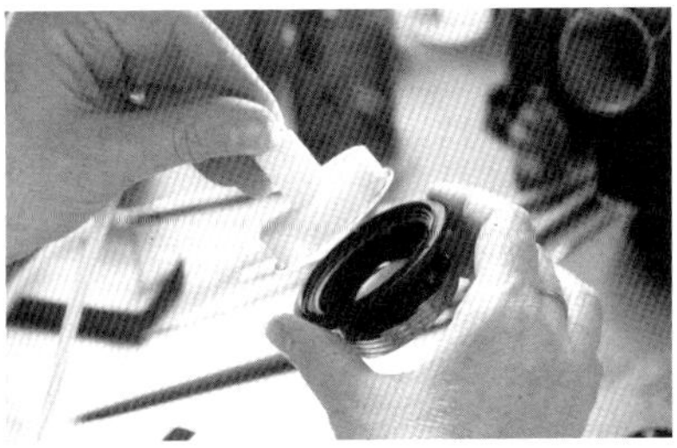

Fig. 41. Each Leica lens is hand built. Special tools are used for handling elements.
Leica Akademie

The most commonly accepted form of modern lens testing used by independent third parties to examine review items in the trade press often refers to the Modular Transfer Function or MTF. In comparing similar objectives, a graph is drawn up showing the number of lines per mm resolved by the lens for high and low contrast at certain aperture equivalents using electronic bench testing instruments. While these tests (which form only a small part of the overall optical testing methods used by some photographic lens manufacturers) can show one aspect of performance, they tend to be terribly misleading. Another popular method of independent testing involves photographing a wall chart, usually at a close distance, and then examining the result under a high powored magnifying glass. The results may show that a particular objective has good edge-to-edge and corner-to-corner resolving power at a particular distance; it may also show whether or not, at that distance, mechanical or optical vignetting, distortion of the object, or chromatic aberration ofcolour is present.

Usually, it is not possible to say that a lens which performs well under these circumstances will perform equally well in the field at all other distances. Without the use of special testing equipment it is virtually impossible to detect slight unevenness in light distribution across the whole field. Without either sophisticated optical bench testing instruments or equivalently sophisticated computers it is impossible to say to what extent coma or other aberrations may be present. What we can say about Leitz and modern Leica objectives is that few, if any, of the commonly known aberrations and distortions which affect some photographic objectives, and are sometimes apparent in the result using other types, exist to the point of being of any significance.

The reason for this, apart from the research carried out to establish formulae for the production of the most suitable optical glass for certain objectives, is that Leitz and Leica have spent decades bench testing to eliminate those flaws in lens design which might otherwise be acceptable for many applications but which would limit its extreme practical capabilities. The company also spent many years pioneering the use of computers in lens design. Many years ago technicians at Leitz developed the special COMO (standing for Correct, Optimize, Minimise, Orthogonalize) computer programme to help speed up the process of mathematical calculation and auto correction. Before its introduction, evaluating comparable lens designs, which may now only take many months to process, would have taken ten men ten years to

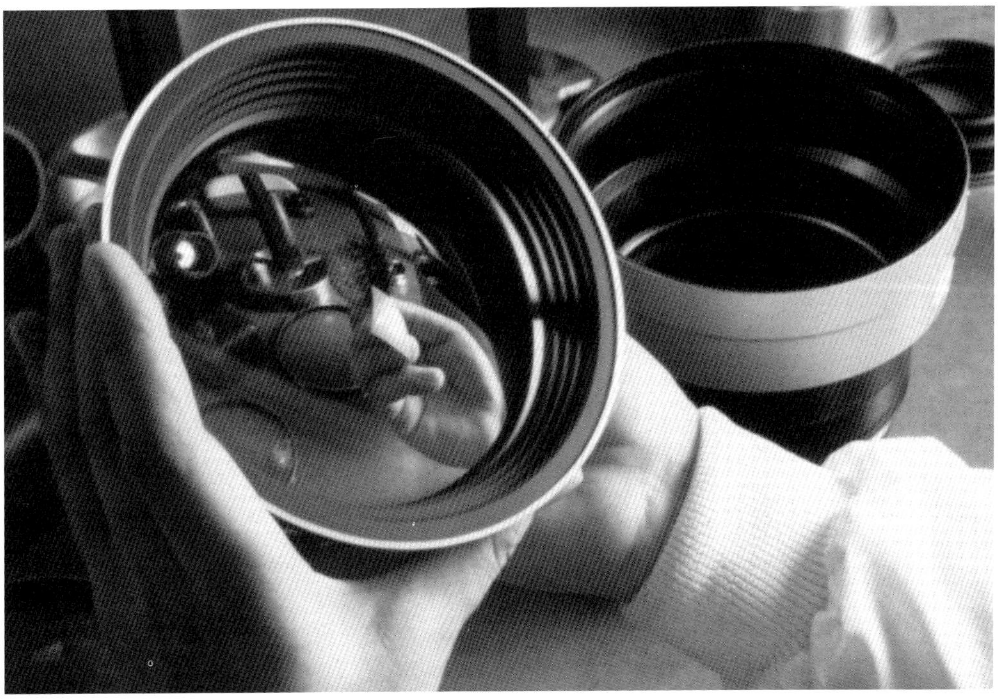

Fig. 42. The working end of the massive Apo-Telyt-R 400mm, f/2.8 objective under construction.
Leica Akademie

finish; even then, they may not have reached the same conclusions.

The development of COMO enabled Leitz to input all of the data collected since the earliest days. It will accept lens thickness, element radii, spacings, all the known glass properties of refraction and dispersion, including anomalous partial dispersion and many other factors. Photographers talk about lens aberrations in simplistic terms, the manifestation of which is only seen by the majority in the contents of a two dimensional print. Lens designers see things differently. Aberrations do not exist in a single dimension but in as many as fifty different mathematical planes. COMO's development enabled Leitz, and later Leica, designers to explore many design concepts that would previously have been unthinkable.

Another point of view concerning cost which deserves some consideration is that to the scientists, technicians and optical engineers involved, there would be little point in housing all this expensive glass expertise in a flimsy mount. The metal engineering side of the equation is thus given equal consideration to ensure stable retention of the glass, considerable longevity in the mechanical life of the lens mount, diaphragm operation and levers, as well as to the life of the focusing mount and durability of the outer shell. Materials used for the basic construction of these parts are brass, hardened brass and aluminium, as well as exotic types of polycarbonate, epoxy materials and durable rubber composites for certain outer casing protection to objectives.

The diaphragm leaves of a Leica R-lens are spring loaded. The closing path – distance of travel to a set aperture – is about twice as long as in many other brands. This ensures high accuracy when smaller f/stops are used and also ensures this same accuracy to within 1/8th of a stop over many years of use. The maximum closing time for the blades is a mere 40 milliseconds. Considering the fragility of this complex mechanical aspect, it is a wonder that lenses sometimes last as long as they do. Recognizing the apparently careless way professional photographers sometimes handle their equipment, and allowing for accidental knocks and bangs, Leitz designers insisted on a specification for mounts and barrels that in the finished form, would be capable of withstanding pressure tests of up to 100G.

These same considerations are given to lenses which are bought-in or subcontracted to independent lens makers. In 1990 when the Vario-Elmar-R 28-70mm lens was launched, some critics noted their surprise that the lens cost five times as much as Sigma's own version. The subsequent reviews in some of the photographic press of the time did little to extol the virtues of the Leica lens, and while this objective sold reasonably well in Germany, it suffered a downgraded public image in other countries and was subsequently discontinued. The features contributing to the additional higher cost of this lens which reviewers conveniently overlooked were;

a. The Leica version was based on a development of the Sigma lens.
b. Much time was spent agreeing a specification for the Leica lens between the two companies.
c. Changes were made to some internal parts; other changes that had to be made included overall finish, design changes to all three control rings; in addition a built-in lens hood, bayonet R-mount, auto-diaphragm coupling, aperture and meter control cams all had to be designed and produced.
d. Considerable differences existed between the two lenses in regard to the auto-diaphragm coupling, requiring design changes necessary to make the Leica version compatible with existing multiple metering systems.
e. To effect production of special parts and sub-assemblies, a variety of special tools, jigs and gauges, as well as performance

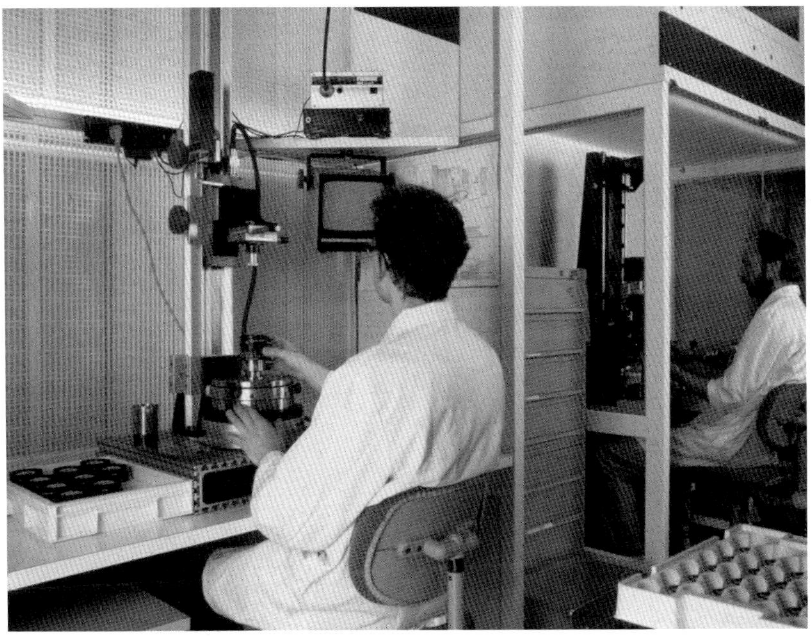

Fig. 43. A Leica laser interferometer automatically checks for collimation and centring errors at Solms. *Leica Akademie*

testing equipment had to be designed and made.

f. Changes in assembly procedures were necessary. Spare parts availability for some years ahead had to be provided for.

h. The total costs incurred by Sigma and Leica in producing this lens were considerable and had to be spread over fairly low volume production.

In practice, this lens proved to be a fine performer, exceeding even the very fine performance of the original Sigma lens on which it was based. In the future it is likely that, in addition to expanding the range of more exotic objectives now beginning to appear in the system, as well as improving and modifying some of the earlier types, Leica will continue the policy of searching out existing independently manufactured objectives which can be optically enhanced and mechanically improved and offered at reasonable cost to the user.

New technology is continually being developed at Leica in the optical research department. One recent result of this is the advent of the suffix ASPH to the name of an objective recently introduced into the Leica-M rangefinder system. The suffix refers to the term 'aspherical' and indicates the presence of certain elements in the overall construction which are not spherical.

Until recently, the formation of aspherical glass elements for photographic use had involved complex grinding and polishing techniques. The technique of manufacturing ellipsoidal elements for other photographic purposes, such as condensers used in slide projectors where tolerances are much greater, has been used for many years. Other manufacturers of camera lenses have produced aspherical lenses with varying degrees of success, but Leica have claimed that until the advent of the new process it has not been possible to produce elements larger than 20mm in diameter which would meet their very high specification.

This new process involves stamping the molten glass with a special die constructed from a ceramic-like material which has been cut with diamond edged tools and polished. The matrix is an exact female replica of the final element shape, finished to exceptionally high tolerances. Leica technicians dubbed the process 'Blankpressen'. It was especially devised to reduce the very high cost of manufacturing the original Summilux-M 35mm, f/1.4 Aspherical (11 873), the elements of which were made by conventional methods. The new lens has an equally complex optical construction but its manufacturing costs are considerably reduced, thus enabling the company to produce an exotic product at a more realistic retail cost.

There is currently no information which would lead one to assume that Leica might take this technology

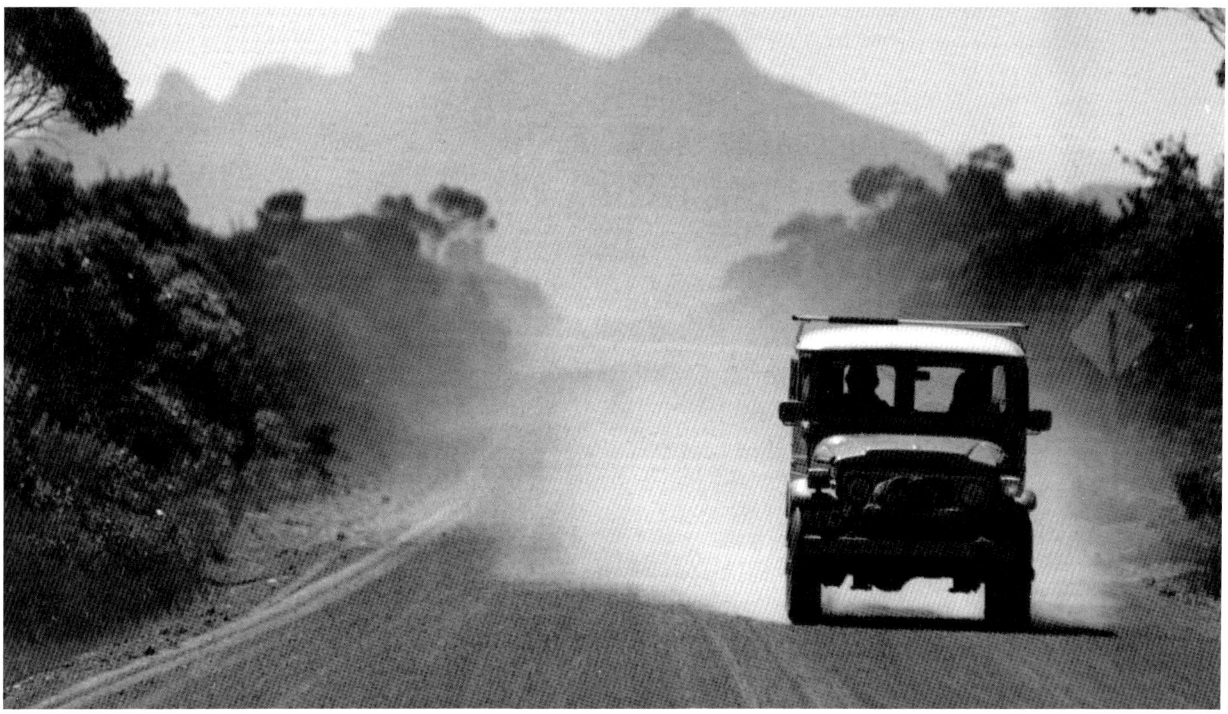

Fig. 44. Western Australia. Leica R lenses are built to endure the toughest environments. Hot-house or ice box, miles from the nearest repair shop, working photographers need cameras and lenses that can be relied upon year in, year out, from one assignment to the next.

further into the realm of R-system lens design; on the other hand, 'Blankpressen' techniques would seem to be ideally suited to the production of the larger diameter elements required for certain fast aperture reflex objectives in the wide-angle to short telephoto range. What chance a Noctilux Leica-R 50mm f/1.0 ASPH ? In the heat ofthe night perhaps.....

As I have already mentioned elsewhere, lens developments at Leica are not confined just to optical redesign of older models. In recent years the company seems to have set something of a precedent in the industry by producing remodelled objectives in a wide variety of focal lengths complete with built-in lens-hoods, obviating the need for photographers to carry additional bits and pieces which are often at risk of being misplaced or lost. One of the latest examples of this updating comes in the shape of the new compact Elmarit-R 28mm, f/2.8. Even though the new lens is heavier (400g) than its predecessor (275g), incorporating the collapsible hood and reducing the filter mount to the common E55 size will make this a popular objective for photojournalists and travel photographers.

The recent addition (Photokina 1994) of the Apo-Summicron-R 180mm, f/2 brings the total number of objectives currently in the Leica-R system to 37, plus two Apo tele-extenders which are perfectly matched to most of the focal lengths from 50mm upwards (see Appendix tables). A series of high grade ELPRO supplementary close-focus lenses for use with objectives in the 50mm to 135mm focal length, and special PHOTAR magnifying lenses for use with Focusing Bellows is also available. Their technical specification follows at the end of the next section.

Leica Cam System

When the original Leicaflex (Standard) was introduced, all lenses for it were fitted with a single curved cam as the meter coupling device, sited between the inner surface of the bayonet mounting ring and the rear retaining rings of the lens rear elements. This can be clearly seen when the lens is viewed from the rear. With the introduction of the Leicaflex SL models (including the SL2), a second curved cam sited directly opposite the first one was required. The diaphragm activating lever was set between the cams. These early lenses are known as single and twin cam types.

The Leica R3 Electronic camera required further addition in the way of a third stepped 'sequence switch' cam which was secured to the inside of one of the curved cams. In most examples where modification has been carried out to enable older lenses to be used on the R3, the additional stepped cam is a thin piece of black curved metal with steps cut out of it. These lenses are known as 3-cam types.

More modern and current lenses for the Leica R-cameras only have this last, third cam fitted. Early 'third cam only' lenses are designated on the underside of the lens barrel near the mount with the words 'For Leica R only' above the name of the country in which they were made. Looking at the lens from the rear with the red button mounting indicator at 12 o' clock, the diaphragm activator is

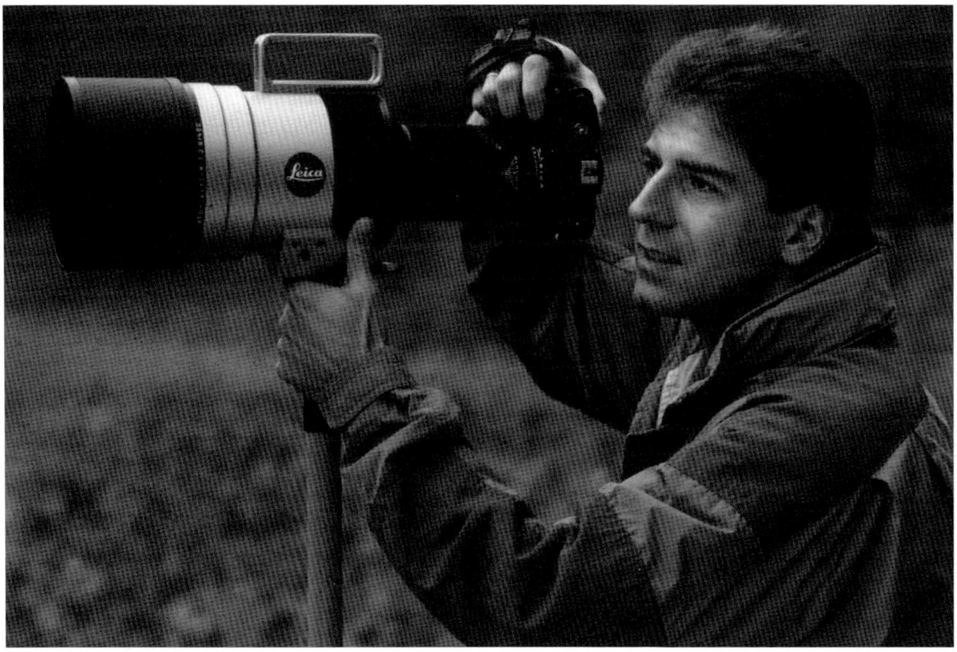

Fig. 45. More than 5% of Leica Camera GmbH turnover is diverted to R & D in the quest to develop high-tech products demanded by today's professional photographers. The Apo-Telyt-R 400mm, f/2.8 lens is a prime example of the company's products. Note the substantial carrying handle and position of the focus control ring, easily operated to achieve pin-sharp focus with a thumb. *Leica GmbH*

seen in the 1 o'clock position and the stepped lens coupling/meter indexing cam at 5 o'clock.

All earlier single and twin-cam lenses (for Leicaflex Standard, SL and SL2) may be used on all models of the Leica R-type cameras in the 'stop-down' working aperture mode only. Single cam 'Leica R Only' type lenses may also be used on the Leicaflex cameras. A conversion service is offered by Leica Camera GmbH to update older single and twin-cam objectives to current specification by adding the stepped sequence switch cam. There is only one lens, the original 1969 2-cam version of the French made Angénieux-R 45-90mm f/2.8 zoom, which cannot be modified to 3-cams. This lens was available with 3-cams to fit the R-3, but the modification to early models was carried out at the factory in Saint-Heand, not by Leitz in Wetzlar. Both the modification service and the production of 3-cam versions was discontinued in 1982 when Pierre Angénieux finally replaced the lens with their own 11 element 35-70mm f/2.5-3.3 zoom manufactured to fit different cameratypes, including Leica R.

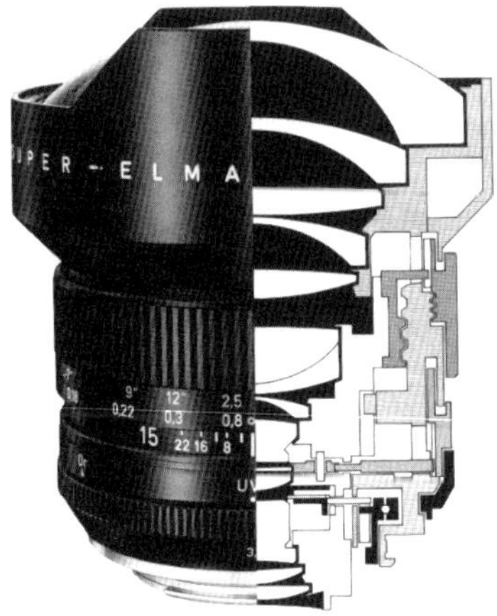

Fig. 46. The Zeiss made Super-Elmar-R 15mm, f/3.5, the widest full-field lens in the Leica R system, an exotic masterpiece of optical engineering.

Current R-Type Lenses

2.1. SUPER-ELMAR-R 15mm, f/3.5

Year introduced: 1980

Earlier version: None

Minimum aperture: f/22.

Angle of view: 110°.

Elements/Groups: 13/12, incorporates floating elements.

Filter size: Built-in turret with Leica UVa – yellow, orange and artificial light blue conversion filter for use with daylight balanced film.

Focusing range: 0.16m – inf. First R-type with hard rubber focusing ring.

Smallest object field: 70 x 106mm.

Lens hood. Built-in anti-flare device part of front mount.

Dimensions: Length 92.5mm, diameter 83.5mm.

Weight: 910g.

Finish: Black chrome.

Product code: 11 213.

Variations: None.

Comment: This lens is made by Carl Zeiss of Oberkochen, Germany, for Leica Camera GmbH and is based on the Zeiss Distagon T* f/3.5, 15mm manufactured for the Contax/

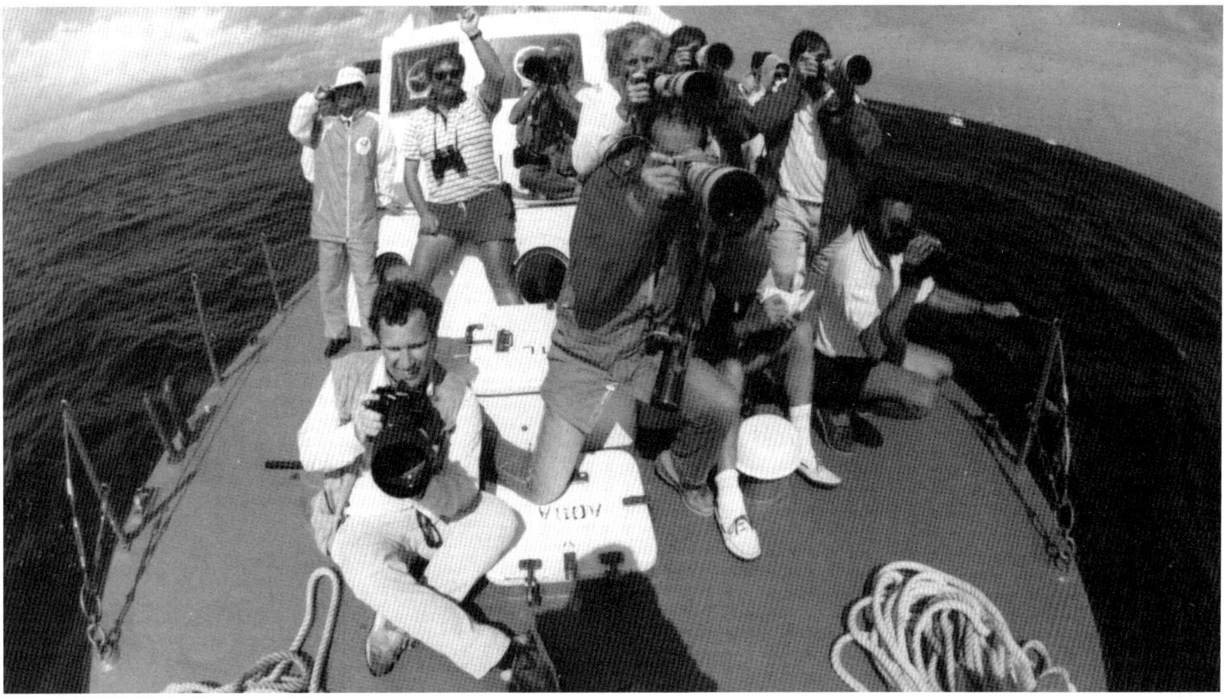

Fig. 48. The distortion effect of a full-frame fish-eye lens increases proportionally as the angle of incidence to the horizon is increased.

Yashica and Rollei 3003 systems. This is a highly corrected, virtually distortion-free lens, producing a rectilinear image and is especially suited to photographers specialising in architectural interiors where horizontal and vertical planes must normally be rendered at perfect right angles without visible bending of the planes at top and bottom and side of the picture. Landscape photographers and those interested in creating unusual effects have also found it a useful lens. Even some press photographers carry this lens for tricky situations where the extreme zone of sharp focus (depth of field) can often make the difference between obtaining a usable image and not (see fig. 165).

2.2. FISHEYE-ELMARIT-R 16mm, f/2.8

Year introduced: 1974

Earlier version: None

Minimum aperture: f/16

Angle of view: 180°

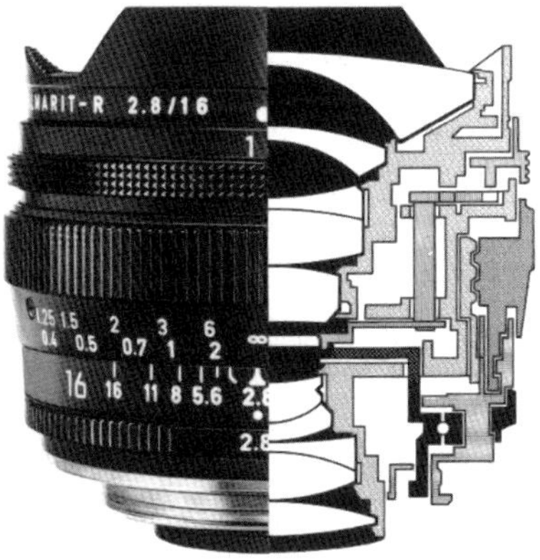

Elements/groups: 11/8

Filter size: Built-in, as 2.1

Focusing range: 0.30m to inf.

Smallest object field: 401 x 601mm

Lens hood: Built-in four-fin type

Dimensions: length 60mm, diameter 71mm

Weight: 460g

Finish: black chrome

Product code: 11 222

Variations: None.

Comment: This is a fish-eye lens designed and manufactured originally for E.Leitz by the Minolta Camera Co Ltd. Osaka, Japan. The image formed covers the whole film frame rather than producing the more commonly associated fish-eye circular picture. The resulting extreme wide-angle image is endowed with planes clearly exhibiting barrel distortion. Ideal for creatively minded enthusiasts, but difficult to use with originality. Current Leica literature specifies the filter combination as being the same as that for the Elmar-R 15mm (see 2.1.); the UVa filter is designated on this lens as a '1A'.

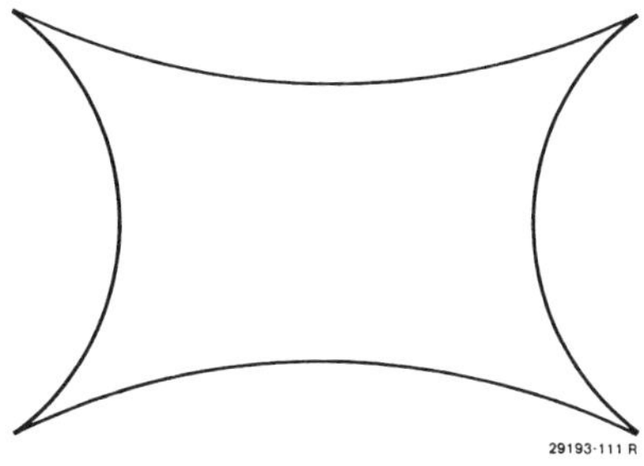

Fig. 47. Fisheye-Elmarit-R 16mm, f/2.8 full-frame fish-eye. The line diagram Fig. 47a, indicates planes of distortion.

2.3. ELMARIT-R 19mm, f/2.8

Year introduced: 1991

Earlier version: Yes, see 2.38.

Minimum aperture: f/22

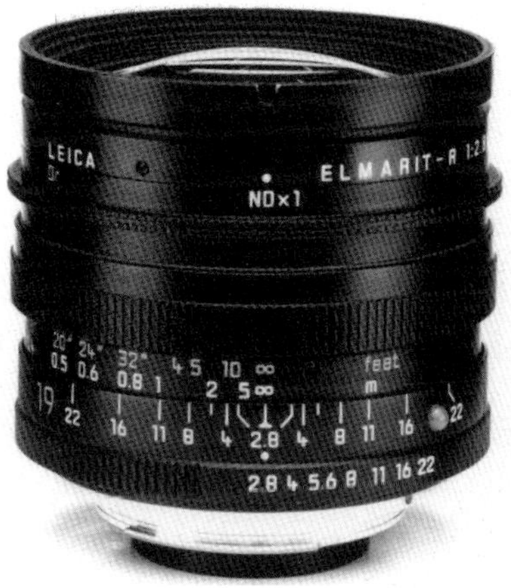

Fig. 51. The new compact Elmarit-R 19mm, f/2.8, is optically superior to its already formidable predecessor.

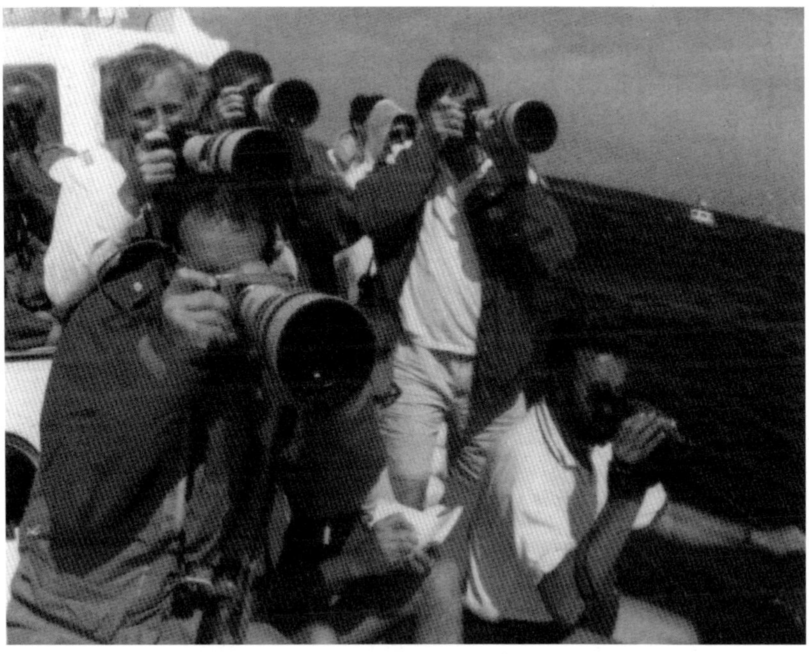

Fig. 48a. A small section cropped from the same picture shows how perspective remains the same, no matter what focal length of lens is used, so long as the photographer's position does not change.

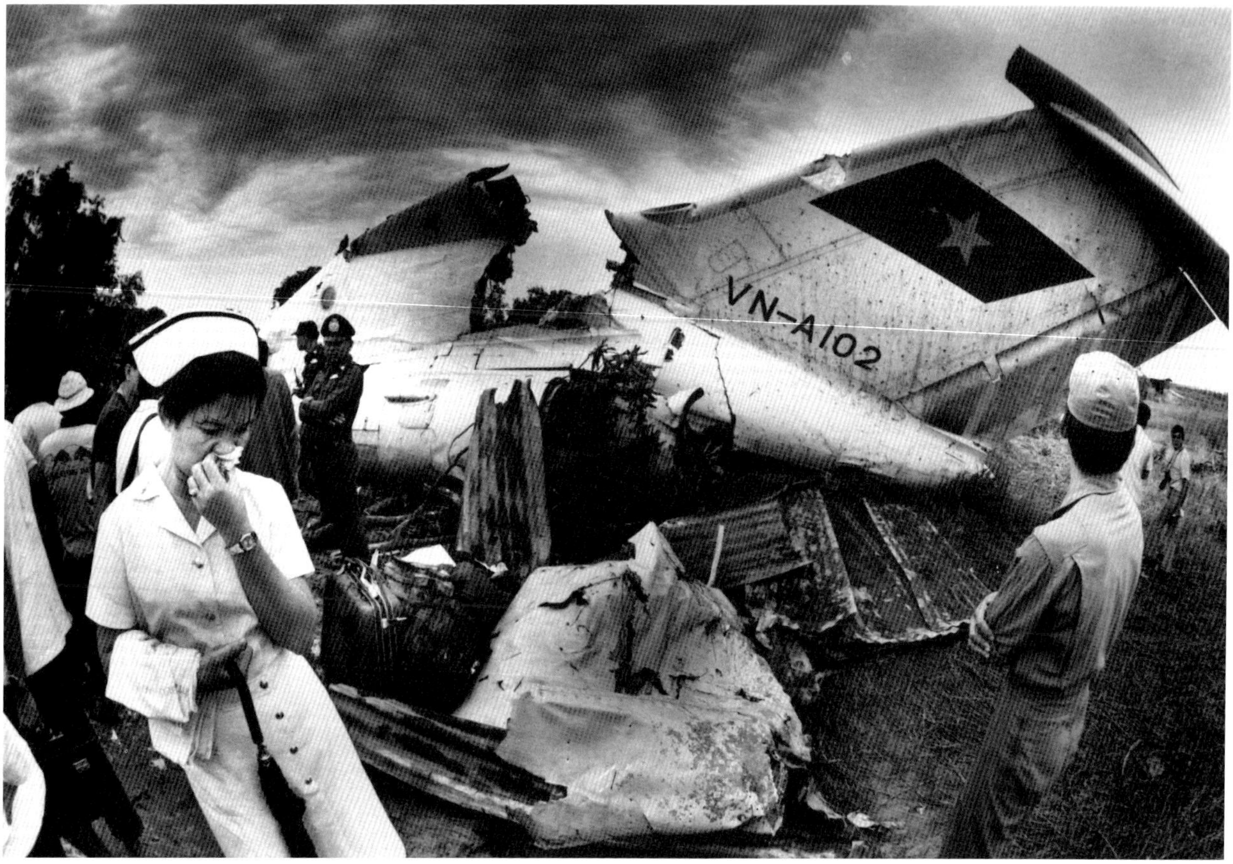

Fig. 50. Imaginative use of a full-frame 16mm fish-eye lens at airliner crash site. The photographer covering this tragedy was hustled away by guards. There was not time to change lenses so the photographer made several discreet exposures and pulled part of the negative in the darkroom to make this effective news picture. *Jeff Widener/Associated Press*

Angle of view: 96°

Elements/groups: 12/10

Filter size: Built-in turret with NDx1, yellow, green, orange, and blue artificial light conversion filter 80B.

Focusing range: 0.30m to inf

Smallest object field: 264 x 396mm

Lens hood: Rectangular clip-on, non rotating

Dimensions: Length 60mm, diameter 71mm

Weight: 560g

Finish: black chrome

Product code: 11 258

Variations: This is the second version of the 19mm lens and was

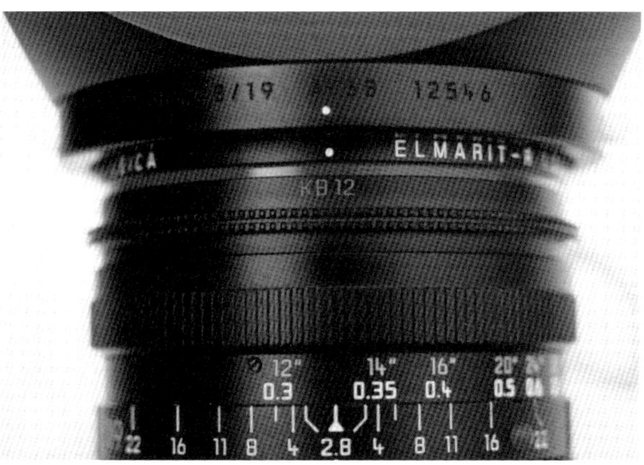

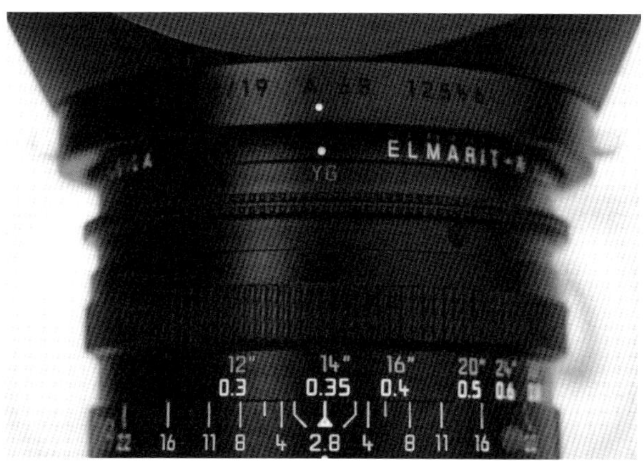

Fig. 52. The new Elmarit-R 19mm, f/2.8 has built-in filters. A red band remains visible at all times when the tungsten/daylight conversion filter is in place. A useful warning indicator. The band is not visible when other filter types are employed (Fig. 52a).

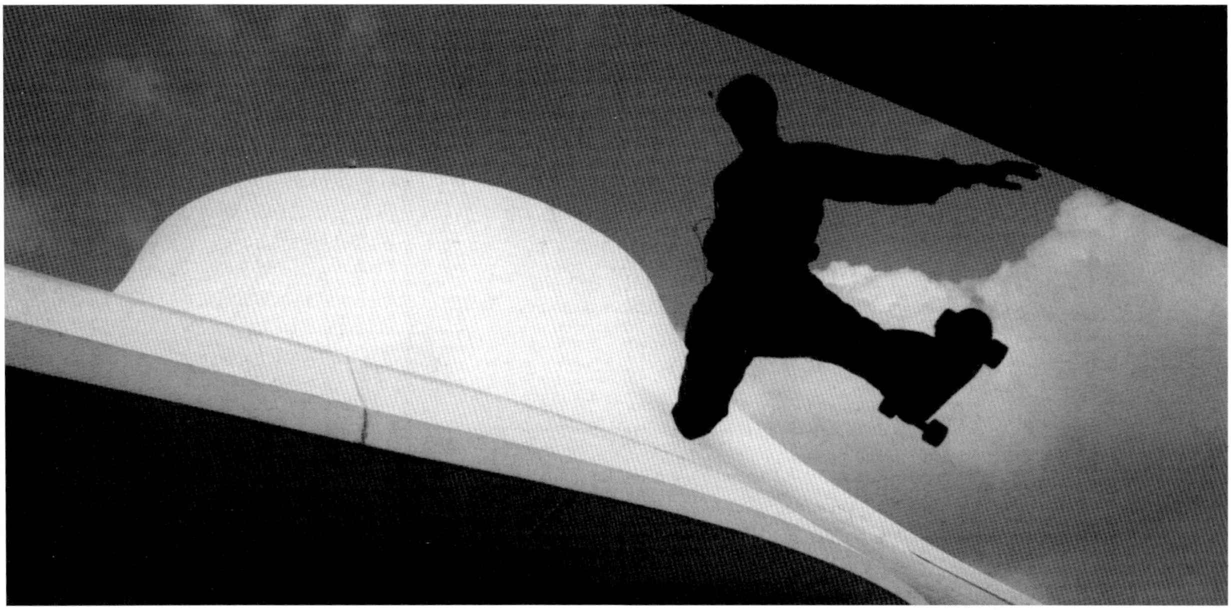

Fig. 53. Extreme wide-angle lenses are useful in confined spaces where a photographer's movement might be restricted. Super-Angulon-R 21mm.

originally recomputed and designed at Wetzlar.

Comment: The filter turret is sited between the fifth and sixth elements. Only the rear group of five elements move when the lens is focused. It is very compact compared to its predecessor and ideally suited for close-viewpoint work or as a general wide angle providing a useful field of view for many subjects. In ordinary use, the filter turret remains fixed with the NDX1 filter in place. The filter ring is spring loaded and when moved forward to enable a change to any of the other three filters, a red ring is exposed and remains visible while the new filter is in use. This is a useful reminder indicating that the correct filter may not be in place when reverting to the use of normal daylight balanced colour film.

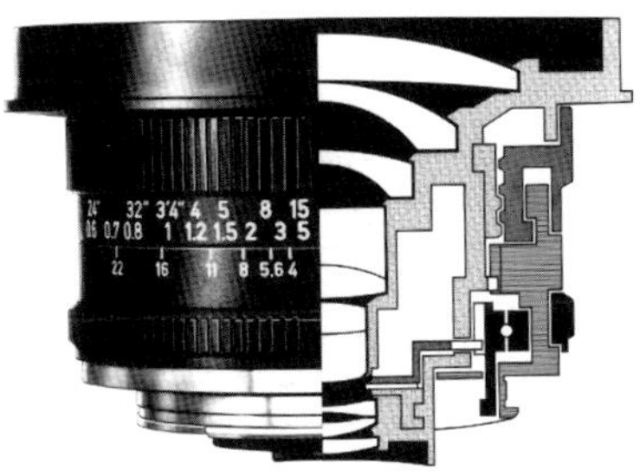

Fig. 54. Super-Angulon-R 21mm, f/4.

2.4. SUPER-ANGULON 21mm, f/4

Year introduced: 1968

Earlier version: Yes, see 2.39.

Minimum aperture: f/22

Angle of view: 92°

Elements/groups: 10/8.

Filter size: Series 8.5

Focusing range: 0.20m to inf.

Smallest object field: 148 x 221mm

Lens hood: Rectangular clip-on, product No. 12 506

Dimensions: Length 43.5mm, diameter 78mm

Weight: 420g

Finish: Black chrome

Product code: 11 813

Variations: The first version of this lens could only be used on the original Leicaflex Standard camera. When the Leicaflex SL was introduced without a mirror lock-up facility (also Leica R3 Electronic) this new retrofocus design was launched by Leitz at the 1968 Photokina show.

Comment: Now nearly 27 years old, this lens is made by Jos. Schneider Optische Werke of Kreuznach to Leica specification. Its age is perhaps indicative of the problems facing lens designers at Leica when endeavouring to improve the optical quality of older models. Its wide angle of view provides dramatic images of outstanding sharpness and even illumination. The lens will focus down to less than 8 inches.

2.5. ELMARIT-R 24mm, f/2.8

Year introduced: 1974

Earlier version: None

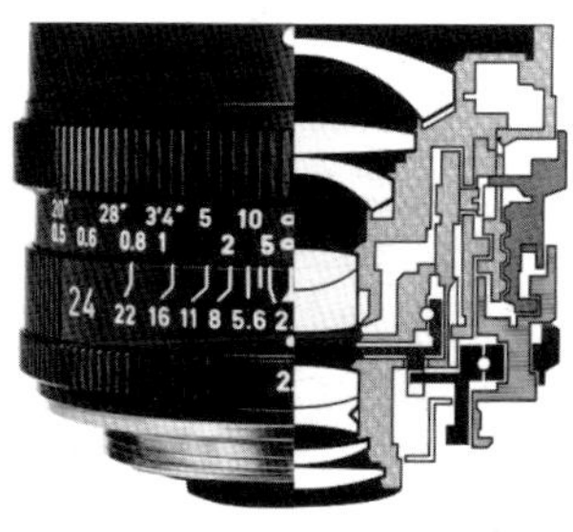

Fig. 54a. Elmarit-R 24mm, f/2.8. A useful compromise in place of a 28mm and 21/19mm.

Minimum aperture: f/22

Angle of view: 84°

Elements/groups: 9/7 with floating elements

Filter size: Series VIII

Focusing range: 0.30m to inf.

Smallest object field: 250 x 374mm

Lens hood: Rectangular clip-on. Product No. 12 523

Dimensions: Length 48.5mm, diameter 67mm

Weight: 400g

Finish: Black chrome

Product code: 11 257

Variations: None.

Comment: This is a Minolta designed lens and they supply the elements to Leica who manufacture it at their plant in Solms. The angle of view of this lens falls exactly midway between the Super-Angulon-R 21mm and the Elmarit-R 28mm. It cannot be used on the original Leicaflex Standard or the SL version. The clip-on lens hood is fitted with a rotating thumb wheel to enable the special polarising filters (13 372) to be used.

2.6. ELMARIT-R 28mm, f/2.8

Year introduced: 1994:

Earlier version: Yes, see 2.40.

Minimum aperture: f/22

Angle of view: 75°

Elements/groups: 8/7, including one floating element

Filter size: E55.

Focusing range: 0.30m to inf.

Smallest object field: 192 x 288mm

Lens hood: Built-in, collapsible, new polycarbonate type

Dimensions: Length 48mm, diameter 65mm

Weight: 400g

Finish: black chrome

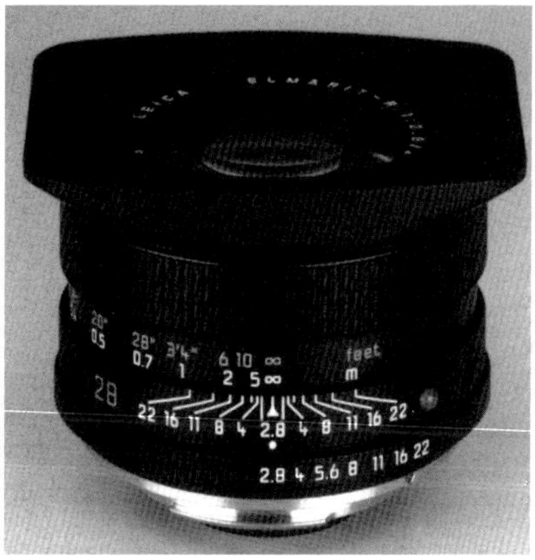

Fig. 55. Elmarit-R 28mm, f/2.8 with floating element and integral polycarbonate lens hood introduced at Photokina 1994. *Leica Camera GmbH*

Product code: 11 259

Variations: None (but see 2.40).

Comment: This new lens is optically different from the first version and incorporates a floating element. The overall size has been reduced, despite the fitting of a long awaited collapsible lens hood. E55 filters may now be used instead of the Series VII type. Initial reviews suggested that the slight vignetting experienced with this lens when photographing a full field of even brightness is eliminated when the

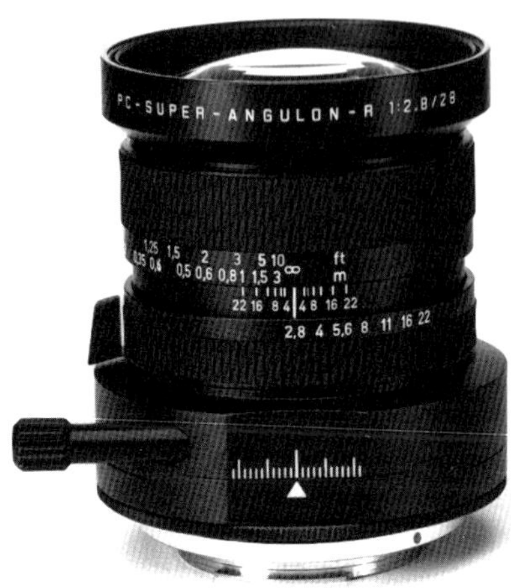

Fig. 56. The impressive PC-Super-Angulon-R 28mm, f/2.8 manufactured by Jos. Schneider Optische Werke Kreuznach GmbH & Co. This objective is a must for travel photographers, photojournalists and studio photographers able to use the small format for product shots. *Leica Camera UK Ltd*

aperture is stopped down to f/5.6. The older polarising filter (13 357) is not recommended for use with this lens as severe vignetting is caused at medium apertures. A new polarising filter (13 335) replaces the old version. The weight increase is due to the fact that brass is used for the inner mount instead of aluminium, providing a better friction coefficient for the floating element.

Fig. 56a. Operating controls of the 28mm PC-Super-Angulon. *Schneider Kreuznach*

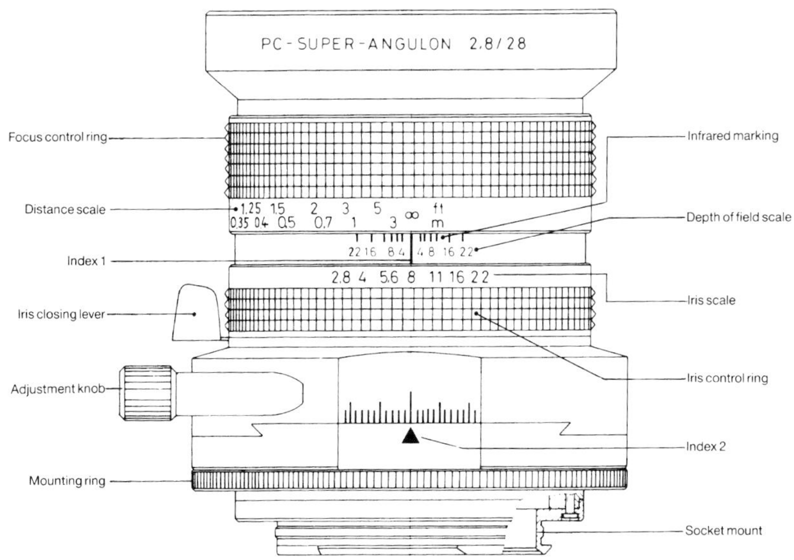

2.7. PC SUPER-ANGULON-R 28mm, f/2.8

Year introduced: 1988

Earlier version: None

Minimum aperture: f/22

Optical offset: 11mm horizontal or vertical, 9.5mm diagonal

Image circle: 62mm

Angle of view: 73/93°

Elements/groups: 12/10 with floating elements

Filter size: special filter 67 EW *

Focusing range: 0.28m to inf.

Smallest object field: 146 x 219mm

Lens hood: Screw in, acts as filter holder. See * below

Dimensions: Length 84mm, diameter 75mm

Weight: 600g

Finish: Black chrome

Product code: 11 812

Variations: None.

Comment: This special perspective control lens is the second of its type, providing a wider field of view than the longer established 35mm focal length described in 2.8. Movements are controlled by a finely tuned operating drive stalk which protrudes from the lens mount on the left hand side seen from the top. Continuous radial movement permits off-sets to be made in any direction. Automatic diaphragm operation is not possible. The lens is pre-set to the working aperture. The 28mm length is ideally suited for many architectural problems, including interiors. It can also be used in the studio for table-top and still life sets. Manufactured by Jos. Schneider, to Leica specification, a similar objective with differently finished control grips and other markings is available directly from the manufacturer's distributors complete with socket type camera adaptor. The Schneider 28mm f/2.8 PC-Super Angulon is outwardly identical in most other respects to the Leica R-version. Optically, the glass and coatings used may differ, although the number of elements used in both this and the lens described in 2.8. below, are the same.

* filter for special wide angle holder with aperture marketed by B&W Filterfabrik, D6550 Bad Kreuznach.

2.8. PA CURTAGON-R 35mm, f/4

Year introduced: 1969

Earlier version: None

Minimum aperture: f/22

Optical offset: 7mm

Image circle: 57mm

Angle of view: 64/78°

Elements/groups: 7/6

Filter size: Series VIII

Focusing range: 0.30m to inf.

Smallest object field: 140 x 210mm

Lens hood: Circular, clip on. Product No. 12 514

Dimensions: Length 51mm, diameter 70mm

Weight: 330g

Finish: Black chrome, distinctive milled black and polished aluminium axis, red figure painted engraved displacement ring

Product code: 11 202

Variations: None.

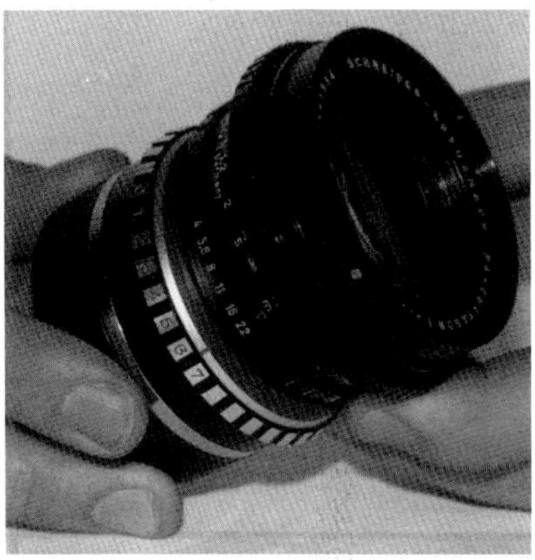

Fig. 57a. PA Curtagon-R 35mm, f/4.0. A more compact lens than the 28mm PC-Super-Angulon with a useful range of movements.

Comment: A narrower angle of view than the 28mm version, this perspective control lens is nevertheless almost half its weight and is physically much smaller. Another superb tool for the photojournalist and travel or buildings specialist manufactured for Leica by Jos. Schneider. Comments regarding the manufacturer's own version (35mm, f/4.0 PC-Curtagon MC) are the same as for its wider sibling, the outward appearance being closer to the Leica version. Again, no automatic diaphragm; aperture must be pre-set.

2.9. ELMARIT-R 35mm, f/2.8

Year introduced: 1979

Earlier version: Yes, see 2.41.

Minimum aperture: f/22

Angle of view: 64°

Elements/groups: 7/6

Filter size: E55

Focusing range: 0.30m to inf.

Smallest object field: 140 x 210mm

Lens hood: Built-in collapsible

Dimensions: length 41.5mm, diameter 66mm

Weight: 310g

Finish: Black chrome

Product code: 11 251

Variations: None, (but see 2.41).

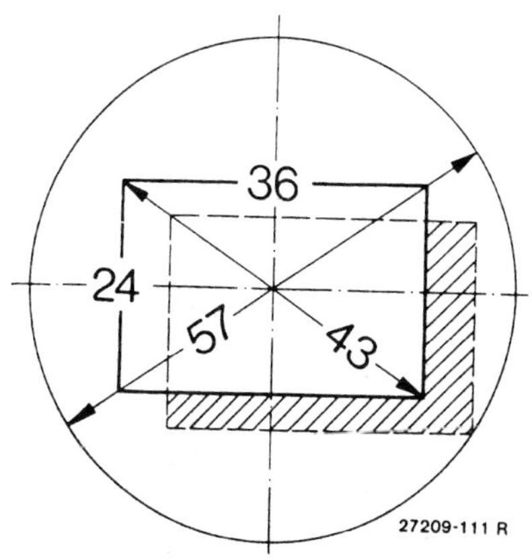

Fig. 57b. The degree of shift available with the 35mm PA Curtagon-R.

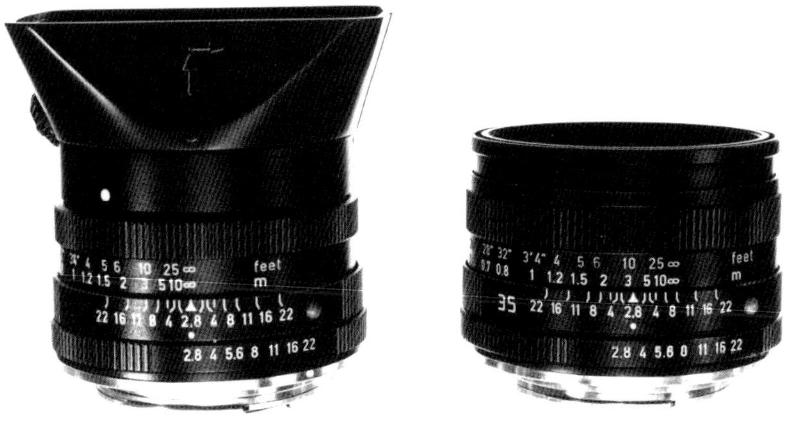

Fig. 58. Elmarit-R 35mm, f/2.8 current version on the right with collapsible hood, compared with earlier, separate hood type at left incorporating polariser filter adjuster wheel. *Leica Camera UK Ltd*

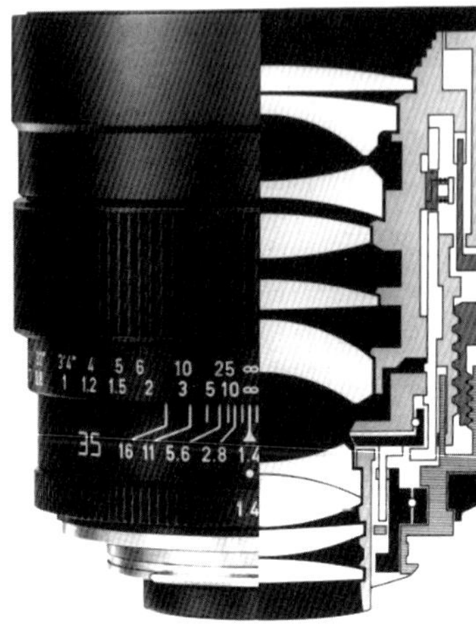

Fig. 60. Summilux-R 35mm, f/1.4.

Comment: A relative lightweight with excellent optical properties. Excellent resolution and contrast are obtainable at maximum aperture. Little or no discernible difference in image quality is achieved on stopping the lens down. Particularly suitable for photojournalists anxious to keep weight to a minimum.

2.10. SUMMICRON-R 35mm, f/2

Year introduced: 1976

Earlier version: Yes, see 2.42.

Minimum aperture: f/16

Angle of view: 64°

Elements/groups: 6/6

Filter size: E55

Focusing range: 0.30m to inf.

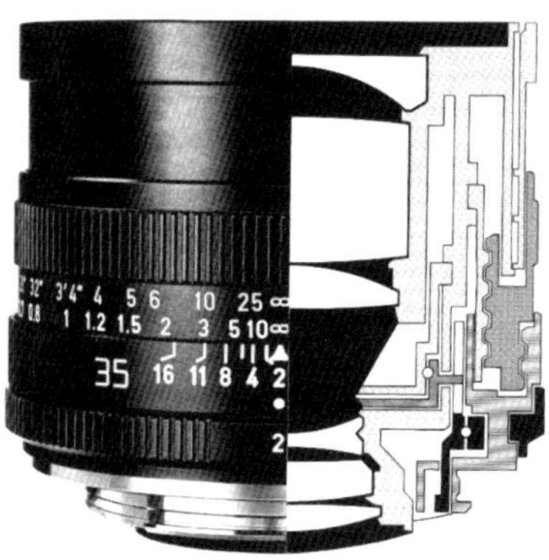

Fig. 59. Summicron-R 35mm, f/2 with integral hood. A brilliant all-rounder.

Smallest object field: 140 x 210mm

Lens hood: Built-in, collapsable

Dimensions: Length 54mm, diameter 66mm

Weight: 430g

Finish: Black chrome

Product code: 11 115

Variations: None, (but see 2.42).

Comment: A completely new optical design over 100 grams lighter than the first version in spite of its having a massive solid second element. This is one of the great all-rounders in the focal length. There are not many subjects that cannot be tackled with it. A fast lens which, like all Leica objectives, can be used wide open without fear of image quality deterioration.

2.11. SUMMILUX-R 35mm, f/1.4

Year introduced: 1984

Earlier version: None

Minimum aperture: f/16

Angle of view: 64°

Elements/groups: 10/9, with floating element

Filter size: E67

Focusing range: 0.50m to inf.

Smallest object field: 266 x 399mm

Lens hood: Built-in, collapsable

Dimensions: Length 76mm, diameter 75mm

Weight: 690g

Finish: Black chrome

Product code: 11 144

Variations: None.

Comment: Cannot be used with the original Leicaflex Standard. This is the fastest lens in this popular focal length group and for many photojournalists is the 'standard' lens. It was designed specially for working in low-light situations and its performance at maximum aperture is remarkable for a lens of this specification, maintaining excellent colour differentiation and contrast, even in candle lit scenes.

2.12. SUMMICRON-R 50mm, f/2

Year introduced: 1976

Earlier version: yes, see 2.43.

Minimum aperture: f/16

Angle of view 45°

Elements/groups: 6/4

Filter size: E55

Focusing range: 0.5m to inf.

Smallest object field: 180 x 270mm

Lens hood: Built-in, collapsible

Dimensions: Length 41mm, diameter 66mm

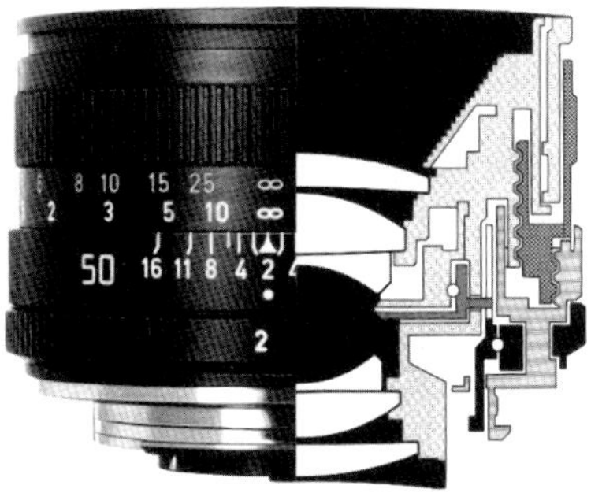

Fig. 61. The current Summicron-R 50mm, f/2 with collapsible lens hood introduced in 1976.
Leica Camera UK Ltd

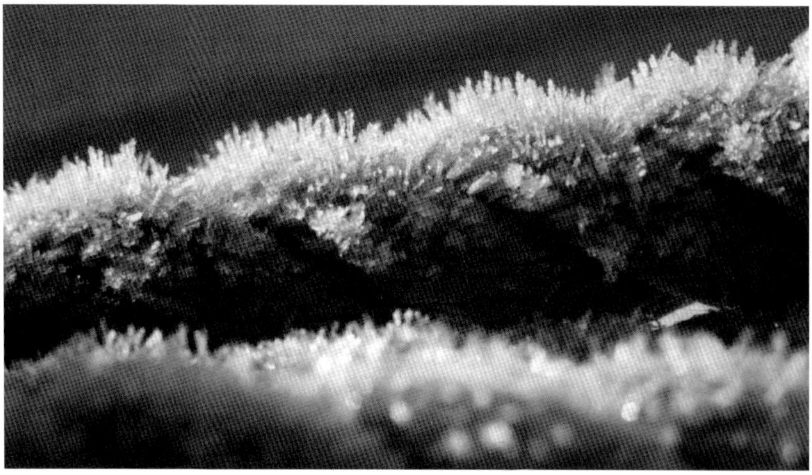

Fig. 64. Ice crystals on rope. Summicron-R 50mm, f/2 reversed and handheld.

Weight: 290g
Finish: black chrome
Product code: 11 216
Variations: None, (but see 2.43).
Comment: Except for the Macro-Elmar-R 100mm f/4, which is the same weight, this is the lightest lens in the R-system line-up. The 50mm focal length has often been claimed as offering an angle of view closely approximating that of human vision. In years gone by, before the advent of compact short zoom lenses covering this as well as medium wide to short telephoto lengths, the 50mm was indeed the 'standard' lens. In the author's view, this much neglected length is one of the most useful for every day picture taking, both as a snapshot lens as well as for serious picture taking. Properly used, it can produce distinctive images. It can be used for portraits, landscapes, copying and a host of other subjects. I particularly like its angle of view for street photography. At the other extreme, it can very rapidly double as a lens for macro-photography without the use of supplementary lenses or bellows.

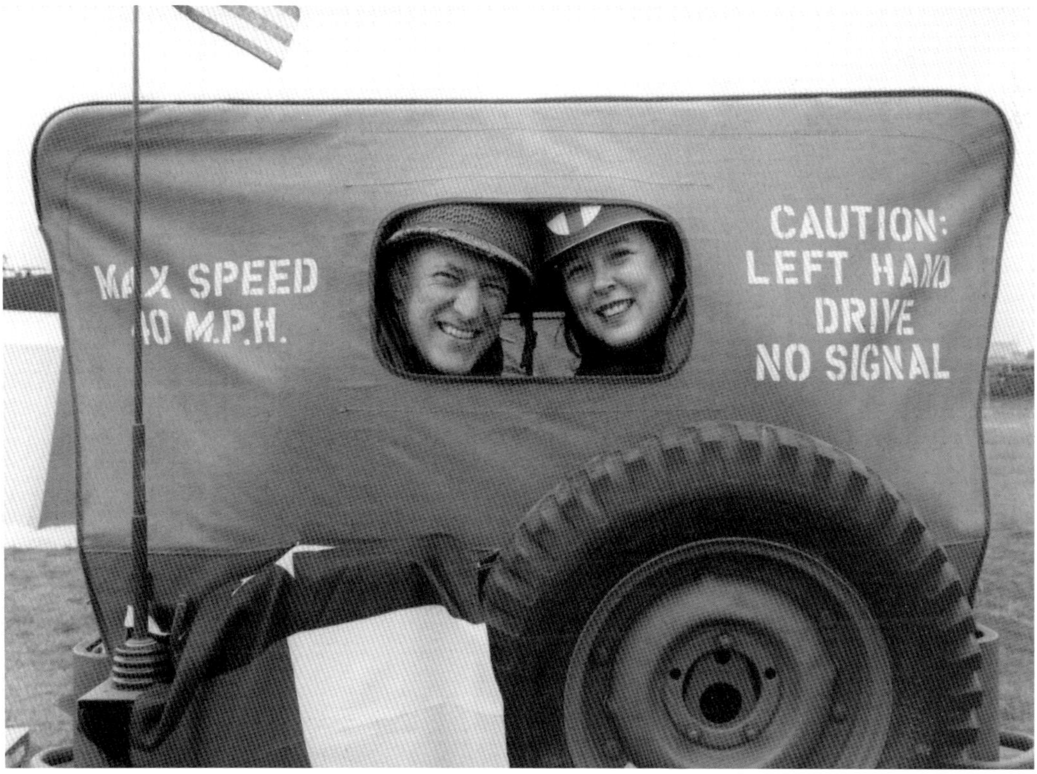

Fig. 63. The 50mm standard lens is one of the most versatile, lending its near human vision angle of view to a wide variety of subjects. Summicron-R 50mm, f/2.

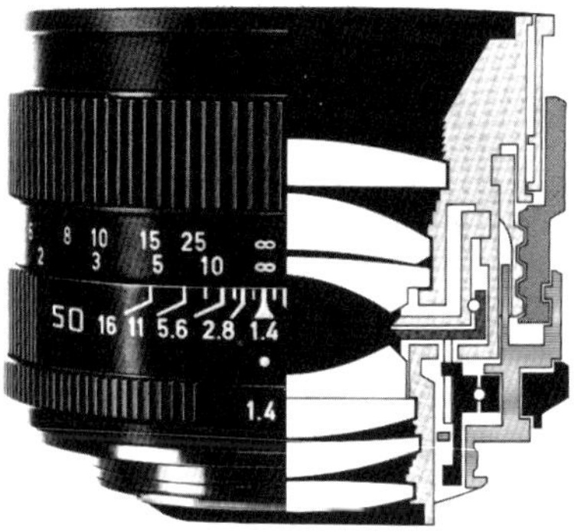

Fig. 62. Summilux-R 50mm, f/2 with collapsible lens hood introduced in 1976.
Leica Camera UK Ltd

2.13. SUMMILUX-R 50mm, f/1.4

Year introduced: 1978

Earlier version: Yes, see 2.44.

Minimum aperture: f/16

Angle of view: 45°

Elements/groups: 7/6

Filter size: E55

Focusing range: 0.5m to inf.

Smallest object field: 180 x 270mm

Lens hood: Built-in. collapsible

Dimensions: Length 50.6mm, diameter 66.5mm

Weight 400g

Finish: Black chrome

Product code: 11 777

Variations: None, (but see 2.44).

Comment: A fast maximum aperture lens ideally suited for photojournalistic work where a wide range of lighting conditions are likely to be encountered. This lens has excellent resolving capabilities and has remained optically unchanged since first launched in 1969.

2.14. MACRO-ELMARIT-R 60mm, f/2.8

Year introduced: 1980

Earlier version: Yes, see 2.45.

Minimum aperture: f/22

Angle of view: 39°

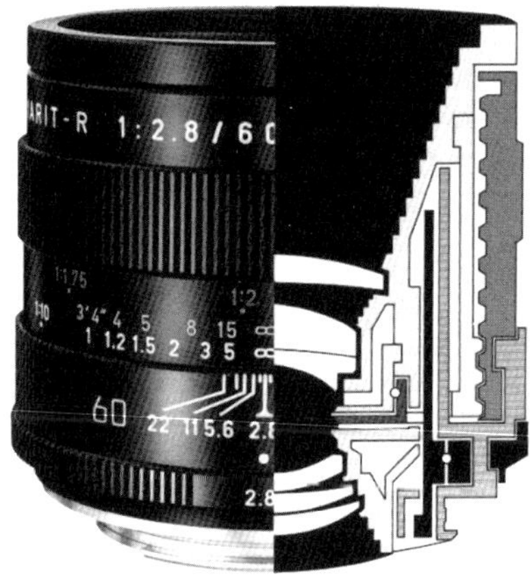

Fig. 65. Macro-Elmarit-R 60mm, f/2.8.

Elements/groups: 6/5

Filter size: E55

Focusing range: 0.27m to inf. 1:1 with Macro Adapter-R

Smallest object field: 48 x 72mm; 24 x 36mm with Macro Adapter-R

Lens hood: Built-in, front portion of mount forms shade

Dimensions: Length 62.3mm (92.3mm with adapter), diameter 67.5mm

Weight: 400g, (530g with adapter)

Finish: Black chrome

Product code: 11 253

Variations: None, (but see 2.45).

Comment: A very versatile lens which, even without the use of the Macro Adapter-R, can focus down to 10.6 inches. This makes it ideal for copying documents while maintaining all the qualities of a standard 50mm objective. Favoured by busy press photographers who may often be required to rephotograph family photographs; at the same time it can be turned efficiently to portrait photography.

2.15. SUMMILUX-R 80mm, f/1.4

Year introduced: 1980

Earlier version: None

Minimum aperture: f/16

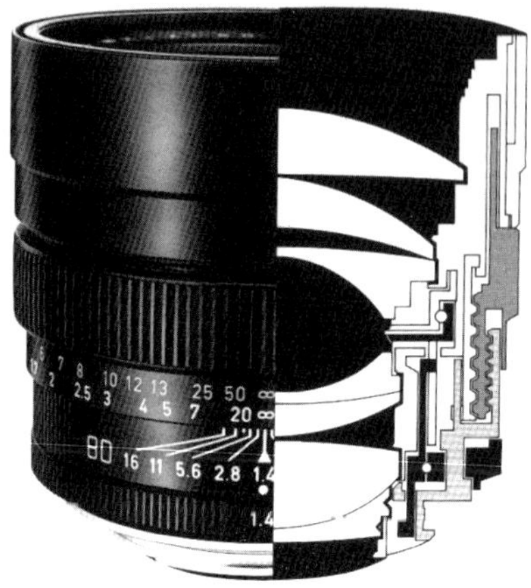

Fig. 66. Summilux-R 80mm, f/1.4, a very fast, wide aperture lens ideally suited to low-light use, portraits and for capturing detail.

Angle of view: 30°

Elements/groups: 7/5

Filter size: E67

Focusing range: 0.8m to inf.

Smallest object field: 192 x 288mm

Lens hood: built-in, collapsible

Dimensions: length 69mm, diameter 75mm

Weight: 700g

Finish: Black chrome

Product code: 11 881

Variations: None.

Comment: An ultra-high-speed short telephoto renowned for its superior performance in low-light situations. A chunky, heavy lens, with fine handling characteristics, perfectly balanced for shooting those tightly cropped portraits.

2.16. ELMARIT-R 90mm, f/2.8

Year introduced: 1984

Earlier version: Yes, see 2.46

Minimum aperture: f/22

Angle of view: 27°

Elements/groups: 4/4

Filter size: E55

Focusing range: 0.7m to inf.

Smallest object field: 140 x 210mm

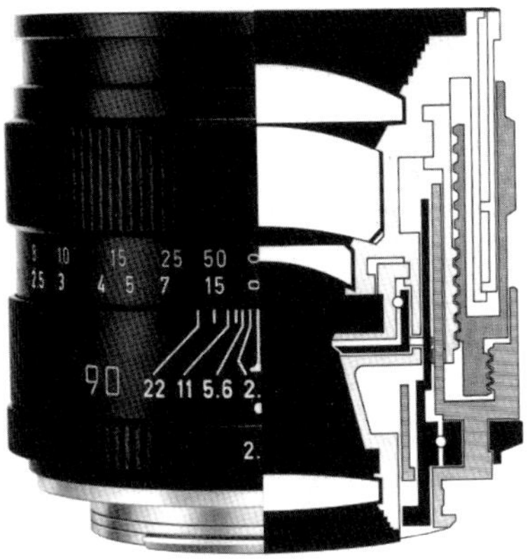

Fig. 67. Elmarit-R 90mm, f/2.8.

Lens hood: Built-in, collapsible

Dimensions: Length 57mm, diameter 67mm

Weight: 450g

Finish: Black chrome

Product code: 11 154

Variations: None (but see 2.46)

Comment: This is a 1983 computer redesign of the first version which was one of the original group of four focal lengths launched with the Leicaflex Standard. The new objective is very small, not much difference between it and the Summilux-R 50mm, f/1.4 in size or weight. The 90mm length has traditionally been the ideal portrait length exploited by Leitz and Leica. This version has excellent edge-to-edge sharpness at full aperture and is computed to give its best performance at near focusing distances. An excellent choice for any photographer concerned with high optical quality and weight.

2.17. SUMMICRON-R 90mm, f/2

Year introduced: 1969

Earlier version: None

Minimum aperture: f/16

Angle of view: 27°

Elements/groups: 5/4

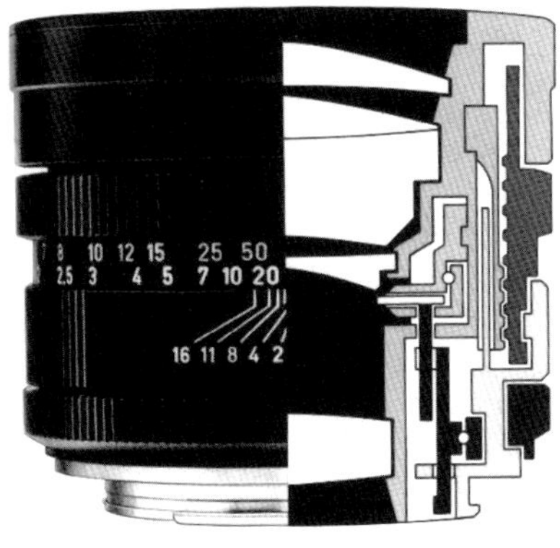

Fig. 68. Summicron-R 90mm, f/2, the ideal portrait lens offering superb performance when used wide open.

Filter size: Series VII with ring 14 161; from serial No.2770951, E55 screw type

Focusing range: 0.7m to inf.

Smallest object field: 140 x 210mm

Lens hood: Built-in, collapsible

Dimensions: Length 61mm, diameter 69mm

Weight: 520g

Finish: Black chrome

Product code: 11 254. (originally 11 219)

Variations: Originally issued in a 2-cam version for the Leicaflex SL. It was factory fitted with a third cam for the Leica R3 from serial No. 2761083. Very early models of this excellent lens had a milled outer ring around the engraved lens designation and country of origin. This distinctive characteristic disappeared as production increased and was replaced by a smooth edged hood retaining ring.

Comment: This fast telephoto was announced at Photokina in 1970 and was designed and manufactured by E.Leitz at Midland, Ontario. Current models were fitted with the single stepped sequence switch cam for Leica-R only from 1987. The five element optical design has remained the same throughout the life of the lens. The current model has a wider focusing ring; the front of the pull-out lens hood is a narrow metal band instead of the wide smooth cover on 11 219 types.

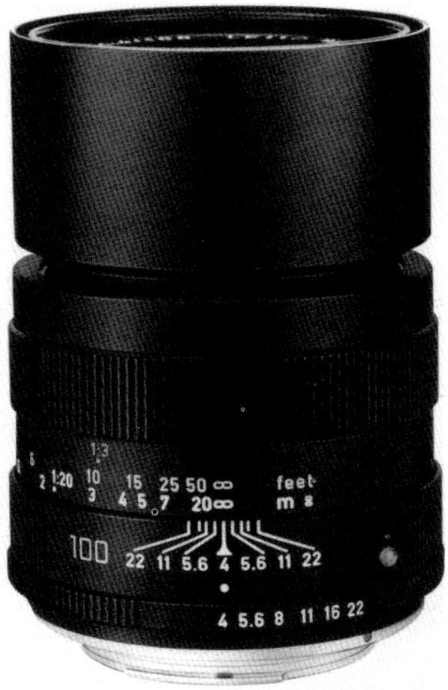

Fig. 69. Macro-Elmar-R 100mm, f/4. This lens is also available in a short, rigid mount for use on the Focusing Bellows-R BR2 when it can be focused down to a reproduction ratio of 1.1:1.

2.18. MACRO-ELMAR-R 100mm f/4

Year introduced: 1978

Earlier version: None

Minimum aperture: f/22

Angle of view: 25°

Elements/groups: 4/3

Filter size: E55

Focusing range: 0.6m to inf. 1:1.6 with Macro Adapter-R

Smallest object field: 72 x 108mm; 38 x 57mm with adapter

Lens hood: Built-in, collapsible

Dimensions: Length 90mm (120mm with adapter), diameter 67.5mm

Weight: 530g, (660g)

Finish: Black chrome

Product code: 11 232

Variations: None, but see Comment.

Comment: This lens was originally launched as a lens head suitable for use with 16 860 Universal Focusing Bellows-R for the Leicaflex SL in 1968 which, in that combination, could focus from infinity down to a reproduction ratio of 1.1:1. The current version of this lens head (11 270), is suitable for use with Focusing Bellows-R BR2 (16880). Older 100mm f/4 Macro-Elmar lens heads (11230) may also be used with the current bellows. The optical design of the lens is of reversed Elmar triplet type designed by Max Berek originally in 1924 or possibly earlier. A special extension tube (14 262) was available separately for 11 232, but the two items were also offered as a package under the code 11 234. 14 262 is now replaced by the Macro-Adapter-R (14 256).

2.19. APO-MACRO-ELMARIT-R 100mm, f/2.8

Year introduced: 1988

Earlier version: None

Minimum aperture: f/22

Angle of view: 25°

Elements/groups: 8/6

Filter size: E60

Focusing range: 0.45m to inf. (with Elpro 1:2-1.1:1)

Smallest object field: 48 x 72mm; with Elpro, 22 x 33mm

Lens hood: Built-in

Dimensions: Length 104.5mm (140mm with Elpro), diameter 73mm

Weight: 760g, (950g with Elpro)

Finish: Black chrome

Product code: 11 210

Variations: None.

Comment: Doubtless, even if this lens had employed Leitz glass of a more modest quality, its performance would have been excellent. As it is, before its closure, the Leitz optical research laboratory perfected the melt of a very special glass using fluoride-phosphate; the result was used in the optical design to create this unequalled high quality objective. The front six elements form an unsymmetrical double Gauss layout which moves when the lens is focused. The two rear elements are fixed. In Leitz tests of the time, no residual traces of coma, curvature of field, astigmatism or chromatic aberration were found to be present. Its correction is complete for the primary wavelengths and extends into the infra-red region. Contrast loss is not detectable across the whole aperture or focus range. This range is extended by employing a custom designed three element ELPRO lens (16 545) which has its own special lens-hood. Use of the Elpro improves

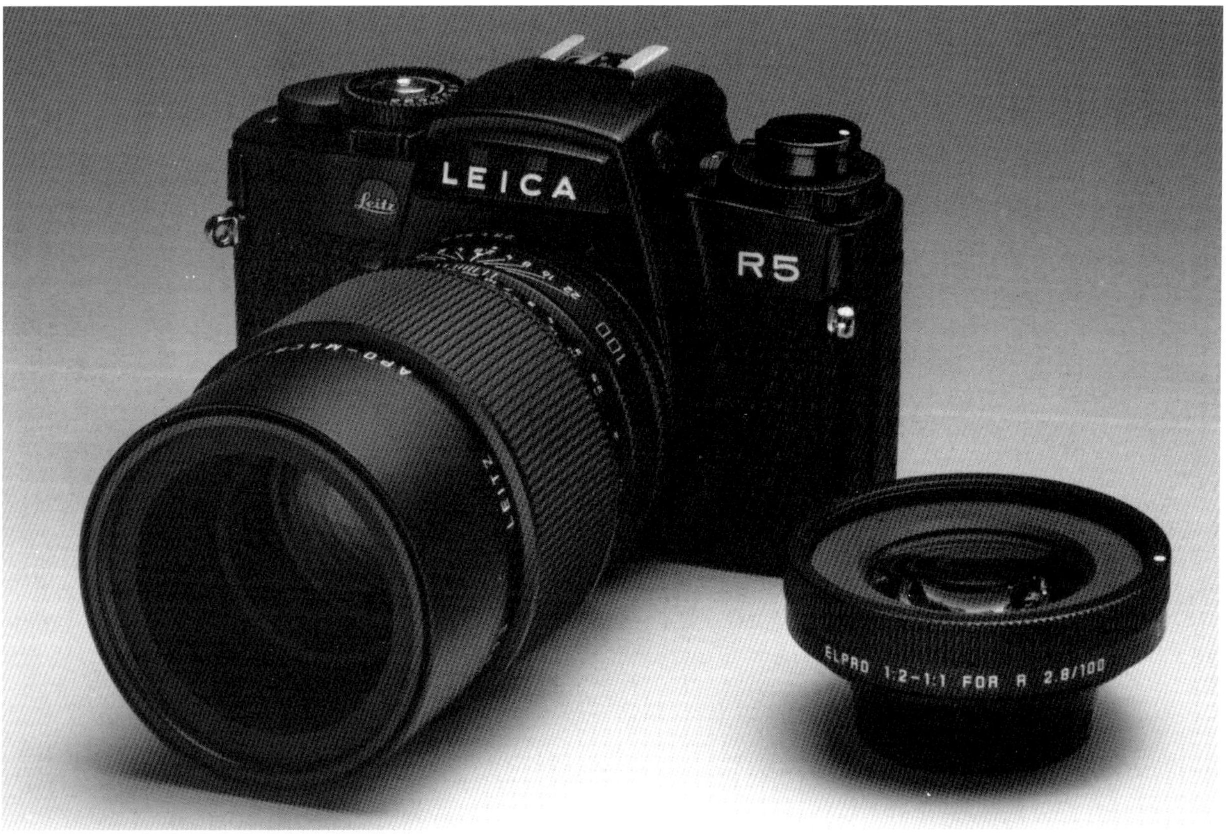

Fig. 70. The Apo-Macro-Elmarit-R 100mm, f/2.8 mounted on a Leica R5, next to it, right, is the special Elpro 1:2-1:1 supplementary lens.
Leica Camera UK Ltd

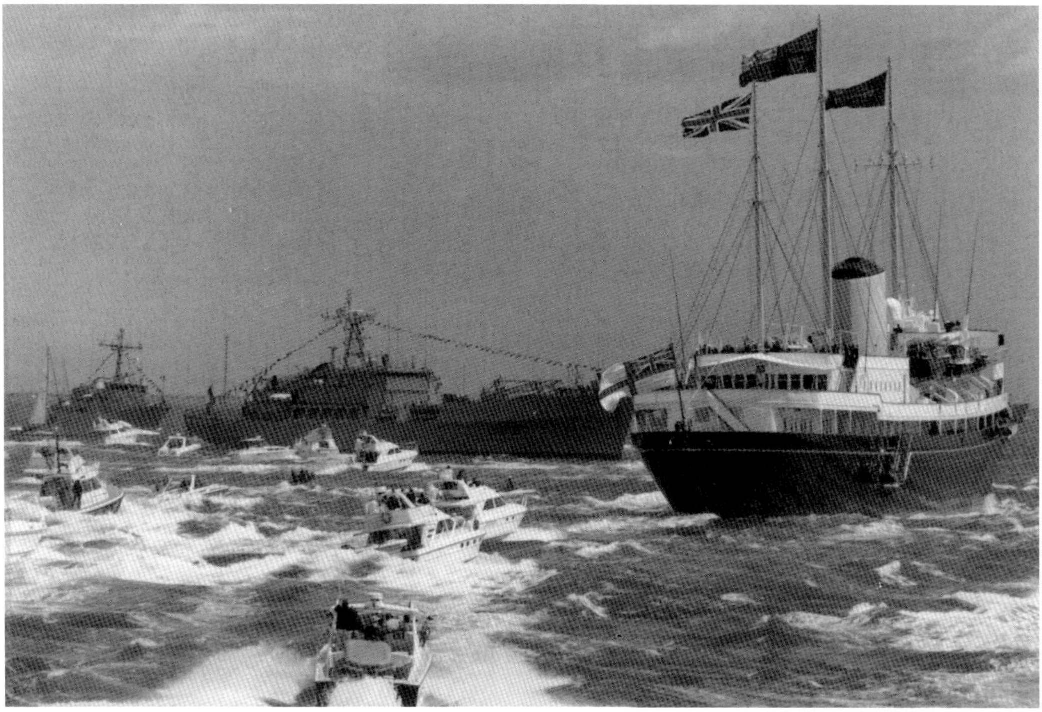

Fig. 71. The Elmarit-R 135mm, f/2.8 is another useful lens, often undervalued for its versatility. Used over relatively short distances it is ideal for maintaining a sense of scale.

the reproduction ratio to 1:1 without loss of optical quality. The Macro-Adapter-R, earlier 2x Extender or APO-EXTENDER-R 1.4x should not be used with this objective as optical quality will be impaired. The current APO-EXTENDER-R 2x may be used however, converting the lens to an effective focal length of 200mm with maximum aperture of f/5.6. A superb lens with great versatility.

2.20. ELMARIT-R 135mm, f/2.8

Year introduced: 1968

Earlier version: Yes, see Variations below

Minimum aperture: f/22

Angle of view: 18°

Elements/groups: 5/4

Filter size: E55 from serial No. 2772619. (earlier version; Series VII with ring 14 161)

Focusing range: 1.5m to inf.

Smallest object field: 220 x 330mm

Lens hood: Built-in, collapsible

Dimensions: Length 93mm, diameter 67mm

Weight: 730g

Finish: Black chrome

Product code: 11 211. (original code. 11 111)

Variations: This was the longest focal length of the original four

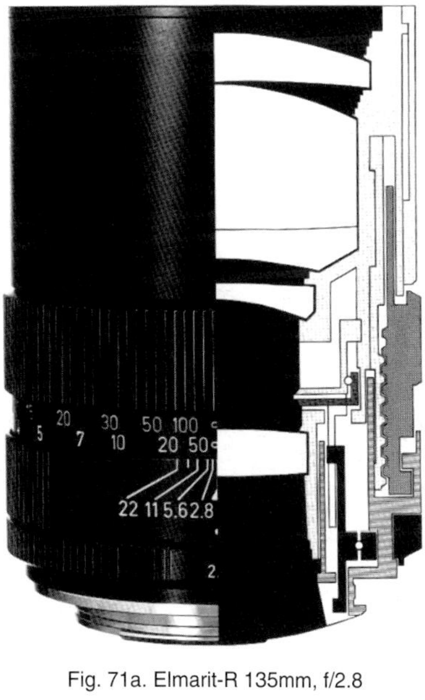

Fig. 71a. Elmarit-R 135mm, f/2.8

launched with the Leicaflex Standard in 1964. A true telephoto design of five elements with four in front of the diaphragm. The rear element of the original has a concave surface when seen from the back; the second and current version is convex in shape. The second version uses the same mount as the first version but was optically redesigned. The only visible difference between current versions and very early examples is that the front ring of the collapsible hood is milled on the latter. These examples were probably made in the Wetzlar factory before production was moved to the Midland plant in Canada. The current model is made in Solms.

Comment: This is an excellent all-round performer and in my opinion probably offers the best value-for-money in the whole Leica R-lens line-up. Its optical properties are excellent across the whole focus range, but its most useful asset is that it can be used for a wide range of subjects, from tight head-and-shoulder portraits to sports and landscapes.

Reproduction ratio of 1:2.8 is possible with ELPRO VIIa, also accepts ELPRO VIIb. Lenses from serial No. 2772619 accept ELPRO's 3 and 4.

2.21. ELMAR-R 180mm, f4

Year introduced: 1976

Earlier version: None

Minimum aperture: f/22

Angle of view: 14°

Elements/groups: 5/4

Filter size: E55

Focusing range: 1.8m to inf.

Smallest object field: 175 x 262mm

Lens hood: Built-in, collapsible

Dimensions: Length 100mm, diameter 65.5mm

Weight: 540g

Finish: Black chrome

Product code: 11 922

Variations: A limited quantity of approximately 4,900 Safari green enamel paint finished Elmar-R 180mm, f/4's were manufactured (11 924) in 1977/78 and marketed with the Safari green Leica R3 Electronic camera.

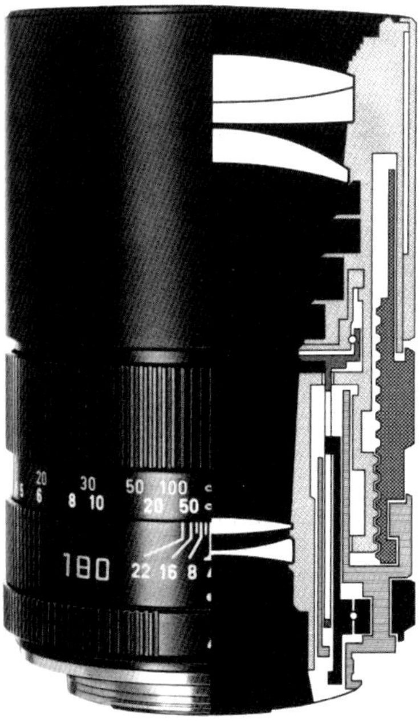

Fig. 72. Elmar-R 180mm, f/4, the lightest and most compact of the 180mm family.

Comment: The optical performance of this and the faster lens in 2.23. is identical. I love those exotic fronted 'dinnerplate' optics of the faster objectives, but there are times when a photographer has to make a choice between humping coal, with its unenviable consequences, or remaining mobile. For the large majority of general outdoor picture-taking requirements, the maximum aperture of f/4 is perfectly adequate, the more so in this case because, as with all other Leica objectives, this lens can be used with confidence wide open. Its focal length is ideally suited to the travel photographer who needs to isolate detail and to the sports photographer as a companion to longer objectives.

2.22. APO-TELYT-R 180mm, f/3.4

Year introduced: 1975

Earlier version: None, but see Variations

Minimum aperture: f/22

Angle of view: 14°

Elements/groups: 7/4

Filter size: E60

Focusing range: 2.5m to inf.

Smallest object field: 276 x 414mm

Lens hood: Built-in, collapsible

Dimensions: Length 135mm, diameter 68mm

Weight: 750g

Finish: Black chrome

Product code: 11 242

Variations: This exotic piece of glass was originally developed at the Leitz, Midland, Ontario plant in Canada in the early 1970's for the United States Navy whose requirement was for a small format, high resolution camera system based on the Leicaflex SL. In this form it was the Elcan 180mm, f/3.4.

Comment: The lens was designed by Dr. Walter Mandler who during the 1950's was responsible for establishing Ernst Leitz Canada Ltd as the centre of Leica lens development for several decades. This APO lens was one of a series of 'extended spectral range' objectives developed by Mandler. It employed special high refracting optical glass rather than glass with artificially grown fluoride crystals. Its performance is outstanding. The apochromatic correction is so good that no adjust-

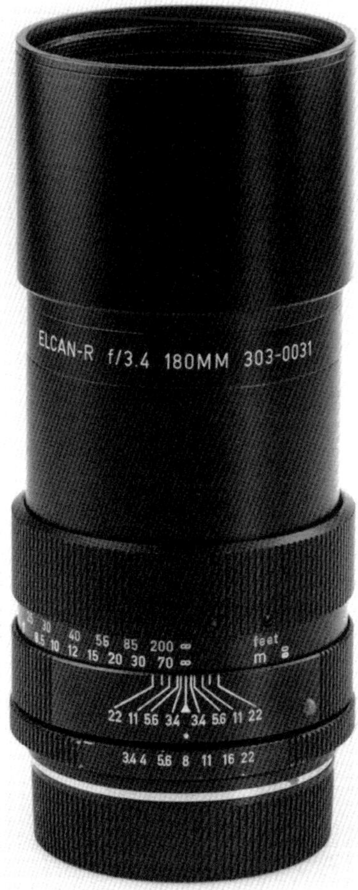

Fig. 73. Designed by Dr. Walter Mandler and developed and built at the Midland plant in Canada for the U.S. Navy, this rare Elcan-R 180mm, f/3.4 was the forerunner of the current Apo-Telyt-R 180mm, f3.4. It has superb colour correction.
Fieldgrass & Gale/Jonathan Harris

ment to the focus is necessary for infra-red photography. Favoured by many professional photojournalists for its superior resolution.

2.23. ELMARIT-R 180mm, f/2.8

Year introduced: 1980

Earlier version: Yes, see 2.47.

Minimum aperture: f/22

Angle of view: 14°

Elements/groups 5/4

Filter size: E67

Focusing range: 1.8m to inf.

Smallest object field: 193 x 290mm

Lens hood: Built-in, collapsible

Dimensions: Length 121mm, diameter 75mm

Weight: 810g

Finish: Black chrome

Product code: 11 923

Variations: None (but see 2.47)

Comment: The faster aperture of this objective has advantages for the photographer who needs an even longer focal length but does not wish to carry a larger prime lens. Using the APO-EXTENDER-R 2x and 1.4x, the 180mm easily converts to a 360mm, f/5.6 or 250mm, f/4

2.24. APO-SUMMICRON-R 180mm, f/2

Year introduced: 1994

Earlier version: None

Minimum aperture: f/16

Angle of view: 14°

Elements/groups: 9/6

Filter size: Series 6 drop-in, built-in protective front filter

Focusing range: 1.5m to inf.

Smallest object field: 158 x 237mm

Lens hood: Built-in, rubber armoured, collapsible

Dimensions: Length 176mm, diameter 116mm

Weight: 2500g

Finish: Black chrome, built-in eyelets for carrying strap

Product code: 11 271

Variations: None.

Comment: This is the second 180mm APO objective; a completely new optical design developed over

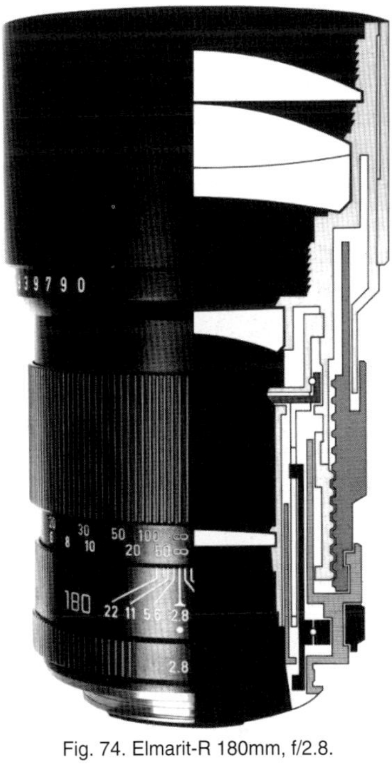

Fig. 74. Elmarit-R 180mm, f/2.8.

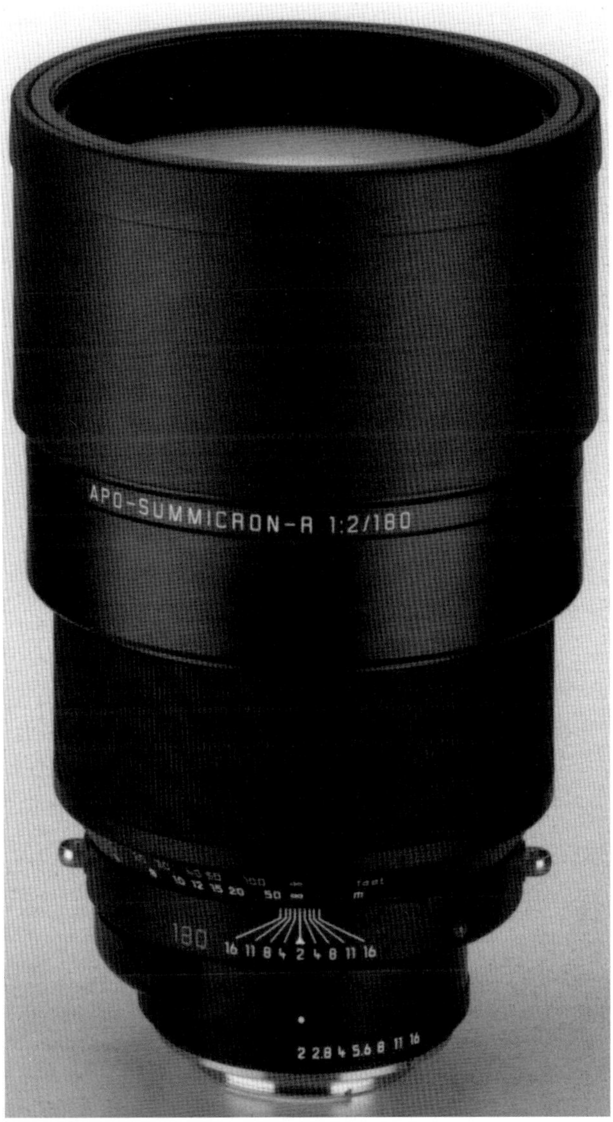

Fig. 75. Apo-Summicron-R 180mm, f/2. Leica Camera have produced several very impressive telephoto objectives during the past decade, but this new 180mm, f/2 takes all the laurels. Optical performance is outstanding. *Leica Camera GmbH*

a period of some 14 months and manufactured in Solms. The glass is to Leica specifications but manufactured by a number of different suppliers. Optical performance is outstanding as one might imagine. It will appeal primarily to sports photographers specialising in indoor events where ambient light levels are often low, as well as to photojournalists. It is also a sumptuous lens for fashion photographers who in recent years have pushed the limits of image making to the edge using longer telephoto objectives. Its weight is not a great deal more than the 1820 grams of the current Telyt-R 350mm, f/4; thus, using the APO-EXTENDER-R 2x, the user creates a 360mm f/4 objective with Apo performance.

2.25. TELYT-R 250mm, f/4

Year introduced: 1980

Earlier version: Yes, see 2.48.

Minimum aperture: f/22

Angle of view: 10°

Elements/groups: 7/6

Filter size: E67

Focusing range: 1.7m to inf.

Smallest object field: 124 x 186mm

Lens hood: Built-in, collapsible

Dimensions: Length 195mm, diameter 75mm

Weight: 1280g

Finish: Black chrome

Product code: 11 925

Variations: None (but see 2.48)

Comment: A handy long focal length of telephoto design with a useful working aperture for photojournalists, sports photographers and transport specialists. Its relatively short length makes it suitable for carrying in a gadget bag. This lens has a comparatively short travel focus ring and its ability to focus at close distances is another advantage for travel photographers intent on isolating detail. Architecturally minded photographers will also find the focal length ideal for maintaining the relative scale of buildings when used at the correct object to camera distance.

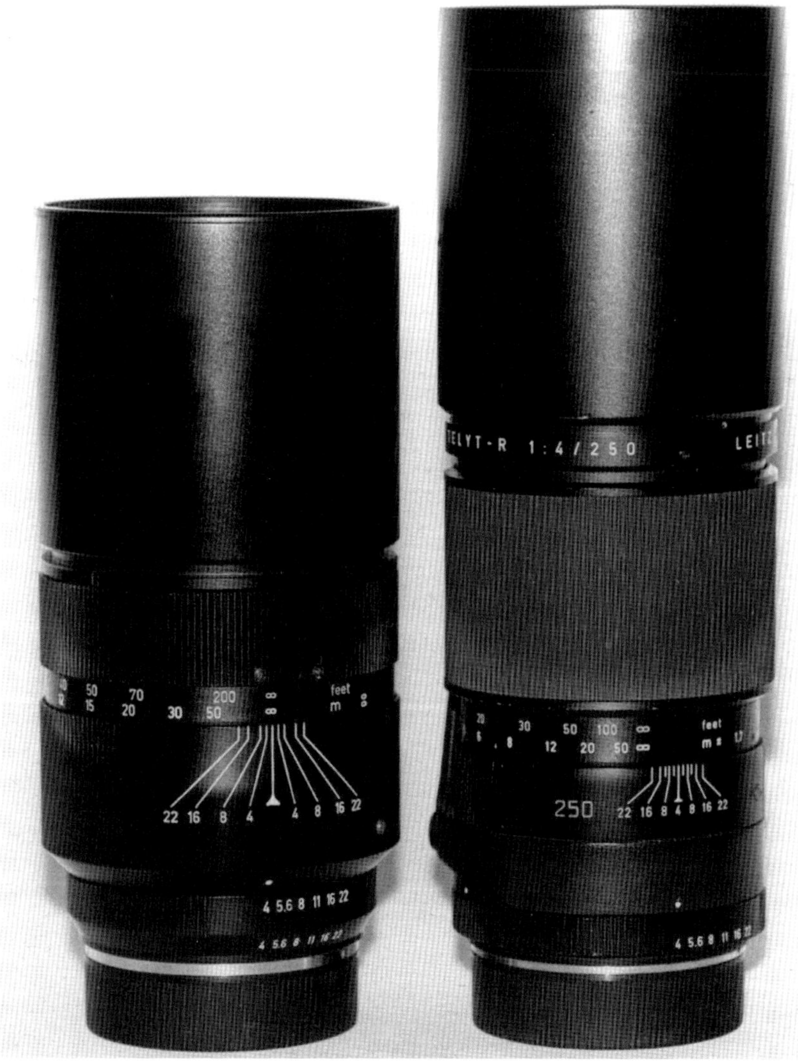

Fig. 76. The long and the short. On the left, earlier Telyt-R 250mm, f/4 (see Introduction and section 2.48 of this chapter) and the later version introduced in 1980. Both optically superb, the later version has a rotating tripod collar, the first version a fixed bush.

2.26. APO-TELYT-R 280mm, f/4

Year introduced: 1993

Earlier version: None

Minimum aperture: f/22

Angle of view: 8.8°

Elements/groups: 7/6

Filter size: Series 5.5 drop-in. Built-in front protection glass

Focusing range: 1.7m to inf.

Smallest object field: 120 x 180mm

Lens hood: Built-in, rubber armoured collapsible

Dimensions: Length 208mm, diameter 97.5mm

Weight: 1875g

Finish: Black chrome

Product code: 11 261

Variations: None.

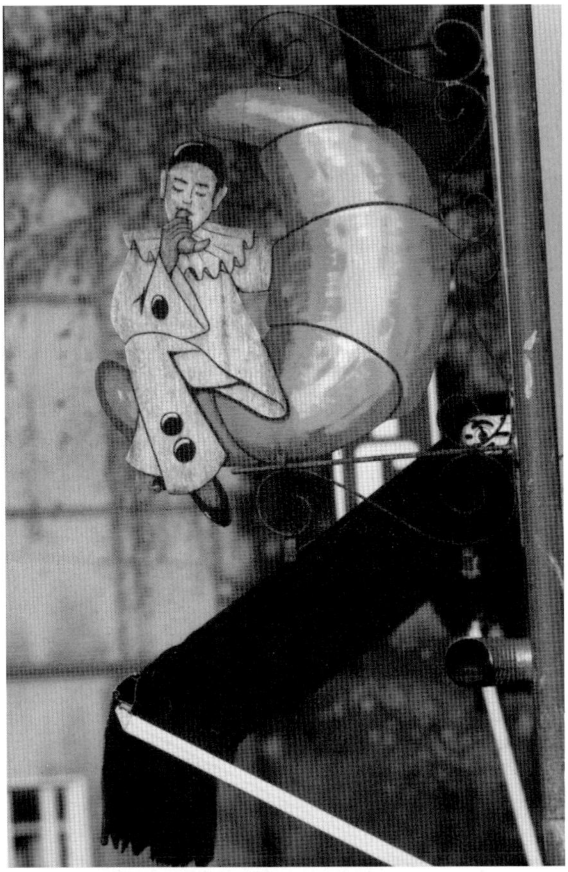

Figs. 78 & 79. The 250 to 280mm focal length range is one of the most useful for travel photographers and photojournalists whose subject range is often varied. Details of street furniture, architecture and those rare ceremonial moments can easily be covered.

Comment: This is the telephoto objective many Leica R photographers have been waiting years for. Built in the Solms factory, it is larger and heavier than most other marque telephotos of similar length but it is nonetheless superbly designed and beautifully balanced when used with an R-type camera fitted with the Motor Drive-R and handgrip. Internal focusing ensures the overall length of the lens remains the same, no matter the focused distance. It is fully apochromatically corrected for extended spectral range (infra-red) photography across the full focus range. Six of its seven specially developed glass elements are comprised of Leica developed Extra-Low Dispersion (ED) glass and each of the seven elements is individually multicoated with up to eight layers of Leica thin-film coatings eliminating virtually all tendency to reflection and ghost imaging in high contrast photography. Point source

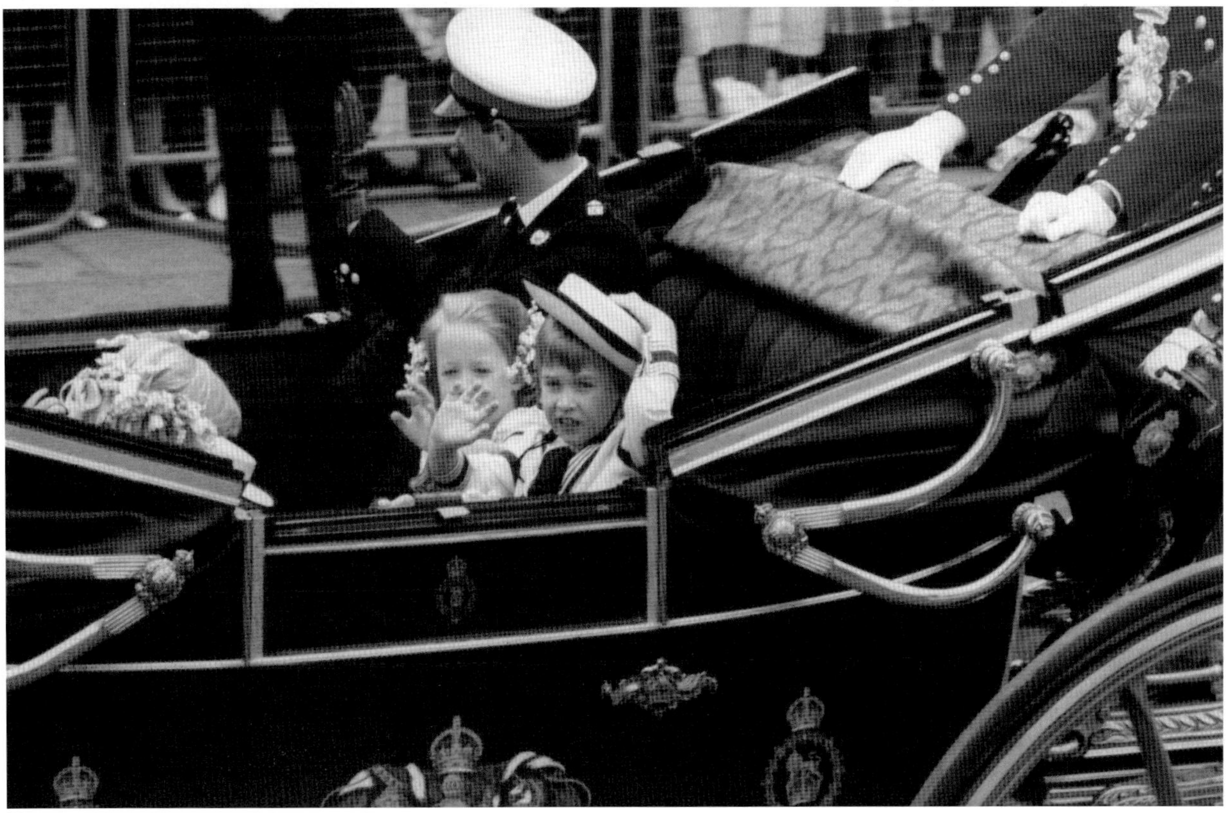

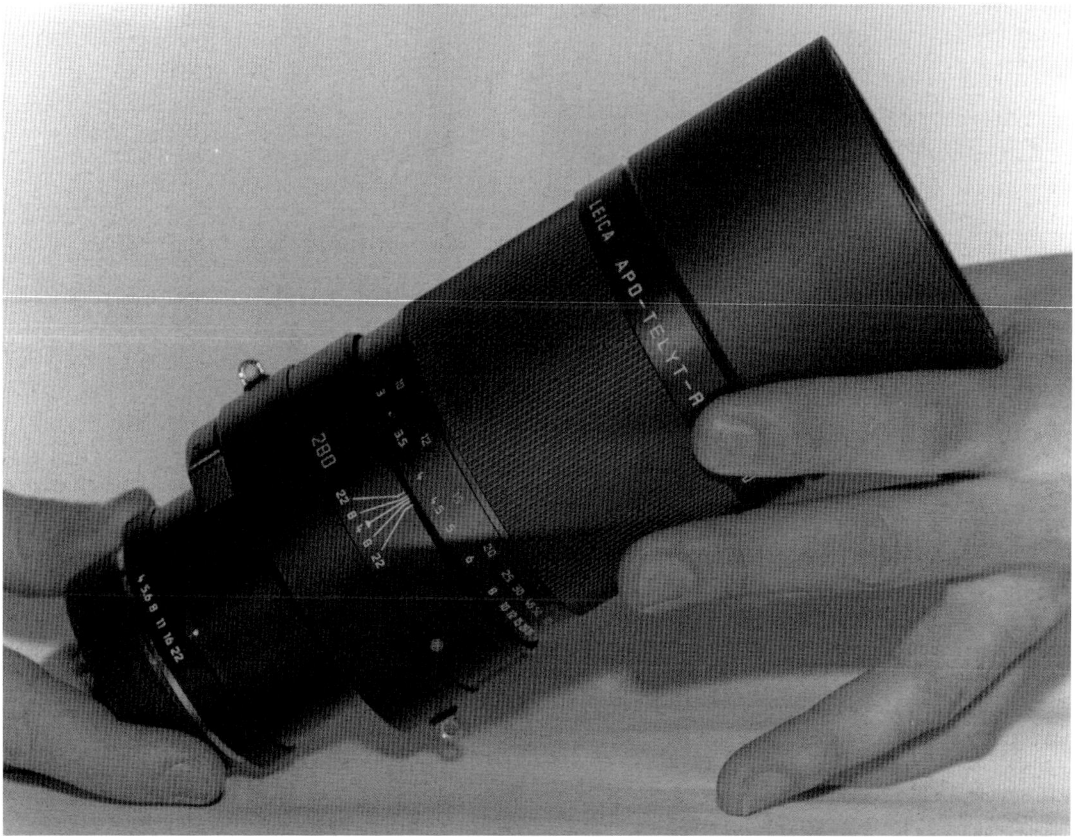

Fig. 77. The Apo-Telyt-R 280mm, f/4, another useful and superb addition to the Leica R lens range, which is surprisingly compact. The very high specification standard is easily seen. The rotating lockable tripod collar is fitted with strap eyelets; a substantial locking filter holder is seen to the left of the collar.

lights and backlighting effects, such as bright highlights are rendered faithfully.

The close focusing distance of 5.6 feet makes it suitable for a wide range of subject material from nature and wildlife photography to sports and landscapes. Results are outstanding with reproduction image definition held to poster size without difficulty.

The lens is fitted with heavy duty eyelets for the carry strap, has a rotating tripod mount with locking screw and comes complete with front and rear caps in a fitted soft leather case.

2.27. APO-TELYT-R 280mm, f/2.8

Year introduced: 1984

Earlier version: None

Minimum aperture: f/22

Angle of view: 8.5°

Elements/groups: 8/7

Filter size: E112, Series 5.5 drop-in (but see Variations)

Focusing range: 2.5m to inf.

Smallest object field: 195 x 293mm

Lens hood: Built-in collapsible

Dimensions: Length 261mm, diameter 125mm

Weight: 2800g

Finish: Black anodising and mottled black enamel effect

Product code: 11 263

Variations: Earliest versions of this lens are not fitted with the drop-in filter drawer which was eventually incorporated into the design in 1992.

Comment: The front element is protected by a solid optical flat which can be removed. This was the first of the truly exotic big telephoto APO-lenses to come out of the factory at Wetzlar and was made possible by the special ED glasses formulated by the Leitz Optical Research laboratory. Japanese photographic companies had supplied similar objectives for some years before Leitz, but when this version was eventually launched at Photokina, it put all others in the shade, such is its optical perfection. The APO-EXTENDER-R 1.4x was specially designed to match the 280mm and converts it to a very useful 400mm, f/4.

Much loved by sports and wildlife photographers, its mechanical design permits easy hand-held use in spite of the weight. Internal focusing is activated by a large focusing ring, the cross section of which is shaped a little like an extreme wide angle lens. The extra wide portion of the focus ring can be moved easily to continuously adjust fine focus with the edge of the thumb.

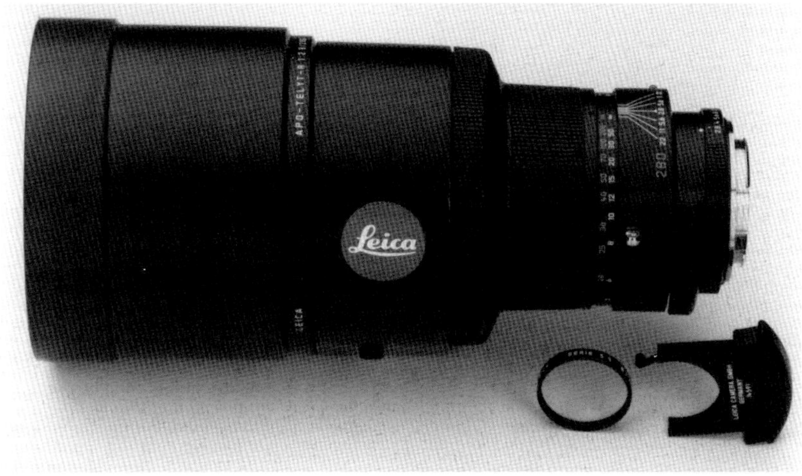

Fig. 80. Apo-Telyt-R 280mm, f/2.8.

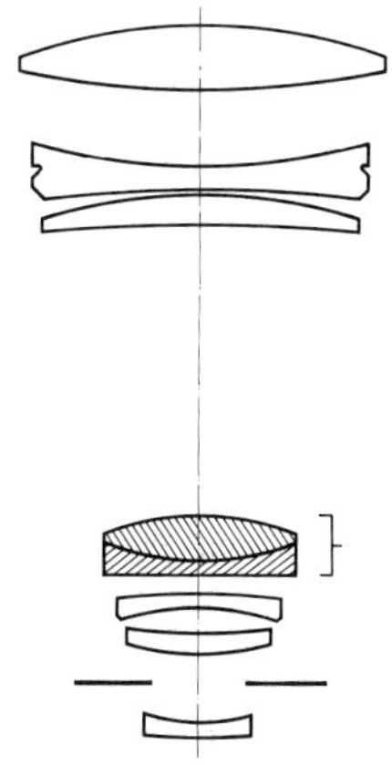

Fig. 80a. Optical diagram of the Apo-Telyt-R 280mm, f/2.8. The hatched elements are the ones which move during internal focusing.

2.28. APO-TELYT-R 400mm, f/2.8

Year introduced: 1992

Earlier version: None (but see Variations below)

Minimum aperture: f/22

Angle of view: 6°

Elements/groups: 11/9

Filter size: Series 5.5 drop-in

Focusing range: 4.7m to inf.

Smallest object field: 280 x 420mm

Lens hood: Bayonet mounted, can be reversed for carrying

Dimensions: Length 365mm, diameter 166mm

Weight: 5500g

Finish: Black and silver chrome

Product code: 11 260

Variations: Earlier prototype versions of this objective were first shown to a handful of selected photographers at the 1988 Winter Olympic Games in Calgary, Canada. This version was some 2kg heavier than the current model!

Comment: The APO 400mm f/2.8 is in a class of its own optically. Fully apochromatically corrected, image resolution and contrast are unaffected when combining the lens with the APO-EXTENDER-R 1.4x which was custom designed for use with this lens and the 280mm version described above. The APO-EXTENDER-R 2x may also be used, but the diaphragm should be closed by at least two stops to maintain optical

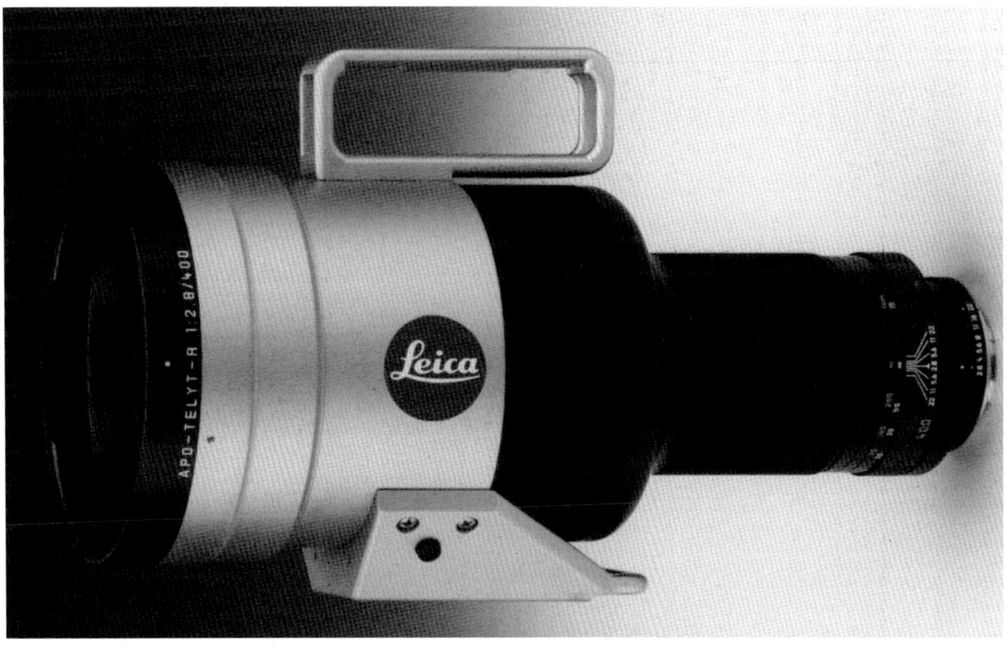

Fig. 81. At five and a half kilos the Apo-Telyt-R 400mm, f/2.8 is no lightweight and ideally needs to be used on a substantial monopod. Ideal for sports and wildlife photography, or even landscapes.
Leica Camera GmbH

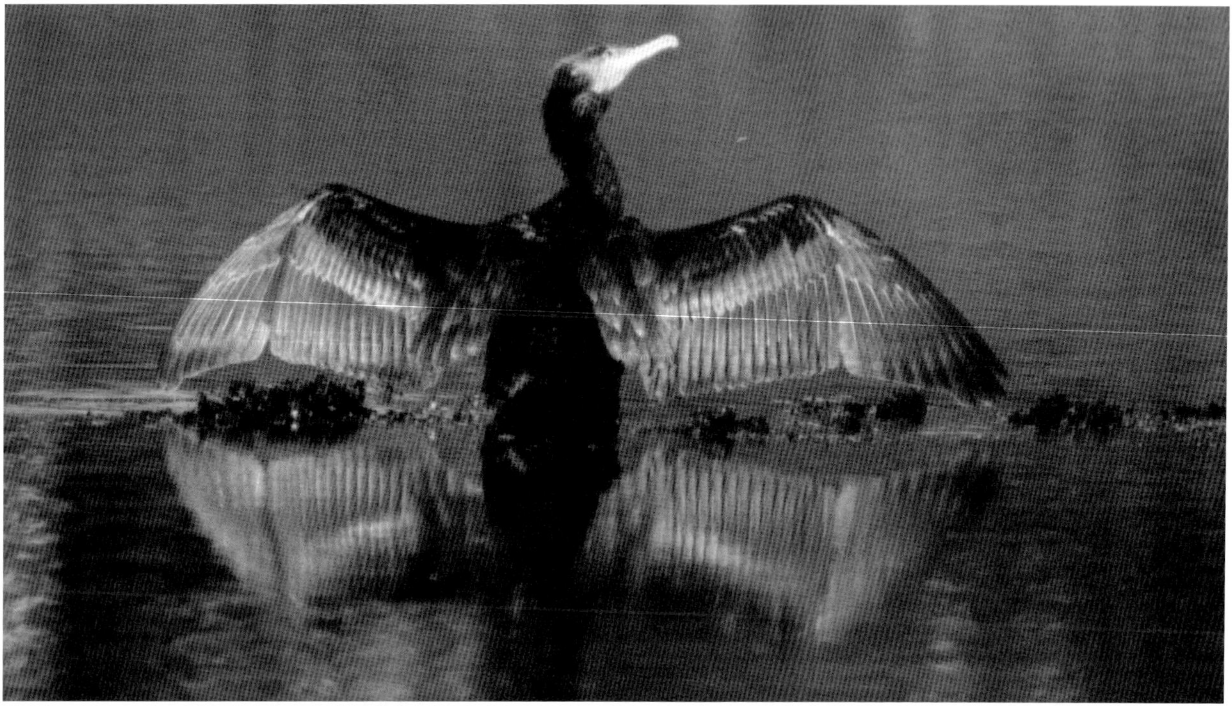

Fig. 82. There are subjects in some environments the photographer can only access with longer tele-objectives; a 1.4x Extender was used with a 400mm lens to reach this cormorant drying its wings.

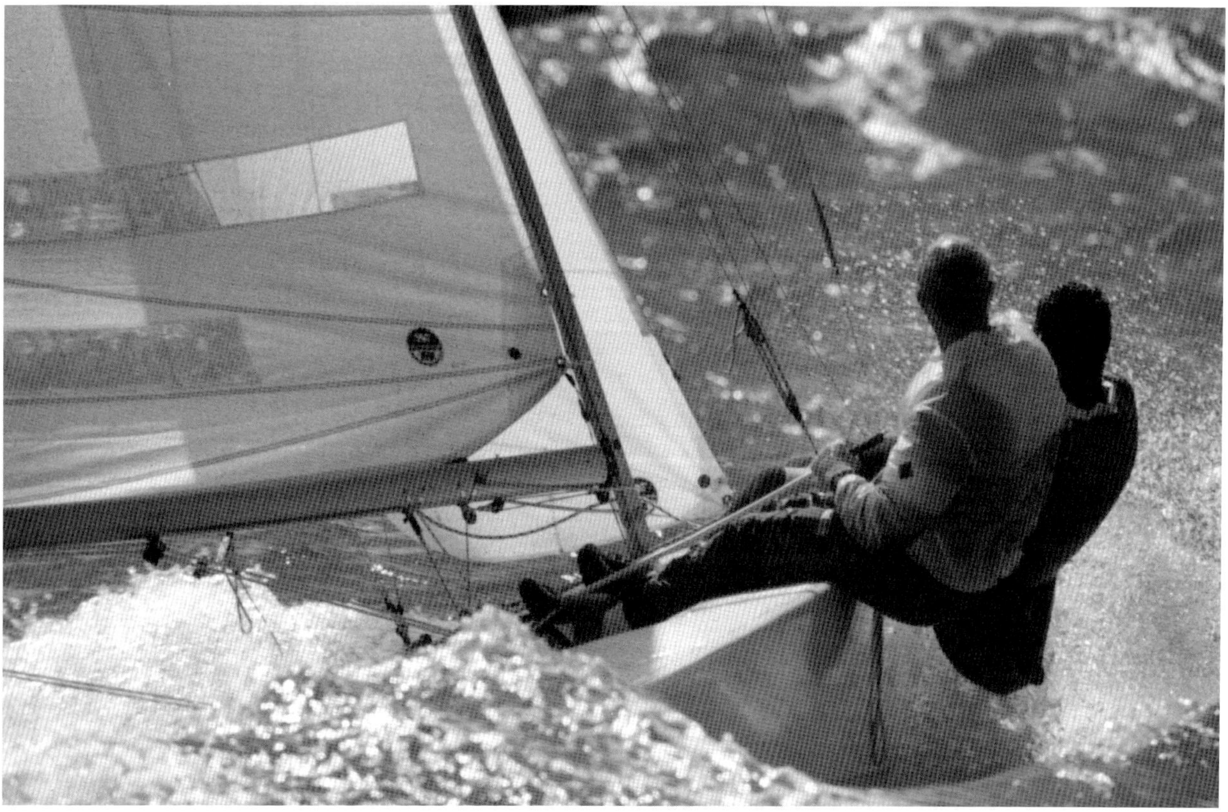

Fig. 83. In brightly lit environments like this, a fast maximum aperture tele-objective becomes an unnecessary burden. The Leica Telyt-R 400mm f/6.8 lens head with Novoflex grip or Leica sliding tube, or the Novoflex 400mm, f/5.6 with Rapid Follow Focus Grip, is perfectly adequate.

performance. The APO 400mm f/2.8 comes with a fitted carrying handle, lenshood, carrying strap and fitted aluminium transport case in which there is an additional compartment for the two extenders and additional filters.

2.29. TELYT-R 400mm, f/6.8. With Novoflex Rapid Follow Focus Grip.

Year introduced: 1990

Earlier version: None (but see Variations below)

Minimum aperture: f/32

Angle of view: 6°

Elements/groups: 2/1

Filter size: Special drop-in filter drawer for Novoflex/Helioplan filters

Focusing range: 7.5m to inf, down to 2.4m using built-in extension tube

Smallest object field: 90 x 135mm

Lens hood: Detachable, bayonet fitting

Dimensions: Length 406mm, diameter 89mm

Weight: 2930g

Finish: Black anodising, lens head covered in black vulcanite

Product code: 11 926

Variations: The lens head supplied with this kit is identical to the Telyt-R 400mm f/6.8 first introduced in 1970 for use with the sliding focus tube 11 906 and which is still currently available as a complete unit (11 953). Outwardly, there are cosmetic differences between the two lens heads. 11 903 is finished in black chrome.

Comment: The Rapid Follow Focus Grip is manufactured by Novoflex Fotogeratebau of Memmingen in Germany and is basically the same as the current D-type Novoflex unit which is available to fit many different camera types with special adapters. The Leica version has been specially prepared with Leica R-type lens mount, Leica logo badge and barrel finish to Leica specification. It also has a special lens head locking bayonet device not featured on standard Novoflex models. The Leica Telyt-R lens heads cannot therefore be fitted to the current Novoflex-D type grip or the previous C-model.

Where these two models differ is in the optics, and the following comments apply equally to the Telyt-R 560mm version. The history of the Telyt's goes back to 1966 when the first 400mm and 560mm, f/5.6 versions were introduced by Leitz to fit the special Televit rapid focusing mount designed for even earlier 280 and 400mm Visoflex lenses for use with the Leica rangefinder cameras.

The optical performance of the f/5.6 versions suffered slightly from curvature of field at the extreme edges. Not enough, claimed Leitz at the time, to degrade image quality. Nevertheless, two slower versions were introduced a few years later, of the type currently marketed. The optical quality is outstanding, considering the simple achromat design. The Leica lens heads use special, highly corrected Leitz formulated glass. Novoflex's own versions, which may be used with their Rapid Follow Focus Grip on Leica R-cameras with the correct lens mount adaptor, are available as 400mm f/5.6 and 600mm f/8 lens units. The 400mm version overcomes the problem of curvature of field encounteredby Leitz, by employing a cemented triplet design. The 600mm version is a doublet. The elements for both types are manufactured by a specialist optical glass sub-division of Agfa at Altenstadt and the optical quality is excellent. The only noticeable difference between the two systems being that Leica images are rendered in typical neutral hues. The Novoflex image is slightly less contrasty perhaps, but equally neutral in colour. The special 2x TEX tele-extender is available to double the focal length of both prime lens heads.

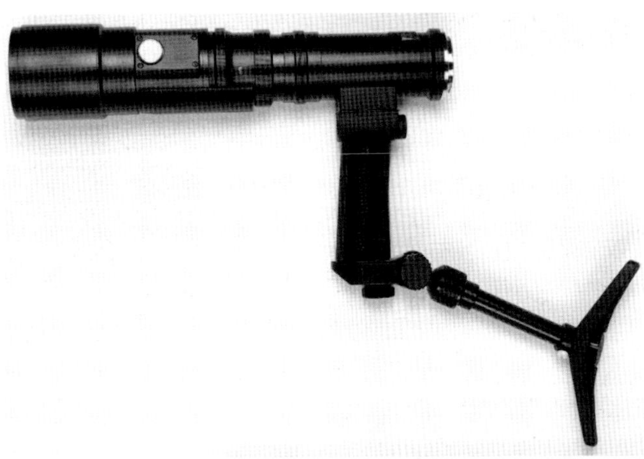

Fig. 84. Telyt-R 400mm, f/6.8 with sliding focus tube (11 906) and detachable shoulder stock. *Leica Camera UK Ltd*

2.30. TELYT-R 560mm, f/6.8. with Novoflex Rapid Follow Focus Grip

Year introduced: 1990

Earlier version: None, but see 2.29 variations.

Minimum aperture: f/32

Angle of view: 4.3°

Elements/groups: 2/1

Filter size: Special drop-in drawer for Novoflex/Helioplan filters.

Lens hood: Built-in

Dimensions: Length 84mm, diameter 74.8mm

Weight: 465g

Finish: Black anodised

Product code: 11 265

Variations: None.

Comment: Manufactured by the Sigma Corporation of Japan to Leica specification. It was officially discontinued in July 1994 but was being offered by Leica UK Ltd and other distributors at the time this volume went to press as a 'free' lens when a current Leica R-type camera was purchased new. Optically, this is a short zoom lens with an excellent performance across the whole focal length and focus range. On the sales front, it faired rather better in Germany than in other parts of the world, notably the UK, where reviewers slammed it as being a too highly priced version of Sigma's own lens (see Chapter 2 text for explanation). The typography used for the engraving of numerals, aperture scale and lens type is slightly at variance with Leica's standard style. It is nevertheless beautifully manufactured and a delight to use. A pity Leica and Sigma could not have come up with an f/2.8 version.

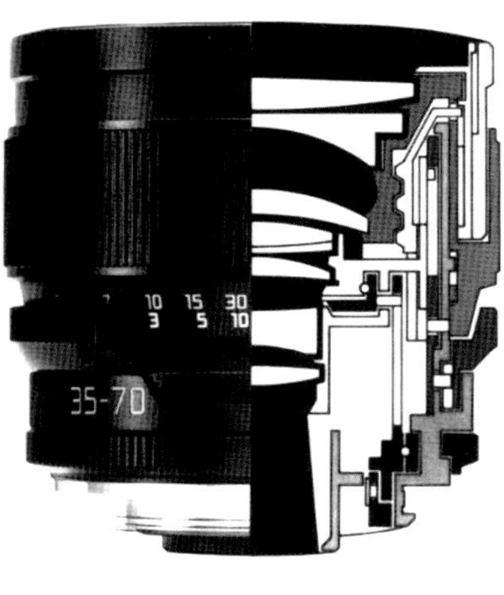

Fig. 89. Vario-Elmar-R 35-70mm, f/3.5.

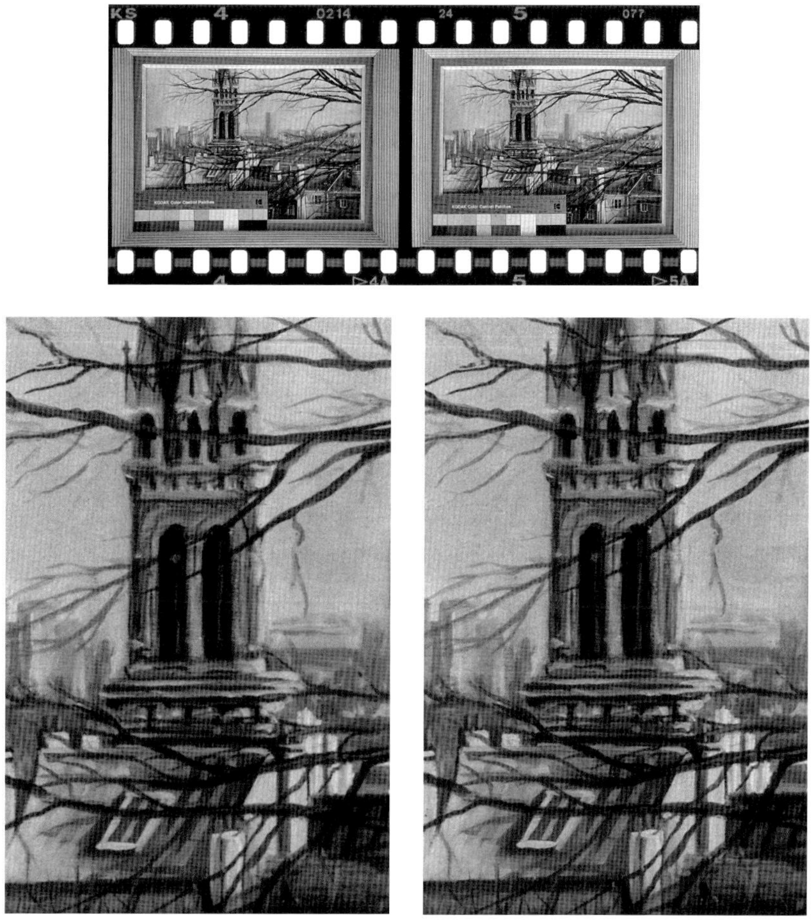

Figs. 91, 92 and 93. With the Vario-Elmar-R 35-70mm lens set at 50mm, the framed size of the object is only marginally reduced (left) compared to the size achieved with the Summicron-R 50mm, f/2 standard lens (right image). The zoom lens definition at this setting and object-to-camera distance is excellent, although some diffusion of the typography edges is apparent. Colour rendition differences in the original transparencies is virtually indistinguishable with the naked eye, and is insignificant for practical purposes.

2.34. VARIO-ELMAR-R 35-70mm, f/3.5

Year introduced: 1988

Earlier version: Yes, see Variations below

Minimum aperture: f/22

Angle of view: 64° – 34°

Elements/groups: 8/7

Filter size: E67

Focusing range: 1m to inf.

Smallest object field: 632 x 947mm to 338 x 507mm

Lens hood: Built-in, collapsible

Dimensions: Length 66.5mm, diameter 76.5mm

Weight: 450g

Finish: Black chrome

Product code: 11 248, (first version 11 244)

Variations: This second version is optically identical to the first model designed and manufactured by Minolta and launched by Leitz in 1983 to replace the Angènieux 45-90mm zoom (see 2.55). Only the mount of the current model was redesigned to eliminate rotation of the front portion of the lens as it is focused. The filter size was also increased to eliminate vignetting. Zooming is controlled by a second ring.

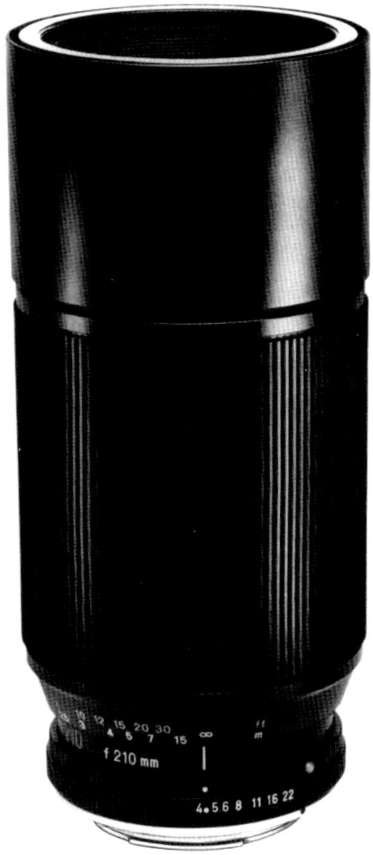

Fig. 90. Introduced in 1984, this Vario-Elmar-R 70-210mm, f/4 zoom lens is probably the sharpest of its type and aperture. Excellent all round performance endears it to those who want to travel light and benefit from its special features.

Comment: Although almost half the size and weight of the French lens, its focal length range does not, in my view, extend far enough at the long end to be of any great use for serious portrait work. Some photographers find it useful however, at the other end of the scale and because it does at least cover the standard 50mm length. Can be used with APO-EXTENDER-R 2x which doubles the focal length and halves the effective maximum aperture.

2.35. VARIO-ELMAR-R 70-210mm, f/4

Year introduced: 1984

Earlier version: None, but see 2.53 & 2.54.

Minimum aperture: f/22

Angle of view: 35° – 12°

Elements/groups: 12/9

Filter size: E60

Focusing range: 1.1m to inf.

Smallest object field: 264 x 396mm to 96 x 144mm

Lens hood: Built-in, collapsible

Dimensions: Length 157mm, diameter 73.5mm

Weight: 720g

Finish: Black chrome with large rubber covered focus/zoom grip

Product code: 11 246

Variations: None (but see 2.53 & 2.54, two earlier models were designed and built by Minolta under the 1970 agreement.

Comment: This third lens has been optically redesigned, but the glass configuration, maximum aperture and focal length are identical to the Minolta MD version. This is a very handy telephoto zoom with a single push-pull-rotate-to-focus ribbed rubber collar exhibiting outstanding image quality for a lens of this type across the whole focal length and focus range. Ideally suited to travel, sports and the general practitioner photographer as well as to the advertising specialist and photojournalist. It cannot be used with the Leicaflex Standard. It should not be used with either of the APO-EXTENDERS.

Teleconverters

2.36. APO-EXTENDER-R 1.4x

Year introduced: 1986

Earlier version: None

Magnification of prime objective: 1.4x

Elements/groups: 5/4

Dimensions: Length 25mm, diameter 62mm

Weight: 220g

Finish: Black chrome

Product code: 11 249

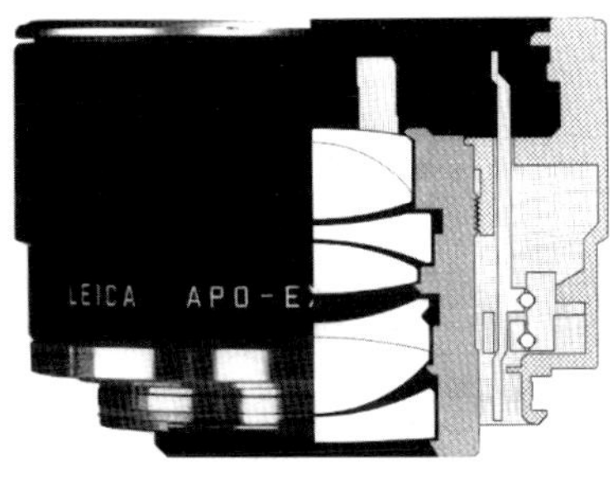

Fig. 94b. Apo-Extender-R 2x.

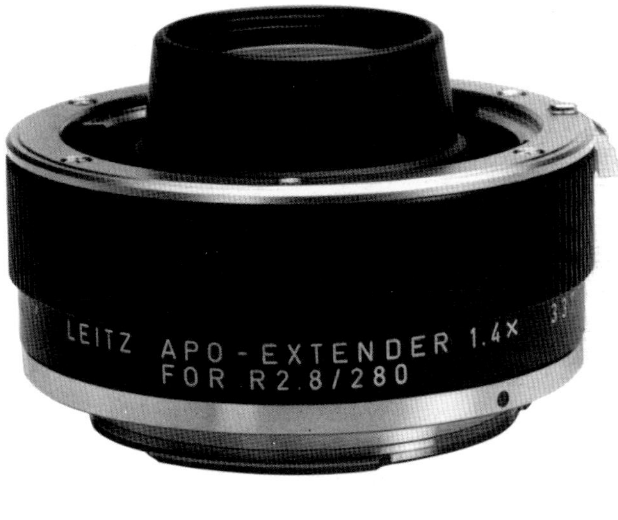

Fig. 94a. Apo-Extender-R 1.4x. See Appendix tables.

Variations: None.

Comment: Produced originally as a matched teleconverter for the APO-TELYT 280mm, f/2.8 lens; may be used with other objectives as described above or see Appendix table.

2.37. APO-EXTENDER-R 2x

Year introduced: 1992

Earlier version: None

Magnification of prime objective: 2x

Elements/groups: 7/5

Dimensions: Length 35.4mm, diameter 62mm

Weight: 245g

Finish: Black chrome

Product code: 11 262

Variations: None.

Comment: This teleconverter is suitable for use with all APO objectives as well as with all other focal lengths from 50mm upward, effectively doubling the focal length and decreasing aperture by 2 stops. (see Appendix table)

Older Lenses for Use with Leicaflex and R-Type Cameras

To reiterate the point made in the *Leica M Compendium* concerning the use of older Leitz and Leica objectives, it is worth noting first that the designs of the oldest Leicaflex lenses are a mere thirty years old, as opposed to eighty plus for the oldest rangefinder types.

At the time design work began on the 'flex' lenses, things were already very well advanced in the world of photographic image making. Much older designs than these, using less sophisticated glass and some with the visible evidence of striations and heaven knows what kind of invisible aberrations, are still capable of turning in respectable image quality.

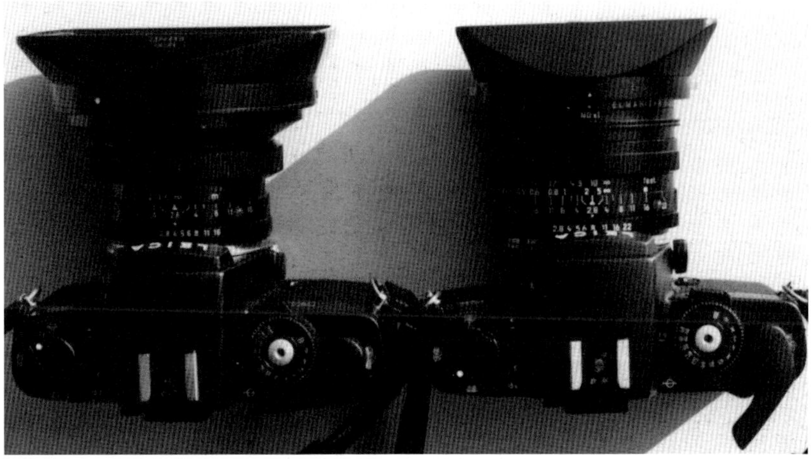

Fig. 95. Old and the new. Dr.Walther Mandler's famous Elmarit-R 19mm left with its very large lens hood. The newer model, right, is more compact but extends almost the same distance from the lens mount flange. Both are mounted on a pair of Leica R-E cameras.

Leitz philosophy from the beginning was always to produce the very best image quality, irrespective of cost, either to themselves or to the customer, and nothing in that department has changed.

Many of the 'flex' lenses, like their rangefinder counterparts, were (and are still) designed to satisfy the demanding specifications of defence procurement departments, science and industry. The discerning Leica camera user has reaped the benefit of all of the research in this respect, and not undeservedly, since much of that research has been made possible on the back of profits made in the good years. Nor has this phenomenal amount of work been without its moments of irony.

When Kodachrome film was invented by the two Leopold's, Mannes and Godowsky in 1935, Max Berek's revolutionary Summar 50mm, f/2 had already been in production for two years. Berek improved the lens by replacing the Summar's large single front element with a larger diameter cemented pair which improved its performance at full aperture. This new lens, the Summitar, was ideally suited to the Kodachrome film and even today, a fine, mint example of this objective produces superlative colour rendering and sharpness when used with modern Kodachrome 25. Never content with what was arguably the finest lens of its type of the day, Leitz pursued the further development of special glasses to produce the 5cm, f/2 Summicron in 1953.

This lens has been in continuous production for over forty years and has undergone several optical design changes in the process. Its optical capability has probably never been fully realised in lay terms; there is hardly a film emulsion made that can match its resolving properties. When the United States Army placed an order with Ernst Leitz Canada Ltd. for the 505 special Leica M4 rangefinder cameras known as the Leica 'Camera Still Picture' KE-7A in 1975, the M4's standard Summicron-M 50mm, f/2 launched in 1969 was considered by the military to be far in excess of the specification required. A cheaper, four-element version was designed by the Canadian plant and dispatched with the KE-7A's. This lens became known as the Elcan 50mm, f/2 and its optical performance is almost, but not quite, as outstanding as the lens it replaced.

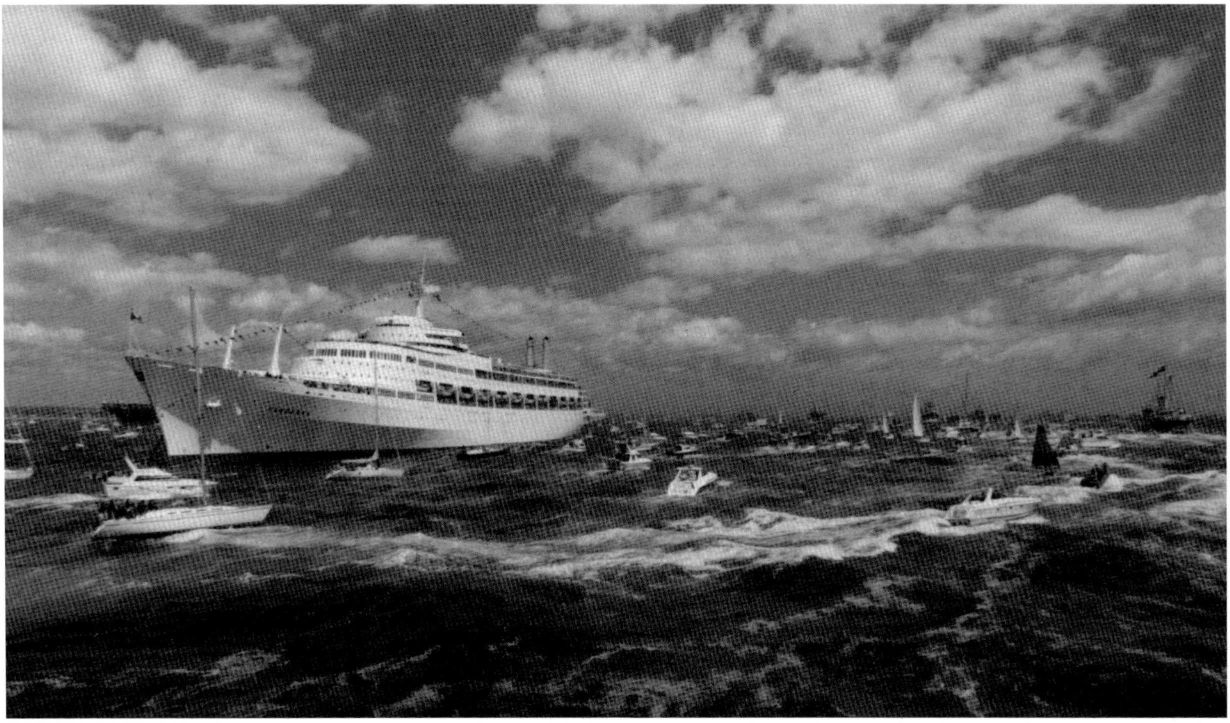

Fig. 96. Extreme wide-angle lenses such as the Elmarit-R 19mm and Super-Angulon 21mm need to be used carefully when attempting dramatic land- or seascapes. The wide angle of view encompasses a great deal, but the mind is more easily impressed by reality. Lenses and cameras cannot think.

In discussing Leica objectives with other Leicaphiles, I have often been asked for my opinion on earlier first and second generation Leicaflex and R-type objectives. The concern invariably revolves around the question of the cost of newer, current types and the optical quality of older versions. The implication considered – as with most products – is that the optical performance of older types is not as good as more recently remodelled versions. To say that older types are 'not as good' is probably misleading; 'not as perfect' would be a better expression. However, it is often the case that in everyday photography – as opposed to scientific applications – the differences are minute, in some cases virtually indistinguishable when the reproduced image is viewed from the normal viewing distance of 30cms (12 inches). Under closer inspection, and, assuming that one has perfect eyesight, subtle differences may be noticeable, but this will also depend on the comparators employed.

Occasionally, we should note that although a second or third version of an objective is introduced, its optical design may not have changed from the first version. Only the mount has been redesigned to take advantage of newer materials or thinking that improves ergonomic aspects. From a user's point of view, I tend to select objectives for work on the basis of handling, balance and weight, as well as for the aesthetic appeal of a particular design. In this regard, there are a number of classic mount designs which I would want just to be able to parade them from time to time! I am also aware, like many other enthusiasts, that some objectives have better reputations than others with regard to optical performance, so I go for those I know to be the best in the focal length ranges most suited to my subjects.

One final point on the subject of optical performance may be of interest. It has been my experience over a period of more than 25 years that only one other manufacturer's lenses have been a particular favourite for certain applications in the field of 35mm photography. However, I have also had the benefit of using other systems for long periods; the accumulated experience of working under a variety of lighting conditions in many different parts of the world is therefore extensive. The physical evidence amounts to more than 150,000 negatives and colour transparencies. Occasionally, when I am editing material on the light box for magazines or a new book, my conscience is sometimes pricked by the fact that a particular story which was not shot with my Leica lenses, should have been. Still, one can go forward, even with older Leica glass.

2.38. ELMARIT-R 19mm, f/2.8, 1975 – 1990. Product No. 11 225

Minimum aperture: f/16

Angle of view: 95.7°

Elements/groups: 9/8

Filter size: 82mm x 0.75 pitch, screw-in

Focusing range: 0.3m to inf.

Lens hood: Rectangular clip-on, product No. 12 529

Weight: 500g

Finish: Black chrome

Product code: 11 225

Comment: Designed by Dr.Walther Mandler and manufactured by Ernst Leitz Canada Ltd. at the Midland, Ontario plant, this lens was (is) an outstanding performer, ideally suited for a wide variety of applications.

2.39. SUPER-ANGULON 21mm, f/3.4, 1964 – 1968. Product No. 11 803

Comment: This lens was introduced for the original Leicaflex Standard and has a protruding rear element which requires the mirror to be locked up before mounting. Required the use of a supplementary viewfinder (product No.12 002) the same as that used for the same lens on the Leica M rangefinder cameras. Cannot be used on any subsequent Leicaflex or Leica R-type camera.

2.40. ELMARIT-R 28mm, f/2.8, 1970 – 1994. Product No. 11 204, 11206, 11 247.

Comment: This version was in production for 25 years. It has a complex optical design of eight elements, all separate. Produced in a compact black anodised mount, the lens hood (12 509) is fitted with a thumb wheel for operating the circular polarising filter. Used Series VII or E 48 screw-in filters. Lighter than the new version. Optically superb. Can be used on Leica M rangefinder cameras in conjunction with adapter mount 22 228. Fitted only with Leica R stepped cam from 1987 on. A quantity were manufactured with a Safari green finish to match the Safari R3 Electronic in 1978. (11 206).

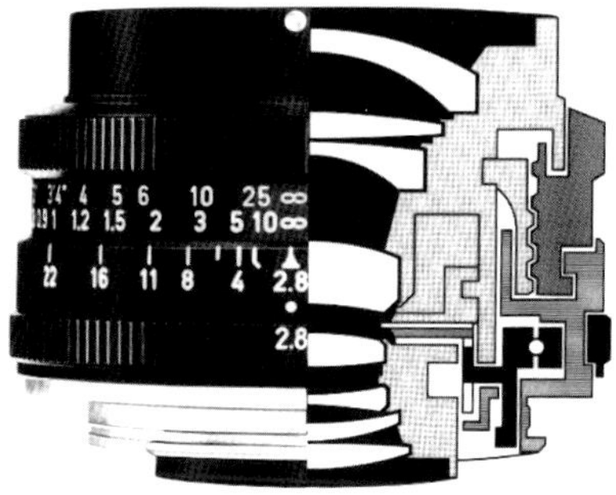

Fig. 97. Elmarit-R 28mm, f/2.8 1970-1994.

2.41. ELMARIT-R 35mm, f/2.8, 1964 – 1974 & 1974 – 1979. Product No's. 11 101, 11 201.

Comment: One of the first group of four lenses produced for the Leicaflex Standard; originally with a silver chrome finish (200 examples). It has been said that light reflecting from the outer silver barrel of these objectives affected meter readings, as did the Summicron 50mm, f/2, and that is why all subsequent versions were finished in black. Available in single, 2- and 3-cam versions. Front mount section rotated when focused. Optically recomputed from seven elements in five groups to seven in six in 1974. Front now non-rotating. Step cammed for Leica R only from 1976 onwards. Excellent all rounder for the general practitioner.

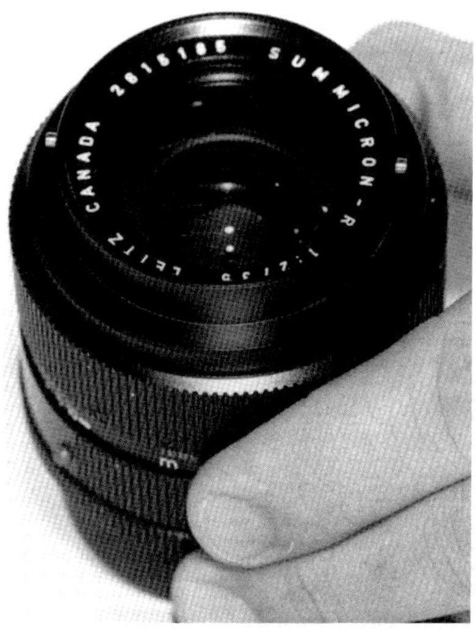

Fig. 98. Summicron-R 35mm, f/2 1972-1976. A real heavyweight, but a great performer, especially with colour film.

2.42. SUMMICRON-R 35mm, f/2, 1972 – 1976. Product No. 11 227

Minimum aperture: f/16

Elements/groups: 9/7

Filter size: Series VII or E48 screw-in

Lens hood: Rectangular, clip-on, (product No. 12 509)

Weight: 525g

Finish: Black anodised chrome

Product code: 11 227

Comment: This is another Dr. Walther Mandler masterpiece of complex retrofocus design, and a heavy one at that. Beautifully balanced with a wide, easily gripped

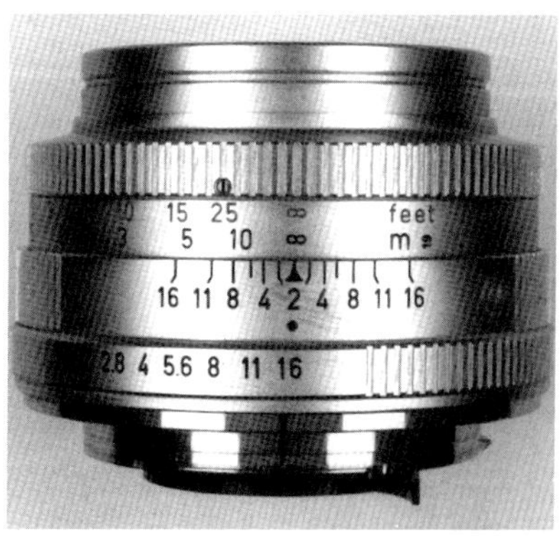

Fig. 99. A rare silver chrome Summicron-R 50mm, f/2 produced for the Leicaflex (Standard). The black chrome version is more common. *Fieldgrass & Gale/Jonathan Harris*

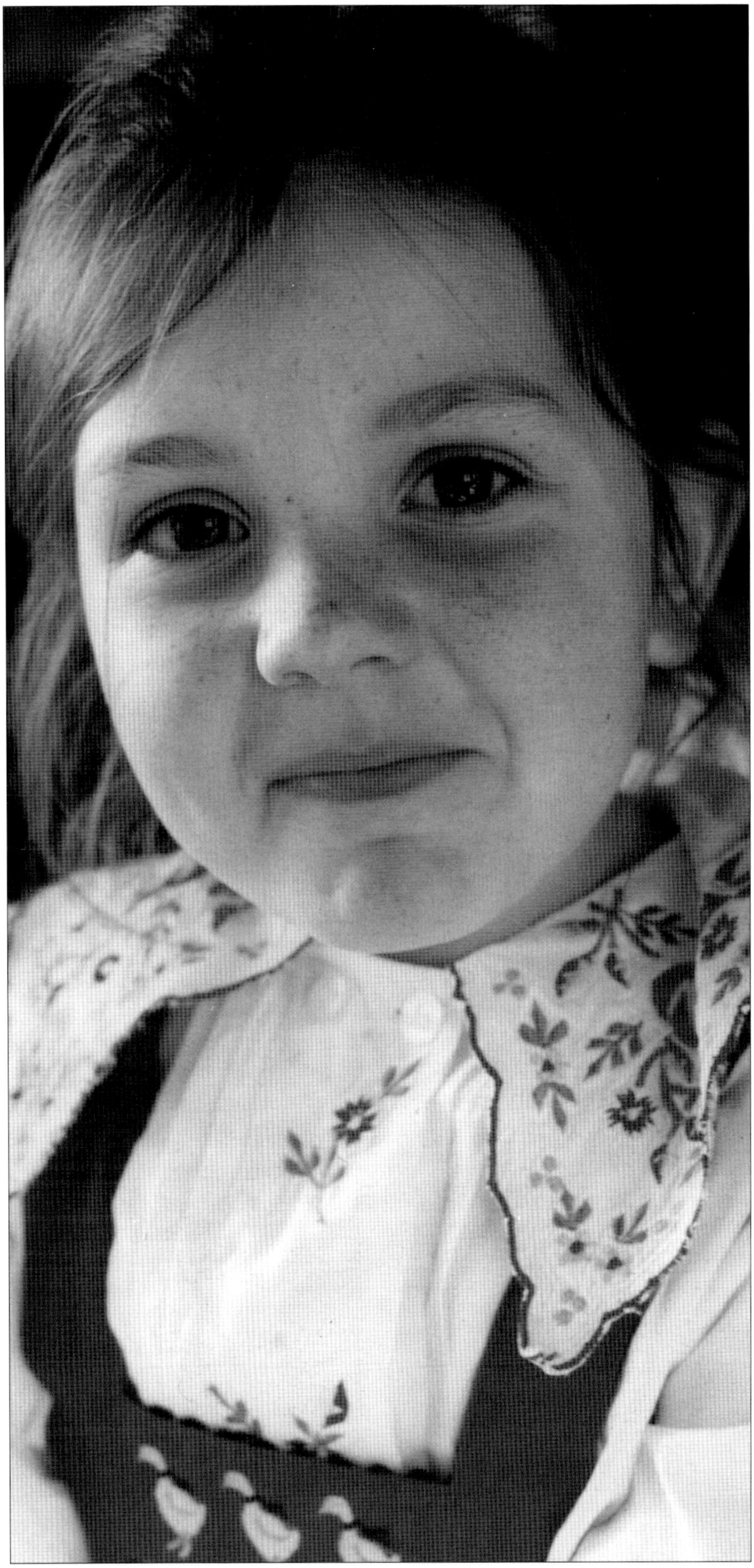

Fig. 101. In the absence of an 80, 90 or 135mm for portrait work, the 50mm focal length can be used successfully. The smaller the focal length, the greater the risk of subject feature distortion the shorter the distance between camera and subject. Keep a respectable distance. It helps to remove the feeling of intimidation some sitters feel when confronted with the camera, and also provides a useful screen area for composition.

focusing ring. Contrast levels are lower than in the current version, but resolution and colour differentiation are excellent. A great lens for use in low light situations where rendering the subtle nuances of colour hues is important.

2.43. SUMMICRON-R 50mm, f/2, 1964 – 1976. Product No's. 11 218, 11228, 11 215, 11 216, 11 217.

Comment: A six-element design similar in some respects to the Summicron-M 50mm, f/2 with two elements behind the diaphragm cemented. The lens is an excellent performer. First 300 in silver chrome finish, black chrome thereafter. Clip-on lens hood 12 564 required, used Series VI filters held in place by ring 14 160. Supplied with single cam for Leicaflex Standard and then with two from 1968 for the SL. Leitz ELPRO two-element achromat supplementary close-up lenses (see Appendix) permitted close focus to 1:2.6. The R3 cam was factory fitted from lens serial No. 2758826 onward.

2.44. SUMMILUX-R 50mm, f/1.4, 1969 – 1978. Product No. 11 875

Comment: A small batch of Safari green examples were manufactured to match the Safari green Leica R3 Electronic in 1977/8 and marketed in Europe. At 460 grams it is no lightweight and differs optically from it's Leica M cousin. Similar in

Fig. 100. On the left, current Summicron-R 50mm, f/2. On the right, earlier version designated on bottom of barrel 'For Leica R only'.

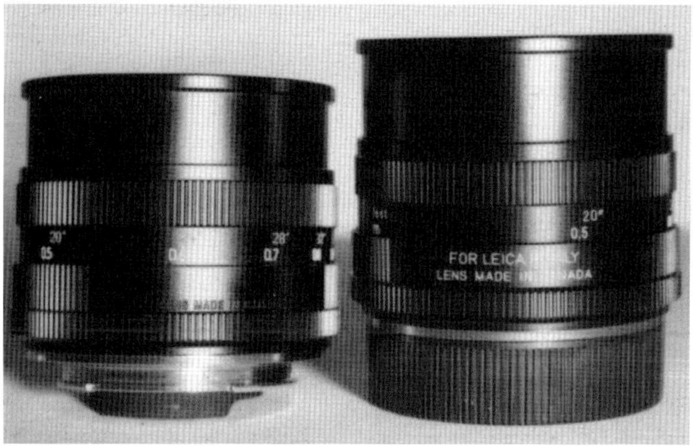

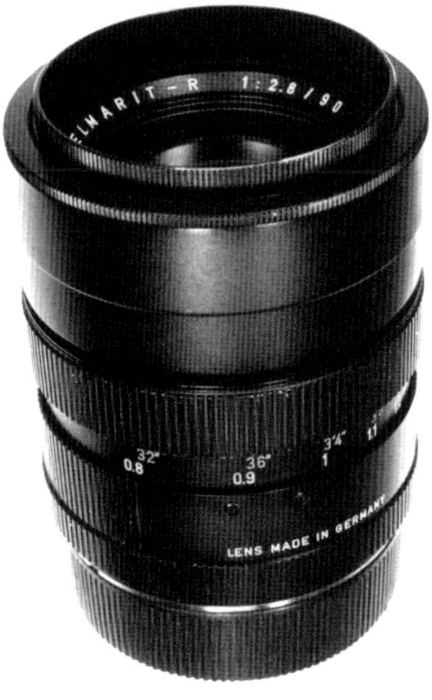

Fig. 103. Elmarit-R 90mm, f/2.8 1964-1983.

shape and size to the Summicron-R 35mm, f/2. Requires circular clip-on lens hood 12508. Manufactured at Wetzlar, this is still an excellent performer in low light situations with flare and coma virtually eliminated.

2.45. MACRO-ELMARIT-R 60mm, f/2.8, 1972 - 1980. Product No. 11 205

Comment: A true macro enthusiast's objective, computed to give the best performance at close object-to-camera distances, but still capable of matching the standard Summicron-R 50mm, f/2, lens at infinity when stopped down to f/5.6. The front element is shaded by the deep conical front mount but requires the special lenshood (12 514) when using Series VIII filters. Additional extension tube (14 198) available to extend focus range down to 1:1 ratio. The tube facilitates full auto diaphragm function but must be connected to the lens with both lens aperture and scale on tube set to f/22. Early versions fitted with two cams, third added for R3 in 1976.

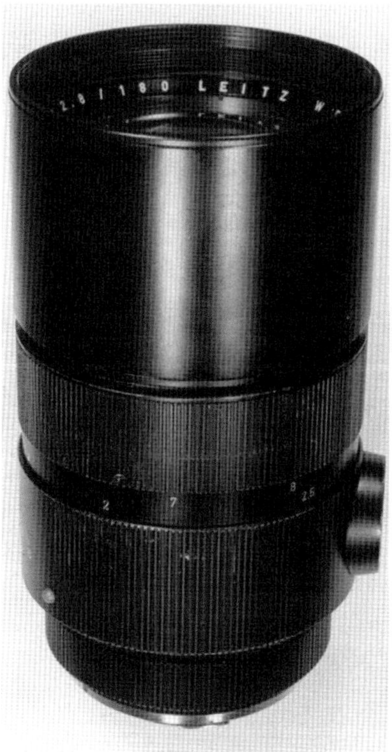

Fig 104. Elmarit-R 180mm, f/2.8, the heavy-weight first version, 1968-1979.

2.46. ELMARIT-R 90mm, f/2.8, 1964 - 1983. Product No's. 11 229, 11239

Comments: One of the most popular focal lengths produced by Leitz for the Leicaflex Standard when it was first launched. Quite a compact lens with a neatly tapered, reverse cone-shaped lens hood, capable of focusing down to 70cms (28 inches). Fitted with the ELPRO VIIa achromat supplementary lens, reproduction ratios to 1:3 are possible. Still plenty about at reasonable prices on the used market with single or double cams.

2.47. ELMARIT-R 180MM, f/2.8, 1968 - 1979. Product No. 11 919

Elements/groups: 5/4

Filter size: Series VIII held in with ring 14 165

Focusing range: 2.1m to inf.

Lens hood: Built-in, collapsible

Weight: 1325g

Finish: Black chrome

Comment: At the time of its introduction this was one of the fastest 180mm focal length objectives available anywhere. It is a real lump with four of the five hefty glass elements in front of the diaphragm. Its not inconsiderable mass, while a pain for the weight conscious, is a great benefit to specialists shooting under low-light conditions with a need to use slow shutter speeds as the lens absorbs virtually all of the camera mirror vibration.

2.48. TELYT-R 250mm, f/4, 1970 - 1979. Product No. 11 920

Elements/groups: 6/5.

Filter size: Series VIII with ring 14 165

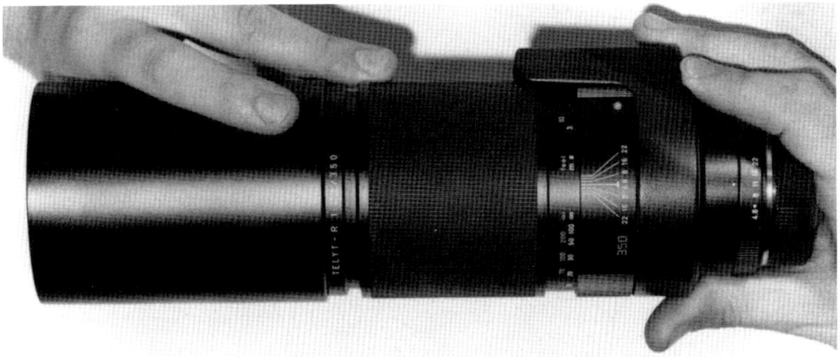

Fig. 105. The Telyt-R 350mm, f/4.8 was discontinued in 1994. It is very compact for its focal length and easy to use. It was fitted with rotating tripod collar.

Focusing range: 4.5m to inf, but less than 4m in some examples factory recammed to R3 specification

Lens hood: Built-in, collapsible

Weight: 1410g

Finish: Black chrome

Comment: Lenses from serial No. 2695343 are factory fitted with the Leica R3 metering cam (but see Chapter 2 text). The tripod base was extended by 10mm from December 1970 on to provide a firm support for monopod, tripod or shoulder stock. Another heavy lens which combined with its wide focus ring and relatively short focus throw makes it a delight to use. Small enough to fit in a gadget bag, it's an ideal objective for the architectural specialist, photojournalist and travel photographer. The new APO-TELYT-R 280mm, f/4. has all but displaced this earlier version and the current model for sports work because of its improved image quality and internal focusing.

2.49. TELYT-R 350mm, f/4.8, 1980 - 1994. Product No. 11 915

Minimum aperture: f/22

Angle of view: 7°

Elements/groups: 7/5

Filter size: E77

Focusing range: 3m to inf.

Smallest object field: 171 x 257mm

Lens hood: Built-in, collapsible

Dimensions: Length 286mm, diameter 83.5mm

Weight: 1820g

Finish: Black chrome

Comment: This lens was dropped from the Leica-R line-up in late 1994, its usefulness having been partly overshadowed by recent APO objectives. Photographers who have a regular need for this focal length, but not the associated weight or expense of the more exotic models, can still purchase the current Telyt-R 400mm, f/6.8 with sliding focus mount. This does not have the benefit of either automatic diaphragm or the extra two stop speed of this objective, but it is lighter and for many subjects, easier to manipulate.

Nonetheless, 350mm is a useful length and I can think of a number of subjects I would use it for – especially architecture – in its present form. Now that Leica Camera GmbH has applied itself to the art of internal focus engineering, there is every reason to suppose we might see this length return with a slightly faster maximum aperture at a price more affordable to the budget strapped.

2.50. TELYT 400mm, f/5.6, 1968 - 1972. Product No. 14 154

(see Variations 2.29.)

2.51. TELYT 560mm, f/5.6, 1968 - 1972. Product No. 14 155

(see Variations 2.29 & 2.30.)

2.52. MINOLTA RF-Rokkor 800mm, f/8, 1970 - 1978

Comment: This one is a bit of an oddball. It was a Minolta catadioptric mirror lens presented at Pho-

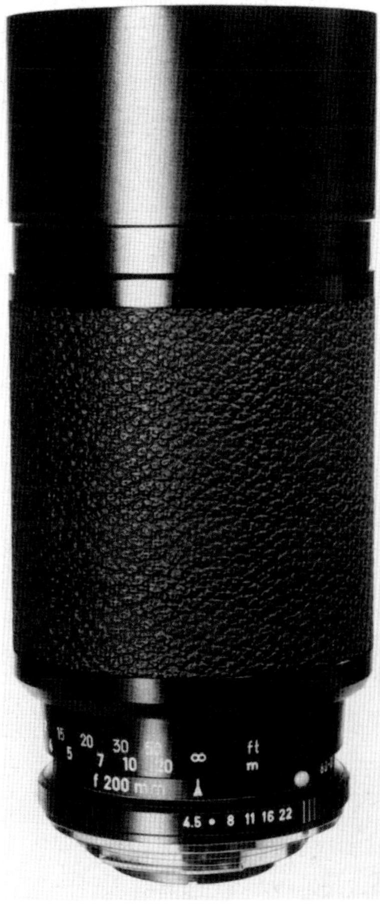

Fig. 106. Vario-Elmar-R 80-200mm, f/4.5 zoom lens. The first long Leica zoom, 1974-1978, had a slightly more restricted focal length range than later versions.

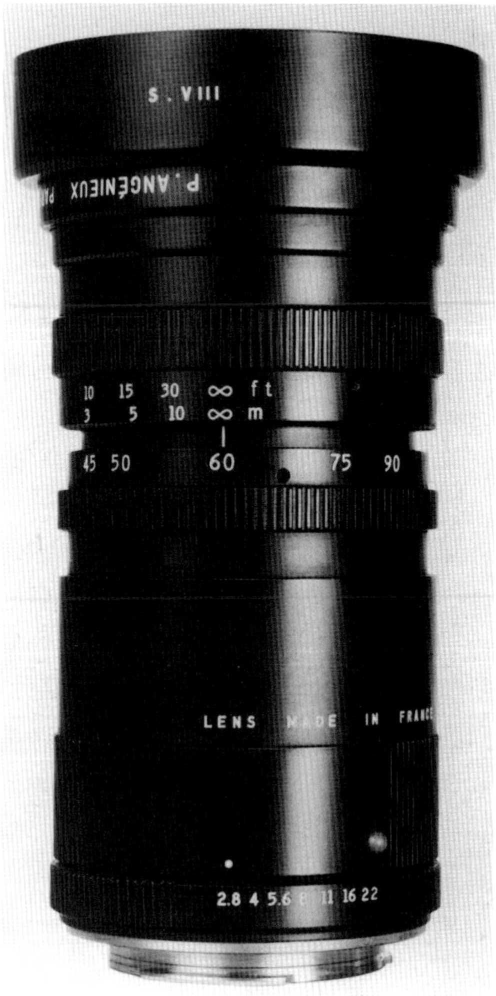

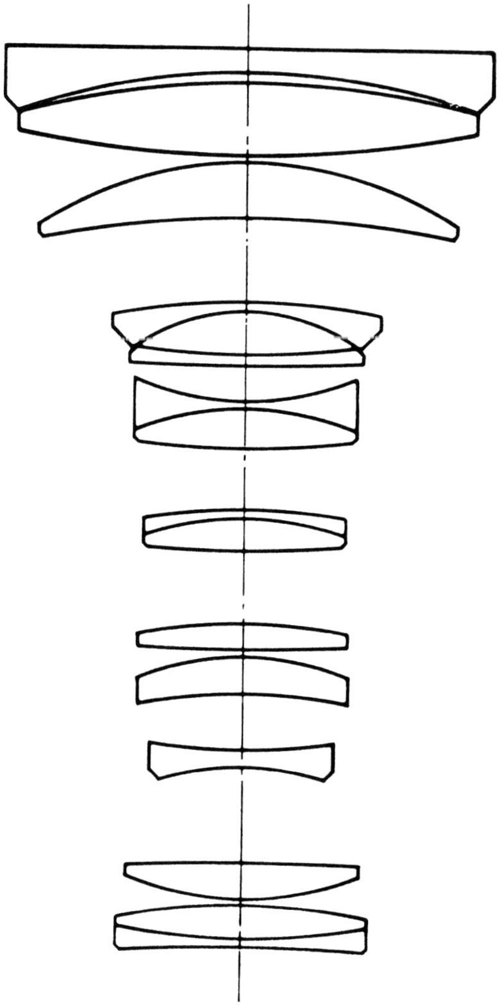

Figs. 107 and 108. The Pierre Angénieux designed Leicaflex-Angénieux 45-90mm, f/2.8 was the first zoom for a Leitz SLR camera. Made in limited quantities in 2- and 3-cam versions, it comprises 15 elements and is finished in black enamel. The drawing shown on the facing page is from the original engineering working plans modified in 1976 and again in February 1980 for the R3. It is a beautifully made lens giving high definition results. At the time of its introduction, and for some years afterwards, it was the fastest short zoom lens in the world and the only lens in the Leitz range which produced slightly warmer than neutral tone results.

tokina in 1972 with a mount for the Leicaflex SL in the Japanese company's livery. It was available first in the United States and had to be ordered from the Minolta Corporation of New Jersey. Later it was offered world-wide and listed in the Leica R3 literature. This was an 8-element lens of 7 groups and measured 166mm in length. It weighed 1800 grams. The MR-Telyt 500mm f/8. replaced this lens in 1980.

2.53. VARIO-ELMAR-R 80-200mm, f/4.5, 1974 - 1978. Product No. 11224. (not for Leicaflex Standard, SL or SL MOT).

2.54. VARIO-ELMAR-R 75-200mm, f/4.5, 1978 - 1984. Product No. 11226

Comment: These two telephoto zooms were designed and manufactured by the Minolta Camera Co. of Osaka under the Leitz/Minolta co-operation agreement. The 80 – 200mm version was introduced in 1974 offering a 2.5:1 zooming ratio with a 'one-touch' zoom and focus control ring. The lens weighs only 625 grams. Its excellent optical performance will still stand up against modern equivalents, but it cannot be used with any of the Leicaflex models.

The 75-200mm version was launched in 1978 and designed to fit all Leicaflex and R-type cameras. Of fifteen element, eleven group construction it can be used in conjunction with ELPRO 3 and 4 supplementary lenses to give a 1:1.7 reproduction ratio at the 200mm setting. An excellent lens with very high image quality supplied across the whole focal length range. Its uses, like any high quality zoom, are many and varied, limited only by the photographer's imagination.

2.55. ANGÉNIEUX-ZOOM 45-90mm, f/2.8, 1969 - 1982

Minimum aperture: f/22

Angle of view: 54° – 27°

Elements/groups: 15/12

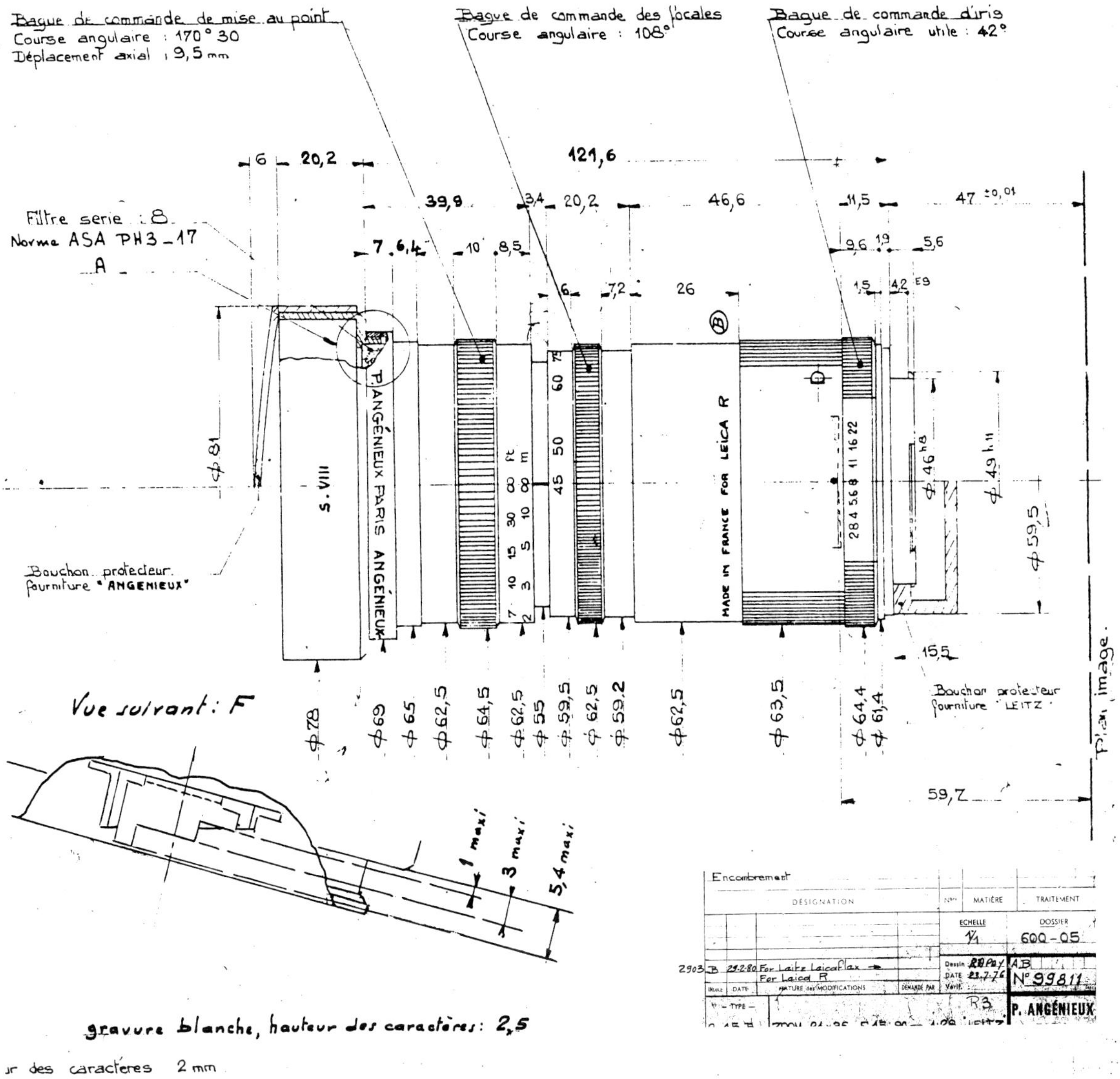

Filter size: Series VIII held in with special lens hood. Special close-up lens, product No. 98 001

Focusing range: 1m to inf.

Smallest object field: 485 x 727mm to 216 x 324mm

Lens hood: Circular, screw-in

Dimensions: Length 122mm, diameter 69mm

Weight: 780g

Finish: Black enamel paint, white paint filled engravings

Product code. 98 000.

Comment: This was the first zoom lens for the Leicaflex SL commissioned by Ernst Leitz from the designer and manufacturer, Pierre Angénieux of Paris, makers of the world's finest cinematographic zoom lenses. The optical construction is complex, with fifteen elements in five groups. The front elements are large, because of the fast maximum aperture which is held throughout the focal length range. In spite of the optical complexity of this zoom, it has a remarkably high light transmission value of 70%.

With the special supplementary lens, a close focus range of between 1.05m and 0.6m (3'5" to 2') is possible. Once focused, the image remains sharp throughout the zoom range, a feat not matched by some brand zooms 25 years later. The glass used in the construction of this lens came from Sovirel in France (now part of Corning Glass Group) and Schott Glaswerke of Mainz in Germany.

At the time of its introduction to the system, this was a truly remarkable optic. It is only recently that photographers have been offered short zoom lenses with a similar maximum aperture specification. The photojournalist David Douglas Duncan selected this lens because of its outstanding resolving ability and unique colour rendering to photograph Pablo Picasso's entire legacy of more than 500 paintings and drawings for his book, *Goodbye Picasso*.

Originally only available with two cams, a third cam was added in July 1976. According to Leica UK Ltd., the 2-cam version is the only lens in the Leica system which cannot be converted to 3-cam. Angénieux S.A. confirmed the conversion is not possible and had never been carried out during the production life of the lens. The lens was available to order only through Leitz dealerships. It was expensive and came in a satin lined wooden box. No records remain at Saint Heand of the total production; An Angénieux spokesman estimated the figure to be between one and two thousand.

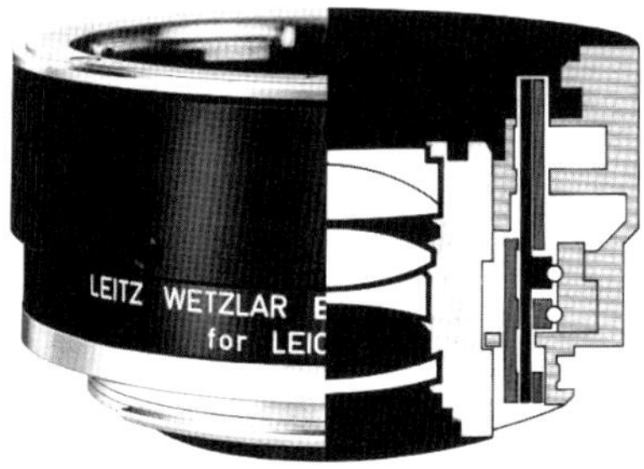

Fig. 109. Extender-R 2x. Superseded by the Apo-Extender-R 2x, this is nevertheless a useful standby for the budget minded who may only have a very occasional need. Results using this extender are quite acceptable, even if a little soft at the edges, provided enlargement does not exceed 10 x 8 ins. The photographer who hopes to maintain near prime optic resolution and print quality should seriously consider the Apo-Extender-R versions described earlier.

2.56. EXTENDER-R 2x. 1980 – 1992. Product No's 11 236 (for R Type), 11 237 (for SL/SL2)

Comment: Introduced in two versions, one with two cams for the Leicaflex SL/SL2 and the other with only the stepped cam for the Leica-R. This is not an APO matched converter; it is a conventional, sophisticated five-element design suitable for press and sports photographers for when occasion demands a picture at all costs. Image quality is very good when used with any prime lens of 50mm focal length or more, up to about 250mm; above this length, the higher magnification of longer lenses increases apparent fall-off in resolution and edge diffusion. The maximum aperture of the prime lens is reduced by two full stops, so an exposure factor increase of 4x should be applied. The automatic 'selective' metering of all Leica reflex cameras from SL to the current R7 facilitates correct exposure in daylight situations; when using flash on TTL flash metering models, a compensation factor of +1 should be dialled in.

CHAPTER 3

Viewfinder Image Control and Metering

3.1. Leica R Reflex Viewing System and Image Control

The reflex viewing system devised by Leitz for use in the PLOOT and successive VISOFLEX models for the Leica rangefinder cameras provided extraordinary quality of viewing for the photographer of the time. Indeed, even today using the Visoflex with long focus lenses provides an extremely clear and bright screen image which has only been marginally bettered in recent years by the advent of laser etched Fresnel screens.

When the Leicaflex Standard was introduced, it was endowed with a carefully designed viewing system offering the brightest and clearest screen image then known in a 35mm-format SLR. Instead of using a more conventional, separate Fresnel type screen sited below the pentaprism, Leitz used a special light gathering condenser lens sited directly below the flat pentaprism base, sandwiched between it and the focusing screen. Further enhancement of the system appeared in the Leicaflex SL. By giving the underside of the prism a convex shape it acted as a condenser lens. Light transmission was slightly improved due to the elimination of the separate condenser used in the original Leicaflex. An optically flat screen etched with tiny triangular shaped microprisms to give a fine groundglass effect was now placed directly under the prism (see Fig. 110) A central circular 7mm portion is comprised of slightly larger precision cut square-shaped microprisms which deflect out-of-focus light rays but have no effect on

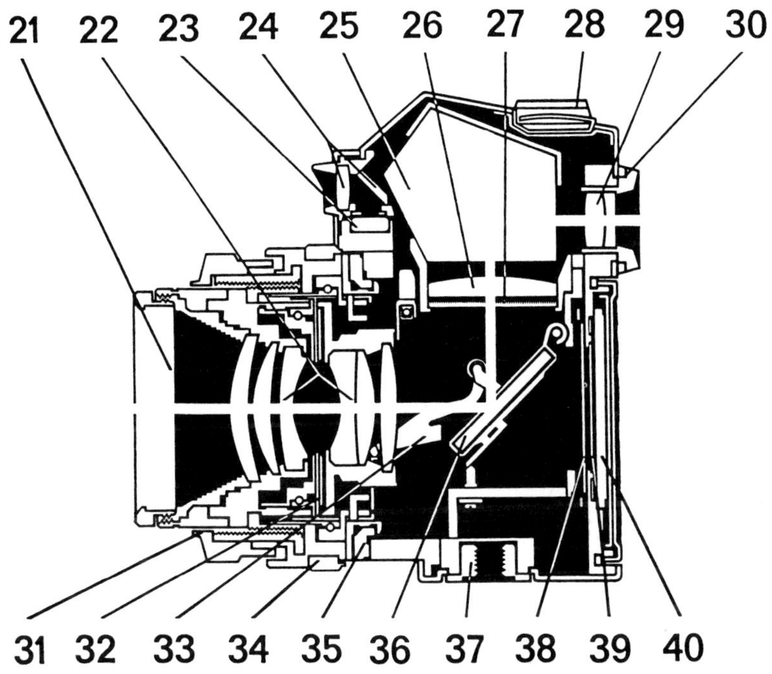

21 Filter retaining ring
22 50mm SUMMICRON-R f/2 lens
23 CdS photoresistor cell
24 Illuminating lens for CdS cell
25 Pentaprism
26 Condenser lens
27 Fresnel lens, with microprism center spot
28 Accessory shoe
29 Eyepiece lens
30 Fitting for eyesight correction lenses

31 Lens focusing ring
32 Automatic lens aperture
33 Auto-aperture operating lever
34 Auto-aperture pre-selector ring
35 Bayonet lens mount
36 Instant-return mirror
37 Tripod socket
38 Focal-plane shutter
39 Film
40 Pressure plate

Fig. 110 shows the pentaprism viewing system devised for the Leicaflex (Standard). It differs somewhat from the description in the text regarding the prism underside, which is flat. A condenser lens is featured between the prism base and the optically flat focusing screen. It seems the underside of the prism was not given a convex shape until the advent of the Leicaflex SL, shown in Fig. 111 on page 80. This presumably was to improve light dispersion.

Fig. 111 See caption re. Fig 110 on page 85

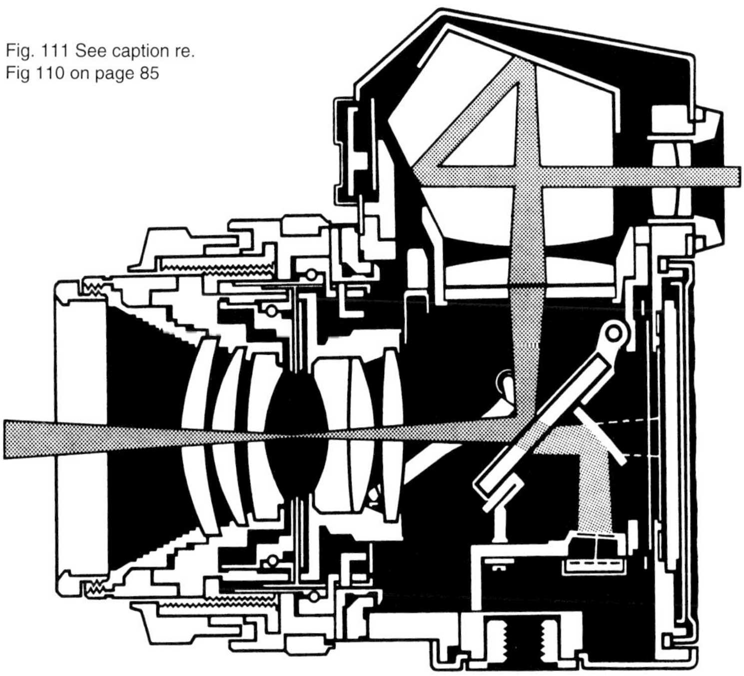

sharply focused images. Slightly unsharp objects centred in the screen are seen as double images overlaid with a shimmering texture. When focus is accurate, the object is clearly defined, the shimmering effect fusing into a single image.

Systems developed by most other brands used pentaprisms with a flat underside surface in conjunction with a separate condenser type focusing screen. Used with moderate wide-angle and short to medium telephoto focal lengths, the arrangement was perfectly suited to general every-day picture taking. The problems for the specialist user invariably began when long focus and telephoto lenses of more than 200mm focal length were required. The central part of the screen, especially in systems which used the split-wedge type rangefinder, blacked out, making it difficult to focus accurately and rapidly.

More sophisticated SLR systems of the period overcame this problem by offering a range of interchangeable focusing screens suited to the use of particular lenses. The Leicaflex Standard and the SL/SL2 models needed no such refinements. Even when fitted with the Telyt-R 400mm, f/6.8, the screen remains as clear as when fitted with a standard lens. The production costs of the Leitz system were high, but as already pointed out elsewhere in this book, cost was not a consideration in perfecting the system.

The viewing system of the Leicaflex SL2 was further modified by incorporating a 3mm-diameter split-image rangefinder into the central 7mm micro-prism focusing section, thus creating an outer collar of the latter. This provides three separate methods of ensuring sharp focus. This extra dimension was designed to facilitate sharp focus in low light situations and has remained an essential part of the viewing system in all models since.

Other contributory factors which ensure an extra bright image in all models is the special pentaprism; ground to an extremely fine tolerance and vacuum coated with pure silver. The reflex mirror, for which Leitz developed a special silvering and multi-layer thin-film vapour-deposit process uses 17 different layers to produce maximum reflectivity. The result is an extremely bright, high contrast image. An extra large eyepiece lens with long exit pupil ensures that even spectacle wearers can see the whole screen image comfortably.

The actual viewfinder picture area of the Leicaflex models measures 23.8mm x 35.6mm – almost 100% of the film frame except for the extreme corners which are rounded. All Leica R-cameras, including current models, have a viewfinder field covering 92% of the film frame size: that is, what the photographer sees measures 23mm x 34.6mm. These dimensions approximate to that of a standard Kodachrome card slide mount. Almost identical measurements have been used in the Leica M-system since 1954.

There is an advantage for photographers who specialise only in producing transparencies for projection using standard mounts. The bulk of photographs taken today, however, are made using colour negative materials. About 5% are made using black-and-white emulsions. The majority of black-and-white enthusiasts develop and print their own work, as do a large percentage of colour negative users. While it is probably of little consequence to the majority of Leica R users that 8% of the image area is unseen when an exposure is made, there are those for whom this loss is almost too great to bear. There is no hope of this situation being remedied while the present camera design continues, but I make the point in the forlorn hope that if a new design ever reaches full production, it will be blessed with a viewfinder covering, at the very least, 99.9% of the film frame area; 100% would be better, of course.

Leica R-models prior to the R5 require clip-in, optional eyepiece

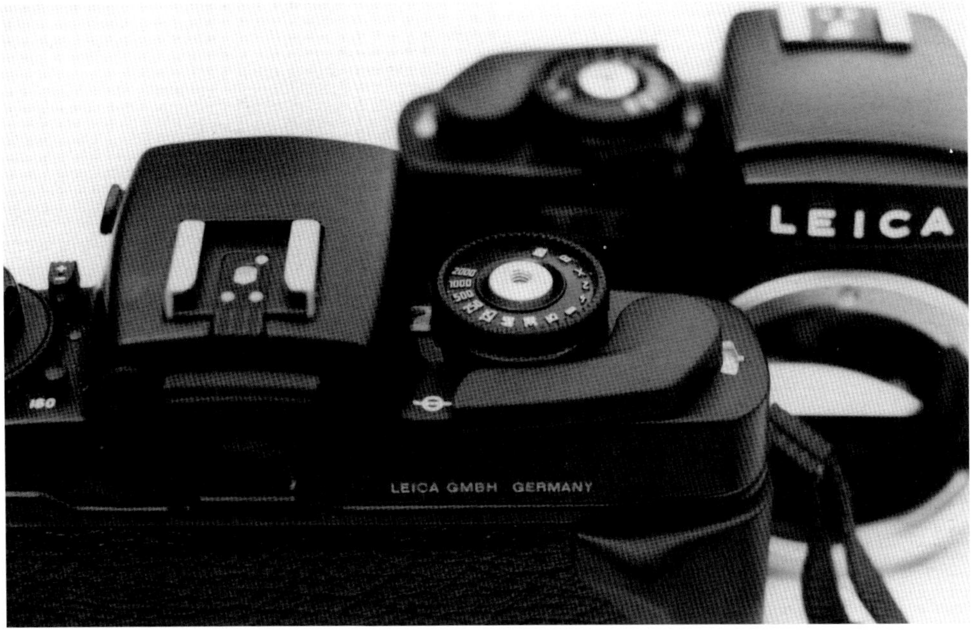

Fig. 115. Automatic eyepiece ocular dioptre correction is fitted to all Leica R models from the R5. The small wheel at top left of the eyepiece is seen above the eyepiece shutter in this rear view of a Leica R-E.

correction lenses (see Appendix tables). This facility has been built into all models since the R5 and comprises adjustment from +2 to -2 dioptres by means of turning a small milled-edge wheel found at the top left of the eyepiece ocular frame.

To obtain exact correction, first remove the lens from the camera. The correction adjustment wheel has two positions; locked and unlocked. In the locked position, it is pushed in firmly towards the camera body. In this position it free-wheels and no correction is possible. By gently inserting the edge of a fingernail under the wheel rim it can be pulled outward. It clicks into the unlocked position. Aim the camera body, without the lens fitted, to a light coloured wall or evenly clouded sky. Avoid pointing the uncovered lens throat towards direct sunlight. Hold the camera so that the screen can be viewed in the normal way and with the left fore-finger turn the dioptre correction wheel left or right until the fine grain of the screen is sharply focused. Once the correct adjustment has been effected, push the adjustment wheel inwards to the locked position.

Additional correction lenses from +3 to -3 can also be used. These are mounted in a special holder or in the rubber eye cup and are fitted by sliding them over the eyepiece mount. The lens and eyecup mounts are fitted with a special sprung locking safety catch.

Before the Leicaflex Standard was launched, various prototype and pre-production models were made. Three of these featured interchangeable viewfinders; a waist-level finder or standard eyelevel pentaprism. The idea never reached production because of the fear of the designers that a removable pentaprism would permit the ingress of dust and dirt which could be sandwiched between the pentaprism underside and the optical flat. In this observation they were correct. Nonetheless, this facility, combined with a 100% image area viewing capability, was just one of the major features of the Nikon-F reflex which helped gain its popularity with exacting professionals and which is still incorporated in the current F4 camera. Had Leitz opted instead for the Minolta XK camera instead of the XE-1 on which to base the R3, the situation today might have been very different.

To overcome the problem of low level viewing with the Leicaflex, Leitz resorted to the production of the 90° angle viewfinder (14 186) which became available in 1971 to fit the SL and later, the SL2. This device could be used with the camera in the vertical or horizontal position and is attached by slipping its right angled connecting plate into the flash accessory shoe of the camera. This viewfinder provides

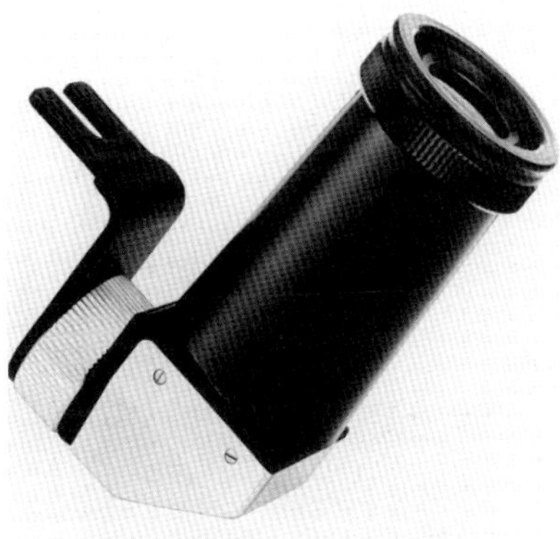

Fig. 116. Right angle finder for Leicaflex.

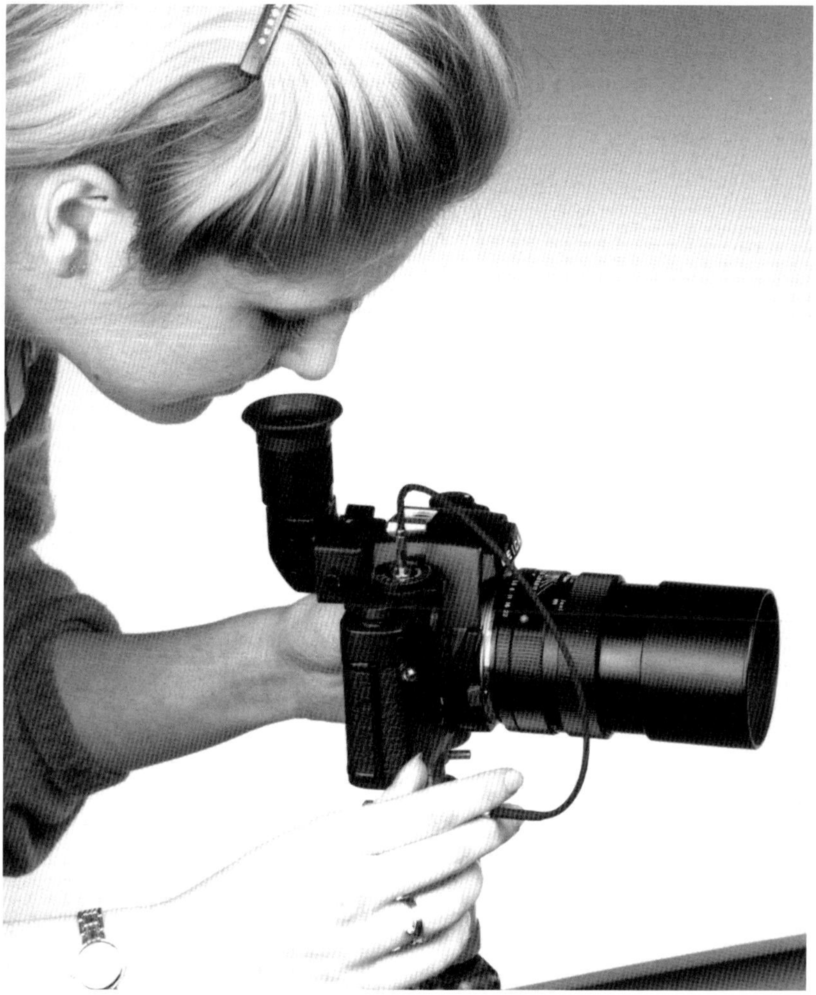

Fig. 117. Current rotating angle finder (14 328) in use. Provides single or 2x magnification of the viewfinder image. *Leica Camera UK Ltd*

the user with a reduced image size which is right-way-round and upright. Subsequent R-model 90° finders were produced, the first for the R3 being essentially the same as for the SL/SL2 and afterwards being fitted with a focusing eyepiece (14 287, 14 286, 14 288 for the R3, 14 326 for the R4). A new right-angle finder with variable magnification (1x for full-field, 2x for the central portion) was introduced for the R4 and Leicaflex SL models in 1985. This item (14 328) also incorporated eye-sight dioptre correction from -6 to +4 and could be rotated through 360° with click-stops at 90° intervals. It is attached to the camera in the same way as the first model. A separate version was available for the Leica R3 (14 329). It was not until 1988 that a version similar in all respects to 14 328 was designed to fit the Leica R5/R6 by sliding into the eye-piece mount (14 300).

3.2. LEICAFLEX AND LEICA R METERING AND VIEWFINDER DISPLAYS

Leicaflex

The origin of the Leicaflex (Standard) meter, and the problems facing Leitz designers at the time, is described in the Introduction and Chapter 1. To re-cap briefly, it can be said that the final choice was based on the design of the early MC-type accessory meter (14 200) for the Leica M-type rangefinder cameras and which was designed and manufactured by Metrawatt, in itself a development of the LC Metraphot meter for screw-thread cameras. This may account for why some prototype Leicaflex cameras featured a Selenium cell in the front

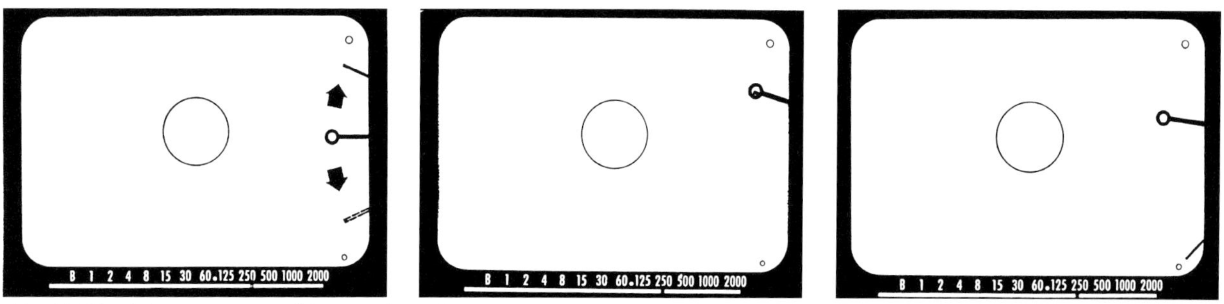

Fig. 112. Viewfinder arrangement of the original Leicaflex. *Left*: Movement of the follow-pointer upwards, towards the larger circle, indicates setting of a larger aperture and downwards, towards the smaller circle, setting of a smaller aperture. *Middle*: Correct exposure is obtained when the follow-pointer is adjusted to cover the meter needle by turning the aperture setting ring of the lens, or the shutter speed dial. *Right*: Battery check feature. When the battery test button on the front face of the pentaprism housing is pressed, the meter needle should drop to cover the small circle in viewfinder if the battery is good. (see notes on use of PX 625 battery.)

pentaprism housing. A later version of the MC meter (14 210), called the Leicameter-MR was introduced for M-type cameras in 1966 and featured a single CdS measuring cell powered by a Mallory PX 625 button cell battery. Was this meter already at an advanced development stage before the Leicaflex was launched? The two types of meter are quite different; the coil windings are a different size and have different resistance ratings. In the absence of concrete information one has to hazard a guess that as the CdS cell was still a relatively new component in the photographic industry at this time, both meters, for the Leicaflex and the rangefinder camera, were probably developed simultaneously.

The biggest problem for Leitz at the time was, of course, that although patents existed for a type of selective through-the-lens meter, its development was not far enough ahead for its inclusion in the Leicaflex to be warranted. Another factor which affected the final choice of meter type was almost certainly connected with the decision not to proceed with the removable pentaprism viewing system. Had Leitz gone ahead with this, the first Leicaflex would have been equipped with true TTL metering. The meter finally selected for the Standard was certainly adequate for most ordinary picture taking with the four lenses originally offered with the system. But there were problems.

The first two hundred cameras were fitted with silver chrome Summicron 50mm, f/2 lenses. Users are said to have reported to Leitz that light reflected from the barrel of these lenses affected meter readings. The measuring field of the meter approximates the angle of view of a 90mm lens and is calibrated for accurate measurement with the camera held in the horizontal position. It has been suggested that Leitz technicians, having realised their 'mistake', soon eliminated the cause of faulty exposures by ensuring all future lens production was finished in the traditional anti-flare black anodised chrome we are now familiar with.

This of course, was a relatively minor problem, except for the few customers who had acquired the Leicaflex fitted with a chrome lens. At best, the Leicaflex meter was a compromise. Beyond the focal length of the longest lens launched with the camera, the Elmarit-R 135mm, f/2.8, Leitz advocated the use of lenses previously designed for use with the Leica rangefinder cameras and the Visoflex mirror box. A Leica-to-Leicaflex lens adapter (14 127) complete with diaphragm simulator, issued in 1966, bridged the gap. Lenses for the Visoflex II and III could be used on the Leicaflex fitted with their focusing mounts and the adapter, but metering became somewhat hit and miss with the longer focal lengths. As none of these lenses were fitted with automatic diaphragms, metering had to be carried out using the stop-down method.

The same problem existed when using the Leicaflex with the Focusing Bellows II (16 556) in conjunction with Visoflex and removable M-type lens units for close-up photography. Separate, hand-held meter readings are the only accurate way to select the correct exposure. At the other end of the scale, the Super-Angulon-R 21mm, f/3.4, optically identical to the Leica-M version, required the mirror to be locked up and the separate viewfinder used. Using the meter with this lens was not possible; the raised mirror blanked off the screen.

The viewfinder meter display of the original Leicaflex features the whole range of shutter speeds in the base of the frame, out of the picture area. A needle indicates the speed set. To the right of the frame, the meter needle free ranges. Correct exposure is obtained when the follow-pointer, a shorter and thinner needle marker, covers the meter needle. This is brought about by adjusting either the auto-aperture ring on the lens, or the shutter speed selector dial. The exact size of the f/stop used is not shown in the viewfinder, but some indication of the stop set can be judged from the position of the follow-pointer. At the bottom of the screen on the right, a small circle indicates the direction of the minimum aperture, while at the top, a larger circle indicates the maximum aperture size.

Leicaflex SL

The Broschkes System of 1962 for selective light metering in single lens reflex cameras employed the reflex mirror to bounce light into the pentaprism where it was measured with a photo-resistor located on the upper face of the prism. Dr. Helmuth Frenk's system for exposure measurement used in the Orthomat promised better sensitivity combined with greater accuracy in the narrow light path required for 'spot' metering and this was the system developed for the Leicaflex SL.

By using a partially silvered reflex mirror and hinged cylindrical shaped sub-mirror, 20% of light reflected from the object is deflected to the collecting lens of the CdS photo-resistor housed in the base of the mirror box. Extraneous light from the lens cannot reach the photo-resistor which is well baffled against this possibility. On exposure, as the main reflex mirror begins to rise, the sub-mirror assembly folds neatly into a recess on the back of the mirror, further preventing stray light from entering the mirror box area.

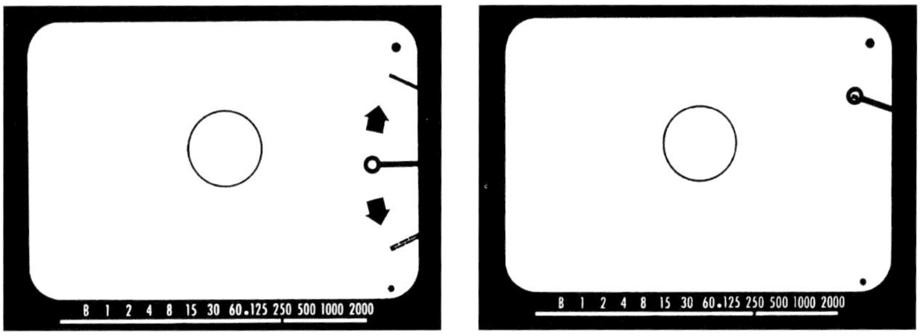

Fig. 113a. Leicaflex SL viewfinder layout.

Thus was born the Leitz 'selective' measurement system which has remained essentially the same in all models of the Leicaflex and Leica R-cameras since. It has proved to be one of the most enduring and accurate systems so far devised for exposure measurement in a 35mm SLR camera.

In the Leicaflex SL, the viewfinder display is similar to that in the original Leicaflex and uses the same match needle – follow pointer system for establishing correct exposure. The aperture scale was again omitted but now it was possible for users to accurately measure exposure using the whole lens and close-up system without the need for an additional hand-held meter. New lenses were added to the line-up and during its six year life, the Leicaflex SL became a best selling SLR with more than 70,000 units being produced at the factory in Wetzlar.

LEICAFLEX SL2.

By 1974, the Leicaflex had been further improved, slimmed down in thickness, had the film track modified, was fitted with an electronic flash hot-shoe, safety lock for the hinged back, as well as a redesigned lens mount with a slightly deeper flange to accommodate three Minolta designed lenses rebadged to Leitz specification.

One of the most important modifications was to the metering sensitivity. It gained 3 stops over the previous SL, in addition to displaying the aperture set in the viewfinder. Another useful feature was the viewfinder shutter/aperture scale display light, activated by depressing a small button on the side of the pentaprism housing. The light is powered by a separate battery which can also be used as a back-up for the meter battery, now located lower down on the right hand side of the body (from the front). The SL2 was by far the best of the three Leitz designed reflexes, and many of the 25,000 units produced are still in use around the world.

Like previous models, the camera relied upon the 'selective' metering method. No full-field, integrated centre-weighted measurement was possible, nor was it considered necessary by the majority of users. The limit of the 'selective' measurement area coincides exactly with the 7mm central coarse micro-prism viewing circle of the viewfinder, covering ⅙th of the diagonal acceptance angle of whichever lens is fitted. The addition of the split-image rangefinder to this model, occupying a 3mm diameter circle in the very centre of the screen, does not affect metering.

The exposure match needle of the SL2 is also different from previous models, looking more like one half of a paper clip, but the follow pointer, match needle system of measuring the exposure is identical. The aperture scale is also incorporated in the viewfinder, alongside of, and to the right of the shutter speed range, which is compressed to the left. Two markers in the underlying white line indicate the shutter speed and aperture selected for the exposure. Now everyone was happy; except the camera was costing Leitz a fortune to build. A year after it was launched, E.Leitz Inc., at Rockleigh, offered the camera complete with the Summicron-R 50mm, f/2 lens for $1,380. It was underpriced. Anyone who bought one then, and still has it unused, boxed, and in mint condition today, would stand to reap considerable profit from the investment.

LEICA R3

Everything about the Leica R3 was a radical departure from the Leicaflex cameras, but in a way, the appeal of the R3 was not difficult to understand. Today, even if its styling is a little dated, it is still a perfectly usable camera, offering a choice of modes and exposure measurement which are more than sufficient to tackle the most demanding subjects. It's a robust machine with many

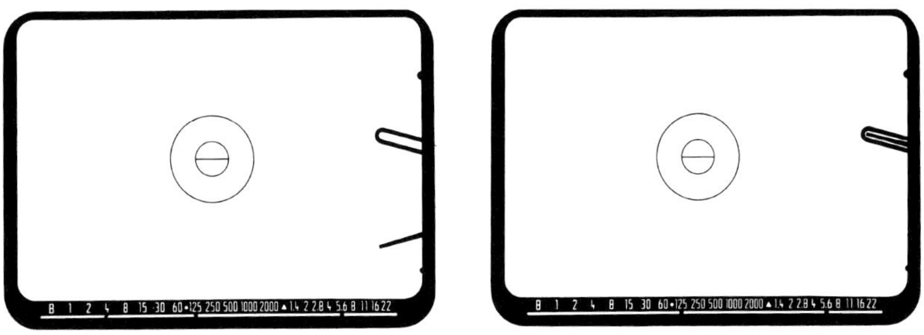

Fig. 113b. Leicaflex SL2 viewfinder layout.

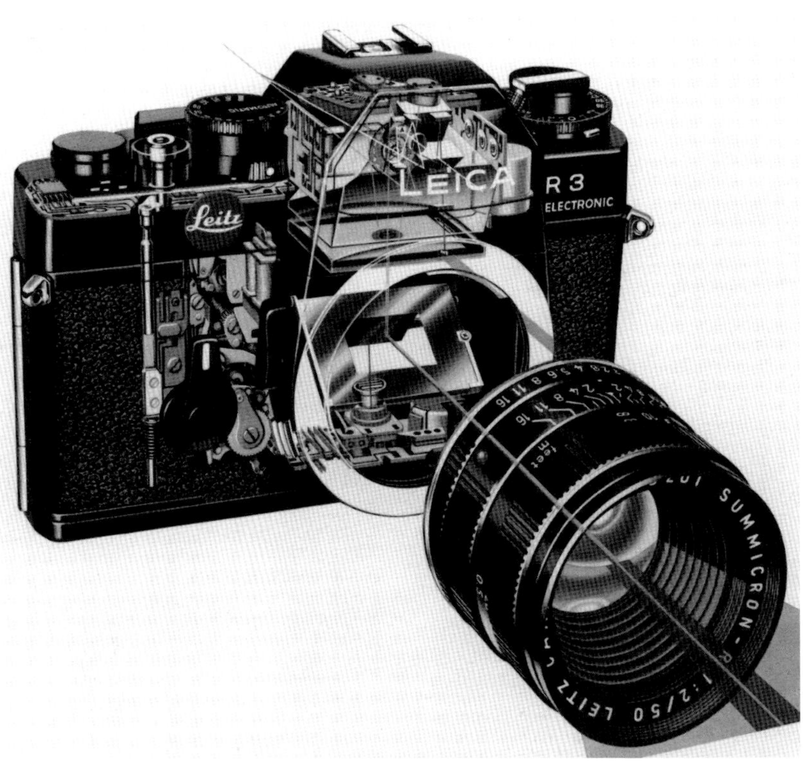

Fig. 118. The third CdS photo cell is clearly visible in the base of the mirror box in this cut-away of the Leica R3 camera. A sophisticated electronic circuit operates the switching device which cuts the third cell in or out when 'selective' metering is selected. *Leica Camera GmbH*

more years of life in it than the 20 or so clocked up so far.

Instead of the single CdS cell used in the Leicaflex SL/SL2, the Leica R3 has three, one housed in the base of the mirror box and two in the pentaprism, thus providing the means to measure the narrow 'selective' light path or alternatively, the full-field, integrated centre-weighted area. A semi-silvered main reflex mirror permits a portion of the light entering the lens to be reflected via a hinged secondary mirror to the lower dual-cell photo-resistor. Apart from the shape of the secondary mirror, which is flat, the principle used is the same as that employed in the Leicaflex SL/SL2 and in the 'selective' measurement mode, the same field area is measured. This is seen in the central portion of the viewing screen, the outer limits of which are the 7mm coarse micro-prism focusing collar.

For full-field measurement, a switch moved at the base of the shutter speed setting dial cuts in the electronic circuit activating the two CdS cells housed in the pentaprism, also of the dual photo-resistor type. Measurements from these are combined with measurements taken from the 'selective' metering cell in the mirror box and electronically computed to give an average, centre-weighted reading.

The R3's shutter speed dial is the control centre for both electronic camera control and metering modes. By turning the dial to 'Automatic', the user may select exposure based on either 'selective' or full-field measurement by moving the exposure mode selector switch from one to the other. This is what is known as the 'aperture priority' mode, whereby the user sets the required f/stop and the camera automatically selects the correct shutter speed.

The second option is the 'manual' mode which again, can be used with either of the exposure measurement fields. Simply unlock the shutter dial from automatic to set a given shutter speed marked on the dial and adjust the lens f/stop until the correct exposure is indicated in the viewfinder display.

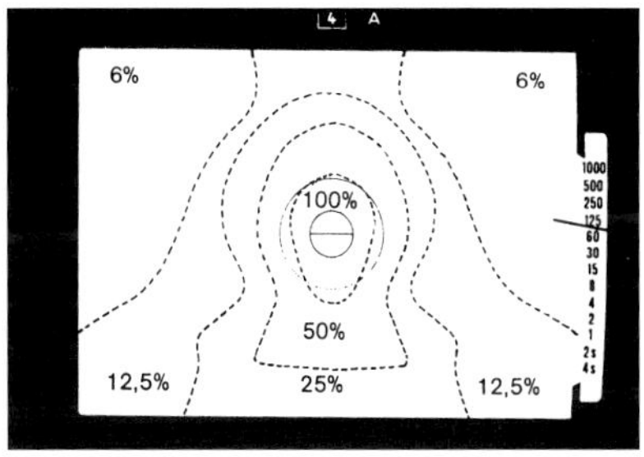

Fig. 120. This diagram illustrates the distribution of metering sensitivity in the integrated full-field, centre-weighted metering mode in the Leica R3.

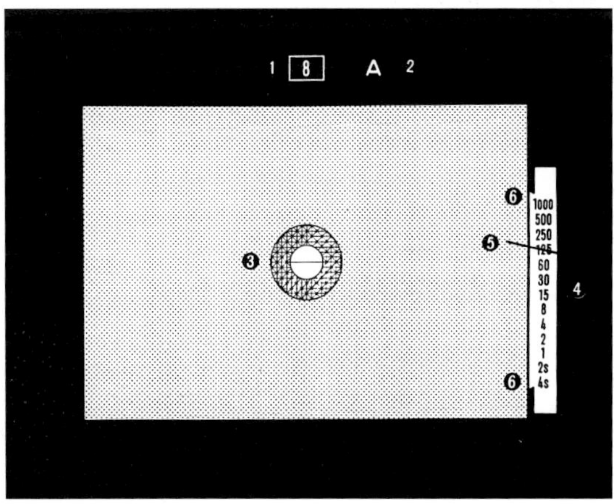

Fig. 119. The viewfinder display of the Leica R3. (1) f/number of lens aperture set; (2) shutter setting status, 'A' for automatic, set speeds indicated when in 'Manual' mode; (3) split image/microprism focus spot covers a 7mm diameter area which also indicates the outer limits of the 'selective' metering field; (4) shutter speed scale; (5) meter indicator needle shows speed set in 'Automatic' mode, indicates correct exposure when in line with shutter speed scale number corresponding to the one manually set and shown in (2); (6) meter coupled shutter speed range in 'A' – when the meter needle extends above or below the range indicated, exposure is incorrect, the remedy is to adjust aperture setting up or down to bring shutter speed within usable 'A' range.

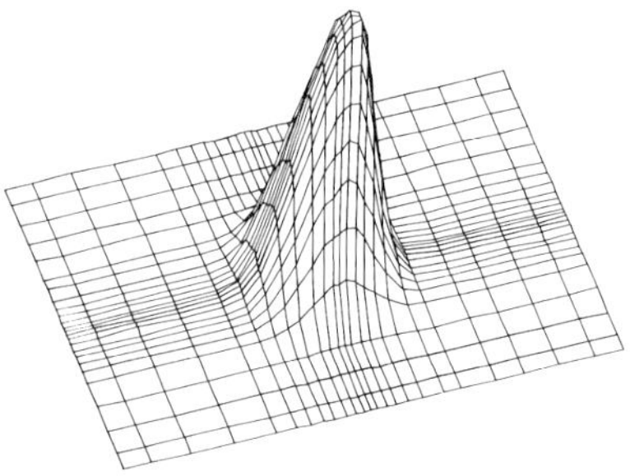

Fig. 125. Computer simulated graphic representing the film frame area metered in the 'selective' exposure mode on all Leica R cameras.

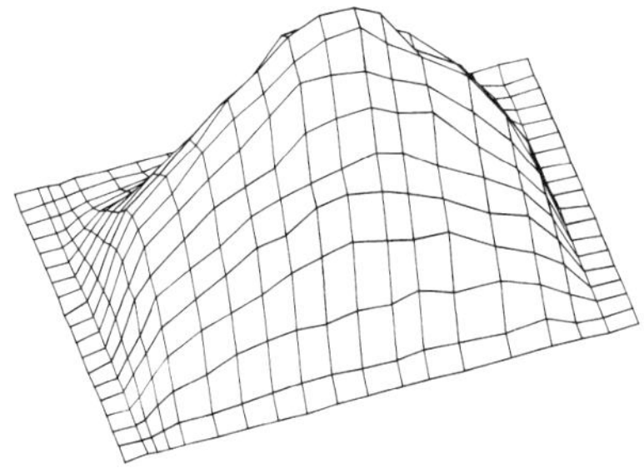

Fig. 126. Computer simulated graphic indicating the area of the film format covered when the meter is used in the integrated full-field mode.

A useful exposure reading memory lock can be activated using the 'selective' measurement when the camera is switched to automatic mode by slightly depressing the shutter release button. The shutter speed selected by the camera for a given f/stop set is 'stored' for as long as the button is depressed; a useful feature which enables difficult exposure measurements to be made before the picture is finally composed.

The viewfinder and scale display is very bright and clear. In automatic mode, the shutter speeds, which are steplessly variable from 4 seconds to 1/1000th second, are seen to the right of the frame. A free ranging needle indicates the speed set according to the aperture selected, which is displayed at the top of the frame. A red letter 'A' shows to the right of the aperture selected to indicate the mode selected. On switching to manual, the red 'A' is replaced by the shutter speed set in white figures so there can never be any doubt as to the mode selected.

LEICA R4 MOT Electronic, R4, R4S, R4S-MOD 2, R5, R6, R-E, R6.2 & R7

The introduction of the Leica R4 in 1980 heralded another design concept for Leitz which has remained to the present day. This was the smallest of Leica single lens reflex bodies, but into it, Leitz engineers had crammed a complete range of electronically operated exposure programmes linked to the (by now) established Leitz preference for 'selective' or full-field, integrated centre-weighted meter control. Whether by accident or design, the electro magnetically operated shutter release button was also back in the centre of the shutter speed dial, as it was in the Leicaflex models, and the dial itself

Fig. 122. Leica R4 profile diagram clearly showing viewfinder eyepiece ocular with auto-dioptre correction lens, pentaprism, focusing screen, main reflex mirror, hinged sub-mirror, silicon photodiode at base. Top left of the pentaprism housing shows the lens aperture reading lens, light gathering window and miniature prism used for transferring the data to the base of the pentaprism.

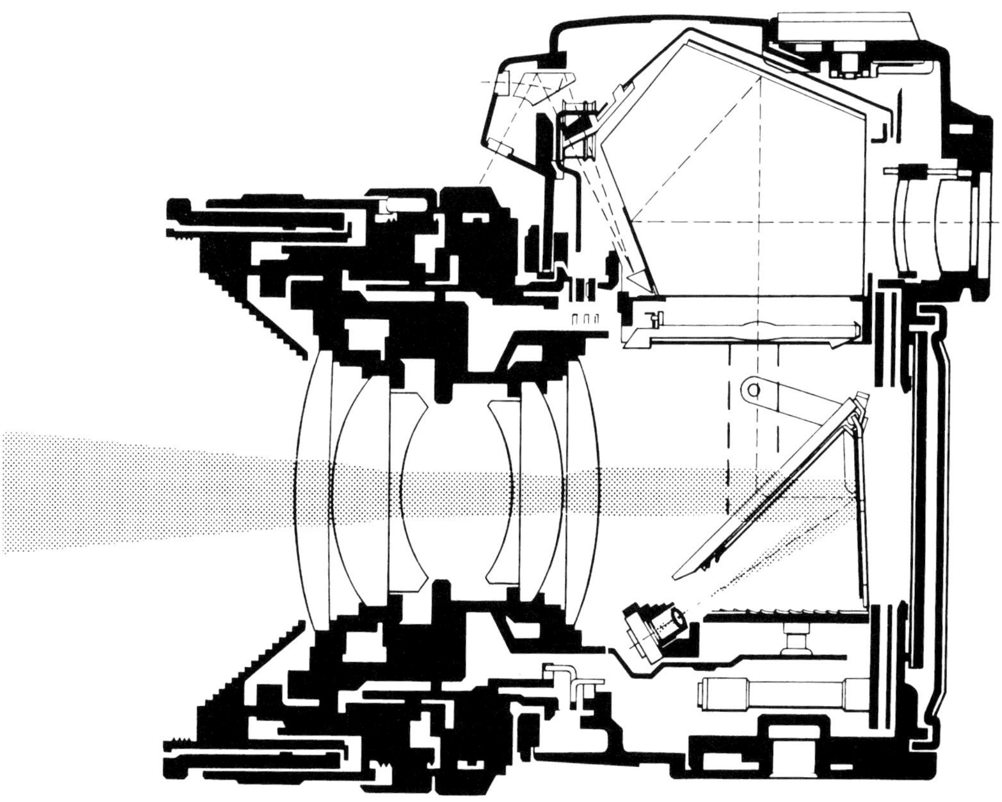

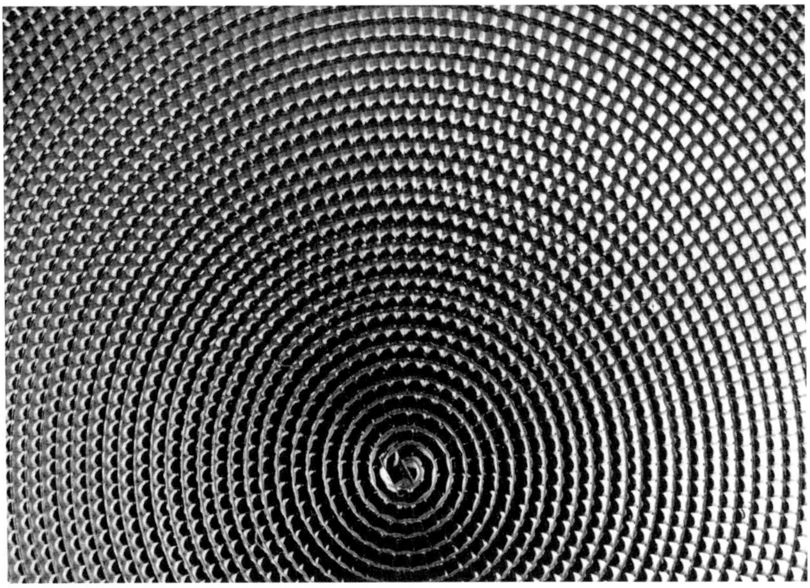

Fig. 127. The Fresnel-type reflector, or sub-mirror, comprising 1345 micromirrors. This hinged mirror is attached to the back of the main mirror and reflects light passing through the lens and the semi-silvered portion of the main reflex mirror to the silicon photo diode. Its optical centre is in the lower portion of the screen for technical reasons.

became the pivotal centre for operating all the main controls.

This operational system has remained essentially the same throughout the fifteen year life of the design. Minor modifications to controls sited on the top plate of the various cameras have not fundamentally changed the manipulative techniques required from one model to another.

Instead of the three CdS cells required for the measurement system of the Leica R3, the R4 and all subsequent models use a single silicon photo-diode which is housed in the base of the mirror box. The original semi-silvered mirror system devised for the Leicaflex SL is also used. A major change was required, however, to facilitate the 'selective' exposure measurement part of the package. By fitting a tiny light-converging collector lens over the cell, the size of the path of object reflected light could be accurately controlled.

Instead of using an electronic switching control, as is used in the R3, R4 types are fitted with a series of connecting levers which move the 4.5mm focal length collecting lens into and out of position over the photo-diode when the switch position at the base of the shutter speed dial is changed.

Different models of the Leica R-types, from the R4 onwards, feature different electronic programme specifications and these are activated in slightly different ways using the shutter speed dial controlled switch.

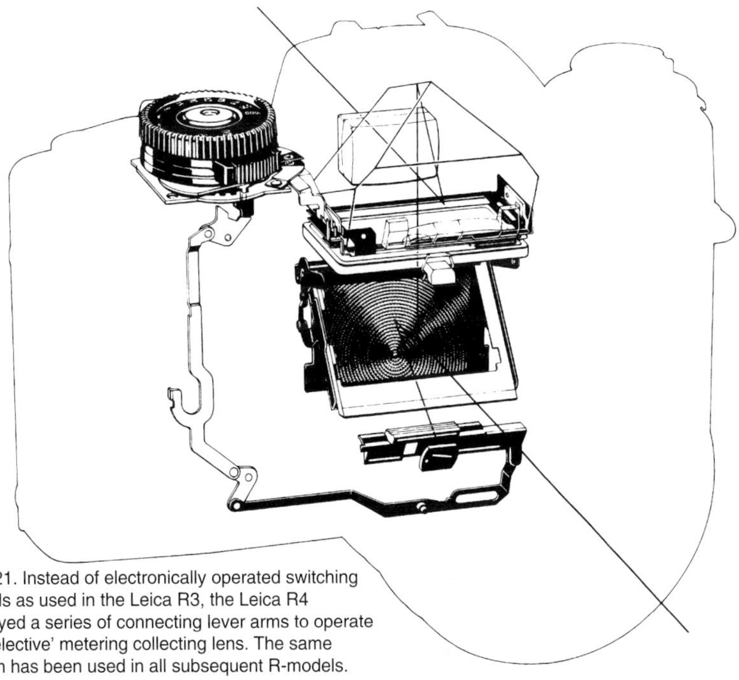

Fig. 121. Instead of electronically operated switching controls as used in the Leica R3, the Leica R4 employed a series of connecting lever arms to operate the 'selective' metering collecting lens. The same system has been used in all subsequent R-models.

LEICA R4

The R4 offers two aperture priority, one shutter priority, one automatic program and one manual mode. The square 'A', circle 'A', 'T', 'P'and 'M' letter indicators are shown in a tiny window between the right hand side of the pentaprism and the shutter speed dial, as the program selector switch beneath the speed setting dial is moved from one position to another. Each one of the respective programs can only be activated when either the shutter release button is slightly depressed, or the push-in button on the front of the program selector switch is depressed. There is no on-off switch as such for the meter batteries as there is on the rear of the top plate of the R3. Fitting the Leica Motor/Winder-R, or Motor Drive automatically cuts out the camera

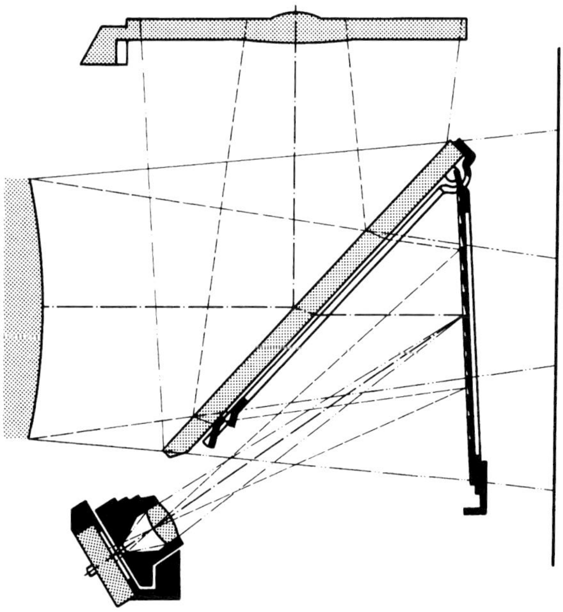

Fig. 123. Condensing collector lens in place over the silicon photodiode and light path schematic showing how a portion of object reflected light is effectively metered in the 'selective' mode.

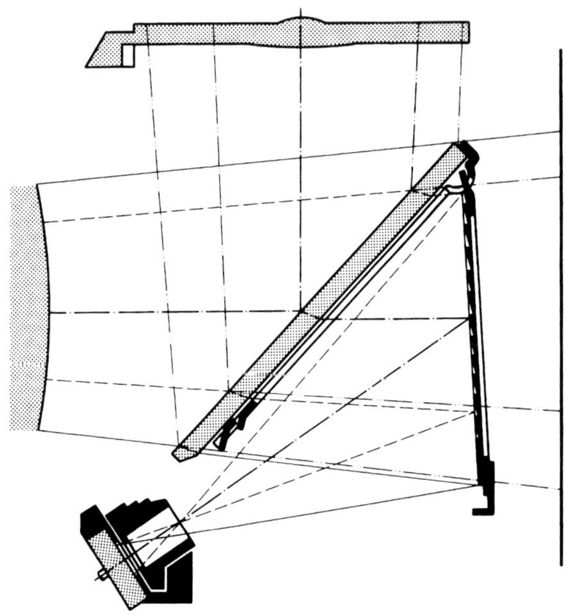

Fig. 124. Schematic showing how light reflected from the sub-mirror is collected by the silicon diode when meter is set to full field measurement.

battery circuit. The meter now receives power from the power pack of the drive unit.

The R4 incorporates an exposure reading memory lock feature in 'selective' measurement. By depressing the shutter release button until the mode symbol at lower left is extinguished, the metered reading is stored for 30 seconds until the object is recomposed and the shutter released. As soon as the exposure is completed, the data previously stored is wiped from the computer memory. All of the selected exposure mode information is duplicated in the viewfinder. The letters and surrounding square or circular symbols indicating the mode selected and the choice of 'selective' or full-field measurement. Shutter or aperture settings are seen to the right; a ranging red light indicates the value set by the computer. Shutter, and or aperture values set by the user are shown at the base line.

The R4 lacks the TTL flash exposure facility of later models. However, dedicated units automatically switch the shutter speed to 'X' regardless of the mode selected. When the flash is ready, a lit symbol appears at the bottom of the viewfinder shutter speed panel.

LEICA R4S

An electronically simplified version of the R4, incorporating only the two aperture priority and manual exposure modes. The viewfinder display arrangement is otherwise the same.

LEICA R4S MOD 2

Essentially the same as the R4S, but with improvements to controls. Maintains all of the electronic

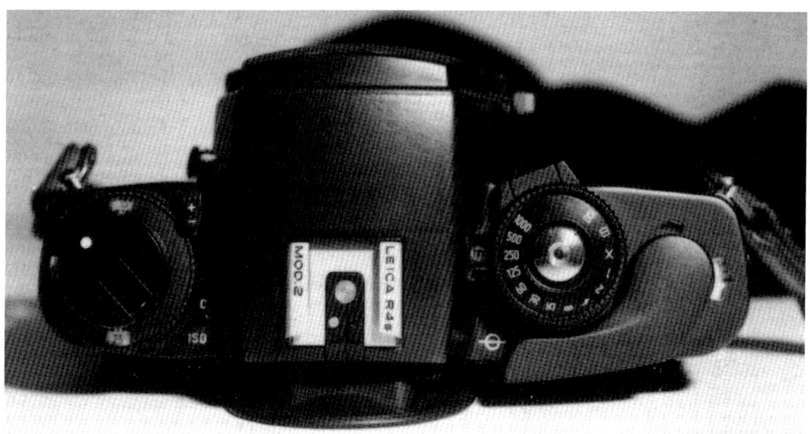

Fig. 128. Top plate arrangement of the Leica R4s MOD 2 (MOD P in the USA). The switch lever below the shutter speed control dial is the key operating mode selector for all Leica R cameras except the R3. In the case of the R4s MOD 2, the camera electronics are switched on as soon as the shutter release button is slightly depressed. There is no 'off' switch. A small window above the film advance lever indicates amount of film advanced. ISO/DIN speeds are set on the dial at left while pressing the button marked ISO which unlocks the ring. +/- switch at top left must be depressed and turned to the left before adjusting for exposure compensation factor visible in the window at 9 o'clock.

exposure mode features, including memory store, of the R4s.

LEICA R5

In addition to increasing the shutter speed range of this model from 15 seconds to $\frac{1}{2000}$th second, the automatic program mode of previous models was upgraded to 'Variable automatic program'. The letter 'P' adjacent to the $\frac{1}{30}$th second speed setting on the shutter dial is sandwiched between a circular wedge shaped graphic.

When the program is set up in conjunction with the selector switch, a 'standard' computer program is activated which covers most of the needs of the snapshooter using focal lengths between 35 – 90mm for shake-free photographs with maximum depth of field. When circumstances arise which require a faster or slower shutter speed than that indicated in the viewfinder, the shutter speed dial is simply turned in either direction to obtain the most suitable combination. Exposure time is always shortened first, while the lens remains at full aperture. Once the required new speed or f/stop are selected, the combination changes simultaneously.

The exposure memory store facility of the R4s MOD2 is incorporated and works in the same way. Exposure compensation is also indicated

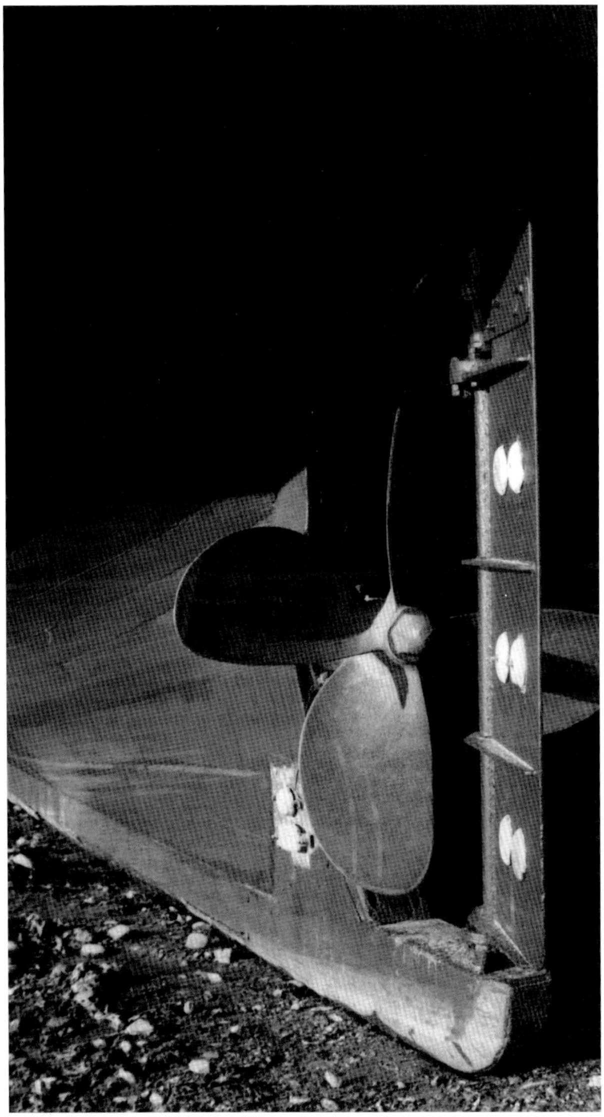

Fig. 129. In many cases, accurate exposure can be easily ascertained using the 'selective' (spot) metering mode of the Leica-R camera. In this picture it was important to retain some detail in the shaded propeller area while maintaining sufficient detail in the brighter parts. The central 'spot' was aimed just to the left of the propeller blade at 9 o'clock.

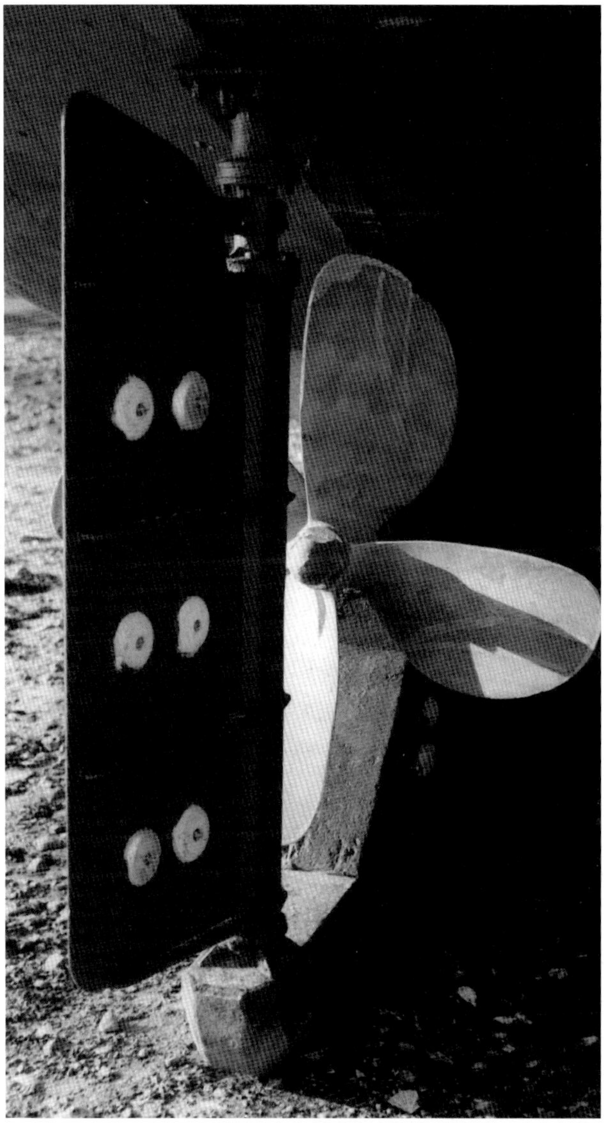

Fig. 130. The important feature of this view concerned the anode placings on the rudder face. The tonal range of the film would not permit retention of detail in all of the propeller blades, but this could be sacrificed for the purpose. The 'spot' reading was taken in this instance directly from the rudder plate at the object-to-camera distance.

in the viewfinder by a flashing mode symbol. Also added to this model is the facility for through-the-lens flash exposure measurement. This is only possible using dedicated electronic flash units supporting the SCA 300 and 500 series adapters. When the unit is mounted in the hot-shoe, or when used with the SCA PC socket module and cable, a flash-ready viewfinder symbol is lit. Flash exposure is controlled automatically and correct exposure is indicated in the viewfinder by a flashing LED which replaces the shutter speed and aperture values previously indicated. The exposure compensation device may also be used in conjunction with electronic flash. It can be set to +/- 2 stops in ⅓rd stop increments and when activated, is indicated in the viewfinder.

LEICA R6

This was the first all-mechanical Leica reflex since the Leicaflex SL2.

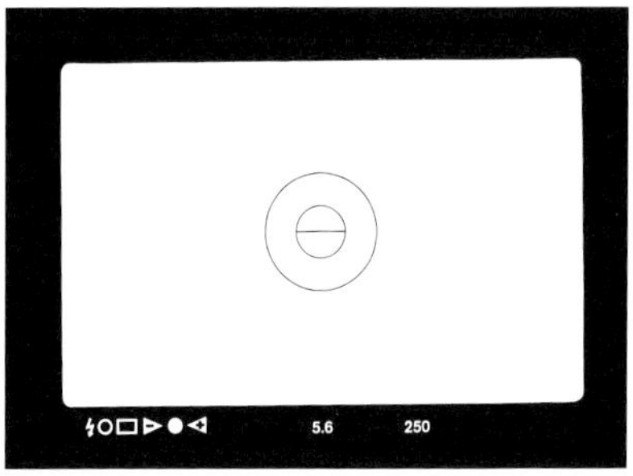

Fig. 134. Viewfinder display of the Leica R6 and R6.2. From bottom left, the symbols indicate: flash ready, selective metering mode, integrated full-field metering mode, under- and overexposure metering balance LED inverted triangle and central 'correct' exposure device, aperture set on lens ring, shutter speed set. Central 7mm circle comprises coarse microprism field and 3mm split-image rangefinder.

It has only one exposure mode; manual, by which the user is required to meter the subject by adjusting the shutter speed and/or the aperture. Correct exposure is achieved by balancing a pair of triangular-shaped LED's at the base of the viewfinder, between which is a circular red dot. When this is lit and the two triangles are unlit, correct exposure is set.

Deliberate over/under exposure can be set using the triangular LED's, so that one or the other is half-lit indicating +/- half-stop exposure increase/decrease. When a triangle is fully lit, i.e. at its brightest peak, the exposure set is increased/decreased by a full stop. The triangles are depicted in such a way that they indicate the direction required for more or less exposure.

The 'selective' and full-field, integrated centre-weighted exposure measurement modes are retained and can be switched from one to the other using the familiar selector switch under the shutter dial. The selector also incorporates the 'off' position which turns off the power to the meter.

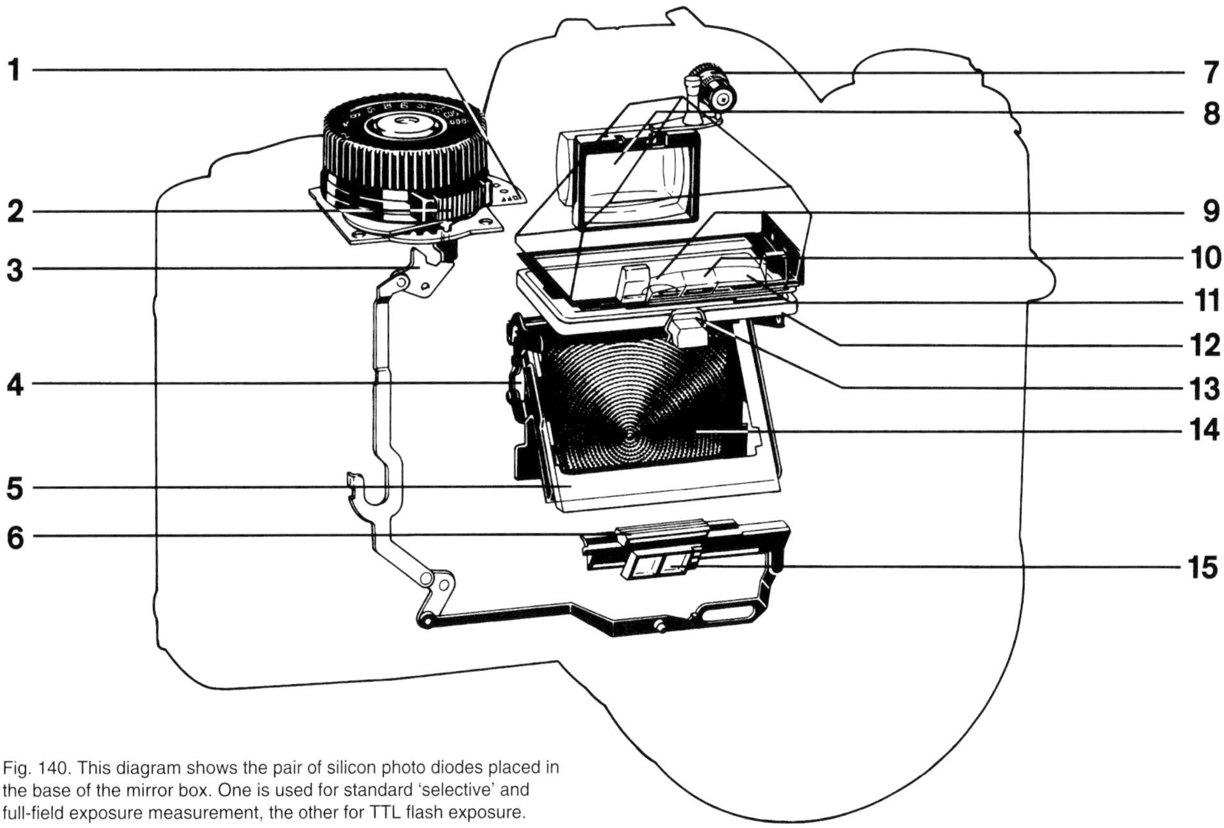

Fig. 140. This diagram shows the pair of silicon photo diodes placed in the base of the mirror box. One is used for standard 'selective' and full-field exposure measurement, the other for TTL flash exposure.

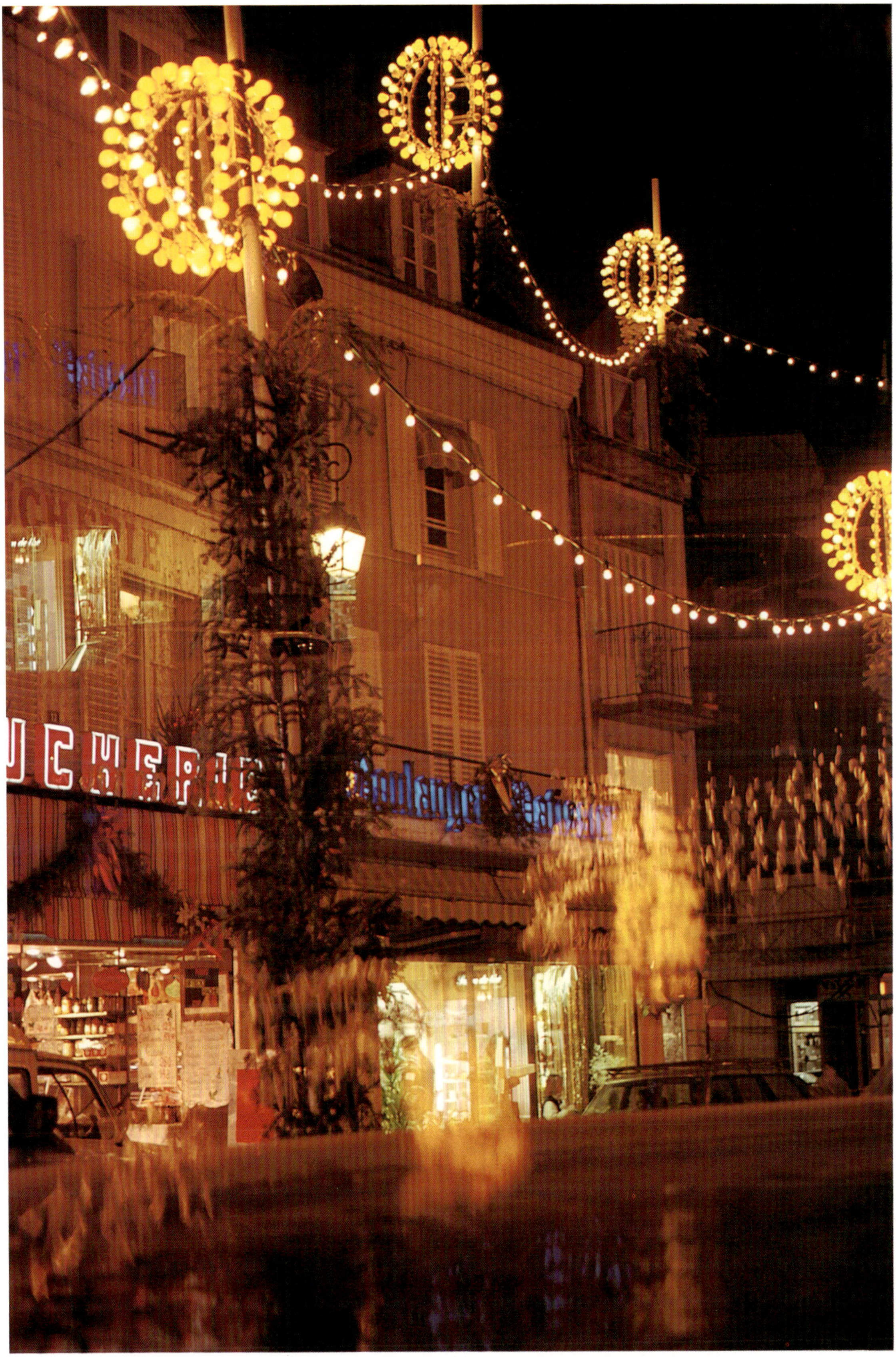

Christmas lights, Lagny, France. Leica R3 MOT, Summicron-R 50mm, f/2 using multiple exposure facility.

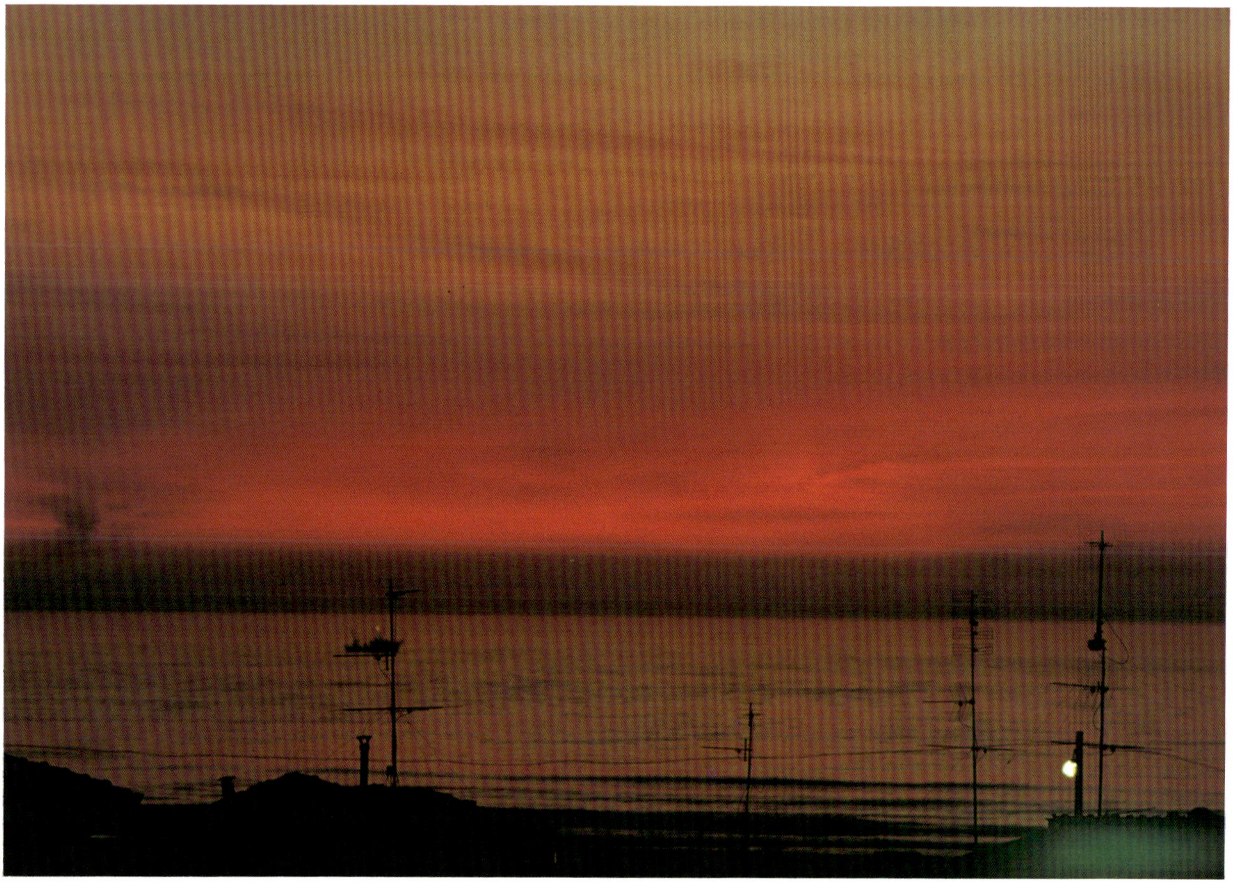

Who can resist a sunset? Viareggio, Italy. Elmarit-R 135mm, f/2.8

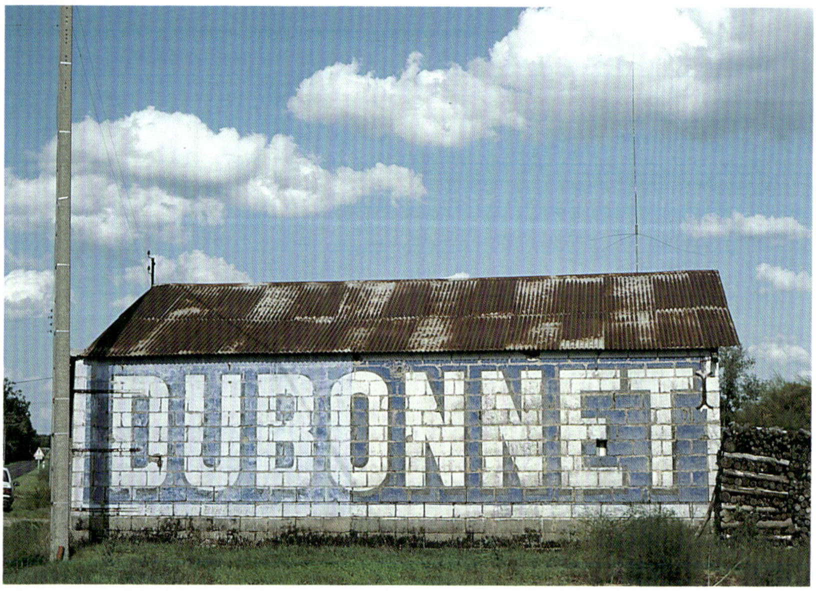

Dubonnet. One sees fewer and fewer of these painted signs in France today, but it was the clouds that stopped me. They look as if someone had pulled out the cotton wool and stuck them up there. Summicron-R 50mm

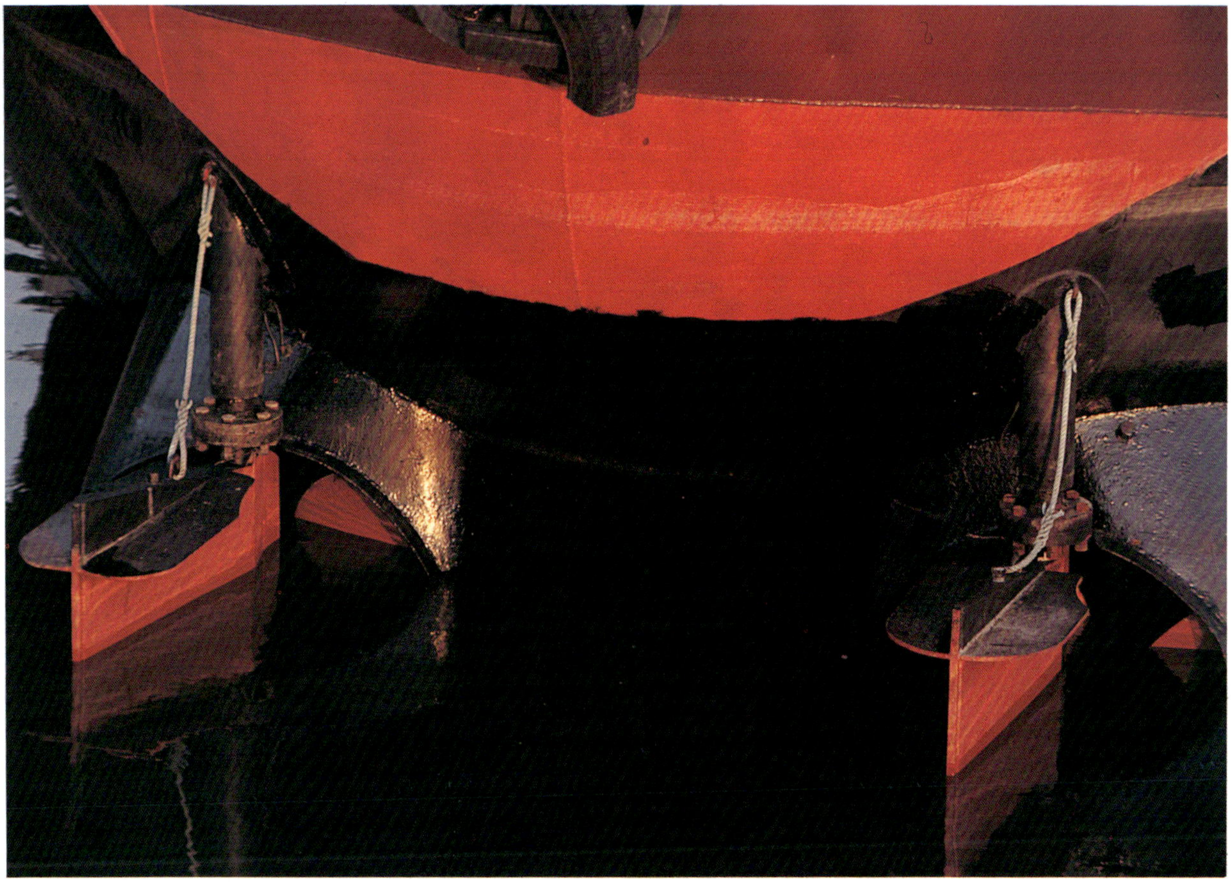

The water, ships and the sea. It always fascinates. Leica R3 MOT, Novoflex 400mm, f/5.6, Motor Winder R3 and Grip

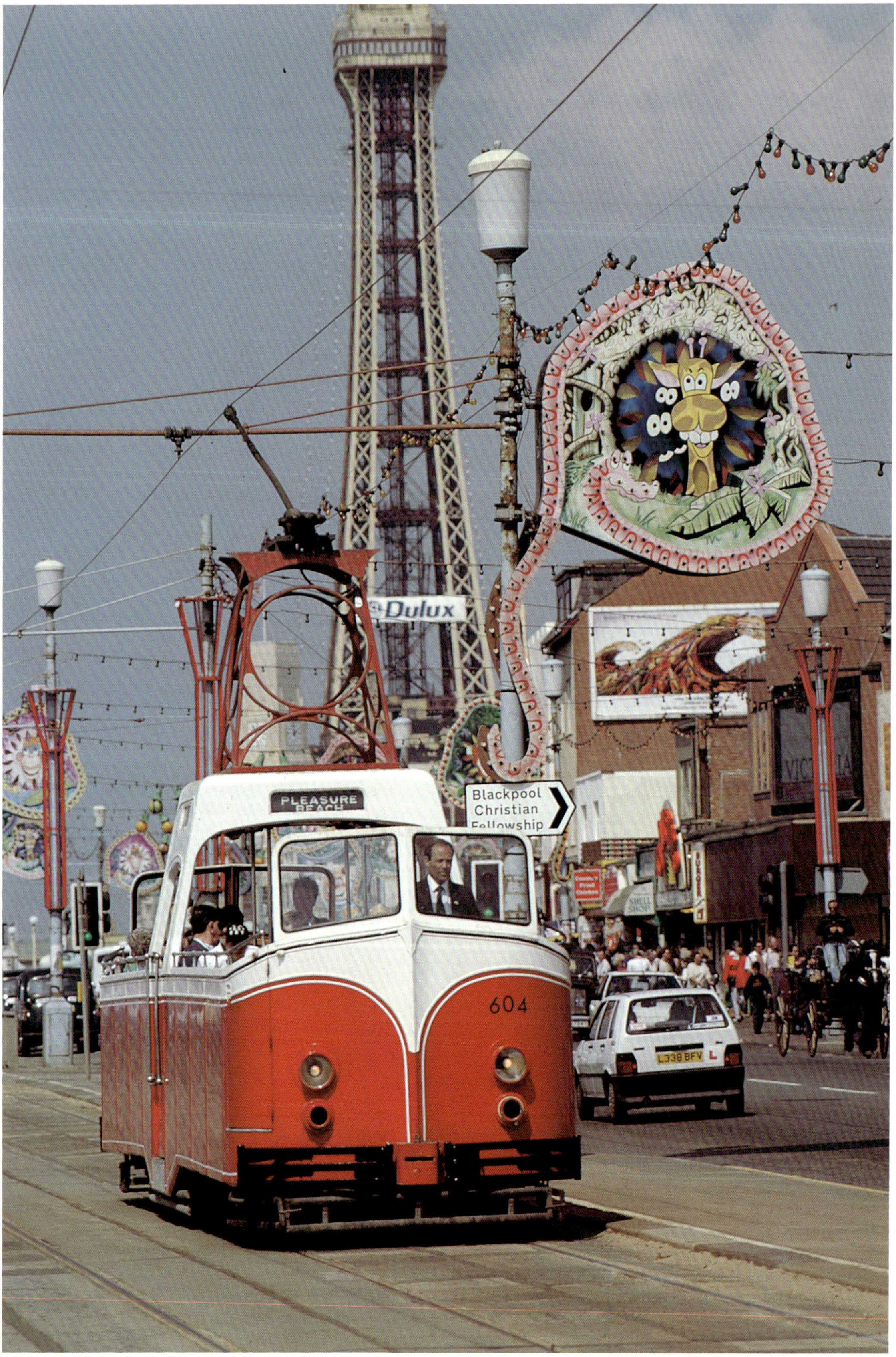

Blackpool, England. A photographer's dreamland at any time of the year. Leica R6, Elmar-R 180mm, f/4

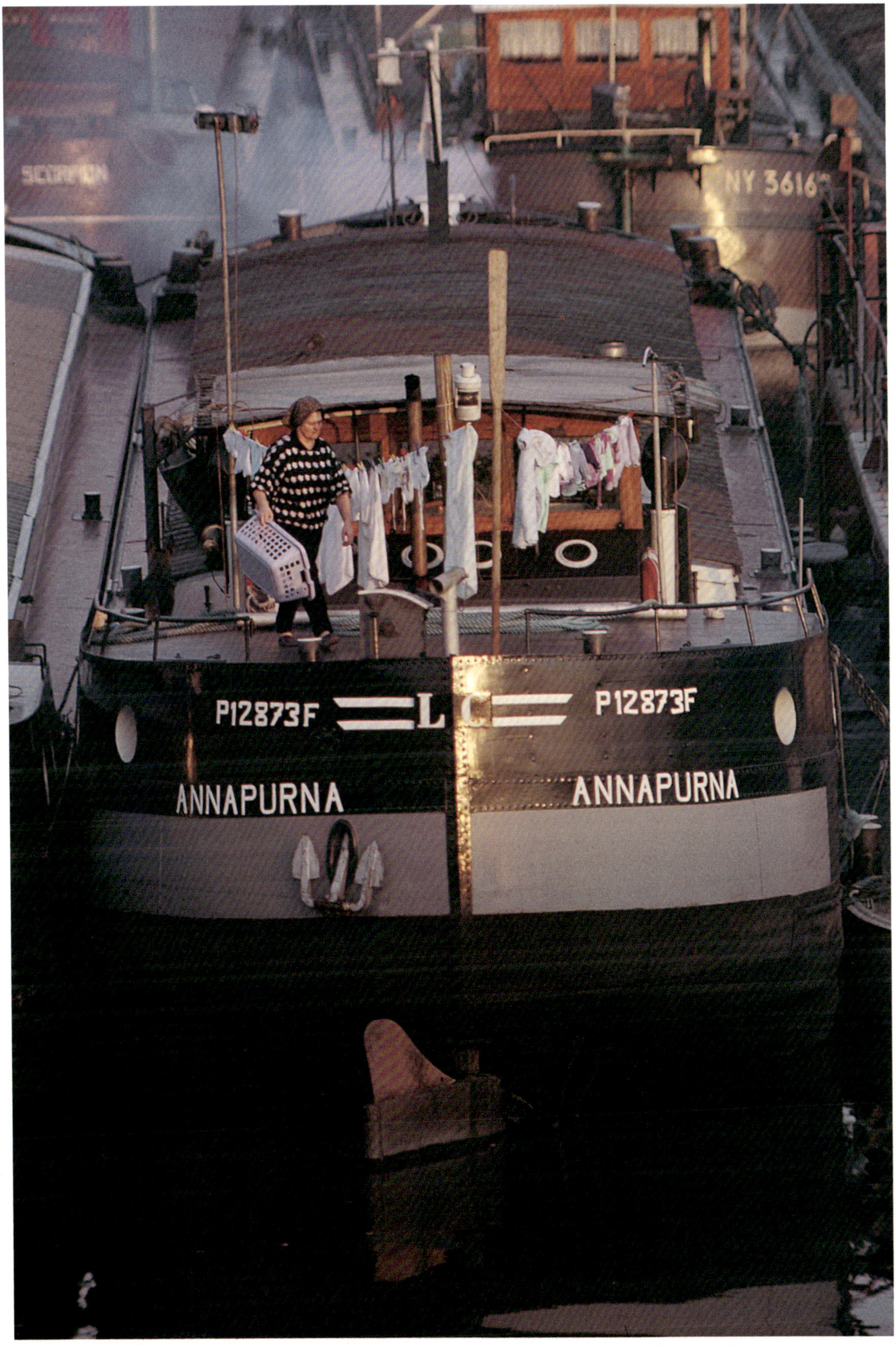

A barge at Conflans, France. Late winter sunshine. Leica R3 MOT, Novoflex 400mm

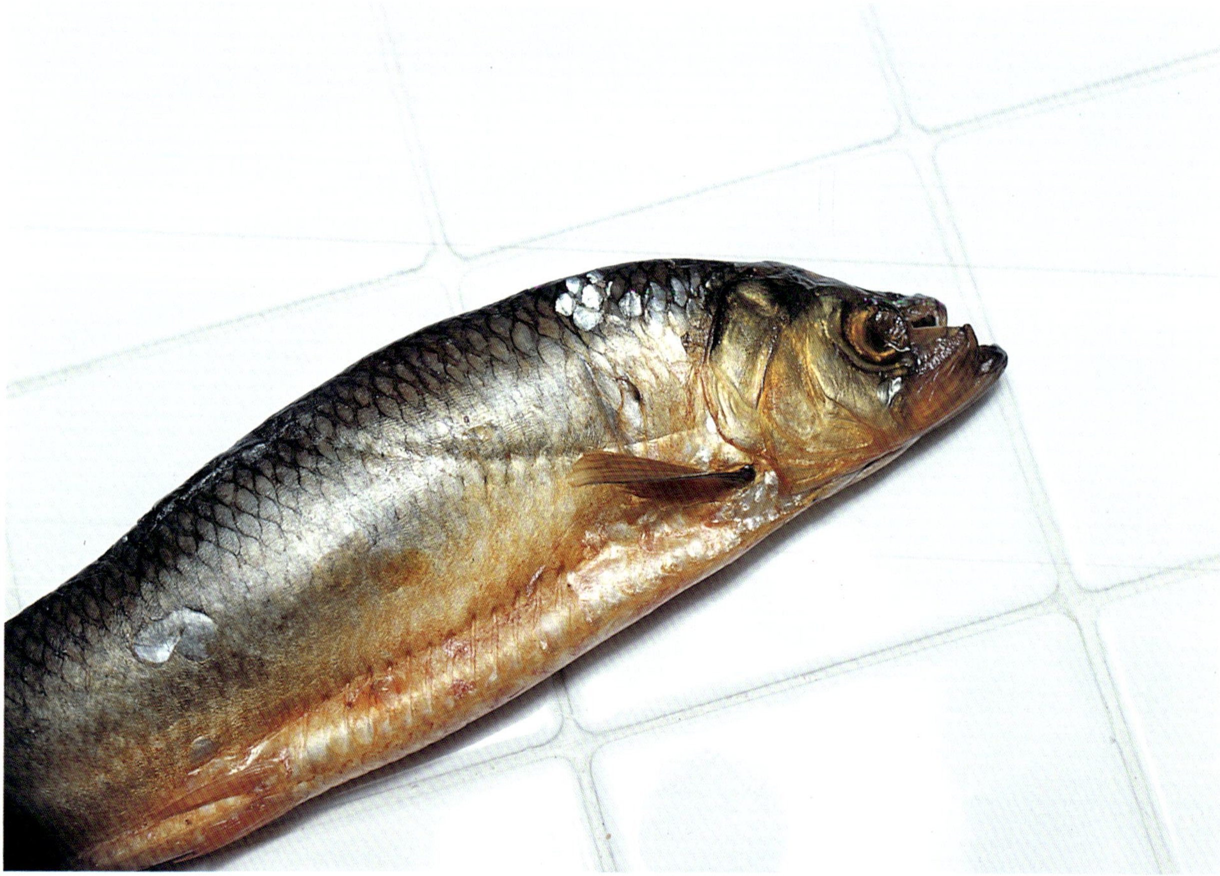

Kipper. I had taken it from the refrigerator to prepare for supper, but, slippery as they are sometimes, it fell from the bag onto the galley tiles.
Leica R6, Summicron-R 50mm, f/2, Metz 36TC electronic flash with SCA 351 adapter, TTL flash, direct with tissue over reflector

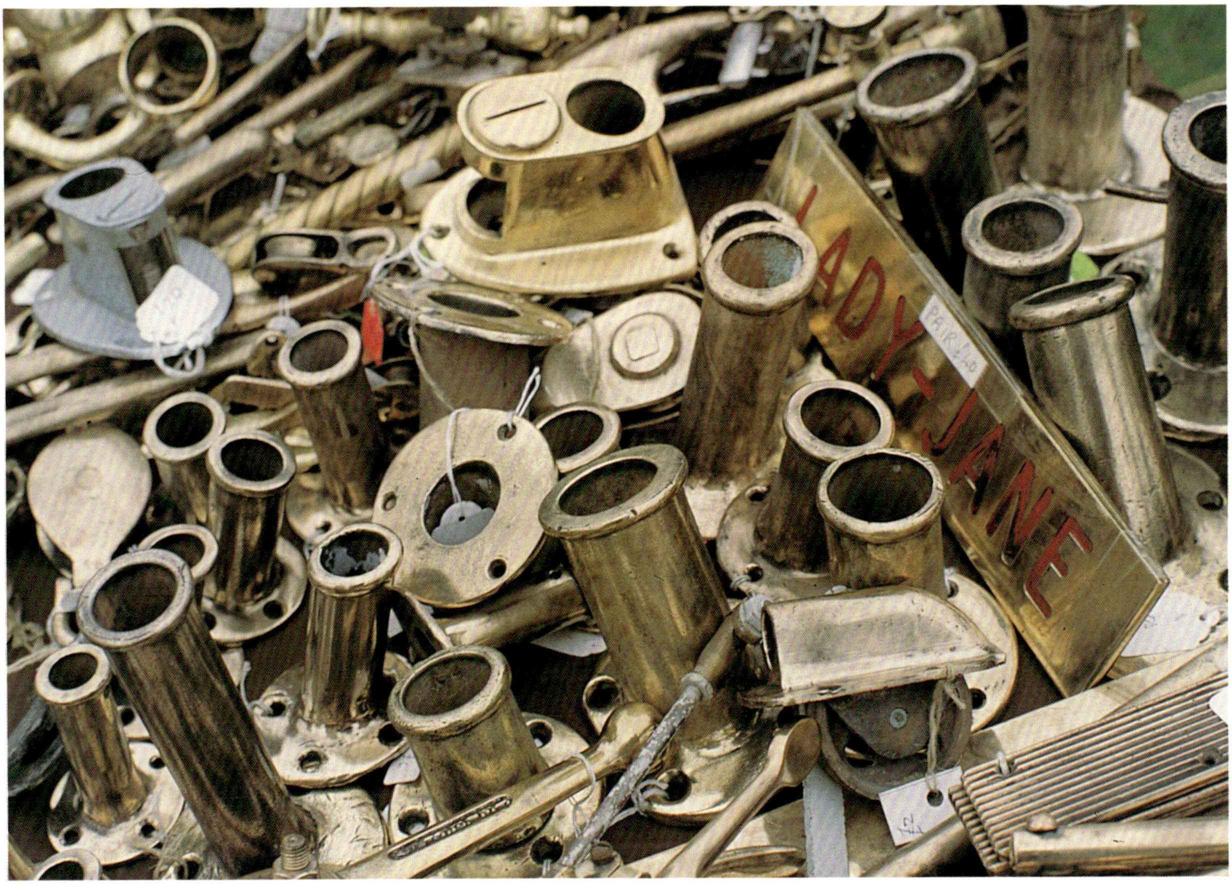

Brass. A table full of this stuff caught my eye at a marine jumble sale.
Summicron-R 50mm

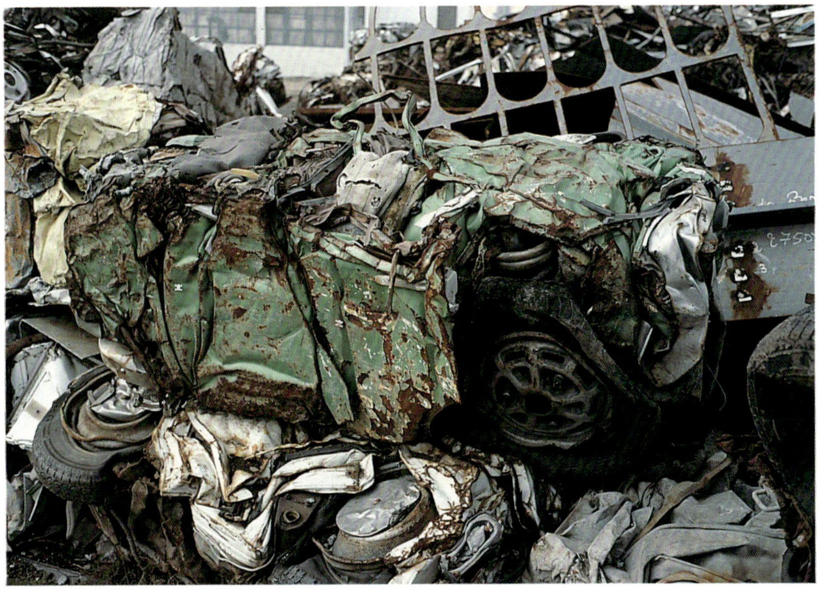

This also caught my eye at a scrapyard in Bordeaux docks one morning. As compact cars go, it was quite small. Summicron-R 50mm

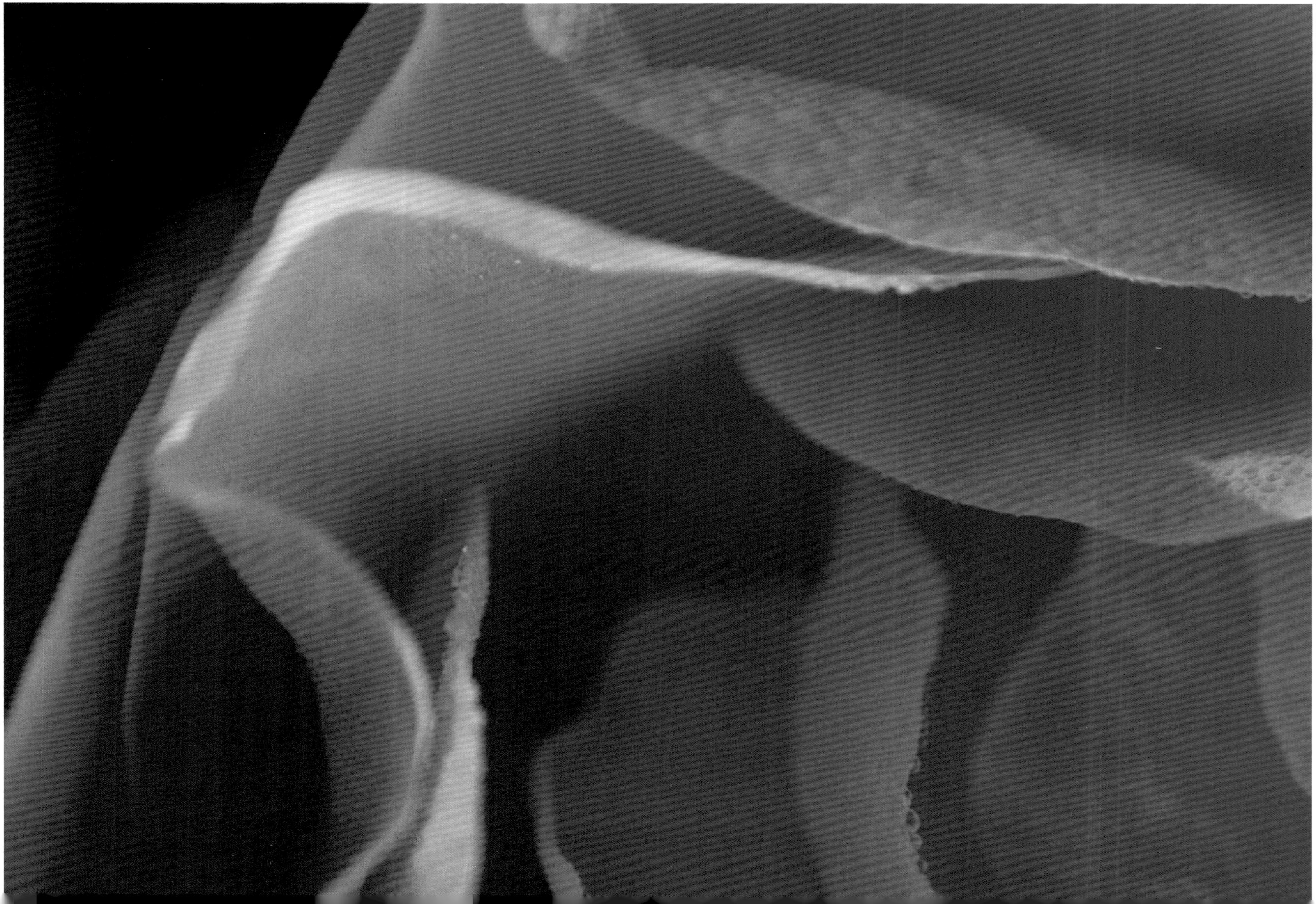

Early morning dew and the soft morning light caught the fragility of this rose.
Leica-R6 with Summicron-R 50mm reversed and hand-held over lens flange

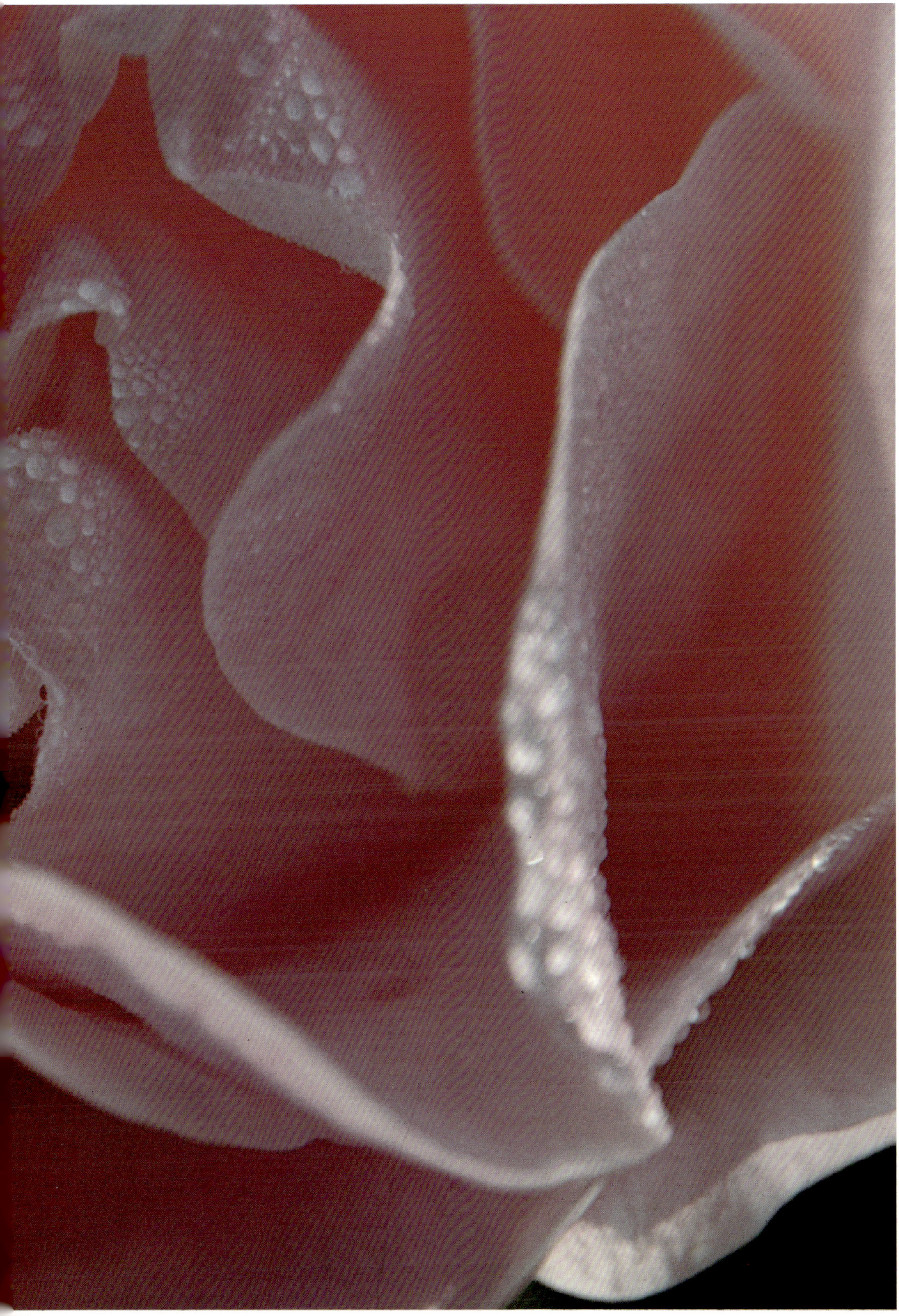

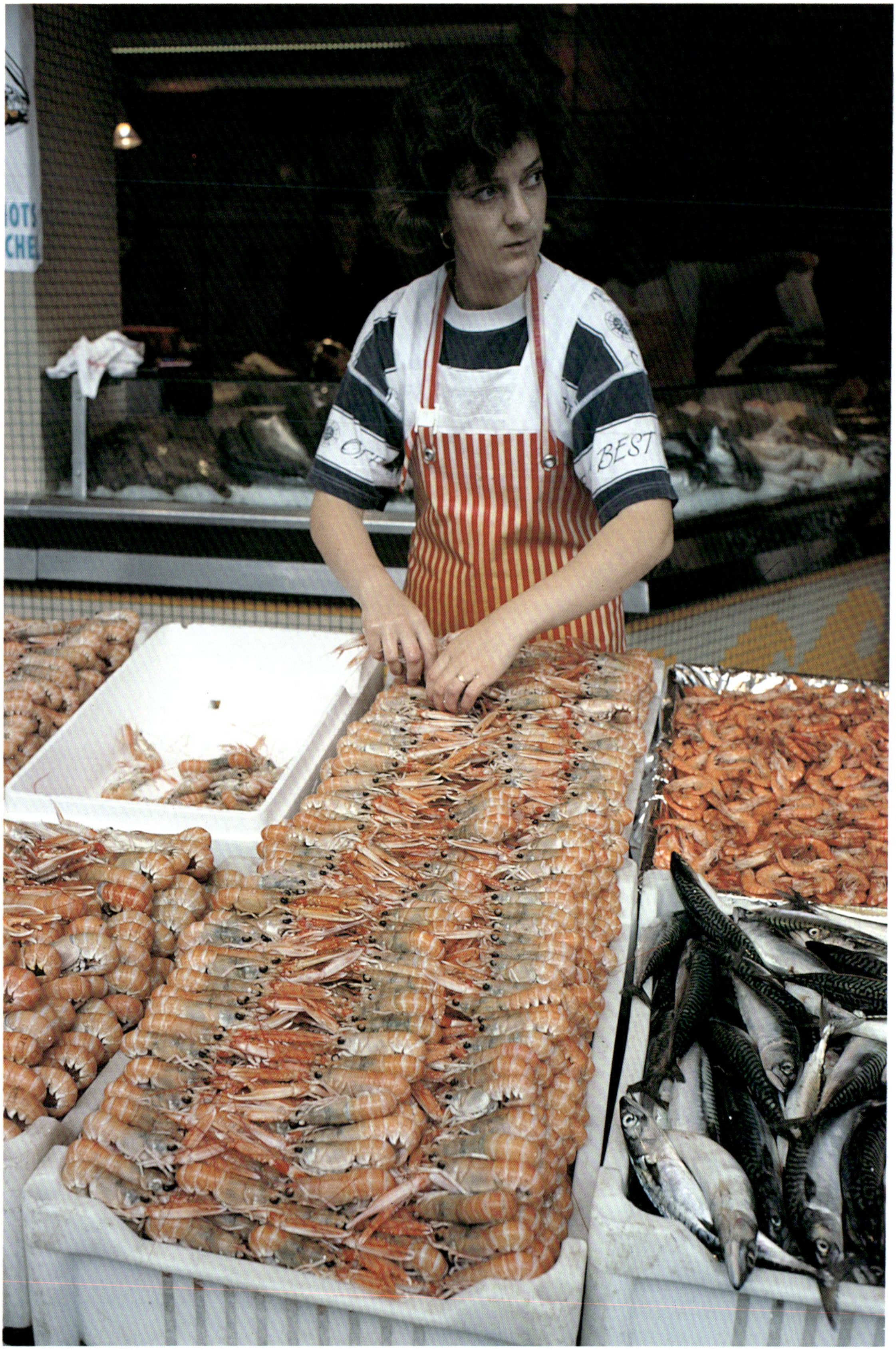

Laying out the morning's catch at Le Havre. You have to get up early to catch these girls at work. By mid-morning the displays have usually gone. I put the sharpest zone in the foreground to emphasise the length of the display. Summicron-R 50mm

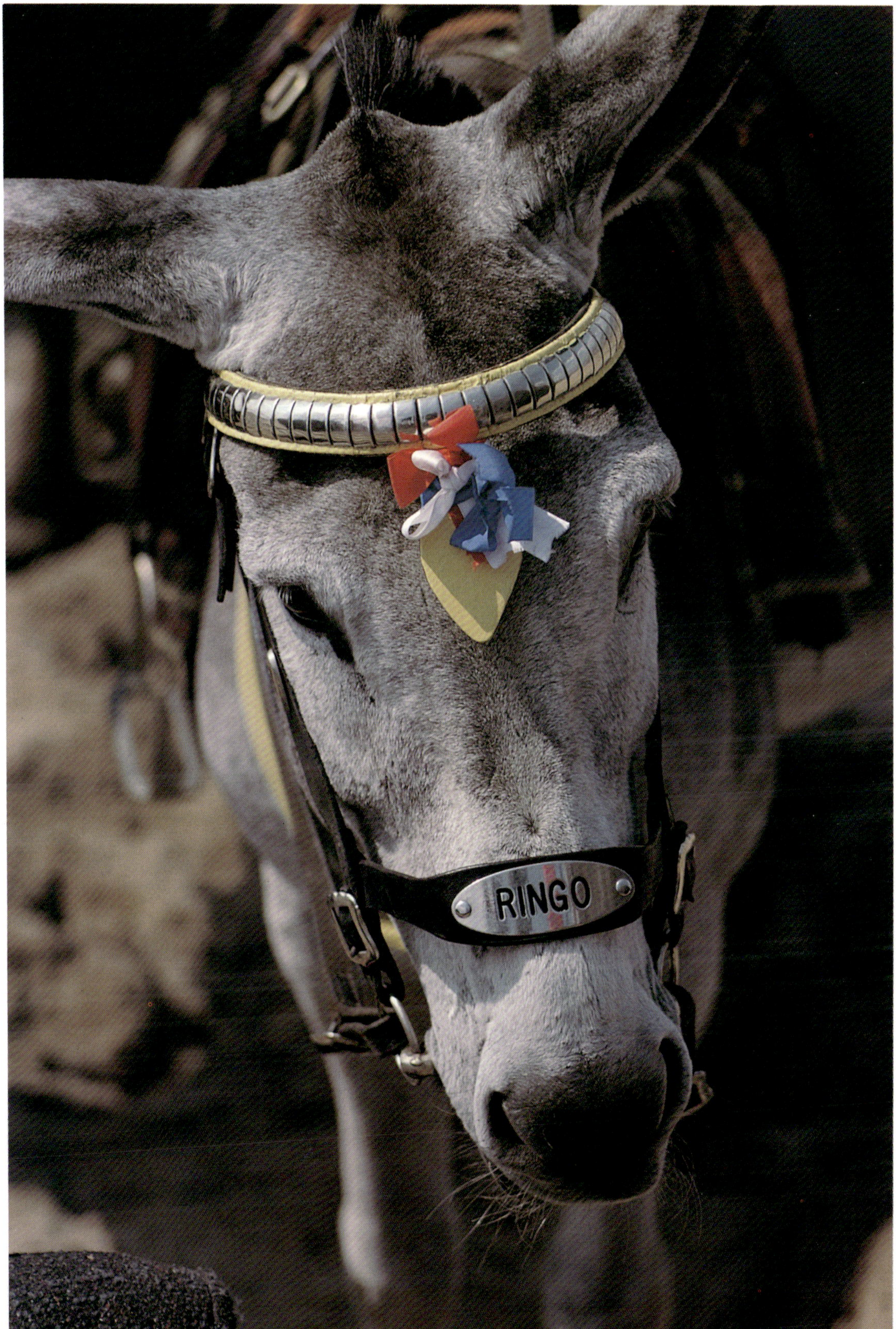

Ringo. It's that tiny coloured rosette which gives this picture balance. Elmar-R 180mm, f/4

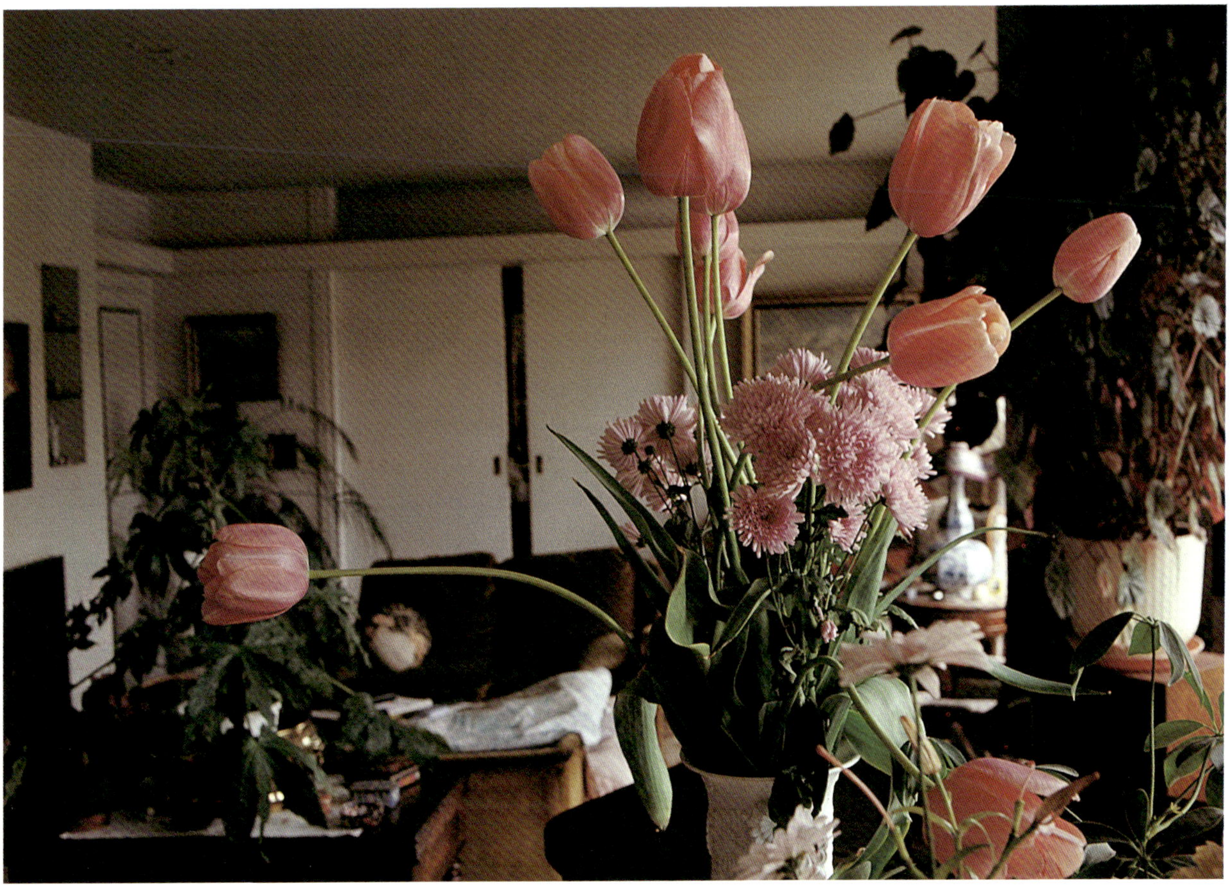

Tulips and available light. A north facing window produces a special quality of painterly light.
Summicron-R 35mm, f/2, Kodachrome 200

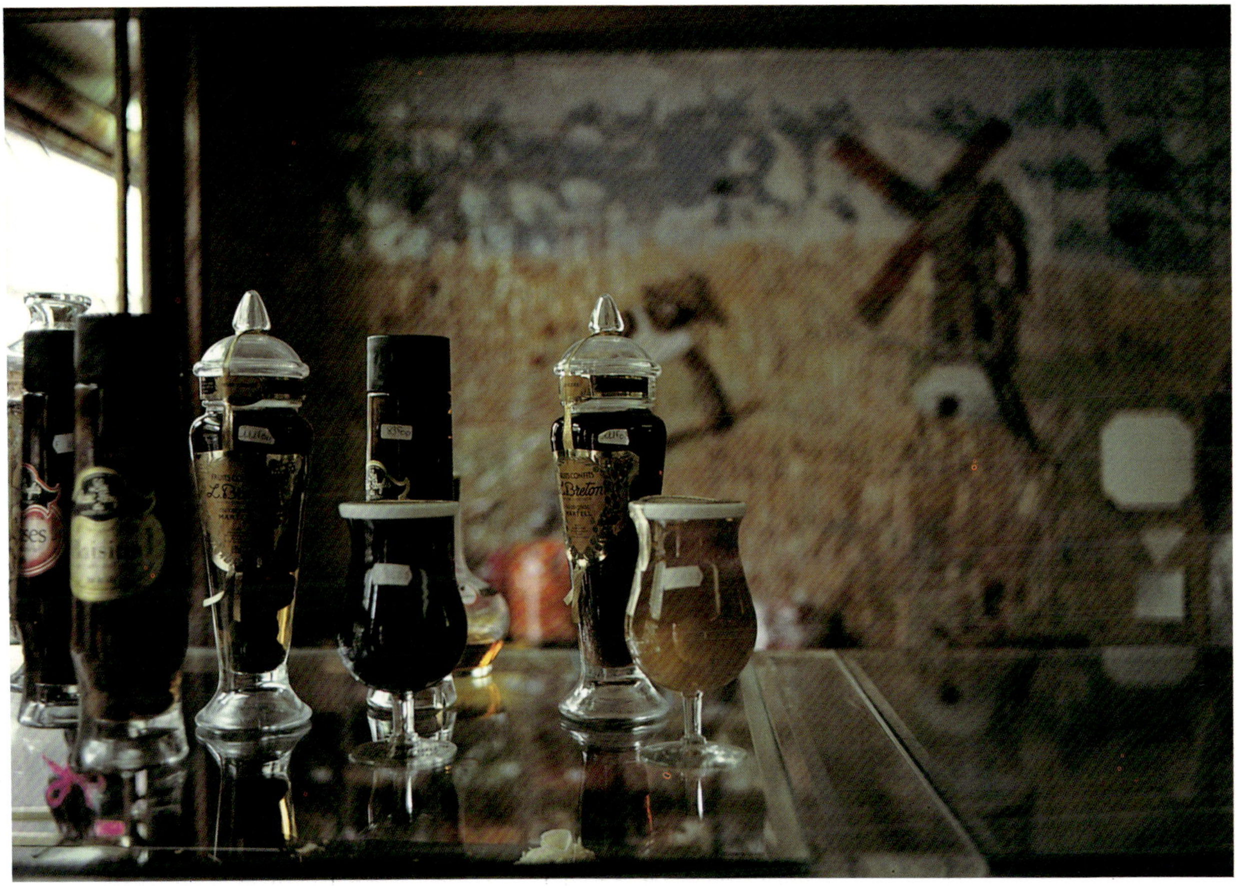

Boulangerie display in Louveciennes, France.
Leica R3 MOT, Summicron-R 35mm, f/2, about 1/8th second wide open

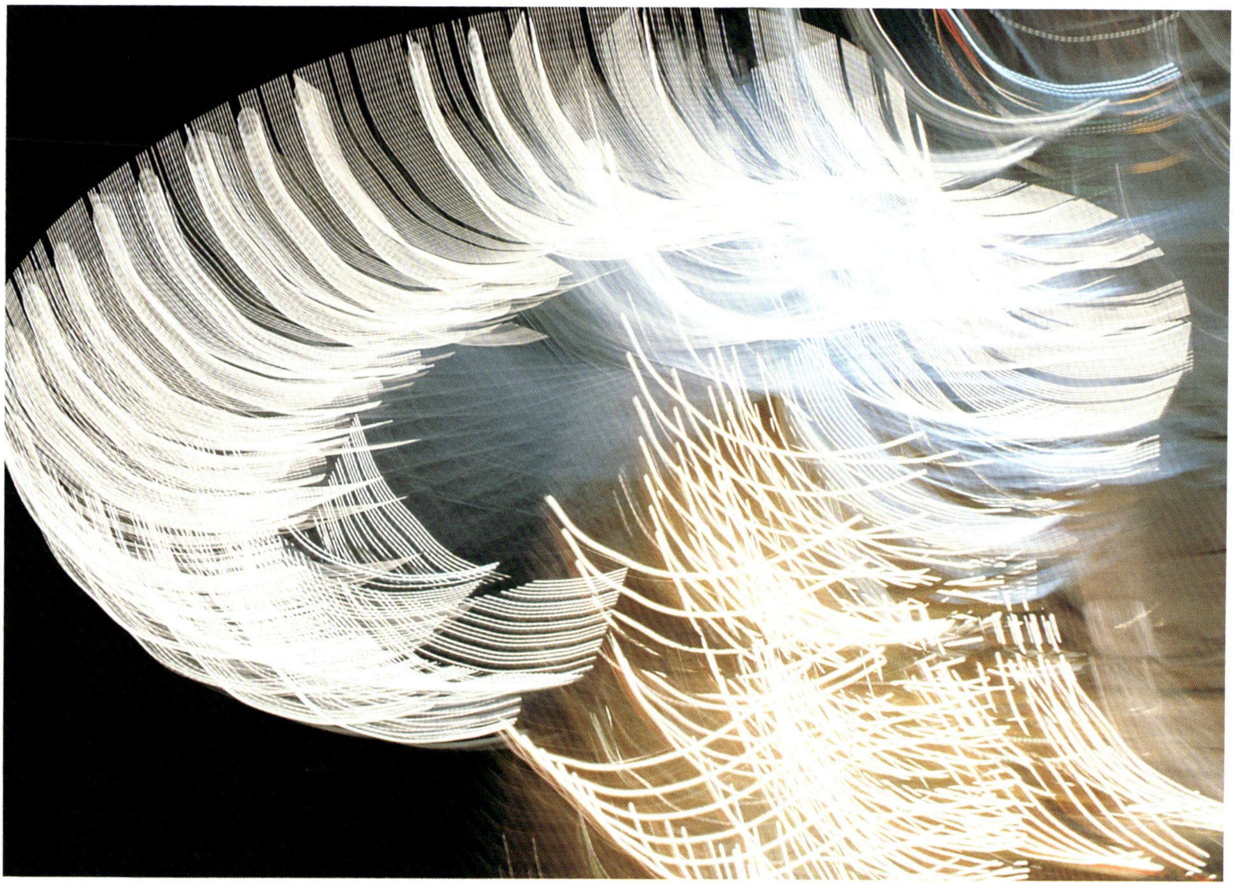

Fairground lights, Paris.
Leica R3 MOT, Summicron-R 50mm, lens panned during exposure

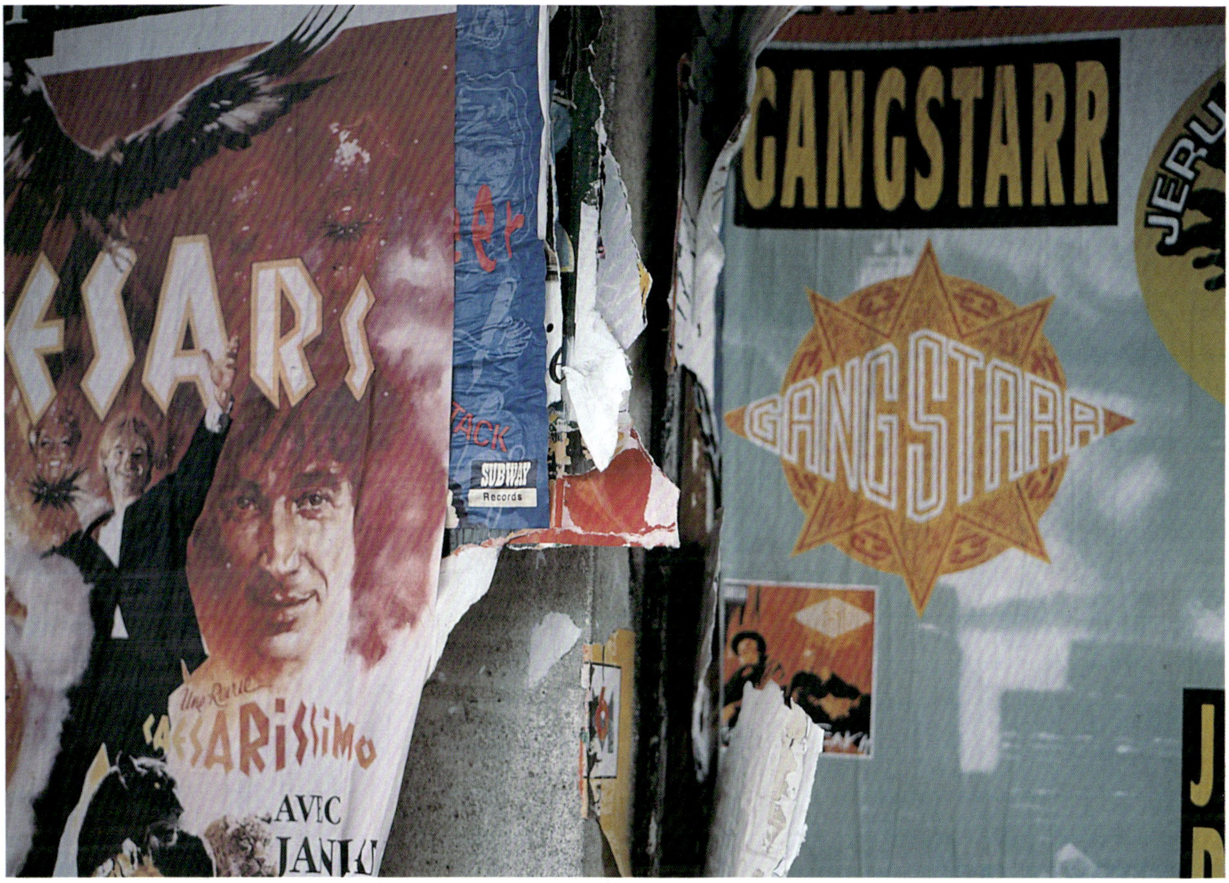

Torn poster, Bordeaux, France.
Summicron-R 50mm

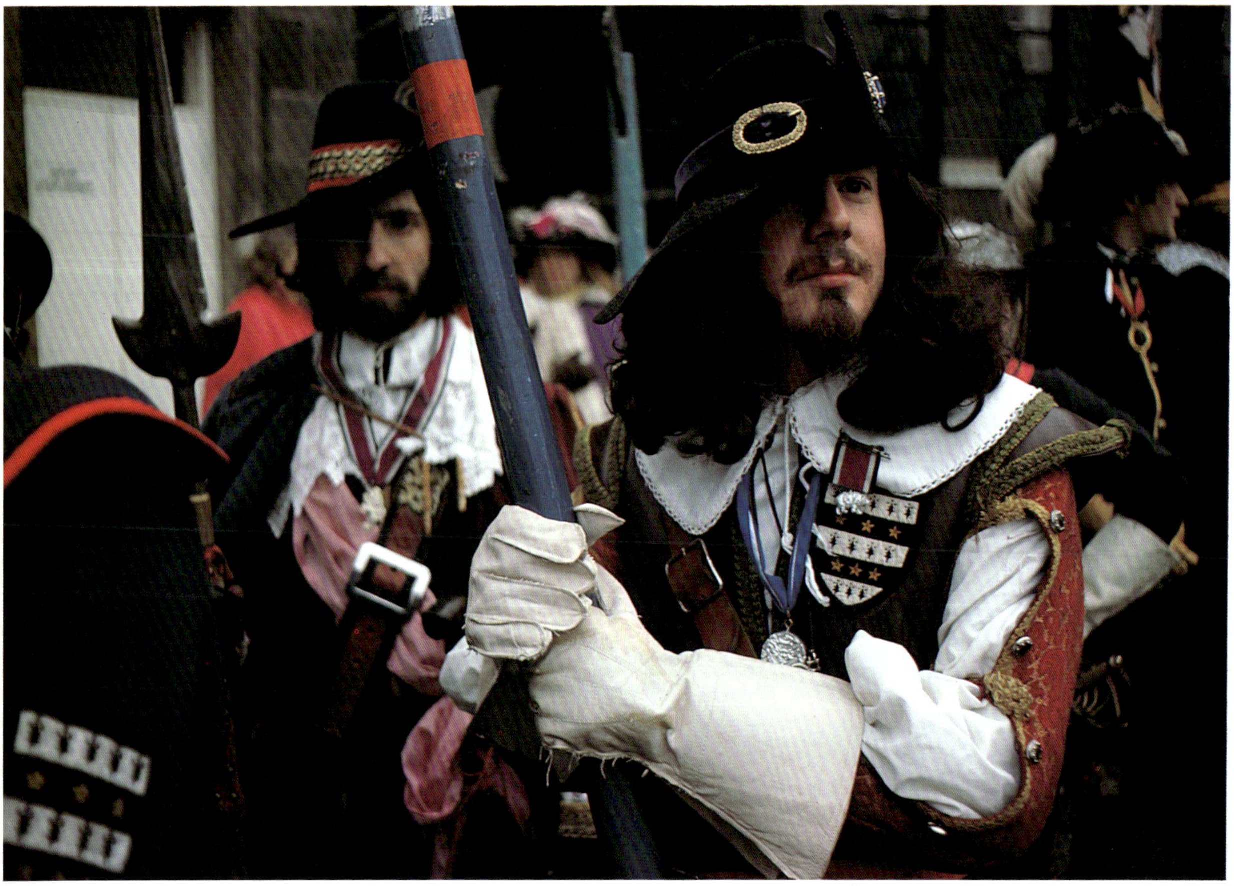

'Old Soldiers'. The King's Army on parade in London. These guys get all dressed up and go around the country re-enacting the English Civil War wherever they can find an empty field. Summicron-R 50mm

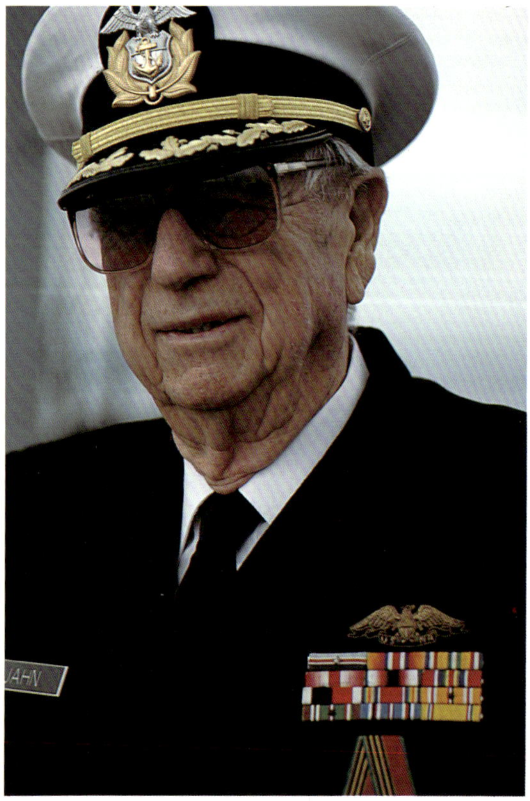

Old sailor. Captain George W. Jahn came out of retirement to bring one of the last surviving Liberty ships from San Francisco to England for the 50th D-Day anniversary in 1994.
Elmarit-R 135mm, f/2.8

This model retains the TTL flash exposure facility of the R5 and is operated using the SCA adapters previously described. Because this is a mechanical camera, the 'X' setting or any shutter speed between 1/60th sec. and 1 second must be set on the shutter speed dial manually. Mounting a compatible electronic flash unit using the SCA 351 or 551 adapters does not automatically set the camera for correct synchronization.

When the shutter is correctly set, the '⚡' symbol appears in the lower left of the viewfinder and is flashing twice a second. If another shutter speed between the range described above is set, the '⚡' symbol is constantly lit. When set to 'B', none of the viewfinder symbols is lit; TTL exposure control is still possible however.

Correct exposure can be ascertained after the exposure has been made by maintaining a slight pressure on the shutter release button. A slow flashing '⚡' (twice a second) symbol indicates that the light discharge is minimal. The flash-ready light should be visible immediately after exposure.

When the '⚡' is flashing at 8 times a second followed by slow flashing, the flash light discharge is adequate but moderate. Slow flashing of the '⚡' symbol indicates the flash is ready for further exposures.

Fast flashing of the '⚡' symbol for two seconds followed by a break (no light) and then slow flashing indicates a heavy condenser discharge. When the flash is recharged ready for use, the '⚡' symbol continues to flash.

No light after exposure followed by slow flashing of the '⚡' symbol indicates the light discharge was inadequate for correct exposure. Once recharged, the '⚡' symbol will continue to flash.

Using shutter speeds other than 'X' in the correct synchronization range causes the '⚡' to remain constantly lit after exposure. No symbol appears when an incorrect shutter speed, i.e. between 1/125th to 1/1000th second is set.

LEICA R6: Optic for viewfinder and exposure meter

1 = Exposure meter mode indicator: selective, integral OFF
2 = Selector switch (selective or integral mode) and locking button, exposure meter switched off
3 = Selector switch for selective/integral mode
4 = Mechanical linkage between swing-mirror mount and hinged Fresnel reflector
5 = Mirror mount, semi-transparent mirror with 17-layer coating
6 = Slide and condenser lens for selective exposure meter mode
7 = Setting wheel for adjustment of eyepiece
8 = Adjustable eyepiece lens
9 = Deflecting prism for shutter-speed display
10 = Deflecting prism for aperture display
11 = Deflecting prism for display of shutter/aperture balance, "flash ready", and exposure meter mode (selective/integral) selected
12 = Mount for focusing screen
13 = Interchangeable focusing screen
14 = Fresnel reflector (1345 micro-reflectors)
15 = Silicon photodiodes to exposure meter and flash-exposure control

LEICA R-E

The top of the range Leica single lens reflex cameras are inherently expensive and in appreciation of this Leica Camera GmbH have continued the policy of producing less highly specified models from time to time to encourage the budget conscious to join the fraternity.

The Leica R-E, like earlier models of the R4s and R4s MOD 2, lacks only a few of the features of the R5, offering Manual, and two Aperture priority modes in conjunction with 'selective' and full-field, integrated centre-weighted measurement. It also retains the TTL flash exposure feature of the other two models.

The viewfinder display for shooting with and without flash is similar to the R5, but lacking the Shutter priority and Variable automatic program mode information.

Sadly, this camera was discontinued in July 1994 after only three and half years of production. I know of several professional photographers who use this model, finding it ideal for their general day-to-day use because of its relative simplicity.

LEICA R6.2

Identical to the original R6 but with an improved shutter blade mechanism and increased range of shutter speeds. Otherwise, the electronic exposure modes and facilities remain the same in all respects.

LEICA R7

The current all-electronic camera with improved specification over the R5, including more sophisticated TTL flash exposure control. This permits dedicated electronic flash to be used as the primary light source, or as fill-in flash for delicate ambient light situations.

In either of the Aperture priority modes, the camera electronics automatically switch the shutter speed to the correct $\frac{1}{100}$th second synchronization speed whenever the correctly dedicated electronic flash unit is mounted. In the Manual mode, any speed between 4 seconds to $\frac{1}{90}$th second may be selected. A built-in computerised safety device automatically switches the shutter speed to the correct setting in this mode, when the wrong shutter speed (i.e. a higher one) is selected. The flash can also be used as a main light source at the 'B' or '100⚡' setting.

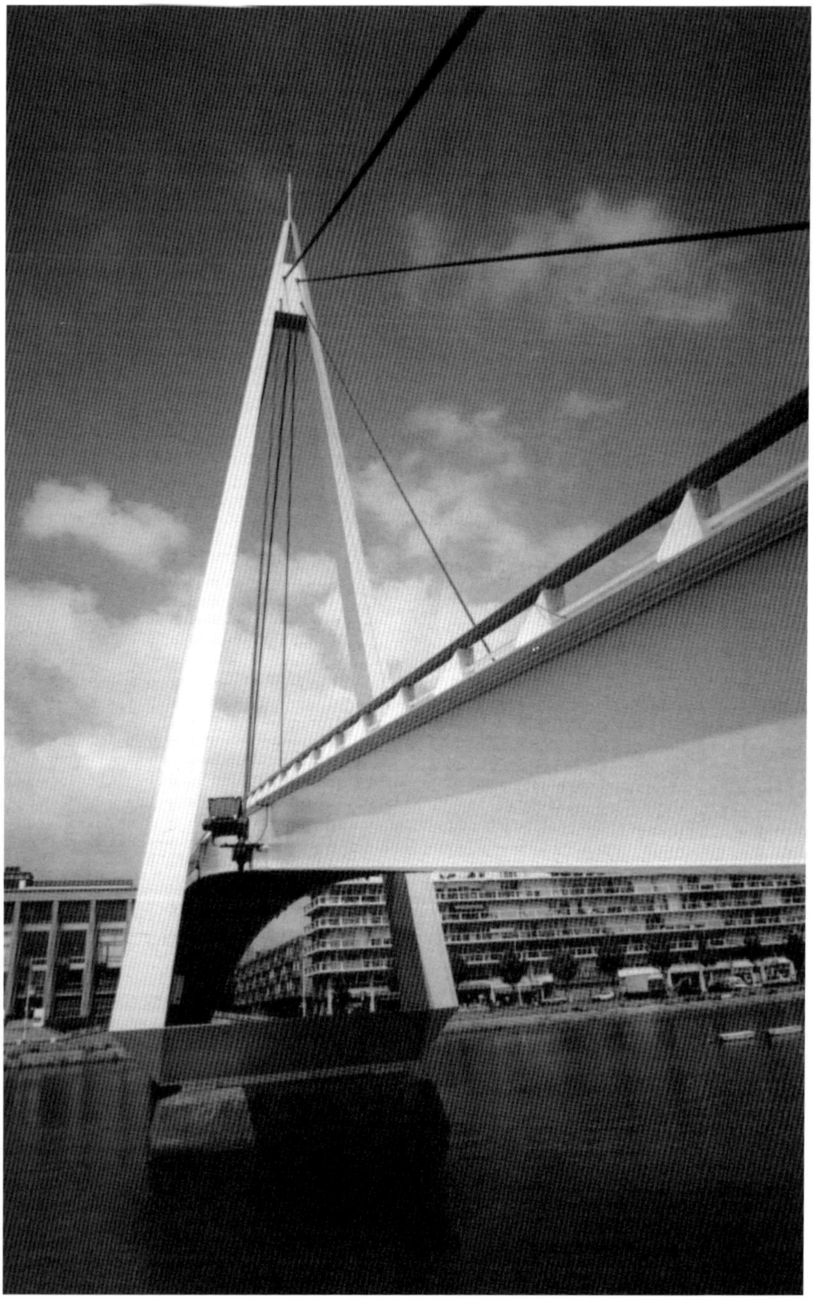

Fig. 131. There are two ways to meter subjects like this, depending on the effect desired. I needed a picture for newspaper reproduction which retained sufficient detail through the tonal range from deep shadow to bright highlight. I could have isolated the white bridge by exposing only for its parts using the 'selective' metering method. However, as this was a colour negative emulsion I opted for the full-field method to give a nicely balanced range.

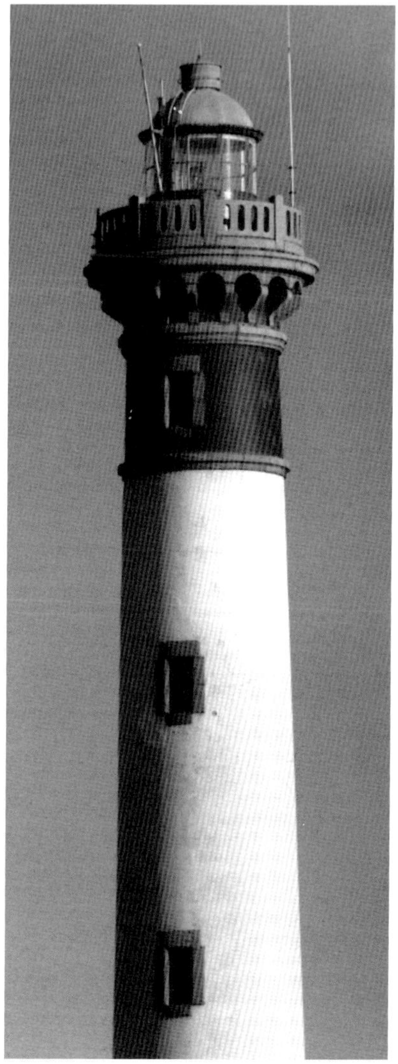

Fig. 133. Another subject example where careful metering is essential to retain detail throughout the tonal range. I wanted to be sure however that some of the colours at the top end of the tower were fully saturated on the colour negative. Retaining detail in the obviously white areas was not so important. I used the 'selective' metering facility on the R6 and measured for an area partially on the light balustrade and the blue sky.

When the selector switch is set to 'P', the variable automatic program takes over flash command at all ambient light levels. Thus, if the ambient light level is sufficient for correct exposure without flash, it is not triggered. In situations where ambient light levels are so low they

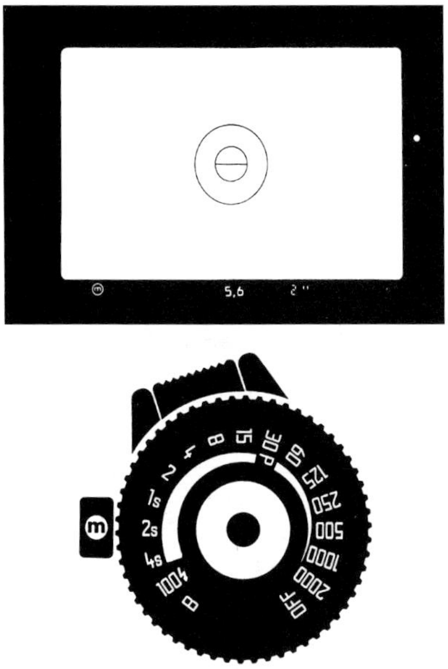

Fig. 135. Manual setting with selective mode.

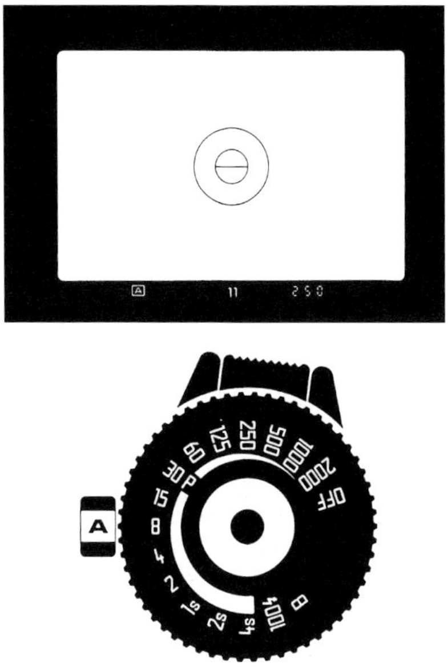

Fig. 136. Aperture priority, full field integral metering mode.

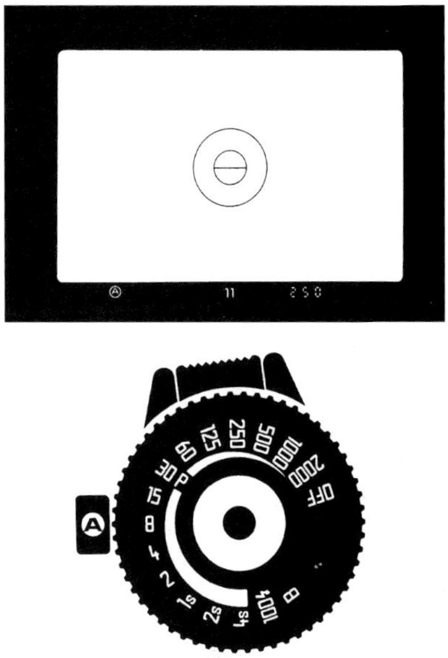

Fig. 137. Aperture priority, selective metering mode.

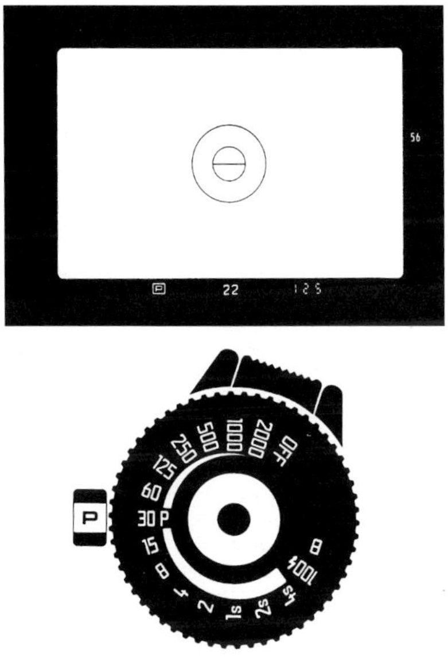

Fig. 139. Variable automatic program mode with full field integral metering.

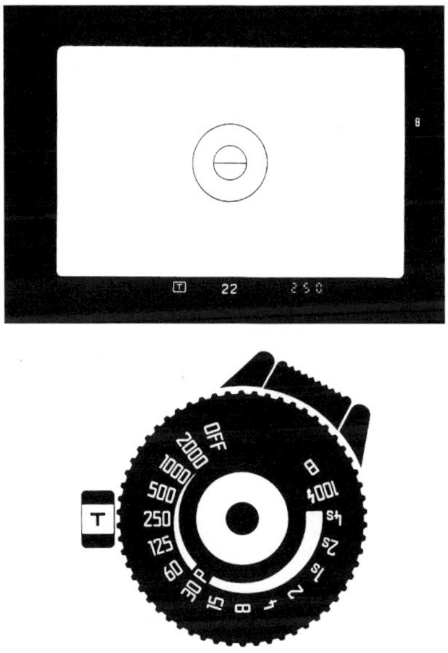

Fig. 138. Shutter Priority with full field integral metering.

would normally trigger the use of a slower shutter speed, the flash automatically kicks-in to fully illuminate the subject.

The viewfinder displays for flash control and exposure operate in the same way as those for the R5, as do the displays for normal shooting using the various exposure modes. All other controls and viewfinder displays are the same as for the R5 and R6/6.2 models. The camera is turned on and off using the mode selector switch.

All of the electronically operated R-cameras since the R3 are equipped with an electromagnetic stepless speed shutter manufactured by Seikosha. The viewfinder shutter speed scale does not show the values of intermediate speeds set using the automatic aperture priority modes, but users can be confident in the fact that if the settings required for correct exposure are computed at, say, 1/99th second, that is the shutter speed used.

All camera models since the R6 are also fitted with a viewfinder shutter/aperture value scale illuminating light. This is a very useful device in low light or night time applications as it uses red LED's to illuminate the scale. The same colour of light is also used to illuminate the aperture scale of the lens so that the f/stop set may be read in the viewfinder. A switch located at the left hand base of the body lens mount turns the ancillary light on or off. It should not be left on unnecessarily as battery power to the meter will be drained more quickly.

Since the launch of the R4, all Leica R-models have also had the benefit of an additional range of focusing screens. Besides the standard Universal focusing screen with coarse microprism collar and split-image rangefinder, there are four other screens, each ideally suited for specific applications. Long focus

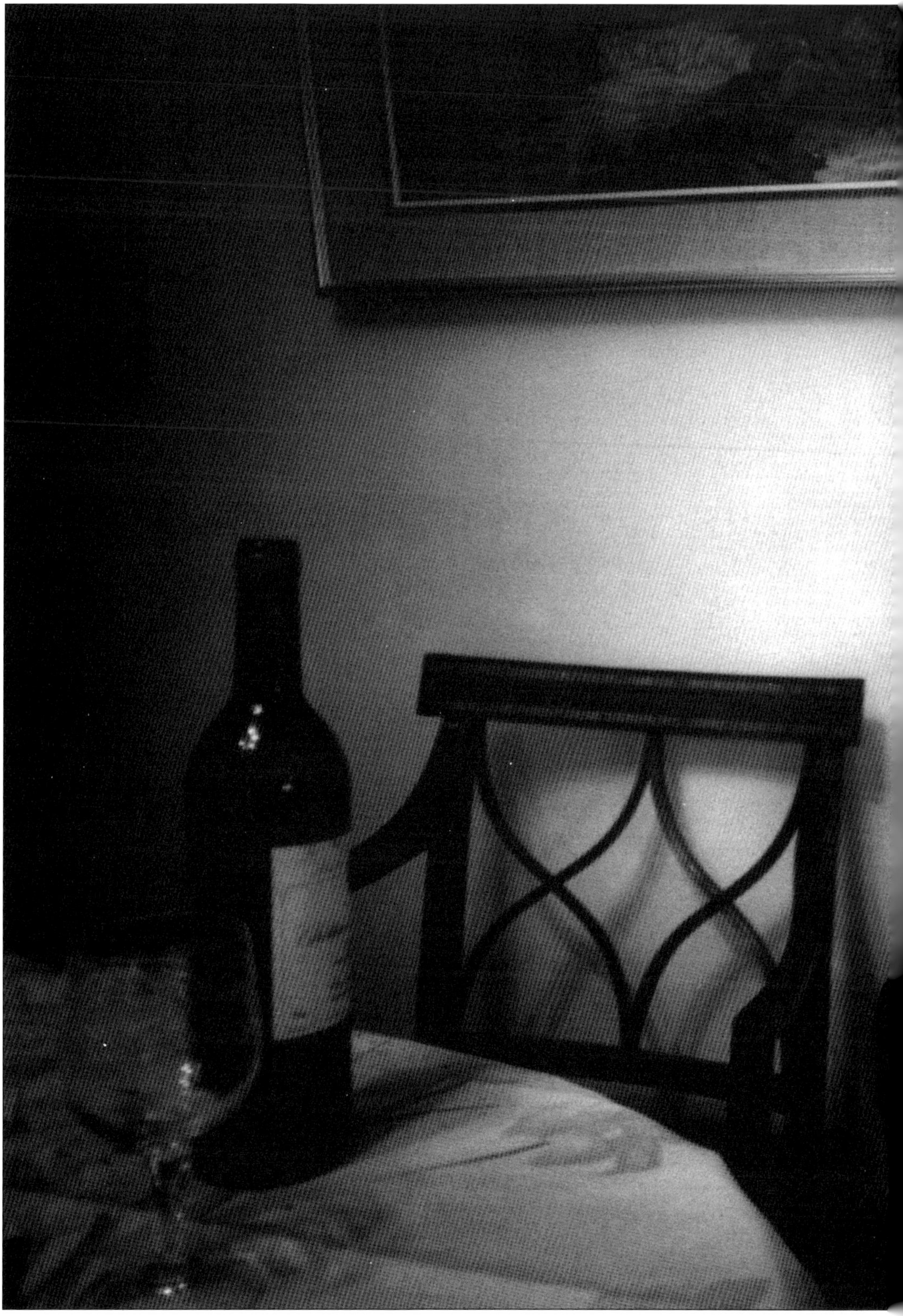

Fig. 144. Lighting for this photograph also came from a window, but its intensity was a lot less than in Fig 143. The important feature here was the sitter's visage which I measured with a hand-held meter and transferred to the Leica. Some burning in at the corners of the print helps to emphasize the subject.

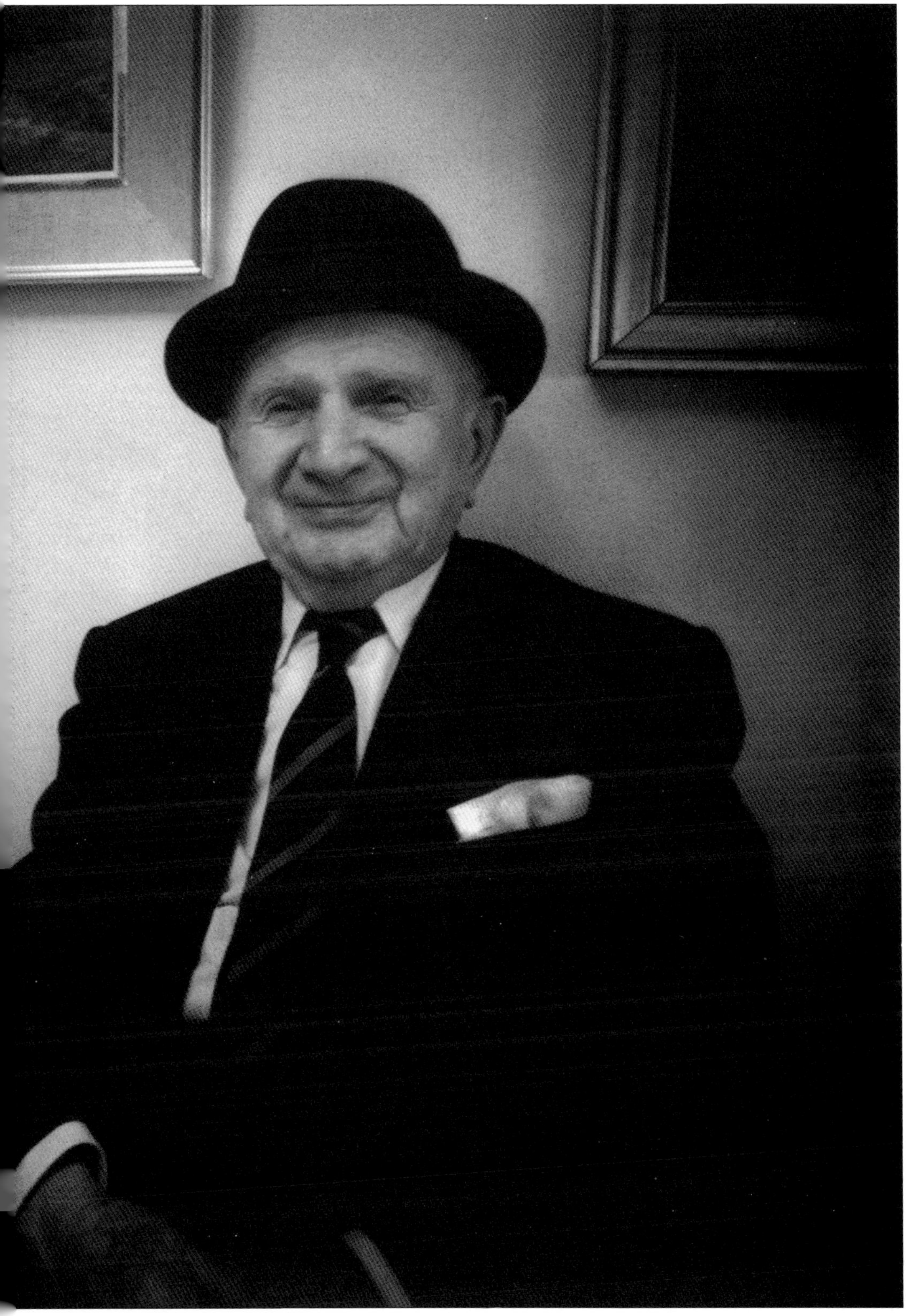

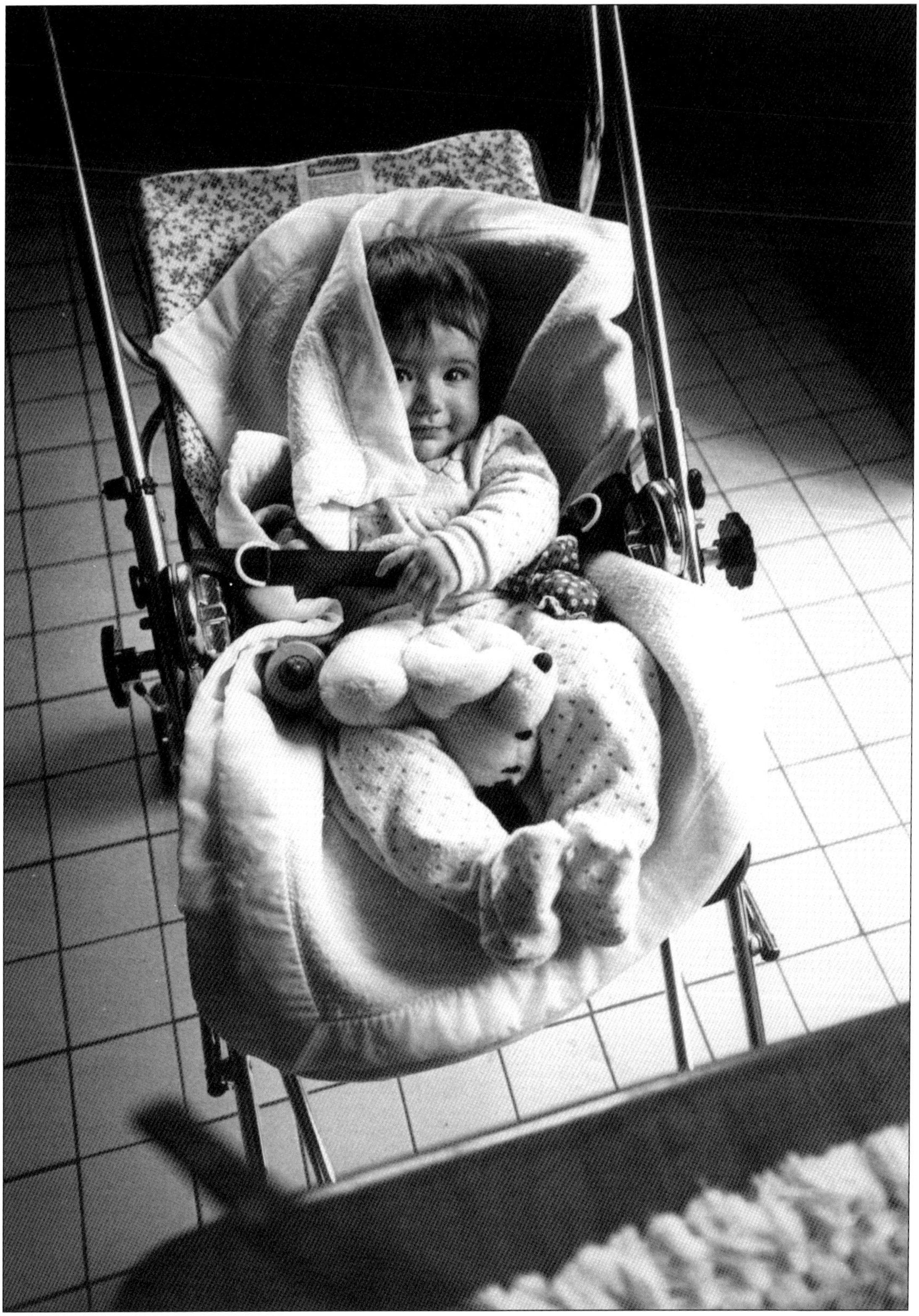

Fig. 143. Many modern colour negative emulsions have a greater exposure latitude than some b/w emulsions. The tonal range in this b/w photograph extends from deep black to bright white. The 'selective' spot metering mode was used to analyse several areas before making a manual adjustment to the lens aperture to 'fit' the film to my own development techniques.

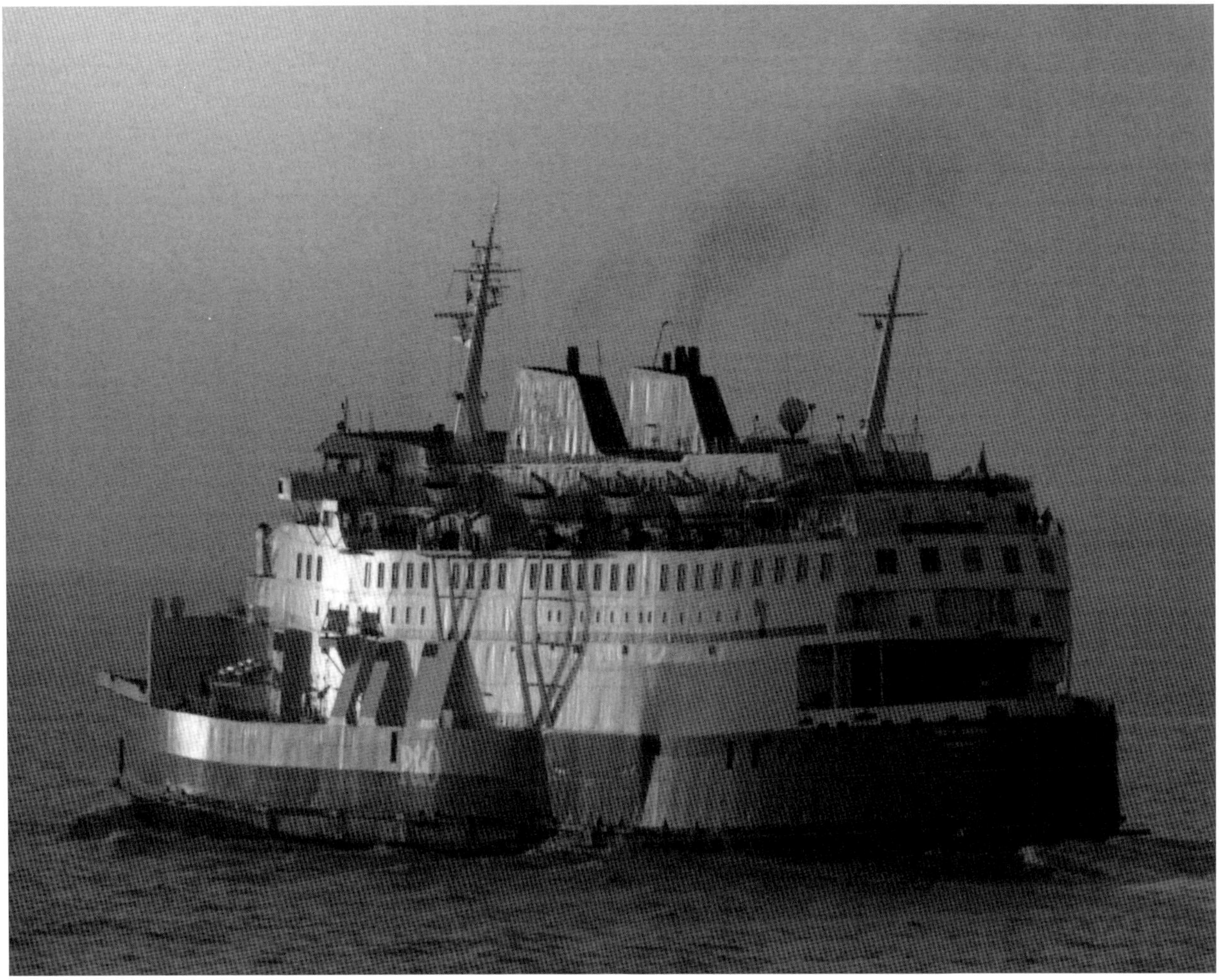

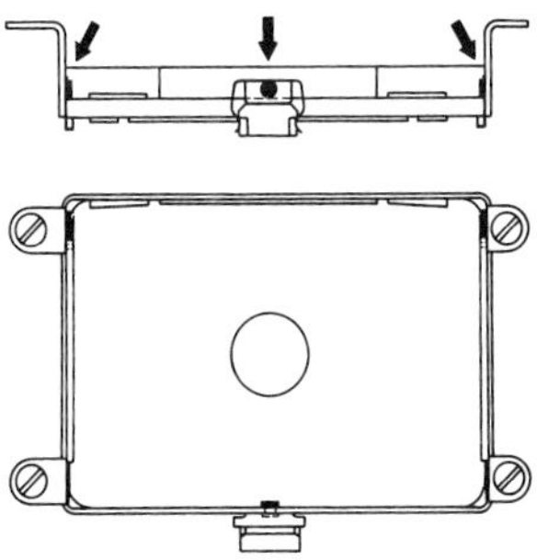

Fig. 141. The focusing screen is held securely in place with a metal frame firmly attached to the inner body chassis with machine set screws.

Fig. 132. The dawn light hitting the side of the ferry was several stops brighter than the areas not affected by it. I used the 'selective' exposure mode and metered off the side of the hull at the back of the ship between the dark patch and lighter areas using a Telyt-R 250mm, f/4 lens on a Leica R6.

and telephoto lens specialists, as well as those working with extreme close-up photography, will find the Uniform Ground Glass screen particular useful. A screen similar to that used in the original Leicaflex and the SL with only a central coarse microprism circle is also available. For reproduction and document copying or architectural users, the Uniform Groundglass screen with grid divisions is available. The Clear-glass screen with central cross hairs is better suited to astrophotography or photomicrography. Each screen has the essential 7mm circle engraved to mark the outer limit of the 'selective' exposure measuring field.

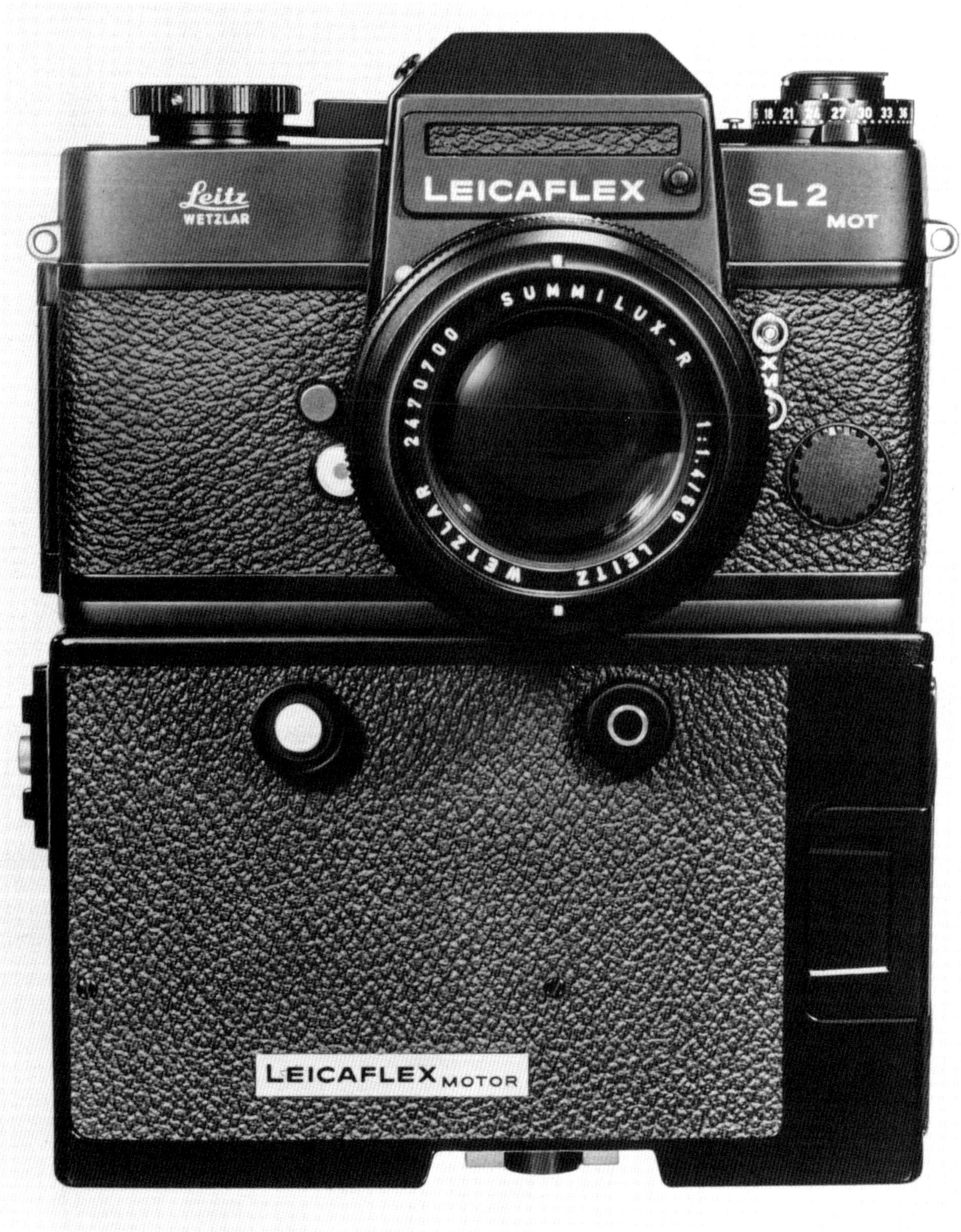

Fig. 145. Leicaflex SL2 MOT fitted with the massive motor drive and integral battery pack. In its day, this was a reliable, first class machine, but like all professional SLR motor drives of the period, it was heavy and bulky. A photographer carrying two SL2 MOT's with drives and a selection of lenses would certainly have grounds for complaint at the end of the day! *Leica Camera GmbH*

CHAPTER 4

Leicaflex and Leica R Motor Drives, Winders and Accessories

4.1. Motor Drive For Leicaflex SL-MOT and SL-MOT.

Apart from the ten experimental original Leicaflex cameras which were manufactured to accept a motor drive, no regular production models of the camera were made which could be fitted with a drive because the modified Leicaflex SL was already at an advanced stage of development and nearing its launch date.

Leitz subcontracted the manufacture of the motor drives for the Leicaflex SL-MOT (1968 – 1974) to the Dresden firm of Max Baldeweg, Balda Werke whose claim to fame is the Baldina range of cameras. The SL itself had to be modified with strengthened winding gear and fitted with the necessary electrical contacts for the drive unit.

Pre-production models of the SL-MOT Motor Drive were fitted with an access panel on the front of the drive; standard production models did not have this facility, but otherwise the unit was the same size and it could only be used on the camera specially designed for it.

The Leicaflex SL2-MOT appeared in 1975. The delayed action device had been removed but in most other respects it was the same as the SL. The Motor Drive unit was virtually the same as the one used for the SL and could be used on the earlier body. Production of both camera and drive unit ceased in 1976 with just over 1000 of the camera bodies having been made. There are no exact figures for the Motor Drive unit but the camera and drive were still listed in Leitz literature until 1980.

The drive unit and batteries are housed in a massive die-cast aluminium casing finished in black, with black vulcanite covering a larger part of the front face. The unit provides automatic shutter winding and film transport for continuous or single shot exposures up to between 3 and 4 f.p.s., depending on the state of the ten AA-sized batteries required to power it, and is fitted with an operating button switch on the front face of the camera at top right where it neatly falls to the forefinger position when held with the special handgrip.

The back of the Motor Drive features a circular frame counter window in the top centre, a resetting switch which also incorporates the exposure sequence rate adjuster (from serial No.2601) and the connecting socket at bottom centre for the remote control cables.

NiCd batteries may be used, but both winding duration and frame speed advance will be lower. During its production life, Leitz advised the use of Varta NiCd batteries DEAC 501 RS in combination with the special Varta battery charger (Varta Code No. 3261 340 011).

Current users of this machine who wish to use more modern AA-size NiCd batteries should obtain the long-life high-power versions and charge them at a rate of not less than 45mA. Previously well charged NiCd batteries should not be used, as even when properly charged, the duration of current supply is quickly diminished. To increase the life of NiCd batteries once discharged, store them in a refrigerator overnight. Cooling the battery has the effect of cancelling the 'charge memory' which is accumulative. Thus when improperly discharged NiCd batteries are recharged, the power retained during charge is quickly dissipated on use. For best results, use a high grade charging unit, capable of the correct minimum charge rate, which is fitted with an automatic charging cut-out device.

Best results will be obtained from the motor when using high-power alkaline or lithium types designed for use with this type of electrical device. AA batteries of the correct type are widely available, but always buy fresh ones as even unused older batteries stored for long periods can dissipate power. Most well known brands are stamped with their expiry date at the time of manufacture; look on the packet, on the battery casing and on the negative end of the battery for dates.

In more youthful times, one thought nothing of the size or weight of professional motor drives. During this period, Leitz, Nikon and Canon all manufactured whopping drives which were substantially manufactured. I regularly toted three and sometimes four bodies, to sports events, all fitted with these monsters and was glad to have them. When Olympus miniaturized the world, other manufacturers were quick to follow suit. Now, one sometimes wonders at the masochistic nature of the species!

Motor Drive Accessories for above

CODE	DESCRIPTION
14 147	Spare Battery Housing.
14 148	(1971) Tripod Holder for mounting Leicaflex with motor on tripod.
14 175	Cable for remote supply.
14 176	8ft Remote Release with push button.
14 177	Remote Release with frame counter – requires 14 178 & 14 179.
14 178	85ft Extension Cable for remote release.
14 179	17ft Extension Cable for remote release.
14 180	Twin Cable for wireless controller and remote release with frame counter.
14 181	(1970) Handgrip for SL-MOT motor.
14 182	see chapter 7.
14 183	Twin flash socket cover.
14 184	see end tables – filters & caps.
14 185	(1971) Tandem coupling device for twin Leicaflex SL-MOT set up enabling simultaneous exposures up to 6-7 fps.
14 186	see chapter 3.
14 187	Cable for connecting Leicaflex SL-MOT with Leicina Super control unit ST-1. (an intervalometer from ½ sec to 360 secs.).
14 188	Universal Handgrip for handheld exposures with telephoto and long lenses.
14 189	Release switch for use with 14 188 on Leicaflex SL-MOT.

4.2 Motor Winder for Leica R3 MOT Electronic

Early production models of the standard R3 could not accept a drive unit. When the R3-MOT appeared in 1978 it was designed with strengthened film winding gears to accept the hybrid Leica Motor Winder R3, manufactured by the cine specialists Eumig in Austria.

The unit is attached to the base of the camera using the tripod connecting port into which the turnkey of the motor winder is screwed home. Alignment lugs and electrical connections on the drive unit permit rapid and secure attachment.

This is a neat and very compact unit using a special winding mechanism to provide up to 2 f.p.s. exposures. Electric motor and drive chain is housed inside a die-cast magnesium body. It can be used on the camera without the special handgrip, and when triggered using the camera shutter release button provides single shot advance only. A separate electro-mechanical release on the front face of the winder unit can be used for continuous exposures, although in the landscape position. Handling the camera with the right hand moved further down the camera body can be a little difficult. The switch is intended for use with the camera in the vertical position.

With the special handgrip attached, the feel of the camera is changed. This accessory, with its leather hand strap, provides a more secure grip and facilitates a continuous exposure mode with the finger-activated grip trigger, which is mechanically linked to the switch on the motor winder.

Compared to the drive unit for the Leicaflex SL/SL2-MOT cameras, the R3 type is about one third the size. It is easily pocketable without the handgrip attached. The winder is fitted with a special battery pack requiring six AA-size batteries (alkaline, lithium or NiCd) which is secured to the winder unit by sliding it into the back section until it locks in place. To unlock and remove, simply press the special locking lever on the front of the unit and withdraw the battery pack. A screw-in bolt unlocks the two sections of the pack. The polarity instructions on the inside of the pack casing for battery insertion should be carefully noted.

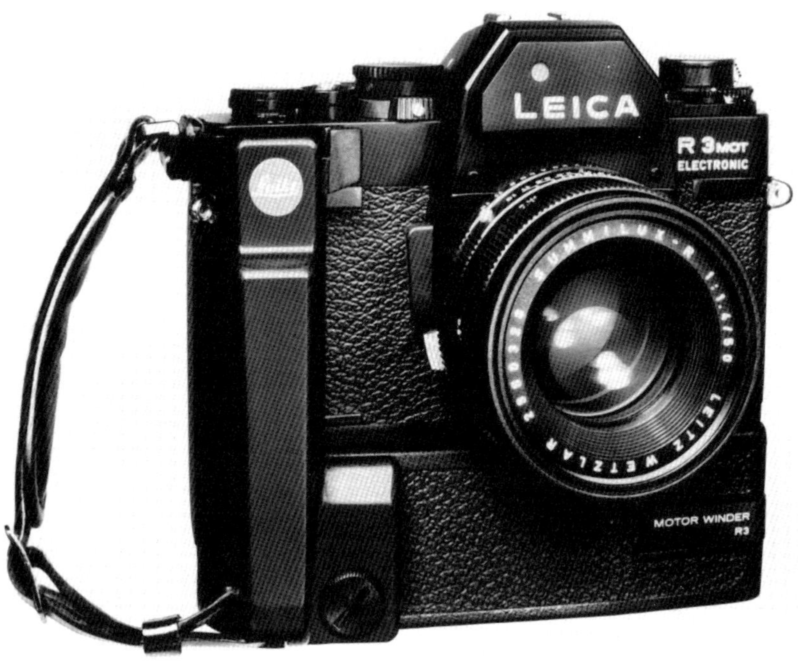

Fig. 146. Leica R3 MOT Electronic fitted with Motor Winder-R3, mechanical link handgrip and hand strap. It had a maximum exposure rate of 2fps. Leitz claimed it was more than a winder, having features of a motor drive. Basically reliable, but nothing like fast enough for sports or wildlife subjects. *Leica Camera GmbH*

A tripod mounting bush offset from the centre is fitted next to the camera securing turnkey in the base of the winder unit. A film wind-on clutch release is also fitted in the unit base. The winder does not have to be removed from the camera when loading or unloading film and this can still be accomplished with the whole unit mounted on a tripod with a head of relatively small surface area. Using the tripod adapter 14 276 permits use of a larger pan-and-tilt head or ball and socket. All functions of the camera can be used with the Motor Winder, including the multiple exposure device.

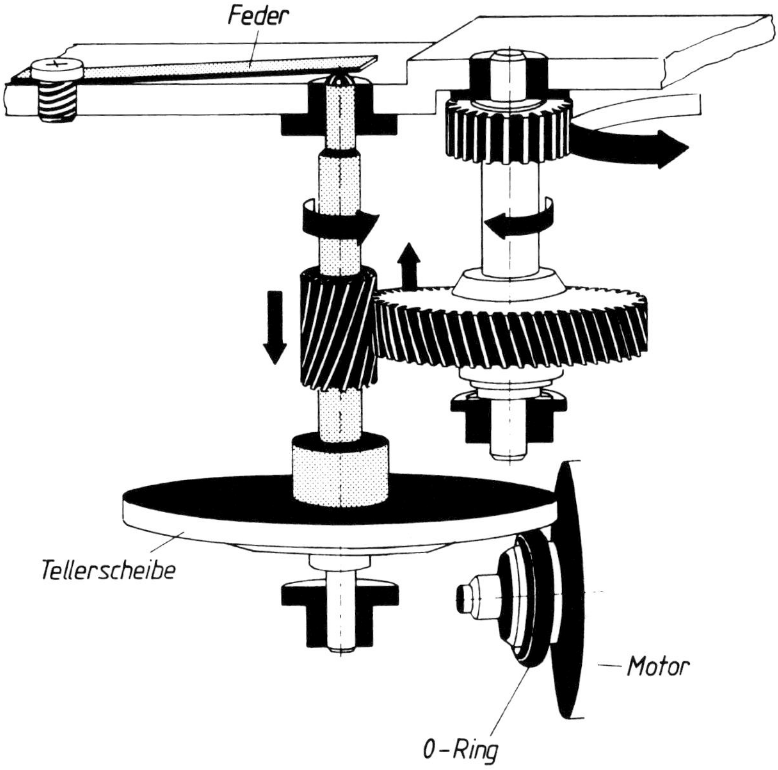

Fig. 148. Schematic detail showing the hybrid motor to drive chain connection of the Motor Winder-R4. The same system is used in all models of the Motor Winder-R. The flywheel of the drive unit is turned by an O-ring fixed to the motor shaft.

Motor Winder Accessories for the Leica R3

CODE	DESCRIPTION
14 271	(1978) Leica R3 Handgrip.
14 272	5m cable with push button release.
14 275	Push button for use with Universal handgrip combined with ext. cable.
14 276	Tripod holder for mounting R3 with motor winder and telephoto lens on tripod.
14 277	Electronic control for remote release built-in timer for remote release digital display confirms exposure.
14 278	Adaptor for remote power supply, to keep batteries in pocket in cold climate.
14 279	Holder for battery housing.
14 280	Spare battery housing.

4.3 Motor Winder for Leica R4 Type and Later

Similar in concept to the Motor Winder R3 with the same specification. It uses six AA cells and has a maximum continuous speed of 2 f.p.s. When fitted to any of the R4 type and later models, the camera's own meter power supply is cut off and the electronic circuit fed from the winder's battery pack. As winders go, it is very robust, housed in a die-cast magnesium body shell and operates at a reasonably low decibel rating. Early models introduced in 1980 (14 282) were replaced with a new model (14 208) in 1986. This is fitted with the electrical contacts which connect with

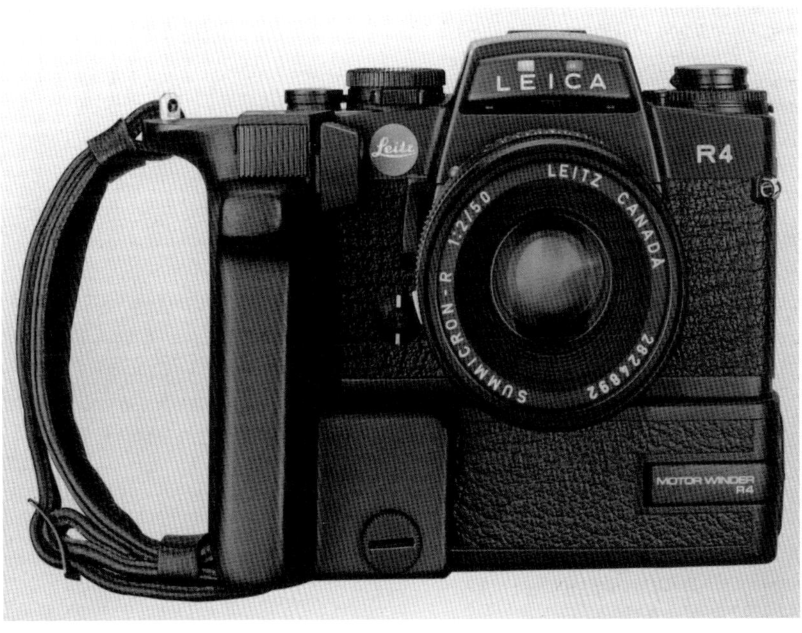

Fig. 147. Leica R4 fitted with the Motor Winder-R4, improved style handgrip but still with mechanical linkage to the winder shutter release and hand strap. *Leica Camera GmbH*

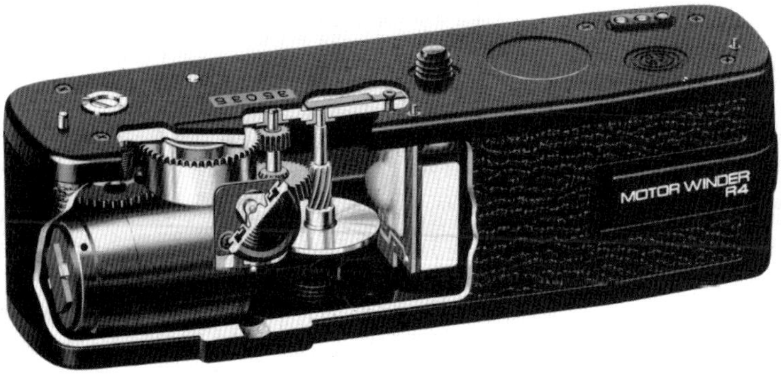

Fig. 149. Cutaway view of the motor and gear chain arrangement in the Motor Winder-R. *Leica Camera GmbH*

the release switch on the later handgrip (14 308).

4.4 Motor Drive for Leica R4 Type and Later

A professional motor drive as opposed to a winder. The Motor Drive-R4 (14 292) was replaced in 1986 with the Motor Drive-R (14 310), designed for use with all models of the R4 camera, the R5, R6, R-E, R6.2 and the R7. Slightly larger and heavier than the Motor Winder-R, its film transport shaft is driven by a more powerful motor and specially geared drive chain offering a maximum film advance and exposure rate of 4 f.p.s., 2 f.p.s. and single shot. The user can quickly reset the rate of advance using the sprung lock slider switch on the front left hand side of the drive unit.

Locating pins at each end of the drive unit and a raised edge on the ten AA-cell battery pack facilitate rapid attachment of the drive to the camera body. A turnkey in the base of the unit screws into the tripod port of the camera base. The battery pack is in two halves, secured by a long bolt which has a coin slot end for fastening. The inner end (right hand side seen from the rear) has plug-in connections to the drive unit and a projecting connecting socket for the remote release unit and connecting cables. A similar socket can be found on the outside right hand (from the rear) end of the drive unit.

The current model (14 310) is used with the Handgrip-R (14 308) on the Leica R4 and later models up to and including the R6.2. Only the Leica R7 requires the special grip (14 317). The extra height of the R7 prevents proper use of the smaller grip.

All camera functions of the models so far described (R4 on) are powered by the Motor Drive-R (and earlier Motor Drive-R4) when it is attached. A set of fresh alkaline batteries provides the camera and drive unit with enough power to expose approximately 150 rolls of 36-exposure film in an ambient temperature of 20°C. Lithium AA-cells will last somewhat longer, but NiCd batteries are less efficient.

Both versions of the handgrip are supplied with a special leather hand strap which is attached to the grip. It fits around the outside of the hand in the form of a girth and can be adjusted accordingly for the most comfortable grip. The earlier grip is a different shape to the current version, with a protruding block at the top end which is ergonomically more secure than the modern version.

The current grip is well shaped to fit the palm of the hand and fitted at the top with a large finger rest platform around the release button. On acquiring my new handgrip, I was appalled to find that while I could certainly reach all the camera controls while using it, my hand frequently slipped off its smooth surface. Unfortunately, I have never been able to use the handstrap supplied with this or the earlier models. I find it too restricting, but it is this item which provides a good deal of extra security when using the motor drive with grip.

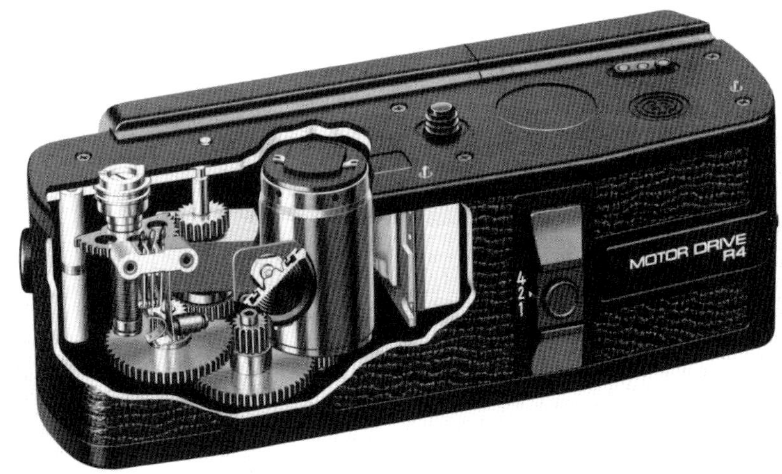

Fig. 150. Cutaway of the Motor Drive-R. A thoroughly solid and reliable accessory with a seemingly endless capacity for work using a ten-cell battery pack. The motor and drive chain unit is far more complex than its slower sibling. A firing rate sliding switch is fitted to the right hand side. The current Motor Drive-R is identical except for the model designation on the battery pack release catch which no longer carries the name R4. *Leica Camera GmbH*

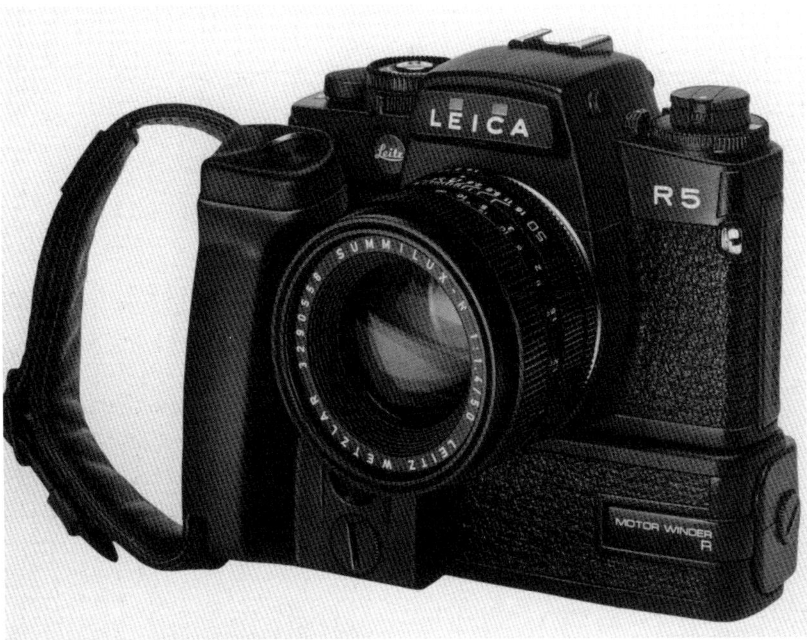

Fig. 152. Current Motor Winder-R and Handgrip seen on R5. *Leica Camera GmbH*

To overcome the problem, I moulded my own customized grip onto the existing polycarbonate base using P38 polyester filler reinforced with glass fibre strands and West system epoxy glue with microfibre filling. It's not something I would recommend you try unless you are fully familiar with the properties of the materials mentioned. The polyester filler will not cure unless a chemical hardener is added to it. The two have to be mixed together in the right proportions before being applied. The only way to obtain a perfect fit for your own hand is to apply large dollops of the stuff to the grip and then wrap your hand around it. However.....

This needs to be done with some caution. As the polyester cures, it becomes warm. It can reach a very high temperature if more than the specified amount of catalyst is added to the mix to speed up the hardening process. DO NOT attempt to shape the polyester mix with an unprotected hand. Use a high quality polythene glove which will enable you to release your hand from the moulding prior to its curing fully. Areas of the grip to which this mix is to be secured should first be abraded to provide a rough surface. Areas of the grip which are not to be covered (such as the release switches and attachment screw, the sides and strap gates), should be masked with poly-vinyl tape. Do not use paper masking tape for this as it will adhere to the filler once cured.

It will pay to spend some time observing how your hand clasps the grip when it is attached to the camera. You will need to make allowances for this when moulding the polyester filler with the grip OFF the camera. A certain amount of reshaping can be done with a modelling knife when the new moulding is almost cured. Cut off all surplus material and then wait 24 hours until the polyester has fully cured. More sophisticated shaping and finishing can now be carried out with an abrasive paper, such as emery cloth, using the wet and dry method. This eliminates the dust factor which can be a skin irritant and for which there is very little cure except constant washing in warm soapy water.

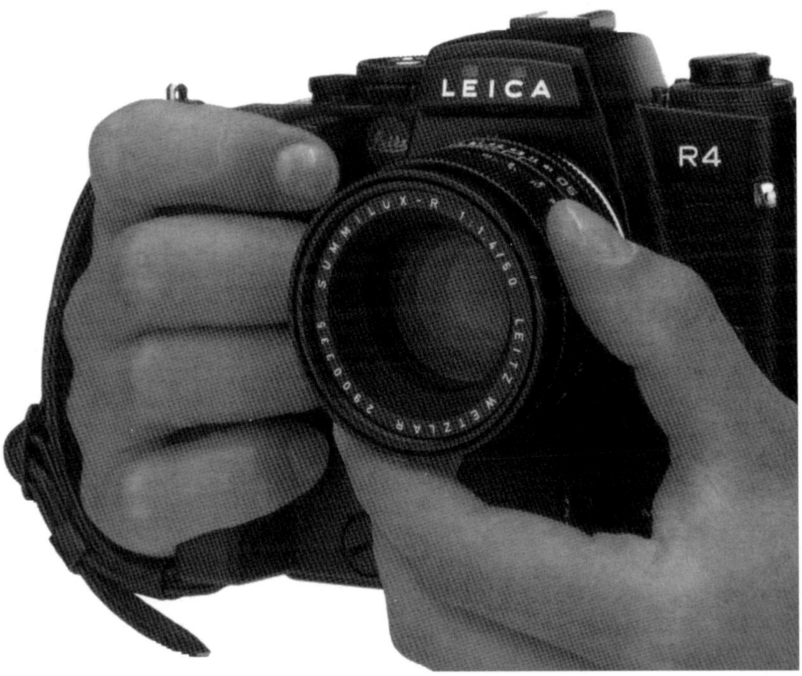

Fig. 151. The correct method of holding a Leica R-type camera when fitted with the Motor Drive or Motor Winder. The hand strap is a useful precaution against accidental slip and provides a firmer but more relaxed grip on the whole rig.

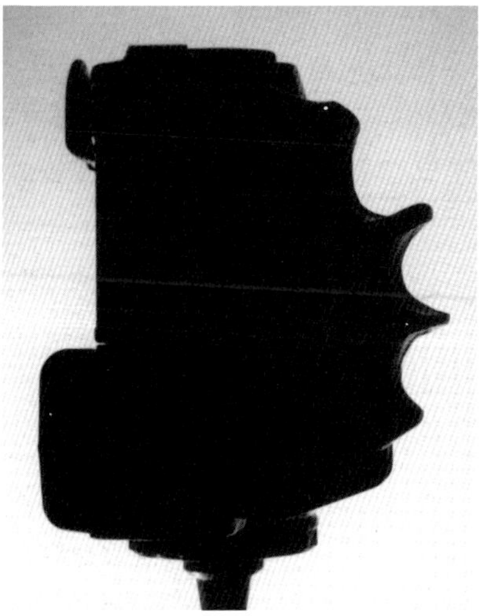

Fig. 153. The author's specially modified handgrip for the Motor Drive-R used on a Leica R6. This provides a true customized grip perfectly moulded to the owner's hand and provides a dramatic improvement in overall handling of the rig. It may be used with or without the hand strap.
See text for construction details.

Once you have achieved the desired grip shape, apply a thin coating of the epoxy fibre filled glue to the polyester, making sure to fill all visible cracks and cavities as well as applying epoxy to the outside and inside faces of the grip so that the polyester filler is completely covered. Allow this film to harden properly before attempting to smooth over the rough edges. Finally, mask off the unmodified portions of the grip and the back with masking tape and then spray paint the new moulding the colour of your choice.

The end result might look like something out of Jurassic Park, but worry not. This will be the best motor drive grip you have ever handled, literally custom moulded to fit your hand only. In practice, my own 'modified' grip works like a dream without the need for the additional strap. I can get a firm but relaxed grip on the whole unit, which even when I am bouncing around at sea, gives me tremendous confidence and a special feel for the camera which does not exist otherwise. That said, I reiterate my earlier warning. DO NOT attempt this process if you are NOT familiar with the properties of the chemicals mentioned, it could be dangerous.

Photographs and a description of this 'customized' grip were sent to Leica Camera GmbH with a plea that they re-examine the existing product to see if it is possible to produce a more ergonomically designed polycarbonate grip, which would be the best all-round solution. However, even the application of a wide strip of composite hard rubber to the palm face of the existing grip would be a step in the right direction.

Motor Winder and Motor Drive Accessories for Leica R4 Types

CODE	DESCRIPTION
14 237	Electric Release Switch-R, for use with Universal Handgrip, 0.3m long. The following items, previously listed for the R3, also suitable for use with this item: 14 280, 14 277, 14 272, 14 274.
14 238	Electric Cable Release-R for remote release with 5m cable or 25m Extension Cables 14 274 up to 100m.
14 239	(1984) Universal Handgrip with shoulder stock. Part of Telyt-R 400mm & 560mm lens equipment but can be used with any lens or bellows. Ideally suited for use with Motor Winder or Drive with 14 237.
14 277	Electronic Remote Control for Leica R fitted with Motor Winder or Drive unit.
14 278	Adapter for external supply MW-R
14 279	Holder for battery housing above.
14 280	Replacement for above.
14 284	(1981) Tripod Holder R4, for use with R4 fitted with Motor Winder or Drive and telephoto lens with Universal Handgrip on tripod.
14 308	(1986) Handgrip with electro magnetic top button release (for landscape position) and electro-mechanical bottom release (for vertical shooting).
14 317	Handgrip R-7 for Motor Winder or Drive. Previous R4 – R6 types not suitable for this camera.
14 322	Spare battery housing. (Following items also suitable for use with this: 14 277, 14 237, 14 272, 14 274.)
14 323	Adapter for external supply MD-R.
14 324	250 exposure Leica R film back for use with Motor Winder or Drive.
14 325	Extension Cable, 5m long for external supply.

4.5 Motor Drive Philosophy

Landscape photographers, macro and photomicrography specialists will probably not gain any continued benefit from using the motor drive or winder accessories described above. On the other hand, some practitioners in these fields may consider the extra weight and bulk added to the camera when fitting a drive a useful enough device in helping to absorb more of the vibration set up in the camera as the mirror is raised and the shutter fired. Entomologists engaged in live action photography with electronic flash might certainly find the motor drive useful when a rapid sequence of photographs is required to depict the wing movements of certain species.

There are times when I find I can do without the extra weight, usually on short travel assignments when personal mobility takes precedence. I figure that if I cannot shoot a cityscape or a landscape without the benefit of a drive unit, then I might as well stop taking pictures. Current Leica R-cameras are so well balanced and correctly weighted for hand-held use that in a way, the idea that the use of a motor drive makes a big improvement, is a misconception.

Where a motor drive scores most points is in the area of fast moving action; news, sports and paparazzi

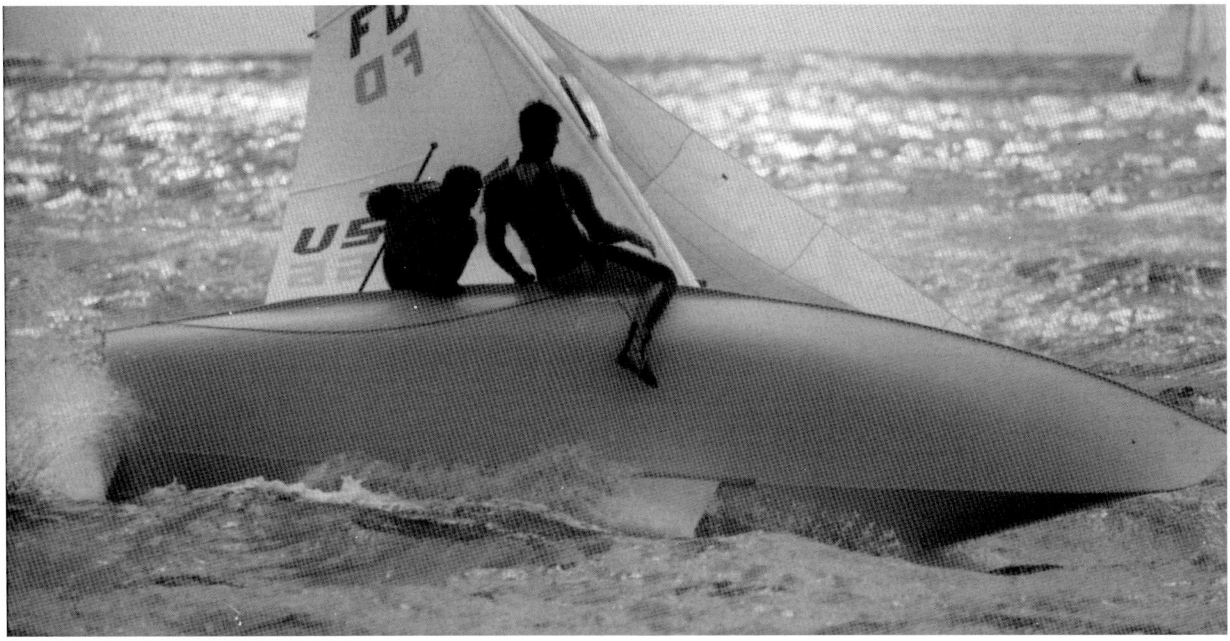

Fig. 155. Going...going... At sports events the motor drive unit is a useful accessory providing the correct balance for long lens rigs as well as the facility which enables the photographer to remain glued to the viewfinder ready to catch the most dramatic moment.

photographers will all benefit from the additional speed with which consecutive frames can be exposed. Oddly, I have never found a need for an electrical drive unit for the rangefinder cameras, but that has more to do with the fact that they are probably easier to fire rapidly without the use of winding accessories. There is also the consideration of objective choice, which for the rangefinder is limited ordinarily at the long end because of its comparatively restricted viewing system.

The professional single lens reflex camera is only limited in this respect by the range of focal lengths supplied by the manufacturer; in Leica's case, a formidable choice of 37 different objectives. In fast moving situations, such as those often encountered by news photographers and photojournalists, the use of a motor drive can definitely be an added advantage in my view. Although I have made many photographs over the years under just such conditions without a motor drive or winder, the times when I have blessed the decision to use one far outweigh those I decided not to. In a real bun-fight, the ability to be able to expose consecutive frames with one hand gripping the camera needs no further explanation as to the benefits enjoyed.

In sports photography, where the choice of objective is more often at the long end of the focal length range, the attraction of using a motor drive or winder is compelling. True, pictures may be made without the use of one. The photographer can always take the 'more measured' stance and bide his/her time, which is perhaps what one should be doing anyway. The flip side of this argument however, weighs heavily in favour of the drive unit as a tool which can seriously enhance the possibility of obtaining the right

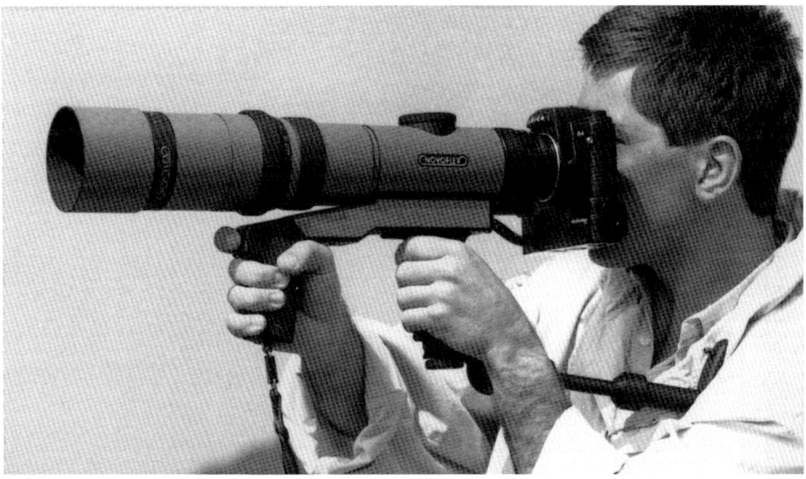

Fig. 157. A Novolfex 400mm f/5.6 lens fitted to a Leica R4 with Motor Drive-R. The front stock of the Rapid Follow Focus Grip is fitted with a micro switch which connects to the drive unit. The detachable shoulder stock is also fitted, increasing the facility to use slow shutter speeds. *Fotoadvise (Mew) Ltd.*

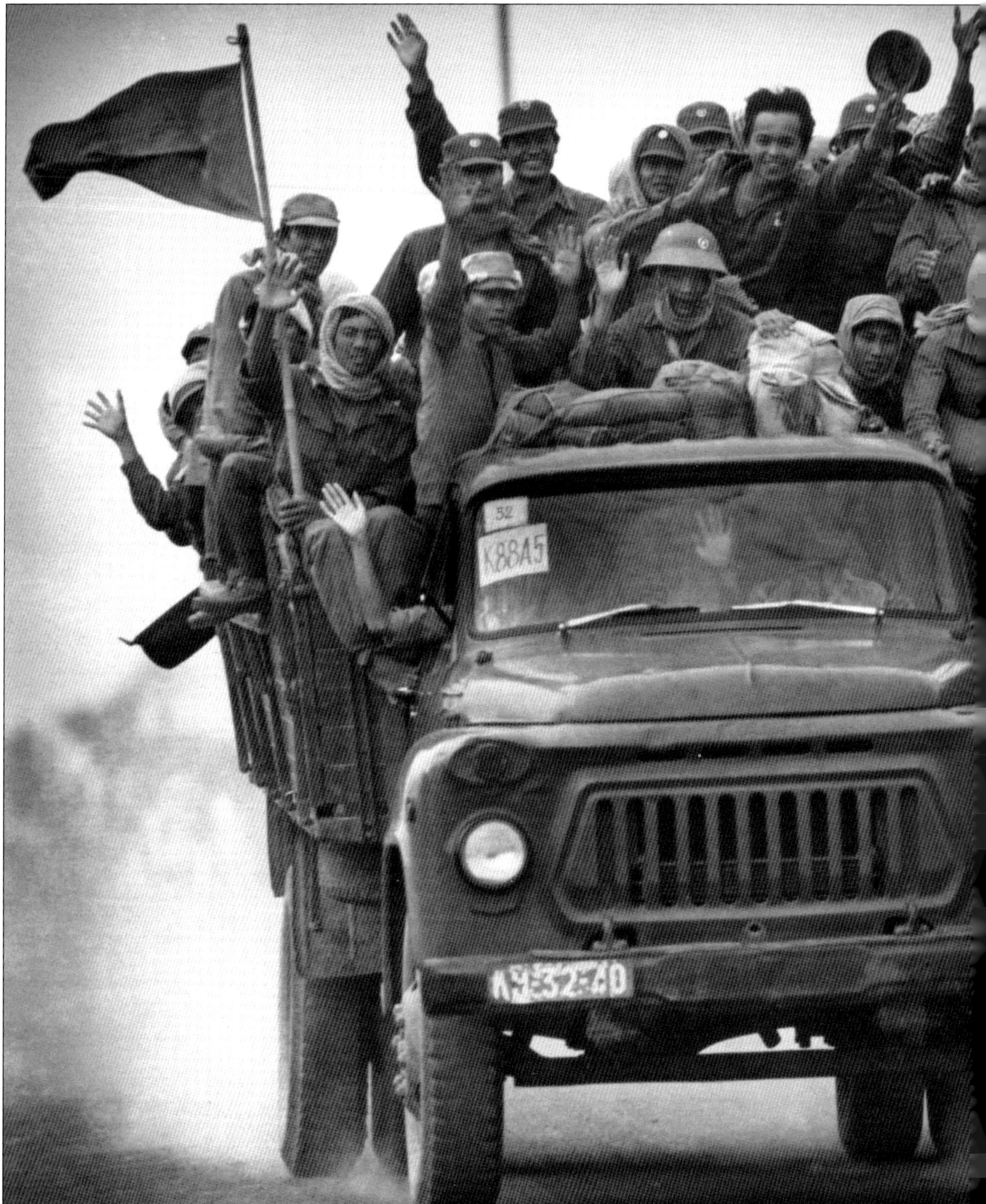

Fig. 154. Vietnamese soldiers withdrawing from Cambodia. Some photographers might argue that pictures like this can easily be made without the benefit of a Motor Drive. It is more practical, however, when using longer and heavier lenses, to fit the drive unit, which helps to improve rig balance while allowing the photographer to concentrate on focus and the moment. It is not necessary to use the drive unit's high speed firing rate, but having the facility enables the user to concentrate on the next frame that much quicker without removing the camera from the eye. *Jeff Widener/Associated Press*

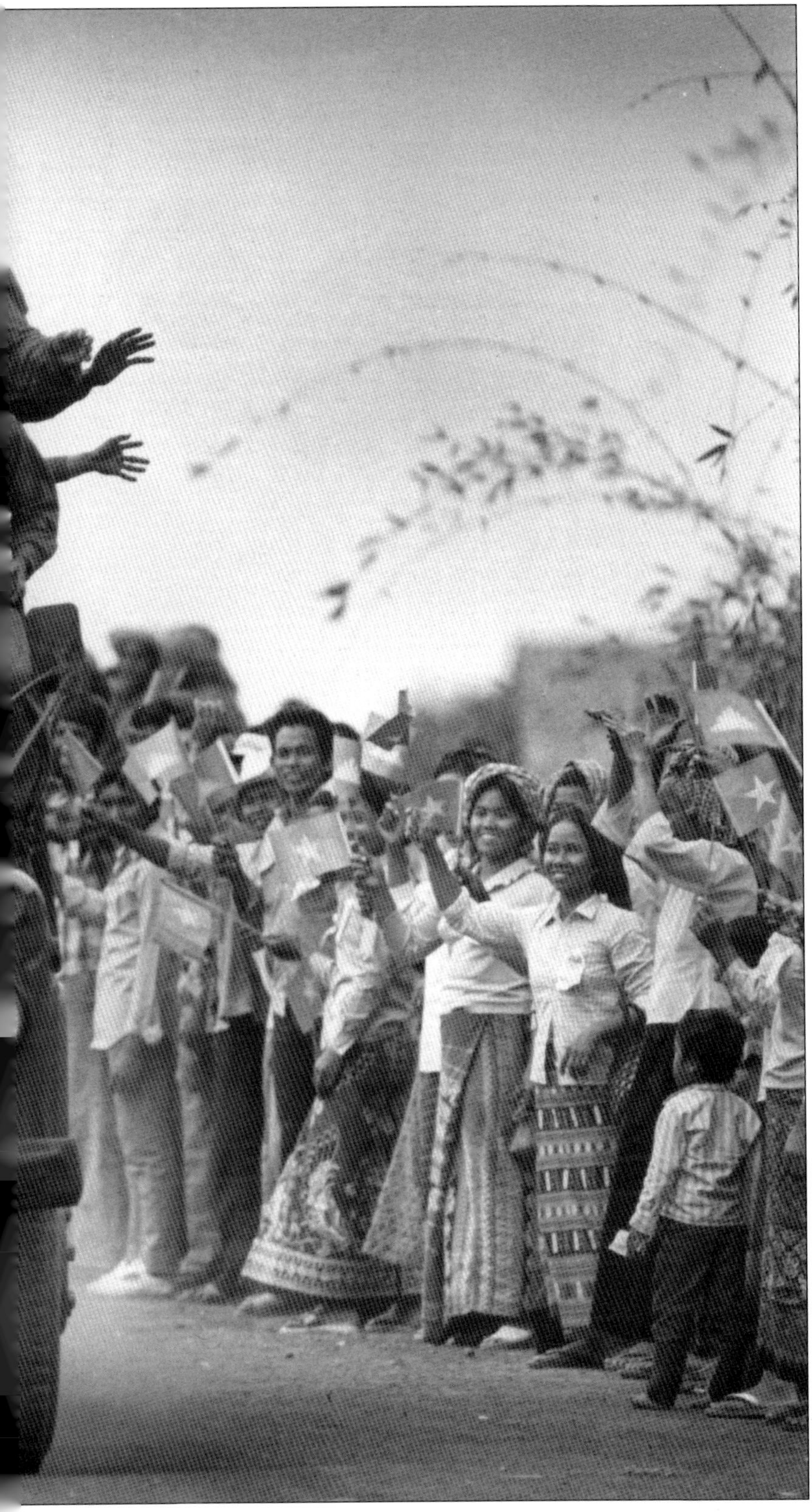

picture or sequence of pictures. The danger of course, is that in inexperienced hands, the drive is permitted to take over. It is not used as a tool to help ensure success, but as a means of exposing film for the sake of it.

Large aperture telephoto and long focal length objectives may all be used on the Leica R bodies without a drive unit attached, but oh, how much more wieldy they become when a motor drive is used. Heavyweight telephoto lenses invariably need the extra weight afforded by the drive just to improve the balance. It gives the user just that little extra bit of confidence in handling a big rig which can make the difference between obtaining the right picture or not, as well as one which is sharp or not. In spite of the availability of high quality, high speed emulsions, many sports situations require exposures to be made with relatively slow shutter speeds. Using the Leica R in conjunction with a motor drive or winder and longer focal length lenses increases the rate of success by quite a wide margin, even when frames are exposed hand-held without the use of additional support.

In air to ground photography, I rarely attempt serious work without a motor drive attached to the camera. The extra mass helps to absorb more of the aircraft vibration, which is transferred through the photographer's body. The higher frequency vibration set up in some single engine high wing monoplanes is often more of a problem than the lower frequency experienced in a variety of helicopters. Shooting with medium to long telephoto lenses simply amplifies the residual vibration not absorbed by the human body or equipment in use, so, aside from any ergonomic consideration advantaged by the equipment itself, the extra mass provided by the drive

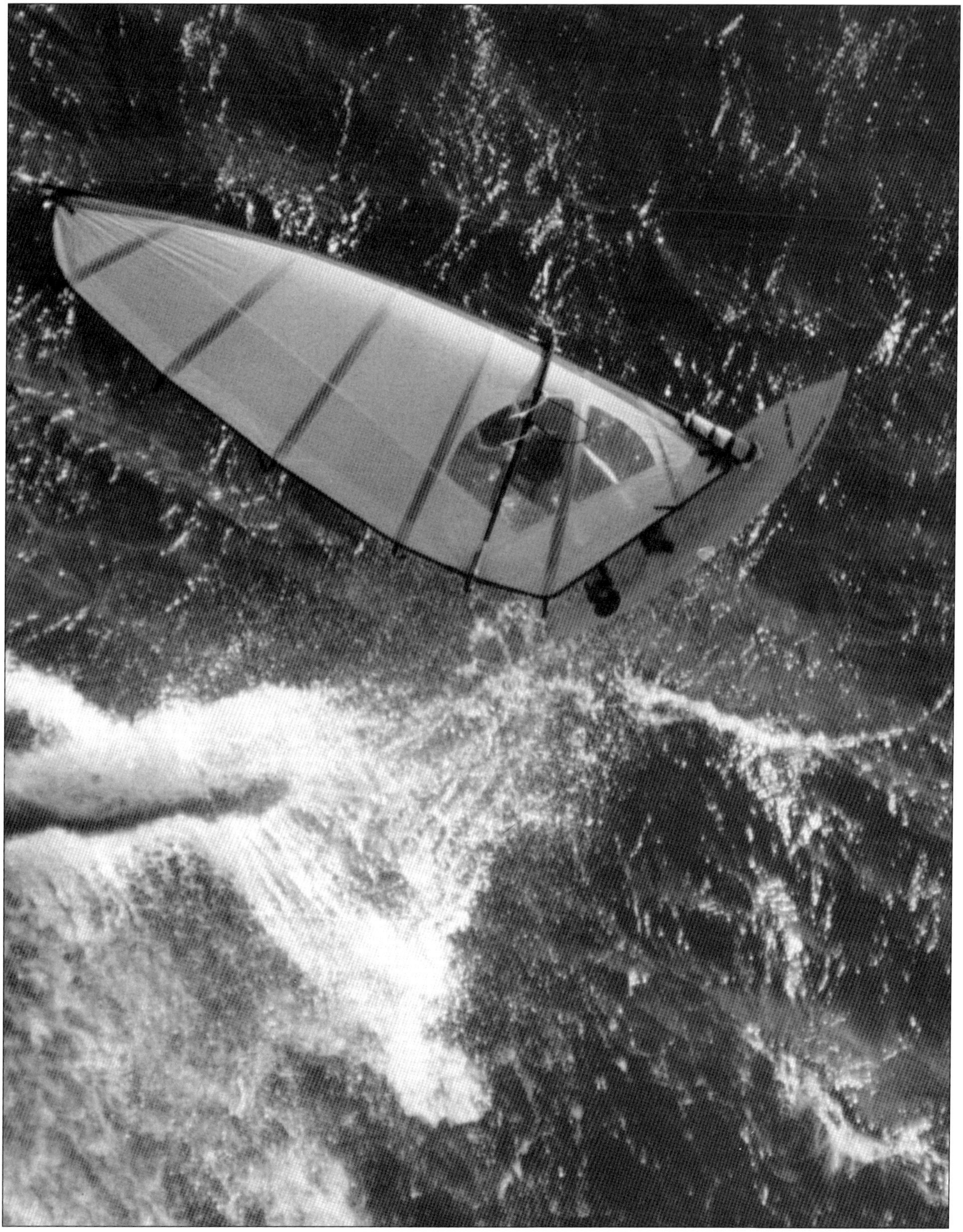

Fig. 156. Leaping windsurfer, Western Australia. This photograph was made from a helicopter at a height of several hundred feet using the Novoflex Rapid Follow Focus Grip fitted with a 600mm f/8 lenshead. This is a section of the original negative and is equivalent to a 16x magnification of it. The motor drive unit enabled me to pick off the jumping surfers as the helicopter rattled around in a circle overhead.

unit is essential to help combat the problem.

And what of the wildlife photographer? Thousands of examples of fine photography exist made with all types of camera to which a motor drive or winder cannot be fitted. Some may argue that a drive unit is unnecessary when photographing birds from a hide, for example. But since the location is static and the operator is mostly hidden from view, the additional noise set up by such a machine is no more likely to disturb the subject than that of an exposure made *sans drive*. My comments with regard to sports photography apply equally in this context. Better to have the facility for that rapidly gained extra frame as well as the ergonomic improvements to balance and feel. In photographing animals and birds on the run, there is no doubt that a motor drive can be a distinct advantage.

Fashion photographers and portraitists might also gain from using a winder or a drive; the former almost certainly as the quick changing scenario often presents many opportunities for photographs in rapid succession. As to the portrait photographer, the demarcation is less clear. One argument is that once the sitter is accustomed to the noise, a more relaxed pose is often adopted, offering the alert photographer a chance to capture the subtle difference between one moment and the next. Of this, I am not entirely convinced. Successful portrait photography requires a special talent and expertise on the part of the photographer. On balance, I would be inclined to the view expressed below regarding the nature of the tool and the kind of reaction it can have with some people, even when they are sitting for friendly photographers.

One final point which might be considered by the more voyeuristically inclined. In this day and age, the sound of a motor drive is one which the vast majority of people easily recognize. In my view, it is a recognizable sound which, for some, is associated with a particular style of invasive photography. In this respect, the photographer's intention may be perfectly harmless; but the alerted subject may not always take the same view and I have experienced a number of incidents when a rapid retreat from a potentially threatening situation has seemed the right course of action rather than pressing home the point. Leaving the motor drive at home affords the candid photographer a better chance of success because camera noise is less audible and perhaps, less distinct. Subjects may see the camera, but because they don't always hear it, invariably smile. By then, the shot will be in the can, as they say!

My Introductory comments with regard to the shape and specification of future Leica R reflex cameras notwithstanding, I have to say that my relationship with the Leica R has been one of pure enjoyment, with or without a motor drive. There are times when, as I have already said, there is no need to carry the extra weight and on these occasions I get a real kick out of using the camera in its 'pure' state. It is surprisingly quiet and an absolute delight to hold when fitted with any of the wide angle objectives through to about 180mm. Beyond that length, experience takes over; the motor drive becomes an integral part of the package which I would not normally consider leaving out for the majority of assignments tackled.

CHAPTER 5

Basic Handling – The Leica 6.2 and Leica R7

5.1. Introduction

Leica single lens reflex cameras conform to a design concept which harps back to an earlier age, to that of the medium format Kine Exakta. 'Traditional' it may look, but many years of subtle design changes have honed the current models to ergonomic perfection. Photographers familiar with this kind of design philosophy will have little difficulty mastering the various controls of current Leica R-models.

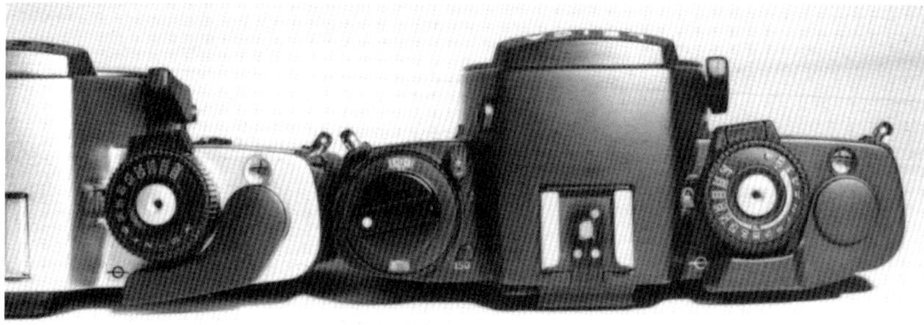

Fig. 158. All Leica R cameras look similar from the top, except the R3. The R7, right, differs significantly from the R6.2, left. The shutter speed dial and program mode operating switch of the R7 permit a variety of electronic exposure programs to be set. The R6.2 lever switch turns the power 'on' or 'off' and is used to select one of two exposure metering methods which are directly linked to manual adjustment of the shutter speed dial or lens aperture ring.

The beginner will find the Leica reflex layout logically simple, even without an instruction manual, but there are various quirks which are markedly different from those of some other brands, as well as subtle differences between current and slightly older models.

Where these differences can affect operating technique they are noted in the following paragraphs and in the main, are confined to Leica-R models from and including the R4-MOT Electronic.

As the reader will have noted from previous chapters, all the models in this group have a family resemblance. They all have control dials and switches in the same place. Back opening, film loading and unloading procedures are identical. With regard to exposure measurement programmes, please refer to Chapter 3.

The two current models, the R6.2 and the R7 are two very different cameras housed in a similar body shell. The R7 is slightly taller than the R6.2, which is a purely mechanical camera. Its only electronic aspect is the TTL meter already described. The R6.2 does not rely on batteries to power the shutter. They only provide power for the meter and should they fail, the camera may continue to be used with the full range of shutter speeds and fully automatic aperture control. All other controls also continue to function. Should the batteries of the R7 fail, it can only continue to be operated using the '100⚡' mechanical shutter speed or 'B'.

All earlier models to the R4-MOT Electronic, except for the R6 which is also a mechanical camera, rely on battery power. So if you have recently acquired an older model of this type as your entry-to-the-system camera, be sure to carry at least one spare set of silver oxide button cells in a pocket or the gadget bag.

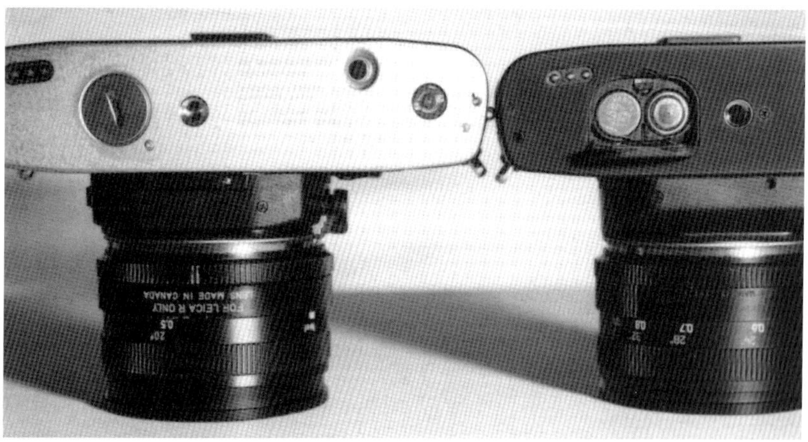

Fig. 159. Base of Leica R6.2 (left) and R7 showing respective battery compartments. The R6.2 has the conventional screw-in/coin operated type covering a housing for two 1.5v silver oxide cells. The R7 features a sprung flap housing twin 3v Lithium batteries.

Under normal operating conditions in temperatures of approximately 20°C, battery life may extend from 1 to 3 years, depending on frequency of camera use. In very cold climates, battery life may be considerably shortened if the camera is not protected from plunging temperatures. A battery test button is provided on the left hand side of the top plate (seen from the rear) which, when pressed, activates the battery test red LED just in front of it. Hold the button down for at least five seconds and note the intensity of the light. If it varies in intensity or begins to flicker, insert a new set of batteries as soon as possible. All previous electronic models of the current R-type can also still be operated using the '100' or 'B' setting placed after the 'X' marker on the shutter speed setting dial.

5.2. Leica R3 Differences

The first all-electronic model, the R3, sometimes manifests a lack of battery power by suddenly coming to a halt with the mirror stuck in the half-way position. DO NOT attempt to force the mirror into its normal position with fingers or metal tools. Turn the master switch to the 'off' position and replace the battery. If no fresh battery is immediately available, turn the master switch to the 'off' position and then reset the shutter speed dial to the 'X' (1/90th second) or 'B' setting. The mirror will return to its normal position and the camera may continue to be used in the normal way. The diaphragm linkage functions normally allowing focus to be carried out at maximum aperture with the working aperture set. The R3 is also fitted with a battery test button sited on the film speed setting ring at the DIN marker which activates a red test lamp on the left hand end of the camera seen from the rear.

Battery failure on the Leica R3 is not a common problem, provided the user remembers to switch the camera power off after use. The switch is located on the rear face of the top plate, right hand side next to the film exposure counter. The 'O' off and 'I' on, positions are not very distinct and are easily ignored. A battery saving device can be simply made using a small triangle of red or orange coloured adhesive tape. Cut and stick this over the 'O' position. It will help to act as a reminder that the power is still on when shooting is finished.

5.3. Leica R Motor Winder and Motor Drive Power Source

When the Leica Motor Winder-R or Motor Drive-R is attached to any of the models described (see Chapter 4), including both mechanical R6 models, the meter and electronic operating system takes its power from the accessory battery pack. The battery test LED will NOT light up when the button is depressed when either of the drive units mentioned are fitted to the camera body. It must be removed before depressing the button.

5.4 Fitting the Strap

Leica R camera straps are unlike most others in their strap-to-camera fixing arrangement. The nylon webbed strap is fully adjustable for length, but its eyelet fitting is a specially shaped stainless steel safety ring which must be properly fitted for 100% security.

1. Slide back the safety loop at the end of the strap.
2. Remove metal hook from the strap.
3. Insert the hook in the camera body eyelet with the bent part of the hook parallel with the side of the camera.
4. Insert the strap through the open end and the narrow part of the hook, then turn through 90° for correct seating over the D-shaped loop.
5. Slide the safety loop over the strap and hook until it is pushed home as far as it will go.

Most Leica R camera bodies from the R4s have polycarbonate inserts fitted to the ends of the top plate above the strap eyelets to prevent body rubbing by the strap fittings. Current straps are thinner and more supple than older heavy coarse webbing types which also had larger steel hooks. The heavy plastic safety loop of this type has a tendency to mark the chrome. Some additional protection in the way of a narrow strip of gaffer tape wrapped around the plastic loop will help to reduce the risk of camera finish marking.

5.5 Fitting the Lens

Hold the camera in the left hand between the thumb – on the front panel – with three fingers on the back and the little finger supporting the base. Align the red mark on the lens mount flange with the red dot on the serrated bayonet lens lock catch. Insert the lens into the mount with the marks aligned, ensuring both faces of the camera body lens mount and lens back face are seated correctly. Twist the lens clockwise until it clicks home.

To remove the lens, hold the camera as described above; press the serrated edge of the lens bayonet lock catch and twist the lens anticlockwise until the red marks are aligned. Remove the lens.

Slightly forward of the engraved red mark on the lens flange, a domed plastic pip is fixed to the lens barrel. This is to facilitate correct alignment of the lens when mounting it on the camera in low light or in total darkness. The raised pip, which is actually a sphere cemented in place, can easily be located by feel in the dark with the ball of the thumb. Holding the camera body as described above in the left hand, extending the left thumb forward locates the lens lock catch. Right and left hand thumbs are easily aligned in the dark, allowing the lens to be correctly fitted. With a little careful practice, owners will soon acquire the necessary confidence for handling the camera under adverse conditions.

As already noted in Chapter 2, Leica R-type lenses are fitted with a single stepped cam. Earlier single and two-cam lenses should not be used on current Leica R bodies or earlier models requiring the stepped cam. (see end tables for diagram and metering cam description.)

5.6 Loading and Unloading the Film

All Leica R camera bodies have a special film take-up spool designed to ensure rapid and secure loading of the film. The base of the take-up spool is fitted with slotted retaining clips. The leader end of the film, emulsion side facing the user, should be slotted behind one clip so that it partially projects across to the next clip. Take the film cassette across the camera back to the cassette chamber on the left hand side of the body, ensuring the bottom row of perforations engages with the tooth on the film advance sprocket. Push the rewind lever home so the cassette is locked in position. With the right hand, advance the film gently until the top set of film perforations is engaged on the advance sprocket. Close the camera back and continue to advance and expose two frames of the film to bring the frame counter to the '1' position.

All photographers using the Leica R for the first time may benefit from practising the loading technique with a spare roll of film. The method employed by Leica is at some variance with other manual loading systems but is very secure, provided the film is properly clipped on the take-up spool in the first place. Make sure that there is no slack in the film between the cassette and the film advance sprockets, or between the sprockets and the take-up spool, before the camera back is closed. If this is the case, it can be taken up with the film rewind lever or by turning the serrated edge of the take-up spool with the thumb.

To remove the exposed film, hold the camera in the left hand, back uppermost, with the right hand end toward the body. Disengage the film advance sprocket by depressing the rewind button in the camera base. Grip the camera securely and with the right hand, flip over the rewind lever arm and begin winding in a clockwise direction. When the film is almost fully rewound, you will feel more pressure as the leader clipped to the take-up spool tugs on the rewind lever. Give a firm extra turn until the leader comes free. Some photographers prefer to wind the leader all the way into the cassette to prevent accidental re-exposure of film. I always leave the leader partly exposed as it is easier to remove the film from the chamber once the back is opened. There is always the risk with the latter method that if the user is in a hurry and the rewind crank is accidentally pushed home at the same time the leader is grasped, that some exposed film will be pulled from the cassette. To prevent this happening, the index finger of the left hand should be placed between the raised rewind crank and the camera body until the film is safely removed.

5.7 Holding the Leica Reflex

It's an odd thing, considering the amount of technical literature that has been published over the years, just how many people hold a camera the wrong way. Even people who know about cameras and who should probably know better, have been seen attempting to focus the lens in a manner one might more

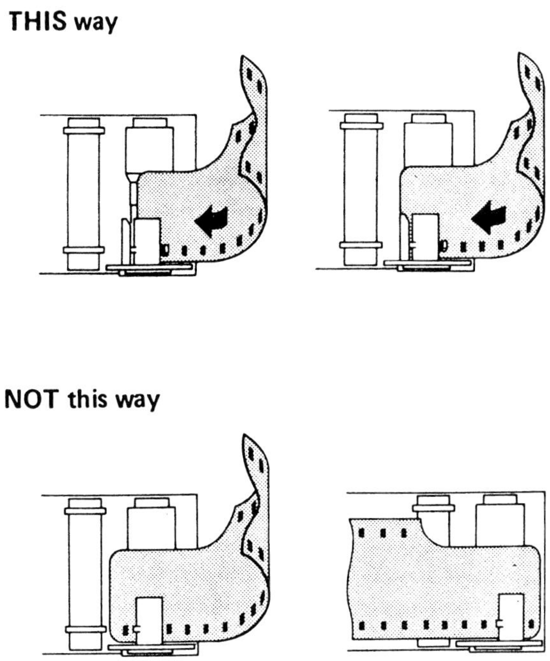

Fig. 161. This illustrates the correct way to load film into current Leica R-type cameras. Always fit the leader end of the film into the take-up spool first, then take the cassette across to the chamber on the left hand side of the body.

readily associate with drinking afternoon tea.

In the absence of any mechanical device, such as tripod or monopod, the more support the user can give the camera the better. Proper handling is a simple matter and is best adopted at the outset so that it becomes second nature.

Hold the camera in the right hand, thumb on the back just below the film advance lever, forefinger lightly resting on the shutter release, the remaining digits spread over the front right side, little finger resting on the edge of, or curled under the base plate. The left hand should be positioned so the base of the palm rests under the front portion of the camera base plate and the camera lens mount, finger and thumb positioned clasping each side of the focusing ring. In this position, fingers can easily be moved back and forth between the focus and aperture control ring.

Keep the left elbow down as far as is comfortably possible. The tendency is to let it flap about like a lame bird's wing. Such movements are invariably caused in the natural order of things, so it will pay to be aware of the likelihood and correct the position. Bringing the elbow down helps to form a more rigid vertical support for the camera and lens; the wrist joint acting in a similar fashion to a ball-and-socket fitted to a monopod.

The Leica R-cameras and the Leicaflex models have an extremely smooth shutter release and subsequent mirror/shutter action. What little vibration is set up by the mirror action is, for most practical purposes, absorbed by the camera mass. Residual vibration is transmitted through the hands and arms to the body. The position of the left arm is fairly crucial in this respect; left to its own device, (i.e. waving), it contributes little to the support function. Properly positioned, it will enable the user to control very long focal length lenses accurately without the use of additional support.

The correct positioning is easier for most people to adopt when the camera is used in the landscape (horizontal) position. In the vertical (portrait) attitude, there are two options. Maintain the horizontal position, keeping a firm grip with the right hand; loosen the left hand grip and raise the right elbow, simultaneously turning the camera anti-clockwise. The left hand end of the camera can now be cupped in the palm of the left hand, the lens control rings adjusted as before. This is probably the most difficult position for many people to adopt naturally. A far easier method is to hold the camera by the lens in the left hand, turning it to the vertical position by pushing the right hand end of the body down. A more comfortable attitude for the fingers operating the shutter release and the film advance lever can then be found. This second position will work reasonably well for all focal lengths, but unfortunately it does not have the same versatility as the elbow-in-air stance, especially when rapid film winding is required.

5.8 Focus and Viewing

Leica R-cameras benefit from a very bright reflex viewing system which enables the user to focus easily even in very dimly lit situations. The Universal screen incorporates three devices which help to control accurate focus (see Chapter 3). The central 7mm collar is comprised of coarse microprisms which flicker when a subject is out of focus. The full field area has the appearance of a fine ground glass screen, permitting subjects to be accurately focused right to the corners of frame. In the centre of the

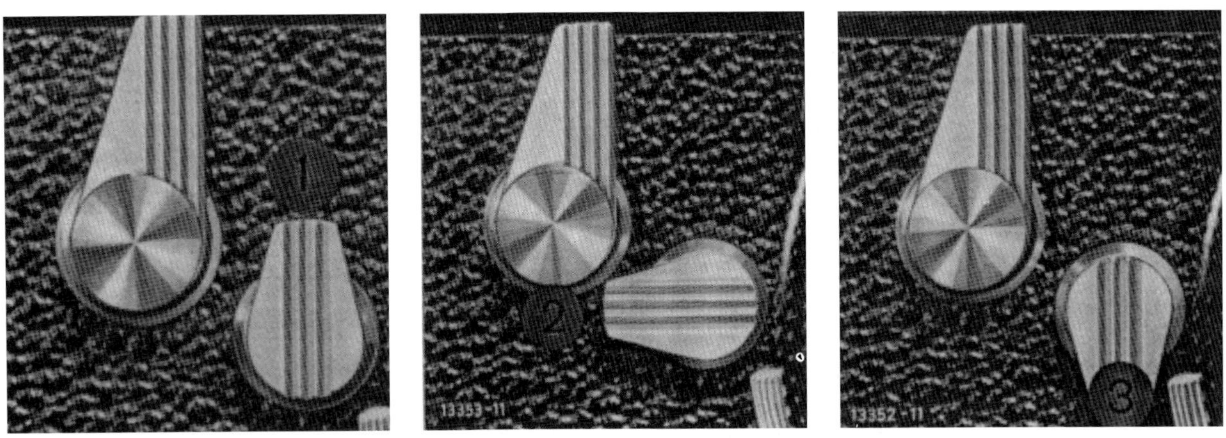

Fig. 162. Leicaflex mirror control lever. 1. Upright = Instant return mirror. 2. Lever moved to side; Mirror-up on shutter release. Remains up until lever position is returned to 1. 3. Lever down. Mirror lock-up facility. Mirror is locked up before shutter is released. Remains locked up until lever returned to position 1. This feature only appeared on the original Leicaflex (Standard). The instruction book gives the following warning: 'After a series of exposures have been made with the control lever in positions 2 or 3, this lever should be returned to position 1 BEFORE retensioning the camera. If the camera is retensioned before resetting to position 1, it will be necessary to make a blank exposure before the mirror will return.'

Interchangeable Focusing Screens

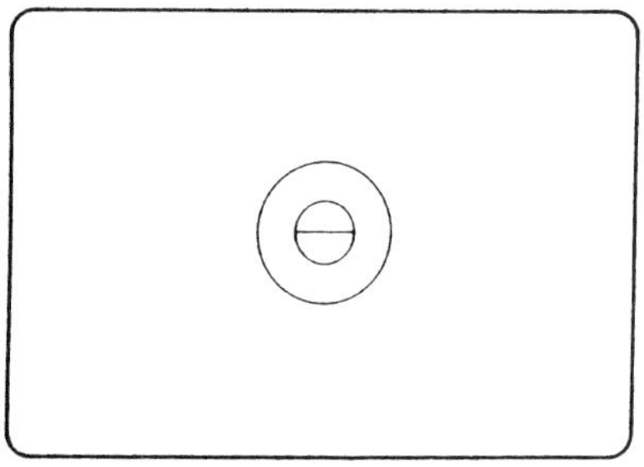

Universal Screen

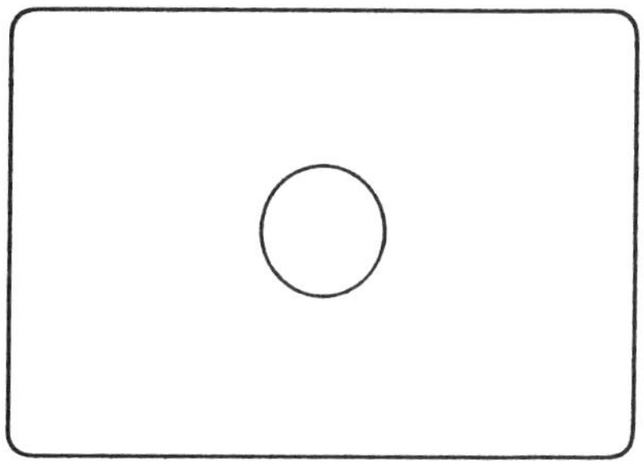

Uniform Ground-Glass Screen

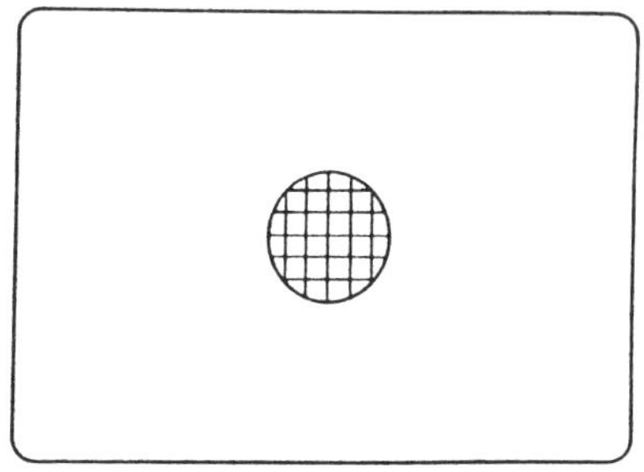

Microprism Screen

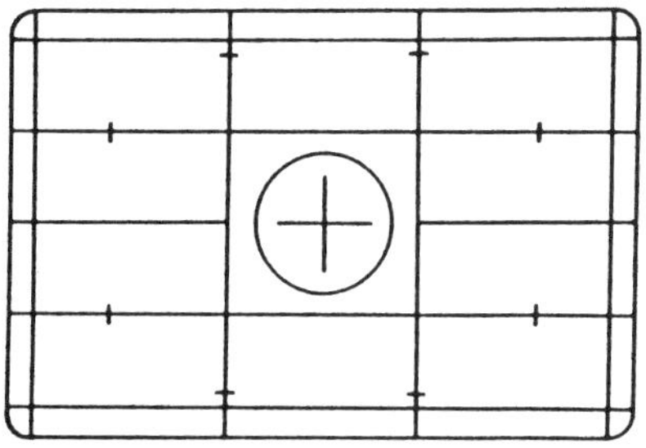

Uniform Ground-Glass Screen with Uniform Divisions

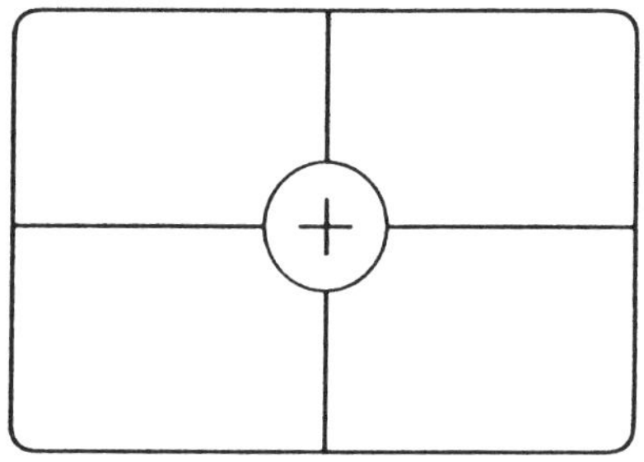

Clear Glass Screen with Crosslines

Fig. 163. The range of interchangeable focusing screens available for current Leica R-type and all earlier cameras back to the R4. These screens cannot be fitted to the Leica R3 or earlier Leicaflex series.

screen, occupying a 3mm diameter circle, is the split-image rangefinder which is useful when the object being photographed has one or more vertical lines or faces. Horizontal lines can easily be sharply focused using this device by turning the camera to the vertical (portrait) position; once focused, the object is reframed with the camera in the horizontal position.

The Universal screen is suitable for the large majority of subjects with lenses in the wide angle to medium telephoto focal length range, and can even be used without black-out of the central rangefinder portion with most of the longest fast maximum aperture lenses. I regularly use a Novoflex 400mm f/5.6 Rapid Follow Focus lens with the Universal screen and have never experienced any practical problems. However, photographers who frequently use focal lengths above 180mm, may find the Full Matt screen a better choice. The object image is clearly seen across the whole screen area with no differential between the centre and the edge. Objects which are sharply focused have the effect of jumping out of the background with extreme clarity. The central 7mm circle marking the outer limits of the 'selective' metering area is still clearly visible, but lacks the coarse microprism collar and the split-image rangefinder.

When the zone of sharp focus is critical, for example when photographing small objects in

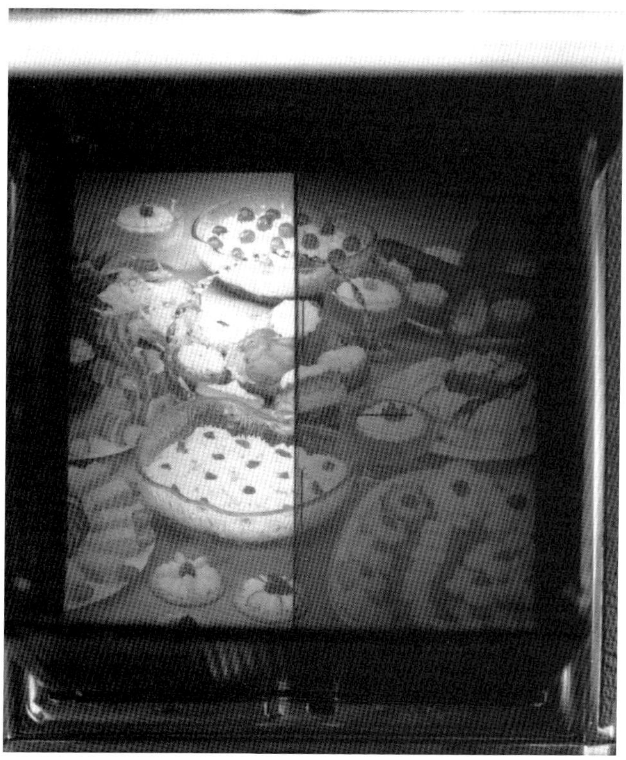

Fig. 164. The Leica R-type viewing system provides the user with one of the brightest screen images available in current single lens reflex technology. There are times, however, when extra brightness can benefit the user, as when operating in dimly lit available-light situations. The Beattie Intenscreen can be used as an alternative to the screens offered by Leica. This photograph illustrates the effect in use on a Hasselblad camera. The brightness of that camera's standard ground glass screen is somewhat less than that of the Leica R Universal type however. *Morco Professional Photographic Products*

close-up, or when wide-angle lenses are used for certain landscape or architectural subjects and when longer focal lengths are used for static or slow moving objects, it is possible to ascertain the zone more accurately by depressing the depth of field lever at the right side of the lens mount. The apparent zone of sharp focus will be visible on the screen and will change according to the working aperture of the lens in use.

As the depth of field lever is depressed, the lens diaphragm lever linkage closes the lens to its working aperture and the image on the screen darkens. The degree of screen darkness will depend on the aperture selected. In practice, the depth of field, or zone of sharp focus, for normally lit subjects can be accurately gauged for working apertures to a level of about f/8. Thereafter, the screen darkens considerably. In very dimly lit situations it may not be possible to see the screen image clearly. This can be overcome to a certain extent where still-life and table top photography are concerned by using a powerful narrow beam torch with which to illuminate parts of the object field while viewing

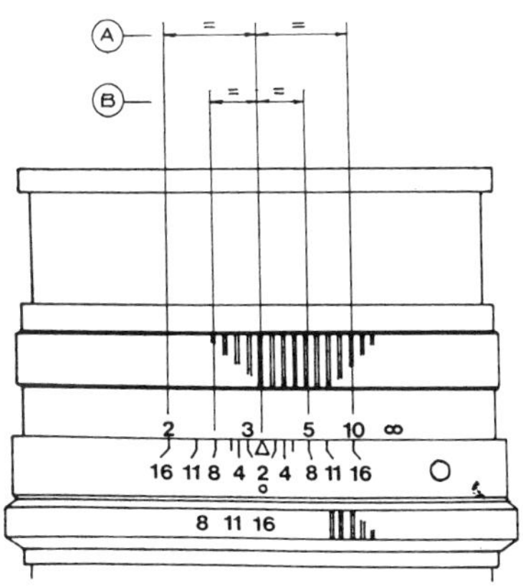

Fig. 165. Depth of field and zone focus techniques. In example 'A' the correct f/stop is f/16 for a zone of sharpness extending from 2 to 10 meters. But a larger aperture may be necessary to effect differential focus where the background and parts of the foreground are thrown out of focus. In example 'B' the zone of sharp focus extends only from 2.5 to 5 meters when an aperture of f/8 is selected.

the scene through the camera viewfinder.

Alternatively, zones of sharp focus can be accurately measured by reading off the distances marked on the lens against respective f/stop settings either side of the central focus index. Measure the distance from the film plane to the point in the scene where sharp focus is to commence. Then measure the distance to the farthest point, i.e. where the zone of sharp focus is required to end.

Set the first distance measured against the chosen f/stop marked to the left of the focus pointer index. Now look to the right of the index and note the measured distance marked on the focusing scale opposite the chosen aperture. If the second distance marked is less than that required to cover the actual object, move the first distance to a position opposite the next smallest aperture on the left of the focus index. Repeat the procedure above for the second distance, reading off the distance shown opposite the right hand side aperture mark. If this new distance is sufficient, remember that the exposure value is changed, a new shutter speed will have to be used which compensates for the change in working aperture.

Once in a while, very small apertures may be required to cover the required distance. The longer the focal length of lens used, the less useful is the depth of field – zone of sharp focus – available to the photographer when the lens is focused at the minimum distance. By gradually pulling back from the object the distance is increased and thus the effective zone of sharpness. But this may now change the framing and object size required.

Many different combinations of object size and zone of sharp focus are possible. These are dependent on three things;

1. Choice of lens focal length.
2. Choice of working aperture.
3. Object/subject to film plane distance required.

In photographing distant objects, such as landscapes, the lens will invariably be focused so that its distance scale indicates a measured distance closer to the infinity mark. Look carefully at the measuring scale and it will be seen that in the majority of cases such as this, the infinity mark on the lens is positioned well beyond the working aperture selected for use marked to the right of the focus index pointer.

Note the closest focused distance marked, opposite the working aperture indicated to the left of the focus index pointer. By resetting the lens focus so that the infinity mark appears opposite the working aperture marked to the right of the focus index, the closest point of sharp focus is increased – i.e. brought nearer to the camera. For most practical purposes, it matters not one iota that the peak of a mountain which for example, happens to form part of the background of a picture, is sharply focused, or just a tiny bit out of focus.

Use of the depth of field lever can give an accurate impression of the apparent range of sharp focus for most outdoor subjects. Accurate control as well as imaginative use of this zone – which is variable depending on 1, 2 and 3 mentioned above, is entirely in the hands of the photographer. Many photographs will benefit from the use of maximum apertures, for example in portraiture where the subject becomes the most important feature, even in snapshots, the use of a maximum aperture can mean the difference between an unsharp and barely recognisable tree growing from the subject's head, or one which is accurately rendered, leaf for leaf.

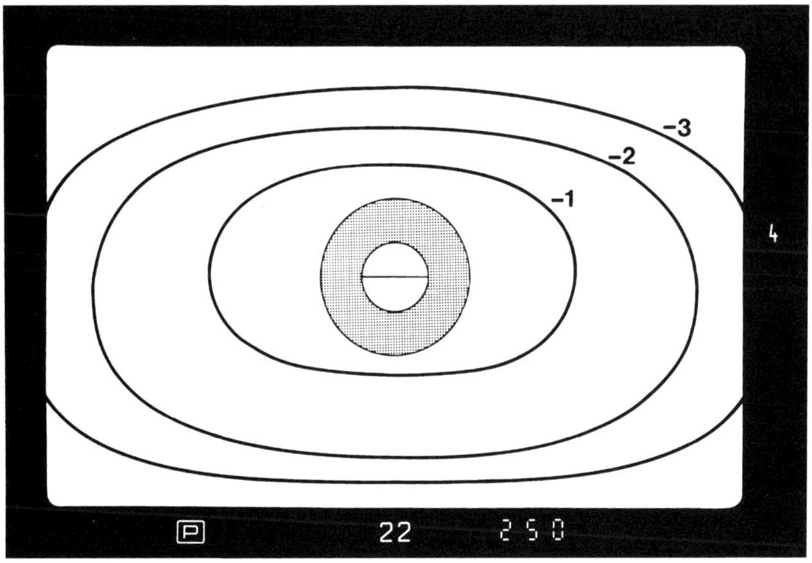

Fig. 167. Leica R7 viewfinder schematic simulation of metered area when the Variable Program mode is used. The rings represent the approximate limits of effective exposure measurement in decreasing EV values.

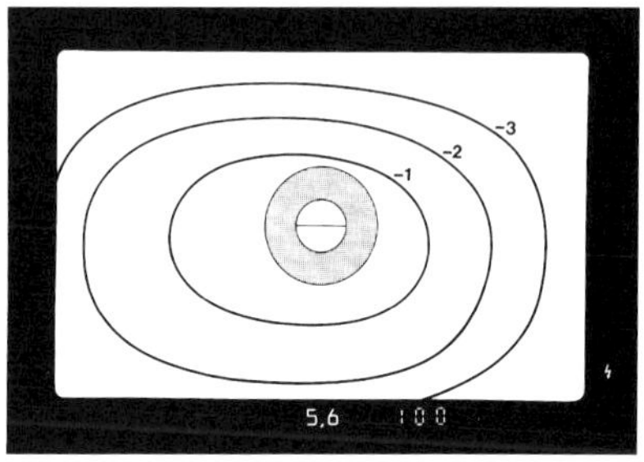

Fig. 167b. A simulation of the screen area measured for TTL flash control on the Leica R7.

5.9 Exposure Metering Choice

The accompanying schematic diagrams clearly illustrate the areas of the film frame covered by the Leica R TTL meter in either 'selective' or full-field, integrated centre-weighted modes.

In 'selective' mode, the silicon photo diode measures approximately 20% of the light exiting the lens in use. The central 7mm marked limit seen in the viewfinder screen is surprisingly accurate as any user will be able to note from aiming the spot at various objects and measuring the brightness range between the brightest and darkest areas. A very definite cut-off point is evident as the central circle is moved around the object.

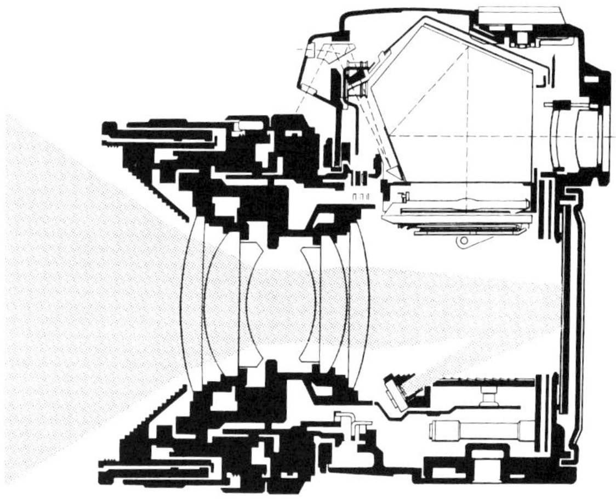

Fig. 167a. TTL flash exposure control is provided in all Leica R models from the R5 onwards. The R7, however, also permits ambient light fill-in flash control. This diagram shows how light reflected from the film plane is measured by the second silicon diode which controls illumination output from the electronic flash unit.

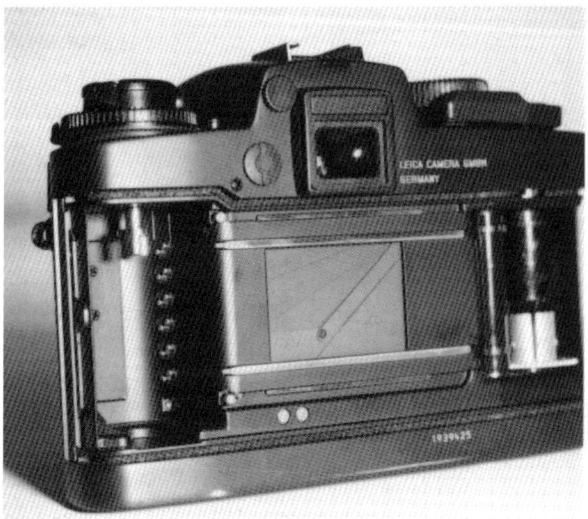

Fig. 166. Back view of the Leica R7 clearly showing the DX film speed datapins in the film cassette chamber at left. In normal use, the ISO speed rating of the film is automatically sent to the main CPU when a DX-type film cassette is used. Manual override is possible, however, by setting the film speed in the usual manner on the dial above the cassette chamber.

The photographer used to a full-field, integrated centre-weighted system will find the 'selective', or 'spot' mode, a useful feature for a great many subjects. It is not, in fact, a fine angle spot meter of the hand-held type measuring perhaps only 2° at most. The selective area in the Leica-R is more of a partial spot, and is of most use in accurately exposing for objects in contrasty lighting situations where, for example with black-and-white emulsions, it is useful to know the range of brightness so exposure may be accurately matched to the brightness range

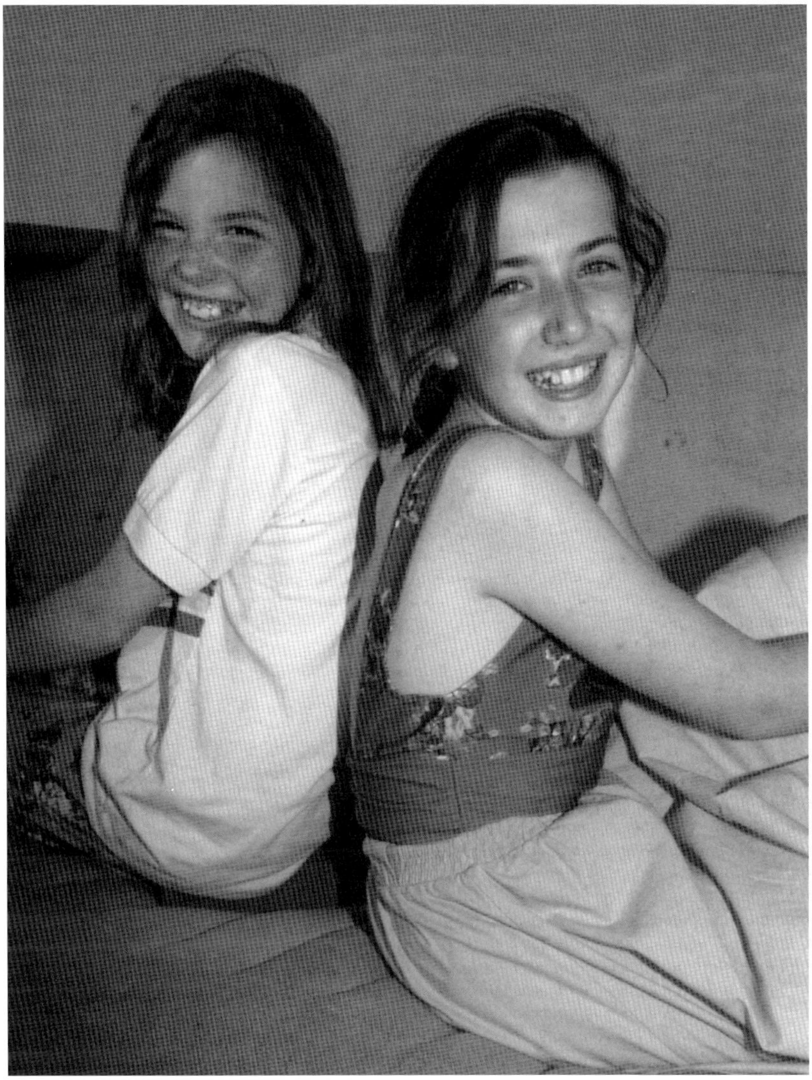

Fig. 167c. A 28mm focal length lens was used with fill-flash to make this picture as the sun was setting.

capability of the film as well as to its development.

The full-field measurement mode can be relied upon to give accurate exposures for virtually all situations where the tonal range is similar throughout the picture. A fruit and vegetable stall for example, may be made up of a display of produce comprising many different colours. Under even, diffused lighting conditions, the difference in tonal range between each item may be very slight. Under these circumstances, the full-field measuring method will provide accurate exposure. The object seen in bright, contrasty light, will have a greater tonal range and in this case, the selective exposure method should be used to determine accurate exposure and the degree of emphasis on certain parts of the photograph.

Backlit subjects are often particularly difficult to expose properly, especially when working from some distance with telephoto lenses. Use of selective exposure measurement eliminates the problem, enabling the user to obtain accurate readings for very small areas of the object. Although the centre-weighted measurement is balanced for a more central reading, with virtually nothing at the extreme edges of the frame measured, the area covered is still too wide for accurate rendition of the object in these circumstances.

Which method is used is largely dependent on the working methods adopted by the photographer. When exposing colour reversal emulsions, I invariably choose the 'selective' mode. Reversal film does not have the exposure latitude of colour negative or black-and-white emulsions. Quite often, a situation will arise when only the essential aspect of the photograph is considered for exposure purposes. Portraiture under a variety of outdoor lighting situations is a good example. Bright sunlight, shade, shadows, contrasting hair and skin tones, the colour and tone of clothing as well as the overall brightness range will all have a significant effect on the exposure arrived at. Using the selective method to concentrate on the skin tones or pick out detail in a dress or other garment, gives me exactly the control I need.

The current Leica R7 offers a wide range of exposure measurement modes enabling the photographer to select the appropriately biased program for the task in hand. Five basic programs are microprocessor controlled; using the Variable Automatic Program mode, the user can customize the program so that it is biased towards slower or faster shutter speeds, small or large apertures. The Aperture priority programs offer full control where the greatest depth of field – zone of sharp focus – is essential using both full-field and 'selective' exposure measurement. Shutter priority will be of most benefit to action photography specialists, while the photographer who wants full control for any creative situation can switch instantly to the

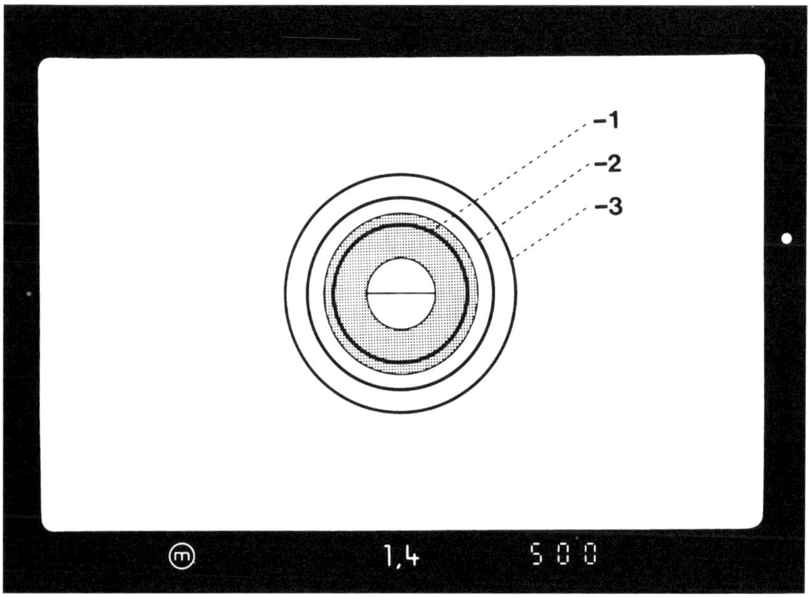

Fig. 168. Effective exposure measurement area when the Leica R7 is set to the Manual program mode using 'selective' exposure metering.

Manual mode using 'selective' metering.

The current Leica R6.2 is a no-nonsense mechanical tool offering the user total manual control over aperture and shutter speeds for any situation linked to centre-weighted and 'selective' metering. The important thing to remember about this camera is that it was designed to fulfil the demands of professional as well as enthusiastic amateur photographers who wanted the sophistication of the Leica TTL reflex metering featured in all of the R-type cameras, but who also required the reliability of a purely mechanical camera. Irrespective of the accuracy of the Leica metering, many professionals prefer to use a hand-held meter for exposure assessment and in certain circumstances, durability comes higher on the priority list than other considerations. That is not to infer the R7 is less durable, just that for some, the mechanical camera is a better option for certain operating conditions.

As a regular reviewer of Leica equipment for the photographic press, as well as a professional user of both R and M types, I am frequently asked by those on the verge of making their first purchase, which is best? It may help to explain that one of the prime reasons for my selecting Leica equipment, is for the quality of the optics. Whether I am using colour or black-and-white emulsion, rangefinder cameras or reflex, the results are identical in most respects. As to the choice of reflex camera, I use both mechanical and electronically operated versions. Neither are current, but they are both R-types. Having reviewed the R7 at some length, I confess to having fallen for its extra height; I think it makes the camera just that little bit easier to grasp, when the motor is left off. I was also very impressed by its range of operating modes. At the end of the day however, only one of these modes can be in use at any one time and invariably with electronic cameras I find I opt for the Manual position more often than not. This is probably nothing more than a legacy from my earliest days in photography when that was the only choice. My second choice would certainly be the shutter priority mode as it is ideally suited to the conditions I often find myself working in. Both the current models are fine instruments, and to my mind the question of which is best only exists in so far as the purpose to which it will be put on a regular basis.

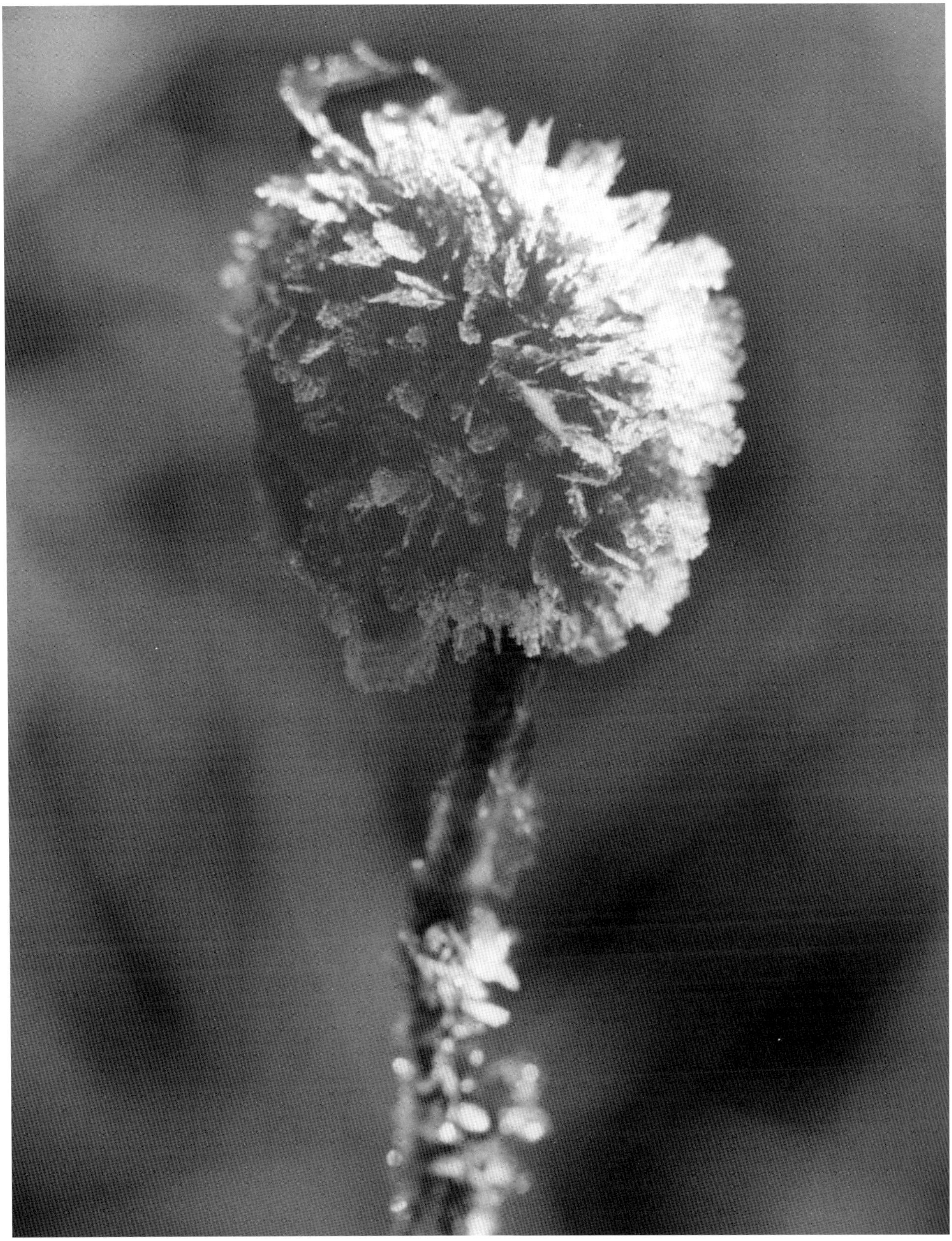

Fig. 169. Ice crystals on a hawthorn berry. This shot was made just as the sun began to rise; the crystals were already beginning to melt. I used a 50mm Summicron-R reversed and held on the lens flange by hand. I set the aperture I wanted and adjusted the exposure on the shutter dial using 'selective' metering.

CHAPTER 6

Close-up and Macro Photography with Leica R Cameras

6.1. Introduction

In the ordinary, everyday routine of life, the majority of people rarely get to see what lies beneath the plane of normal close focus. Our eyes are not equipped for it. Once in a while, an old magnifying reading glass might be called upon to inspect a work of art or an antique, but generally, few of us pay much attention to what lies beneath the surface of what is ordinarily visible.

Close-up and macro photography represent an aspect of photography which can provide a whole new world of subjects, with a range only limited by the imagination of the specialist. Photographers equipped with only a Leica R-body and standard lens, such as the Summicron-R 50mm, f/2, need nothing more to make exploratory forays into this world.

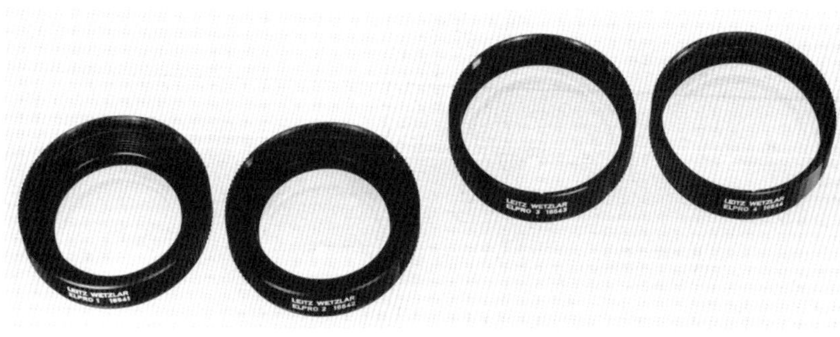

Fig. 170a. Elpro close-up lenses.

Leica manufacture a special range of supplementary close-up lenses, extension tubes, automatic focusing bellows, three special short focal length magnifying lenses, an automatic macro extension ring, and three special close-focus objectives already detailed in Chapter 2. A number of other, older accessories may still be used with current and earlier Leica R-type cameras, and these are itemised further on.

Macrophotography and photomicrography have traditionally been Leitz and Leica strong points. The original Leitz company was involved in manufacturing apparatus for use with microscopes and the scientific field long before it became involved in the design and manufacture of cameras. The origins of the company are well documented in other volumes dealing with Ernst Leitz history, but a brief outline may be useful to set the scene.

Karl Kellner founded the Wetzlar based Optical Institute in 1849. Wetzlar lies on the river Lahn in a traditional iron working area of Germany, some 30 miles north of Frankfurt. Kellner's family owned a number of mines in the district and he chose Wetzlar as the base for his astronomical telescope manufacturing business because of the wealth of highly skilled metal working craftsmen living in the area.

Within a few years, Kellner's operation had added a range of microscopes to the production line, but he did not live long enough to witness the real growth of the business. His partner, Friedrich Christian Belthie, took over the business in 1855, but he was not in the best of health either, and he hired as his assistant a young engineer by the name of Ernst Leitz. Leitz was a precision fanatic and thrived on the problems involved in endeavouring to create the world's finest microscopes. Eleven years later, Belthie died. Ernst Leitz had already been made a partner and now found himself in the position of sole proprietor. The business was renamed, Optisches Institut von Ernst Leitz. By the

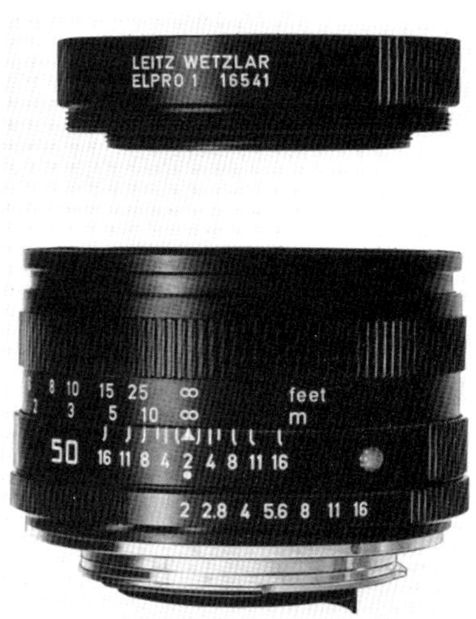

Fig. 170b. The Elpro screws into the filter thread of the lens.

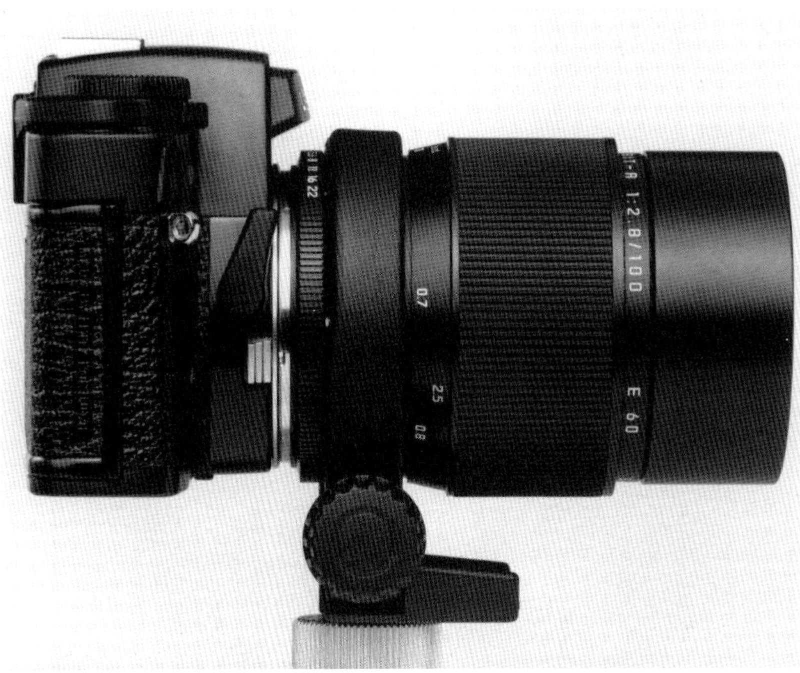
Fig. 179a. A useful device for the close-up and macro worker is the special tripod clamp SRA-1 (14 636) which was designed for the Apo-Macro-Elmarit-R 100mm, f/2.8. *Leica Camera (UK) Ltd*

turn of the century, 50,000 microscopes had been manufactured. This achievement was recognized by presenting the first special serial numbered instrument to the Davos Tuberculosis Sanatorium. Presentations of cameras with uniquely collectable serial numbers to organisations, eminent citizens, royalty and photographers were to follow in the years ahead.

By the time Leitz produced the first Leicaflex, what the company did not know about the close-up, macro and photomicrography end of the business would probably have required a microscope to find it written on the head of a pin. A huge range of accessories already existed for the Leica rangefinder cameras, which facilitated high definition photography in the world of medicine, science and technology. Some of these accessories were developed and modified for use with the Leicaflex and Leica R-systems.

6.2. Universal Camera Attachment for Microscope

One of these items was the Universal Camera Attachment brought to the market in 1971 which allowed both Leica rangefinder cameras, as well as the Leicaflex SL, to be microscope mounted. Exposure metering was carried out using the TTL built-in meter of the Leicaflex SL or that

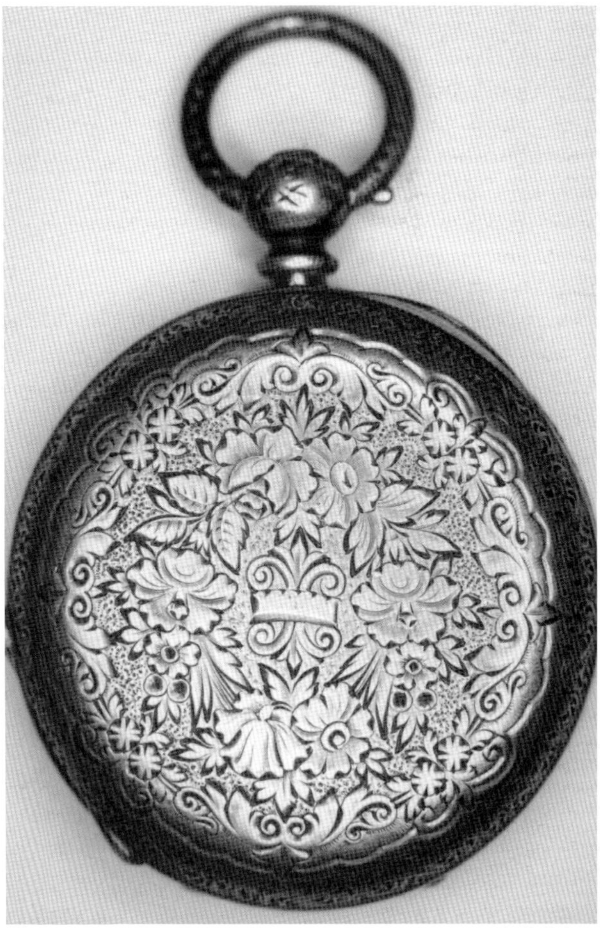
Right: Fig. 180. The Leica Macro-Adapter-R, standard lens and a small ringflash is easily assembled into a hand-holdable rig which can quickly be used to record items of importance, heirlooms or small items of jewellery for insurance purposes.

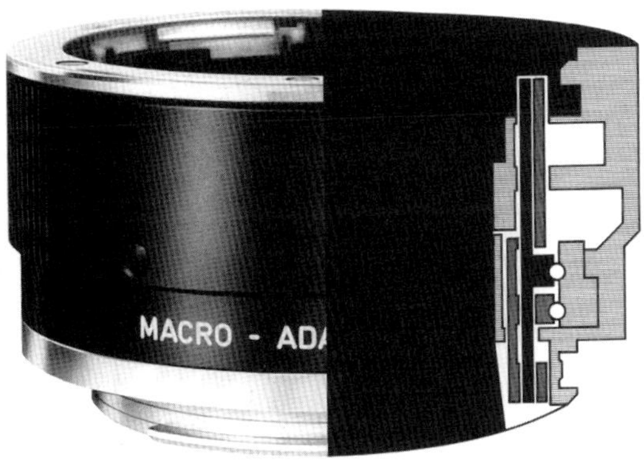

Below: Fig. 179. Leica Macro-Adapter-R (14 256) which maintains automatic diaphragm operation with any Leica R lens with that facility. Gives 1:1 reproduction ratio when used in conjunction with Macro-Elmarit-R 60mm and replaces 1:1 adapter 14 198 originally supplied for this lens.

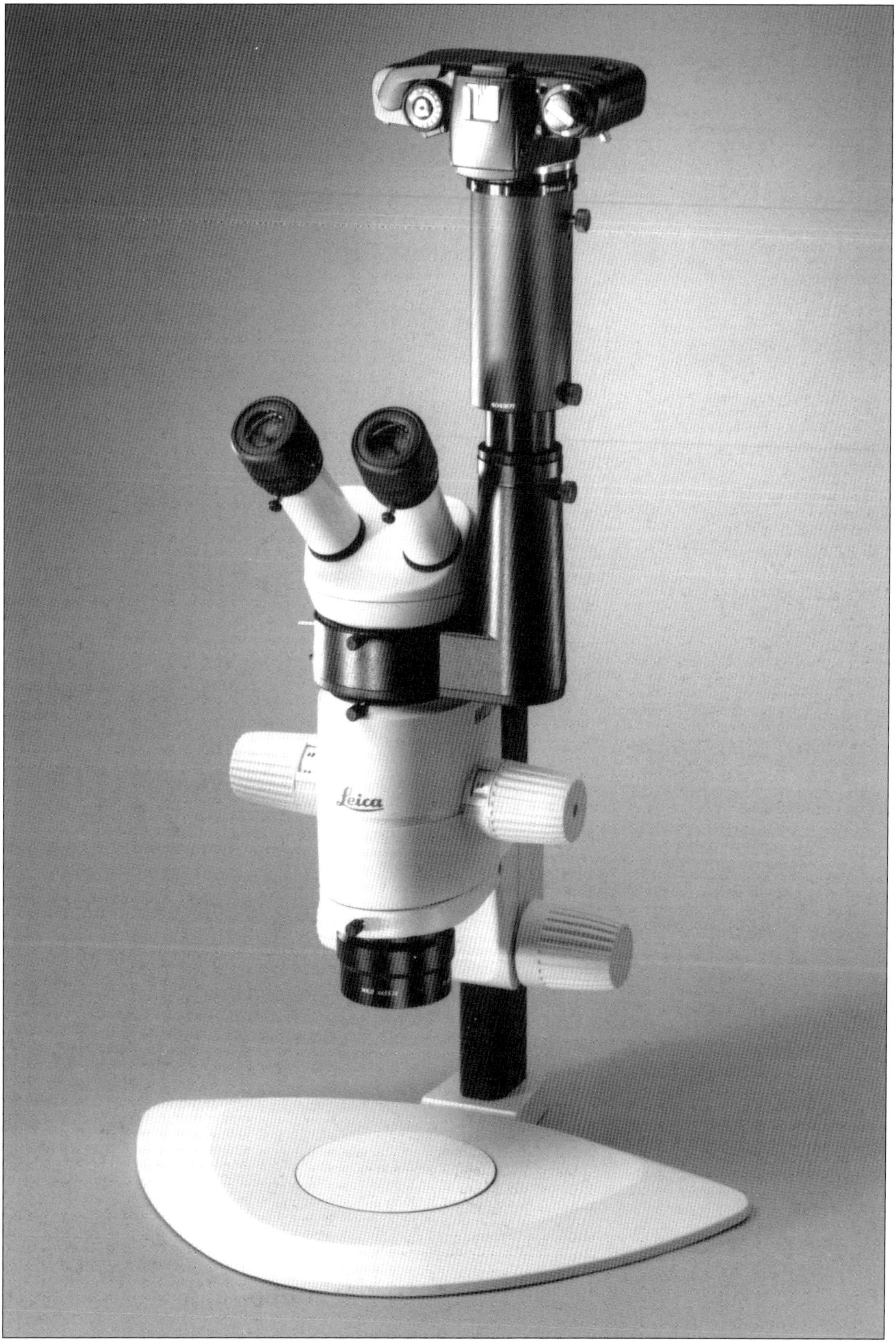

Fig. 171. A Leica R5 camera body fitted to a Wild M3Z stereo microscope. This is the modern version of the Universal Camera Attachment.

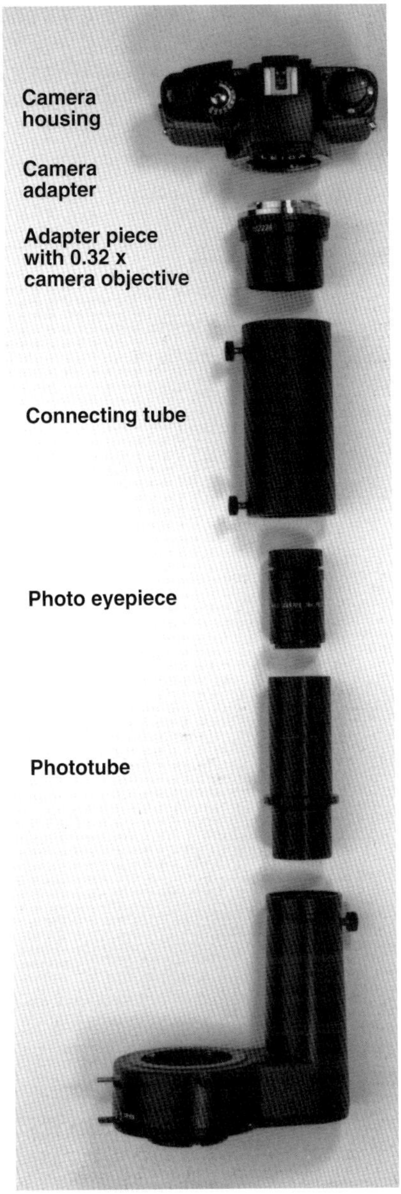

Fig. 172. The separate parts of the Universal Camera Attachment for Microscope.

of the Leica M5. A separate port permitted the probe of the Microsix-L exposure meter to be inserted for accurate measurement when non-integral metered cameras were used. The unit was also fitted with a special anti-vibration mounted Compur type leaf shutter. This was used instead of the camera's focal plane shutter. There was also a facility to attach a simple 35mm-format film transport housing as well as a large format 9 x 12cm (5 x 4in) cameras and a Polaroid back.

Photomicrography, or as it is sometimes called, photomicroscopy, has traditionally been an area for scientific and medical exploration and recording. The artistically inclined photographer has also discovered that this area is as yet, relatively new and holds the promise of discovering patterns of incredible complexity and vibrant colour beneath nature's veil of secrecy. This is an area which is well beyond the scope of this book but for those who are interested in tracking down the various pieces, I have listed below the Leitz product codes.

6.3. Universal Camera Attachment Accessories

CODE	DESCRIPTION
54 3192	Shutter part with exposure measuring port.
54 3058	Microsix-L exposure meter.
54 3194	Clamping collar to microscope which required fitting below 54 3192.
54 3218	Adapter (to microscope) for high-point photo eyepieces.
54 3193	0.32x Camera objective for use with Leica or Leicaflex.
54 3195	Adapter for Leica M-type camera body (fitted above 54 3193)
54 3195	Adapter for Leicaflex (fitted above 54 3193)
54 3197	0.32 Camera objective for use with simple film transport housing.
54 3077	Simple film transport system (fitted above 54 3197)
54 3235	0.8x Camera objective, alternative to 54 3236.

6.4 Special Macro and PHOTAR Lenses for Focusing Bellows-R

Ordinary camera objectives are designed to produce optimum optical performance in the range from the middle distance to infinity. One or two have special qualities in the close to medium distance range, but none, except the Macro lenses, are designed for photographing tiny objects close up. However, for the majority of reproduction work involving handmade photographic prints up to 30 x 24cms, or equivalent size on the printed page, many of the standard range of Leica R-lenses will provide better than average definition when used for close-up work. Where a high degree

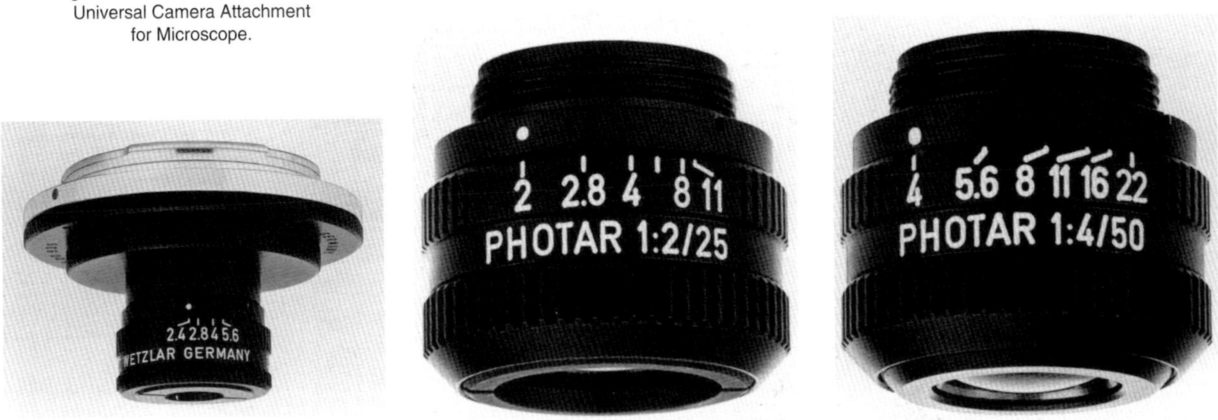

Fig. 173 Photar lenses. Left to right: 12.5mm, f/2.4 Photar in adapter (14 259) for fitting to Focusing Bellows-R BR2; 25mm, f/2 and 50mm, f/4

of accuracy and minimum distortion is required, Leica market a special trio of 'PHOTAR' lenses in different focal lengths which are specially designed for high magnification work to produce exceptional image quality.

The original 'Photar' lenses were first introduced in 1970. They replaced the earlier Summar and Milar lenses which had been manufactured since the early 1930's for the Leica rangefinder camera. These two types had special qualities, the Milar being advised for use where high contrast in the final image was required, and the Summar recommended for superior colour correction.

These lenses had maximum apertures of f/4.5. The postwar versions were coated, and they continued in production until the 1970's when they were gradually replaced by the first of the Photar series. The Summars ranged in focal length from 24mm (Micro-Summar) through 35, 42, 65, 80, 100 to 120mm. There was also a Repro-Summar 24mm, f/4.5 with special mounting ring for magnifications up to 4x (7x with 16 615 ring) which could be obtained with a special L39 threaded adapter (16 615) to fit the Leica Reprovit I (1951), Reprovit II (1956) and IIa (1963) Universal Copying Equipment. The Milars began at 20mm and ranged through 30, 40, 50, 65, 80 to 100mm. The same L39 adapter ring just mentioned could be used with these lenses.

The Photar lenses

CODE	DESCRIPTION.
54 9017	Photar 12.5mm f/1.9.#
16 783	Photar 25mm f/2.5.#
54 9020	Photar 50mm f/4. *
?	Photar 80mm f/4.5.*
?	Photar 120mm f/5.6.*
16 783	Repro-Photar 25mm f/2.5.
16 615	Repro-Photar extension ring, height 26mm, for 16 783.
50 0935	Adapter rings for Focusing Bellows-R (code 16 860) for use with lenses marked * with Leicaflex cameras.
54 2121	ditto 50 0935 (Leitz General Cat.1/73).
54 2185	Adapter rings for Focusing Bellows-R (code 16 860) for use with lenses marked # above with Leicaflex cameras.
14 259	Special Photar Adapter-R ring permits use first set of Photars as well as the following on Universal Focusing Bellows-R (1968, code 16 860) and Bellows-R BR2 (1992, code 16 880).
54 9025	(new 1984) Photar 12.5mm f/2.4.
54 9026	(new 1984) Photar 25mm f/2.0.
54 9027	(new 1984) Photar 50mm f/4.0.

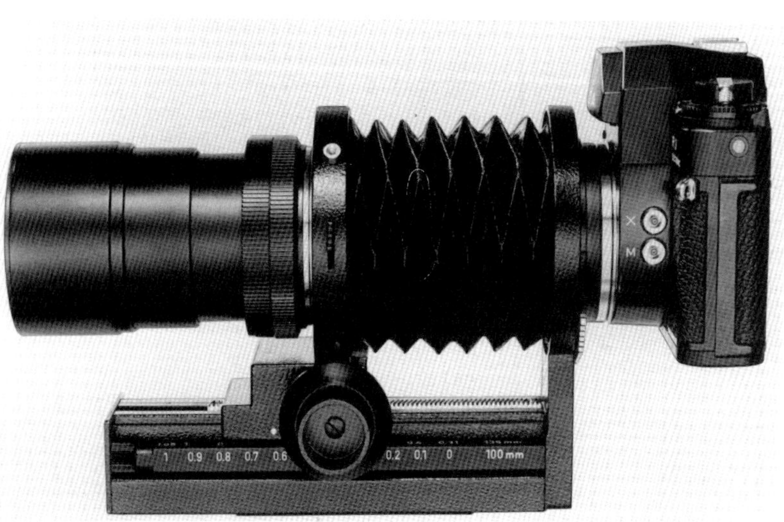

Fig. 174. The original 16 860 Bellows-R fitted to a Leica R3 Electronic. The Macro-Elmar-R 100mm f/4 with lens hood extended is fitted to the bellows. *Leica Camera UK Ltd*

6.5 Leitz/Leica Focusing Bellows for Leicaflex and Leica R

The first Universal Focusing Bellows-R (16 860) was introduced to coincide with the launch of the Leicaflex SL in 1968. The Bellows-R can also be used with the Leicaflex (Standard). The unit can be used in the upright or horizontal format. It is fitted with a rotatable scale rod with reproduction scales for the 90mm, 100mm and 135mm focal length lenses, the apertures of which have to be closed to a pre-set value with the twin cable release (16 494). The Bellows-R also accept the Macro-Elmar 100mm, f/4.0.

Leica lenses designed for use with the rangefinder mirror box housings, Visoflex II, IIa and III can also be used with the following adapter rings.

CODE NUMBER	SUITABLE FOR USE WITH:-
16 863	(1970) Elmar 65mm f/3.5 (1:1.5 to inf.) Elmarit 90mm f/2.8 lens head only (1:1.1 to inf.) Tele-Elmar 135mm f/4.0 (1:1.3 to inf.)
14 167	Adapter for Leica lenses of the Visoflex II/III on the Leicaflex SL (height 21.8mm).
14 127	Adapter for Leica lenses of the Visoflex II/III (with aperture stop simulation device for the Leicaflex (Standard) with external exposure measurement) (height 21.8mm).

The Macro-Elmar 100mm, f/4.0 could be supplied as the lens head unit only for use with the Bellows-R, giving a reproduction range of 1:1 to inf. (16 494 as lens head only).

The current Universal Focusing Bellows-R BR2 is fitted with a cam enabling the automatic diaphragm features of the majority of current Leica-R objectives to be used, thus retaining full use of all electronic exposure programs in current Leica-R models.

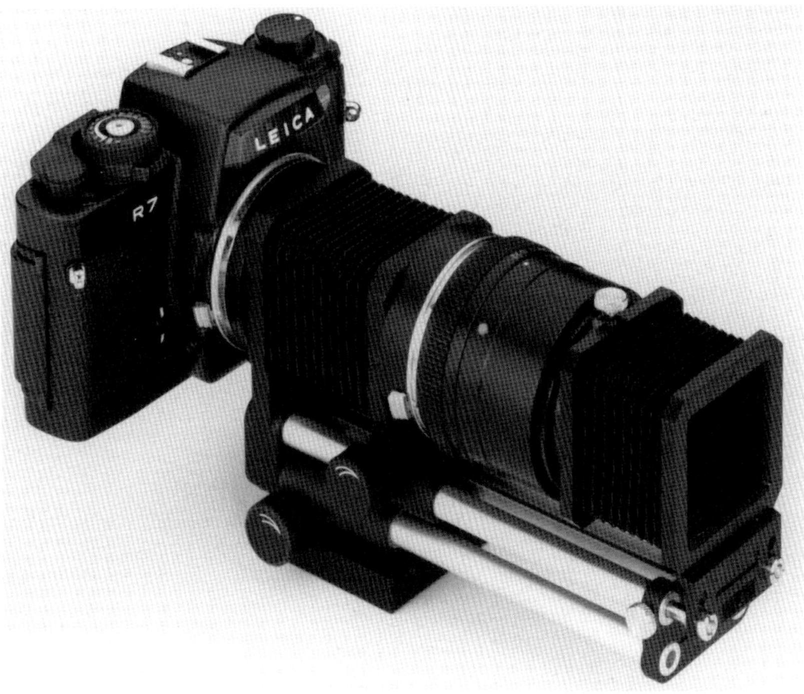

Fig. 175. Current Universal Focusing Bellows-R BR2, manufactured for Leica by Novoflex, with automatic diaphragm connector, on a Leica R7. The current 100mm Macro-Elmar f/4 lens fitted permits continuous focusing from infinity to 1:1.1 The special bellows lenshood is also fitted.
Leica Camera UK Ltd

The maximum extension of the bellows unit is 11cms, and it is supplied complete with a special bellows-type lens hood carried on twin guide rails. It is attached to the lens head with a set-screw-operated clamping ring. These new bellows are superbly manufactured by Novoflex Fotogeratebau of Memmingen for Leica Camera GmbH.

6.6 Third-party Accessories for Close-up and Macro Work Suitable for Leica R-Cameras

Since the break-up of the family owned Leitz group and the formation of Leica Camera GmbH in the 1980s, a great deal of rationalization within the new company has resulted in some accessories manufactured for the Leicaflex and early Leica R-type cameras being discontinued. Many of the accessories for close-up and macro-photography manufactured for the Leica rangefinder cameras had previously been discontinued. One of the reasons for this was so that a more rapid development plan could be instigated to expand the Leica R-system in the lens department, which for some time had lacked many of the more exotic objectives produced by other marques.

Two companies manufacturing the type of accessories suitable for use with the Leica R-models are based in Germany. One, as has already been noted, has been involved with Leitz and Leica for some years in manufacturing special products. Both Novoflex and Kaiser make a wide variety of products from special clamping sets for small objects to focusing bellows units, adapter rings and electronic lighting units.

The Novoflex Macrolight Plus can be operated from an electronic flash or cold-light source. The Macrolight unit employs a system of mirrors and fibre optics in three flexible light guides 50cm long to deliver the light which may be placed by the photographer in exactly the right spot. The Novoflex cold-light source unit will accept a variety of electronic flash units, including the range of Metz and Mecablitz guns which are ideally suited for use with Leica R-cameras in conjunction with the SCA adapters. This facility enables macro specialists to maintain full use of the TTL flash exposure program with all Leica R-bodies from the R5 to the present R7. For setting up, the unit is fitted with a 24 volt, 150 watt tungsten halogen lamp. This system is available with a number of accessories, including a focusing lens with 18 colour filters, three additional focusing lenses and three filter holders. The manufacturer's product code is MAKL-150.

Kaiser Fototechnik GmbH of Buchen manufactures a system for close-up and macro photography which is modular in construction and requires a variety of components. The company's Macrospot 1500 illuminator employs 150 watt halogen lamps with a regulated emission of 3400°K. Up to three extra flexible light units may be fitted as well as a ring-light for shadowless lighting.

Some Minolta electronic flash units may also be used with Leica R-cameras. In particular, the Minolta Auto Electroflash Macro 80PX ring-flash is an ideal lighting unit for photographing a wide variety of objects. To mount this accessory on the Leica R5/R6/R6.2 and R7 you will required the special Leica RBA Ring Flash Adapter (14 410).

Another excellent type of ring-flash suitable for use with all Leica R-cameras featuring TTL flash control is the Yuzo Automatic Macroflash. This unit employs a

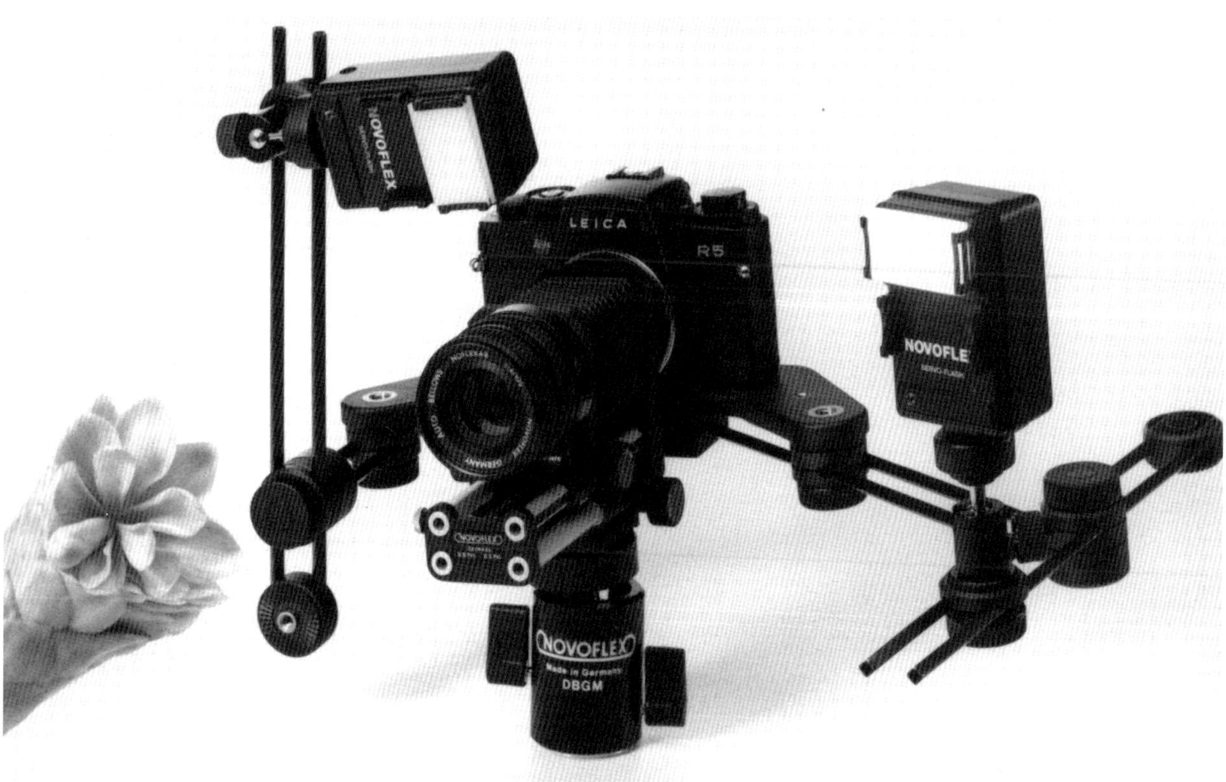

Fig. 178. A Leica R5 fitted with Novoflex Auto Focusing Bellows, Noflexar 105mm, f/4 auto lens and Novoflex Uniset multi-bracket system.
Fotoadvise (Mew) Ltd

similar interchangeable type of hotshoe control module to the Metz SCA type which maintains all the normal camera functions. The Yuzo flash unit is unusual in that, in addition to the ring-flash, it incorporates a point-source flash moulded into the main light ring. Either light source may be used separately. The unit is attached to the Leica R-lens by means of a substantial milled-edge, step-down filter thread adapter ring.

Novoflex manufacture what is probably the most comprehensive

Fig. 177. An exploration into the world of Leica minutia using the Yuzo automatic Macroflash, a Summicron-R 50mm, f/2 lens and the Macro Adapter-R. These pictures were all made on colour negative 100 ISO film using the 1/16th power feature on the Yuzo Macroflash. Very little reflection is apparent on objects with bright metal finishes, such as satin chrome. Shiny surfaces are more at risk, however. If the object can be easily cleaned and is of no great value, some of its reflective properties can be reduced by spraying the item with a light coating of hair spray.

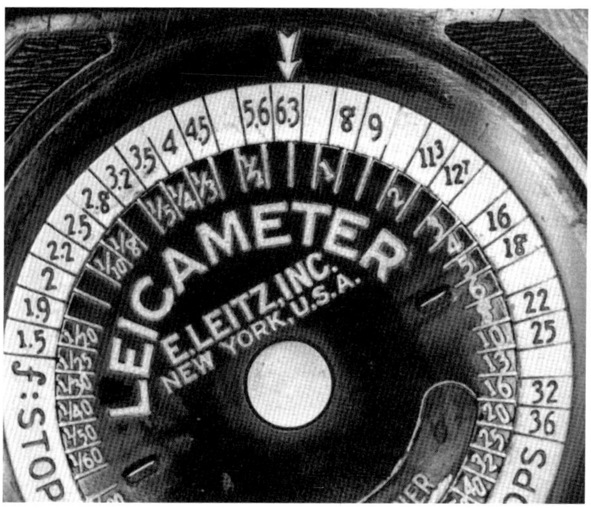

1. Front dial face of Leicameter, Weston Model 650 of 1936.

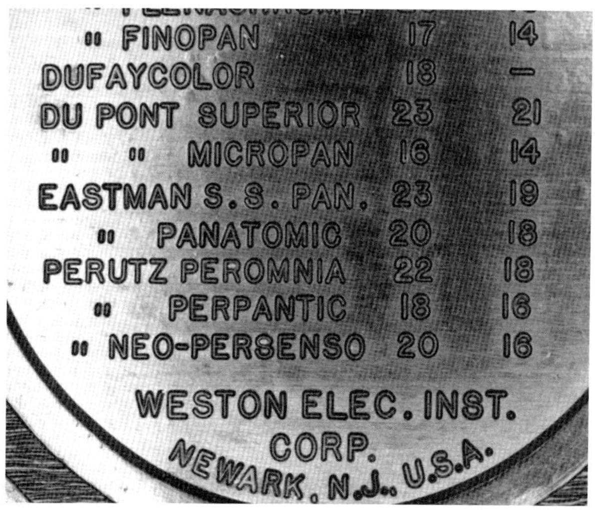

2. Maker's name and address on rear of Leicameter.

range of accessories for repro, close-up and macro photography suitable for the Leica R. The following is an abbreviated list of some of the main items.

CODE	DESCRIPTION.
MACRO-S	Macro-ReproStand. Consists of solid 420mm column with movable carriage and 230mm x 220mm base, taking originals for copying and objects up to 165mm. Can be used in horizontal mode.
MAWA	Object carrier, translucent plexiglass reflector specially coated for back ground projection without hot-spot.
MAKLEM	Object holder.
CASTEL-PRO	Adjustable focusing rack. Length 20.6cm, movement range 31 cms, weight 760 gms.
MARM	Flexible swan neck arm of 45cms with removable ball-and-socket head and flash shoe.
KLEMME	Clamp with rubber jaws for supporting background reflecting screens.
UNISET	Multi-bracket system consists of camera plate with jointed mounting rods. Flashes, reflecting screens, filter, special masks and lights can be fixed in any position around the camera.
UNIVER-S	Vertical extension rod.
UNIVER-W	Horizontal extension rod.
BLITZ-S	Servo flash with two diffusor discs, tilt head and synchro cable.

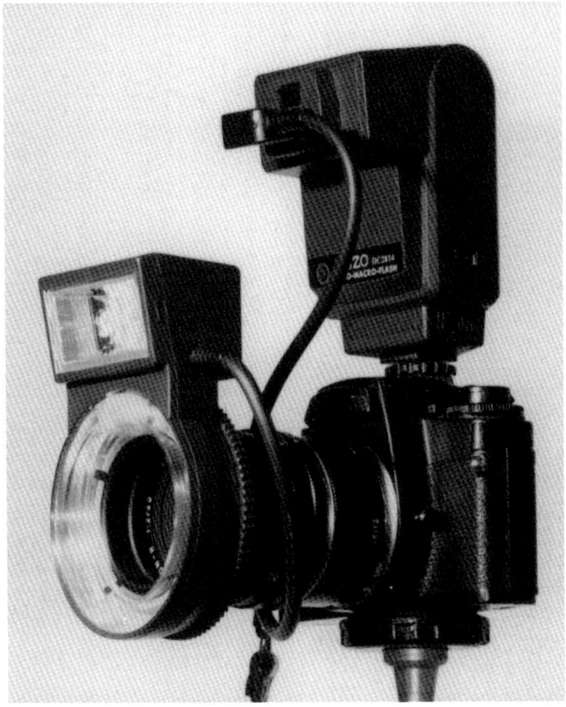

Fig. 176. The Yuzo Automatic Macroflash in use on a Leica R4s MOD 2. This electronic ring-flash unit can be coupled to Leica R-type cameras using a special adapter which provides Automatic TTL flash exposure and 1/16th power output control. An unusual feature of this unit is its point source flash, which is an integral part of the front ring unit, which can be switched on or off at will.

The advantage of the UNISET Multi-Bracket system is that all light sources and accessories remain in the same position relative to the camera when the camera position is adjusted. It allows both hands to remain free, permits hand-held macro shots without the need for a tripod, can be used with background lighting, the key light and fill-in light can be easily balanced, shadow-free illumination is possible, and it allows unlimited lighting possibilities for special effects.

X-SET III	The Macroflash-Set is attached to the filter thread of the lens using an adapter. The

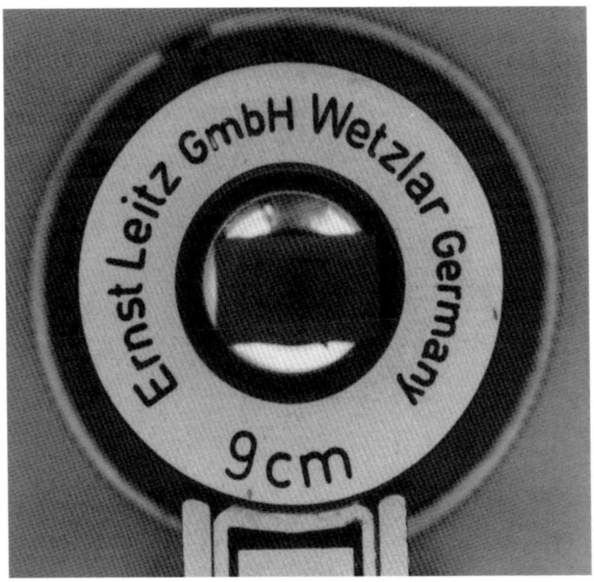

3. Typography engraving features on 9cm brightline finder.

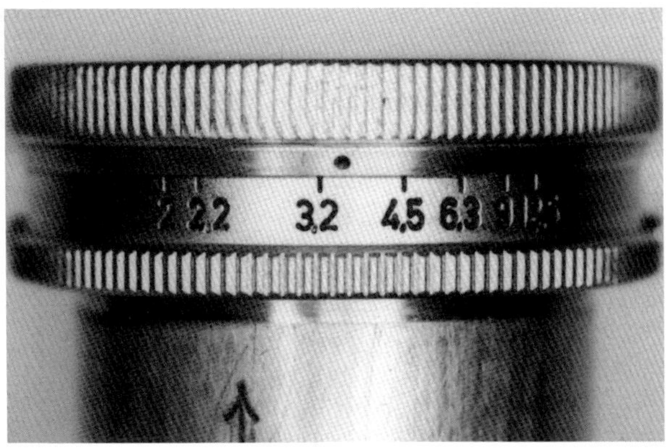

4. Old European aperture scale on 1934 Summar 50mm f/2 standard lens.

two servo flashes may be positioned in any way relative to the camera with light intensity being controlled by two diffusor discs. Servo flash unit has a GN of 20, duration 1/500 second powered by 2x 1.5 AA cells.

X-SHOE III Macro flash brackets without the flash units. Ideal for other system flash units.

KABEL-X Replacement synchro cable.

X-55 Adapter mounting ring for X-SET III for E55 Leica R lenses.

STASET Versatile Rod Support system. This is an ideal system for use in the field when attempting to photograph wind-blown plants, for example. It has unlimited potential when combined with many of the accessories already listed above and the following STAER sets:-

STAER-1 Accessory Set 1. 2 rods @ 30cm, 1 rod @ 15cm, 1 ground pin, 1 connection screw.

STAER-2 Accessory Set 2. 3 clamp sockets, 2 ball-and- socket heads with flash bracket.

STAER-3 Accessory Set 3. 3 plant brackets, 2 retaining clamps.

6.7. Leitz/Leica Copying and Reproduction Equipment

A number of accessories suitable for use with the early Leicaflex models were still being listed in Leitz catalogues in the late 1980's and these can occasionally be found today on the used market. If you own and use a Leicaflex camera, the following items may be of interest. Most of the items are accessories which are used with clamping stands and the various arms required for lighting.

CODE	DATE/ITEM DESCRIPTION
16 761	Framing box for use with Reprovit IIa and Reprovit 35.
16 786	1964. Object stage for reproduction of slides and macrophotography. A Micro-meter screw permits very fine focusing adjustment.
16 798	1978. Universal camera holder for Reprovit II. Can be used with Leicaflex cameras.
16 707	1967. Copying stand, comprising 80cm tall columnwith guide rail and arm with coarse and fine adjustment, baseboard. Can be used with Leica M and Visoflex or Leicaflex with or withoutUniversal Focusing Bellows-R and Bellows-R BR2.
16 773	1967. Transparency light box, inc. masking cloths and twin fluorescent light tubes. 18 x 16 ins.
16 792	1977. Transparency light box of grey metal 614mm x 400mm.
16 774	1971. Docuflex 35 camera. This was a special 35mm film single lens reflex camera fitted with a clear glass screen permitting a variety of formats on a maximum bulk load of 35mm film. The camera is electrically driven and operated with motorized film transport and shutter controlled by a foot switch. Fitted with a standard 70mm, f/5.6 lens interchangeable with other focal lengths. The camera is fitted with a special vacuum suction device for keeping the film perfectly flat during exposure. In normal use, the camera is focused by projection and is fitted with a clear glass screen which shows all the different format frame sizes and test marks for focus control. A special version of the camera with a ground glass screen could be obtained for close-up work and I have seen these around on the used market for reasonable prices. Used on a lighting stand the camera was listed as Reprovit 35. Complete with control unit for 110-240 volts, 50-60 hz (max load 1000watts) and foot switch. The following items are its exclusive accessories:-
16 778	Camera carrier.
16 782	Extension ring for close up photography to obtain 1:1 ratio, 4 rings are required.
16 779	4x magnifier.
16 486	5x vertical magnifier.
16 488	5x 90° angle magnifier.
16 714	Stand with 4-lamp lighting array on special Docuflex carrying arm with 66 x 67 cm baseboard.
16 717	REPROVIT-R, comprised of baseboard, adjustablecolumn and twin arms fitted with halogen lamps balanced for artificial light type film. 220-250v, 300 watt version.
16 718	REPROVIT-R as above but, 115-120v, 650 watt version.
16 774	REPROVIT 35, Docuflex camera and 16 714.
16 788	REPROVIT IIa. consisting of 67 x 68cm baseboard, column with carrying arm, coarse and fine adjustment, built-in projection device and magnetic release, special focusing slide, angle magnifier and 4-lamp lighting unit, forked lever and lens diaphragm lever for automatic lens stop-down. Focotar 50mm, f/4.5 lens and exposure timer, Complete system for use with Leica MDa, MD2 and Docuflex 35. 220v version.
16 789	As 16 788 but 110v version.
16 761) 16 773) 16 786)	Described above, may all be used in conjunction with Docuflex and Reprovit 35

6.8 Equipment for Film Duplication

For a while, Leitz product catalogues carried the ILLUMITRAN-D, made by Bowens of London, a semi-automatic electronic flash controlled slide copier. This machine is still manufactured by Bowens but no longer listed in Leica catalogues.

Leitz gave this item and its accessories the following product codes.

ILLUD	Semi automatic slide copier.
UNIHA	Universal holder for film formats of up to and including 6 x 6cms.
VERLE	9 x 12cm Sheet film attachment.
PFASZ	Extension cable for photo cell.
BALGT	Screw-on focusing bellows.
ADRLC	Leica rangefinder camera adapter ring.
ADRLX	Leicaflex SL adapter ring.
ADR 50	Adapter ring for Focotar 50mm, f/4.5.
ADR 65	Adapter ring for Elmar 65mm, f/3.5.
BLIAU	Flash release button.

The recommended camera for this set-up was the Leicaflex SL with Focusing Bellows-R and Macro-Elmar 100mm, f/4, complete with copying stand for same.

The modern Mark III unit can be purchased complete with adjustable column and the correct fittings for the Leica R-system, but it is no longer marketed by Leica Camera

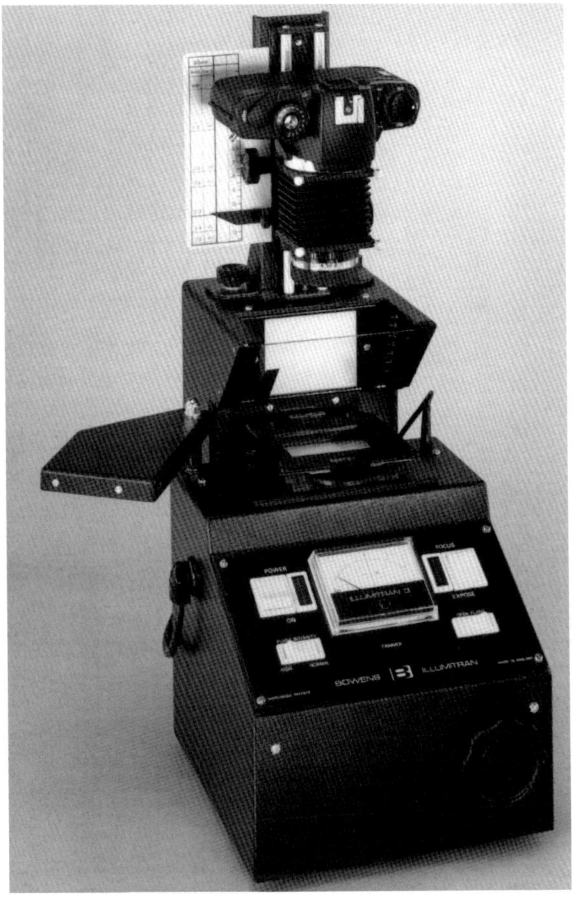

Fig. 186. The Mk III Bowens Illumitran transparency duplicator with built-in density control, Leica R4s fitted. The original to be copied is placed in the mask; the screen image of the duplicate to be made is easily sized and focused using the focusing bellows unit. A built-in reproduction scale on the machine column helps to ensure accuracy in setting up the camera. *KJP Professional Sales, London*

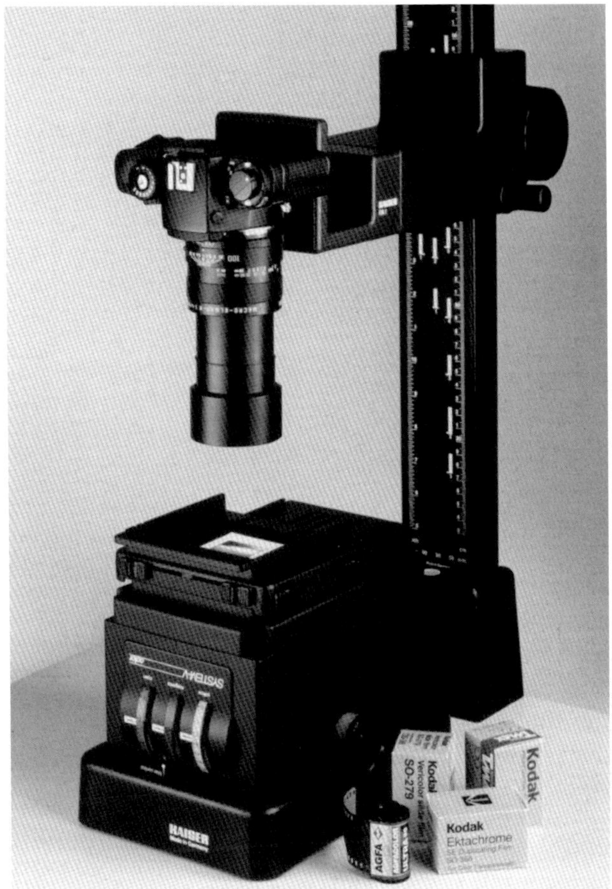

Fig. 187. A Leica R5 camera fitted with Macro-Elmarit-R 100mm f/4 attached to the Kaiser copy column in conjunction with the Kaiser 4444 Colour Mixing Head. The built-in dichroic filtration provides for accurate colour cast correction in duplicating transparencies or for making print film transparencies from colour negative originals. *Kaiser GmbH, Germany*

GmbH. Only stockists of Bowens professional lighting equipment will have it.

Another semi-automatic slide copier is the ELINCHROM which, like the modern Bowens machine, is fitted with a contrast control unit. This instrument was not widely advertised during its 20 year life. It was finally discontinued from the maker's catalogue in 1994, but new units were still available from some dealers at the time of writing.

The Kaiser 4444 Colour Mixing Head with 12v/100 watt halogen cold-light mirror lamp is probably one of the best systems on the market today for amateur and professional duplicating. This unit is basically the colour head used for a Kaiser enlarger which has been adapted with various accessories, including the baseboard, adjustable column and camera support arm. The complete Slide Duplicating Set (Kaiser product No. 5979) consists of a holder and covering hood for the reversed colour mixing head, providing adequate ventilation and secure positioning. You will need a transformer (4451), conversion filter for using daylight balanced film stock (5974) and one or all of the various negative masks: (4489) is for mounted 35mm format slides, (4484) is a Compound Negative Carrier for 6 x 6cm slides with built-in adjustable framing masks and (4483) is a similar accessory for all formats from 24 x 36mm to 100 x 72.5mm.

6.9 Data Recording Equipment

The imprinting of alpha-numerical data on to the film negative at the time of exposure can provide useful information for the photographer as well as specialists in the technical, medical and scientific fields. Ernst Leitz first began manufacturing special cameras which could be used for data recording in the early 1930s. The Leica Standard, Model E, of 1932 was also intended for use with the copying, macro and photomicrographic devices the company was

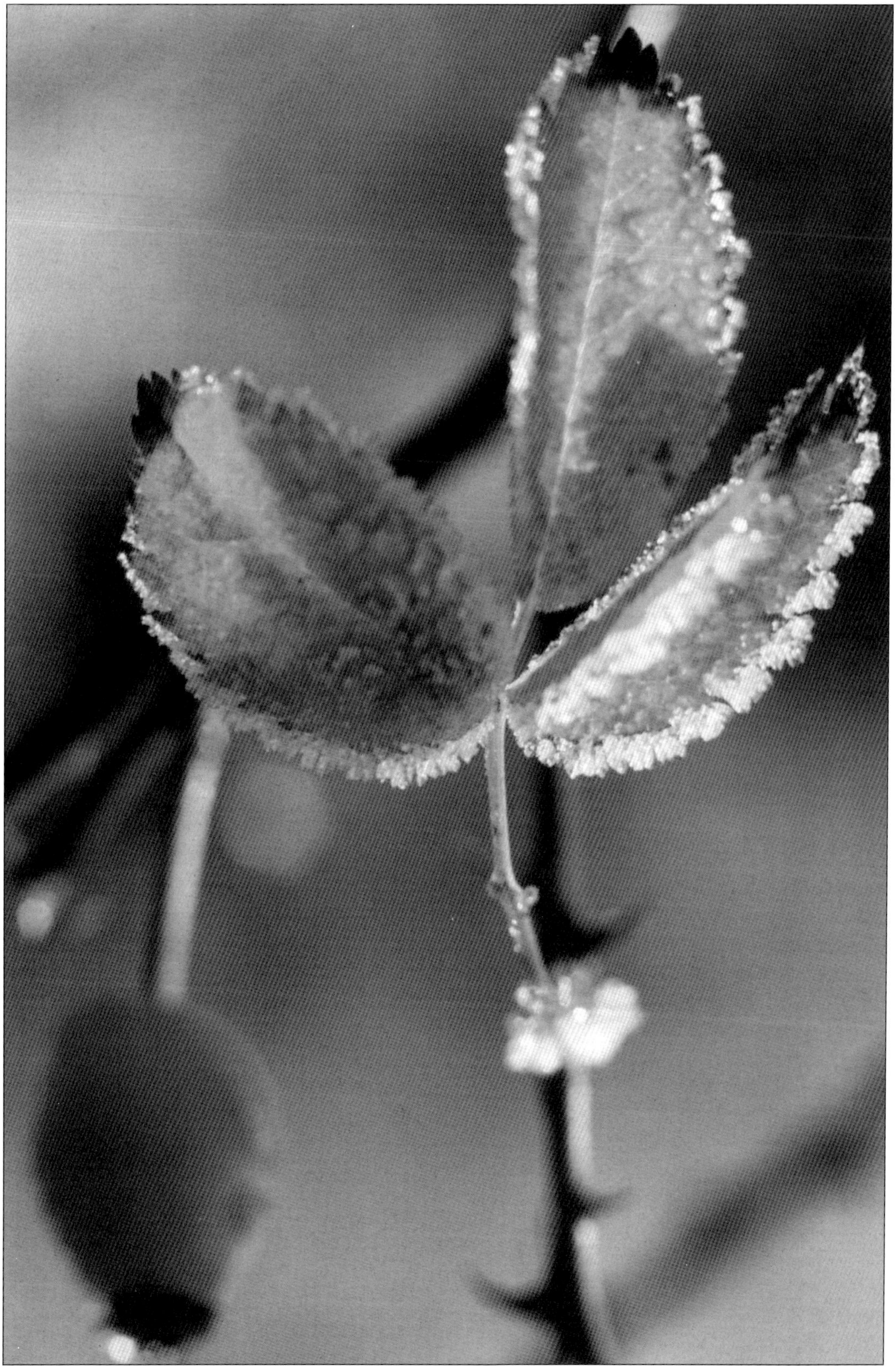

Fig. 181. Frosted leaves. Summicron-R 50mm f/2 reversed and held over lens flange by hand. Aperture pre-set and exposure adjusted using shutter speed dial in combination with integrated full-field metering.

control (Electronic remote control unit RC Leica-R 14 277) is used to photograph the opening and closing sequences of plants; timelapse records of wildlife behaviour, monitoring instrument readings, etc.,

The DB or DB2 back gives the Leica R a different feel when in place and of course, once fitted, it can only be removed when the entire roll of film has been exposed, or after a certain number of frames if these are rewound into the cassette. The electronic components add nearly a centimetre of extra thickness to the back. If you have no need of either of these accessories for regular work but still wish to record important data on the film, there is a simple solution. Write the information in bold letters with a felt tip pen on a reasonably sized sheet of paper, cardboard, old envelope and photograph it.

6.10. Simple Close-ups with a Leica R Camera

The photographic novice who has joined the Leica-R fraternity may be wondering, especially when budget strapped for some of the sophisticated accessories and objectives mentioned in this chapter, how to get started in the world of close-up photography. I say close-up, because the following procedure is a little Heath Robinson, probably would not technically qualify for the term 'macro' and is only used in the absence of any other accessories.

Using a standard Summicron 50mm, f/2 set at its infinity distance setting, and with the diaphragm initially cranked to maximum aperture, it is possible to photograph an object measuring approximately 46 x 31mm; equivalent to a matchbox label, a large colourful stamp, possibly a pair of smaller ones – at any rate, a fairly small object.

No other accessories are required except a steady hand. Remove the

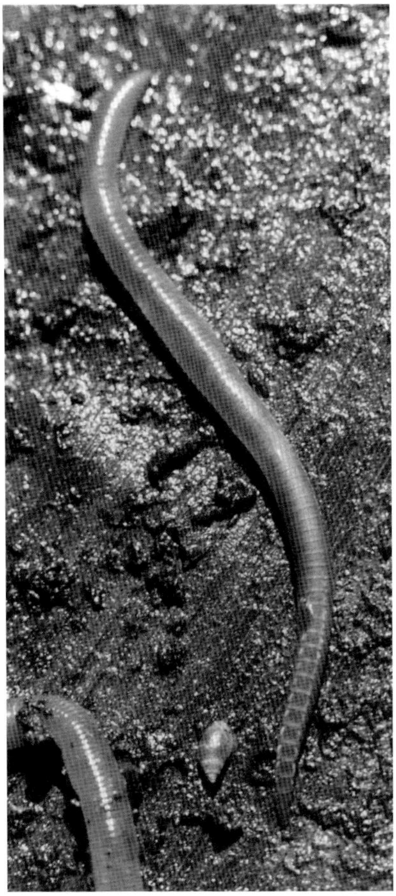

Fig. 184. Endangered species ....? Yuk. But this is just the kind of shot the specialist nature photographer building a picture library can shoot easily without any special equipment using the technique described in the text.

lens from the camera and turn it back to front, so the front element is at the back. Ensure the collapsible lens hood, if there is one, is pushed home. Set the aperture to f/2. Set the distance marker opposite the infinity mark on the focus ring. Hold the lens between thumb and forefinger and very carefully place the outer rim of the collapsible hood flush against the camera body lens mount flange. Hold the camera with the right hand in the normal way and look through the viewfinder at the object to be photographed. Gradually move the camera and lens closer. At about 110mm, the object will be sharply focused. Slight rocking movement towards and away from the object will position the camera and lens at the sharpest plane of focus, but the depth of field or zone of sharp focus will be very shallow.

Practice this a few times before attempting to squeeze the shutter release. One thing you have to try and ensure is that the lens is firmly held against the lens mount flange of the camera, so that as much extraneous light as possible is excluded from the camera. If you are worried about this aspect, you could try taping the lens in place with black PVC tape, ensuring that once taped, you keep a good grip on it and the camera. Now try stopping the diaphragm down, to say about f/5.6 or f/8 and follow the procedure above to obtain the sharpest possible focus. Lightly depress the shutter release button of your Leica R to activate the exposure meter and note the correct exposure. The Aperture Priority mode using 'selective'

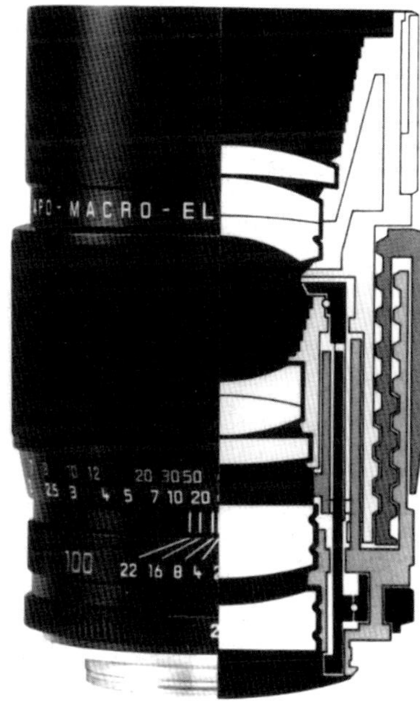

Fig. 189. Optical construction details of the Apo-Macro-Elmarit-R 100mm, f/2.8. Eight elements in six groups give a very high all round performance at both ends of the focusing range. Close focus reproduction ratio extends to 1:2; with the special Elpro (see Fig. 70.) near focusing attachment, a ratio of 1:1 is possible. The lens design became possible after formulation of special fluoride-phosphate glass developed in the Leitz laboratory at Wetzlar. *Leica Camera UK Ltd*

metering will provide the most accurate measurement. Make a mental note of the shutter speed selected by the camera. If you think it is too slow for successful hand-held exposures, open the diaphragm half or a full stop and try again. Once you are ready to make the exposure, begin to breath slowly but deeply. Release the shutter as you exhale. Don't attempt to hold your breath, you'll just get stuck there.

Because stop-down metering is possible with all Leica R-cameras, there is no need to worry about exposure control, provided there is sufficient light reflected from the object. This is not a difficult procedure, though if you have never done it before, I can understand the concern about dropping a lens. So long as you clasp it firmly – not a vice-like grip – and take your time, avoid all distractions, you should have few problems.

Some of the photographs in this volume were made in this way, usually on the spur of the moment when I have been out and about and have only the camera and lens over my shoulder. Illustrations using this technique are so indicated in the captions. They were all made free-hand, i.e. no tape, and hand held.

Larger magnifications can be obtained using longer focal length objectives the right way round or back to front in the same way. However, for this trick you will need a stiff cardboard tube of appropriate diameter to enable the lens to be slid inside at one end. The fit should be tight, but not so tight the lens cannot easily be moved in and out. A rough approximation of the length of tube required can be ascertained by holding the lens and camera body as already described. Move the lens away from the lens mount slowly while watching the image formed in the viewfinder. The closest focus point will soon become apparent. Ask a colleague or partner to measure the distance from the lens mount to the new front element with a tape measure. Cut the tube to the approximate length, minus sufficient length for finger and thumb focus control of the lens inwards and outwards in the tube. Now spray-paint the inside of the tube with matt black paint – available from any hardware or auto supplies store – and allow to dry. Be sure to give the inside a good coating from both ends before applying a couple of coats to the exterior. This should be enough to maintain a high percentage of light transmission and to block residual flare. Once the tube is dry you can begin experimenting with a world of subject matter which might not otherwise have existed.

CHAPTER 7

Visual Thinking with the Reflex camera

I have a theory concerning the condition of modern photography in England. To be specific, it concerns the state of contemporary photography made with the small-format, single lens reflex camera. In my view it is a sorry state, in spite of the fact that in recent years the medium of photography has been elevated to a higher academic plane. Specifically in England, exhibitions of new works can be seen every week of every month of the year in just about every city throughout the land.

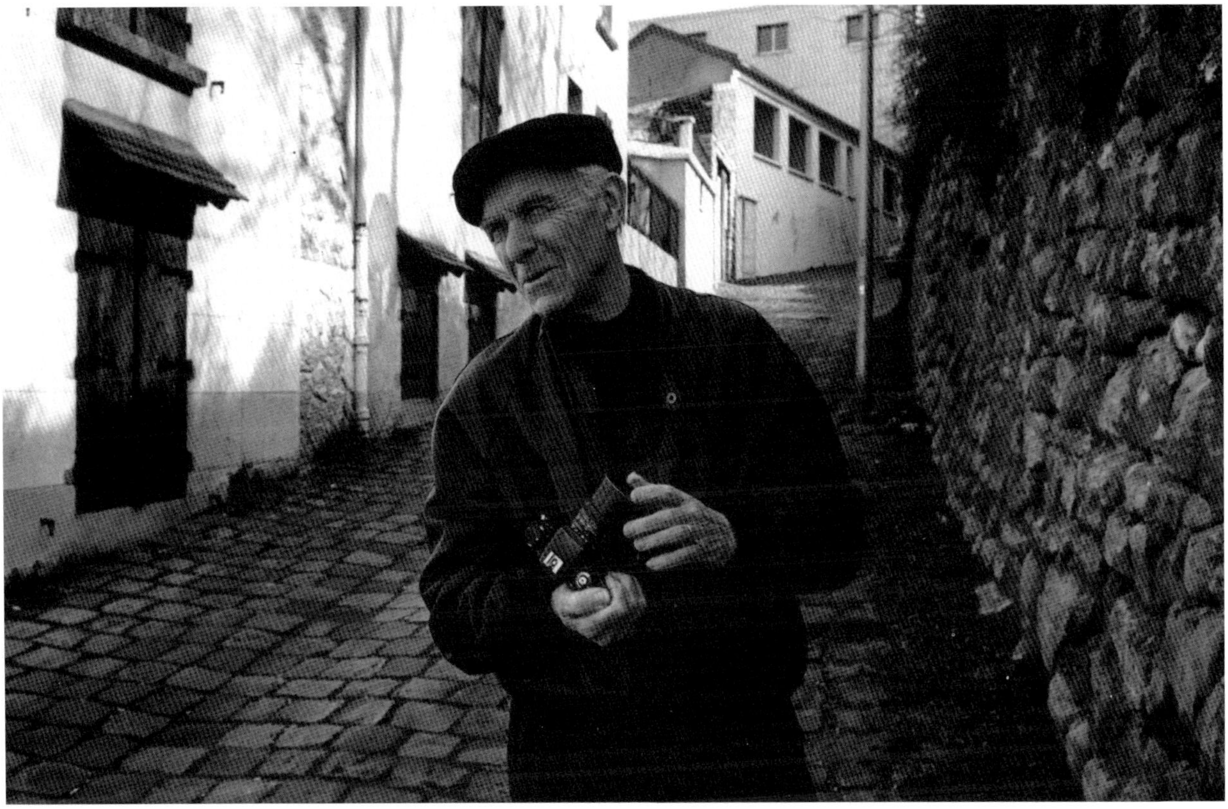

Fig. 191. The late Robert Doisneau on the streets of Paris, armed with his Leica. *Eamon McCabe/The Guardian*

This is exactly how it should be. Photography is at last on the agenda of ordinary mortals. However, the problem as I see it is that while the number of exhibition venues and galleries have increased significantly, the quality of their content has diminished by roughly the same proportion.

The proliferation of photographic galleries up and down the country is due in part to the new photographic culture begun in the 1950's and 60's, which spread its message through the pages of glossy fashion and Sunday newspaper magazines in soot-and-whitewash black-and-white. Curiously, colour was only a serious consideration in the minds of a handful of *avant garde* practitioners of the day. Photographers Ernst Haas and Art Kane made startling new contributions. How these, and many other powerful new images impacted on society is perhaps best illustrated by the huge demand in the 70's and 80's for the type of icon images which contributed to the great sociological changes of the times in the form of wall posters and framed prints. Photography got publicly promoted; something that had long been a part

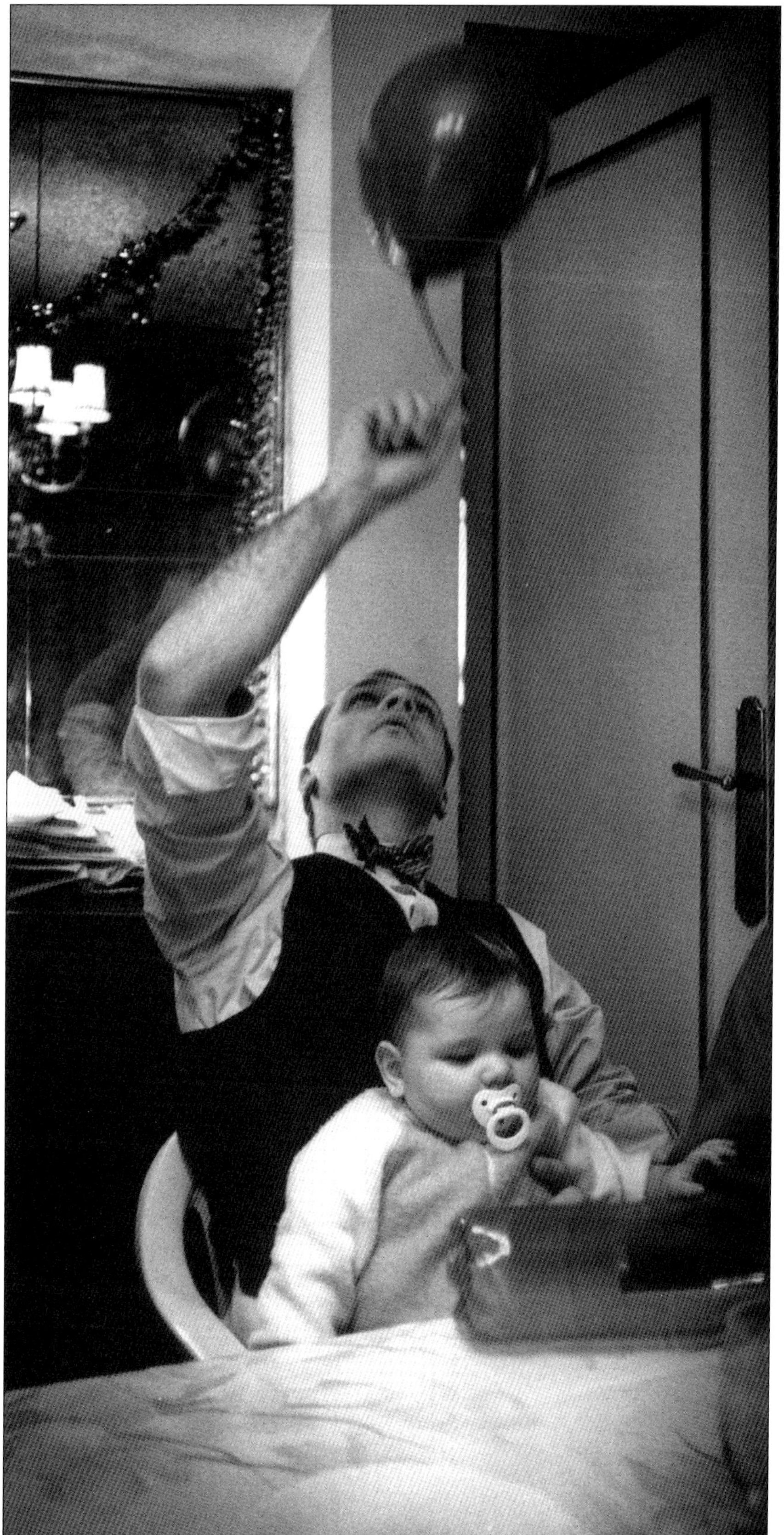

Fig. 190. The balloon.

of the underlying culture in other countries such as France, Hungary, Czechoslovakia, the USA.

This promotion did not happen overnight. It was a gradual process, perpetuated by academics, exhibition critics, pundits, writers and journalists. It was also inextricably linked to the mass importation of the ubiquitous 35mm camera from the Far East. Well made, and sporting the level of sophistication only previously associated with the very best and very expensive German manufactured models, these imports were marketed as affordable toys for the masses. And masses of people, would-be and wannabe photographers became proud owners. Now the learning curve began.

Traditionally, the English could be described as a nation of tinkerers. When something breaks, like the washing machine or the car, our natural instinct is to want to fix it (increasingly more difficult as the level of electronic sophistication increases). Nonetheless, it is in our nature. We are a nation of do-it-yourself freaks. 'The English imagination', said Lord Gowrie in a talk delivered to the Royal Society of Arts early in 1995, 'seems to work best, or most consistently, when faced with the scruffiness of human life, the untidy familiarities of hearth and home, the challenges of making do.'

This attitude, if it is an attitude, affects everything we do and are about. It is one of our great strengths, manifestly exemplified by our ability to cope in times of stress and hardship. When the going is easy, complacency rules. How does this affect photography?

That photography is one of the most popular leisure pursuits in this country can easily be seen from the statistics published by the industry. We buy new cameras, expose miles of film and do much of the processing and printing of it ourselves; we consume thousands of journals devoted to the hobby and join camera clubs in the hope of learning from those more experienced in the art of picture making.

Many do. Learn, I mean. At least, they seem to acquire a sound knowledge of the fundamental rules, about composition, lighting techniques, about what makes a 'good' photograph. But here it stops. Very few progress beyond this stage of 'basic' photography to the more hallucinatory plane where the primary concern is about the image and the effect it might have upon the viewer.

As a nation of photographers, we, the English, are stuck in first gear. We are still learning about what cameras do and what they cannot do, about which lenses are sharp and

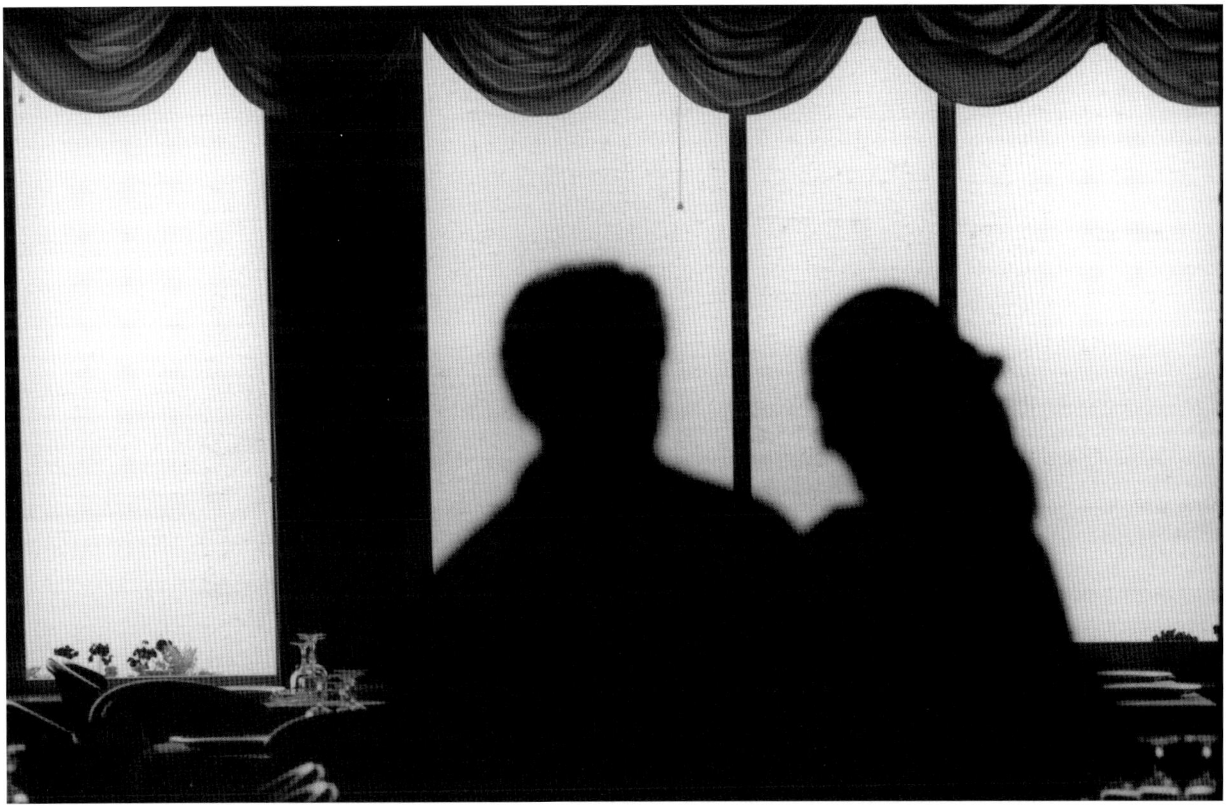

Fig. 192. The aim is to develop a way of seeing whereby ordinary life is framed. French restaurant. Elmar-R 180mm f/4.

which are not. Our concern is more about camera functions, about the detail of engineering quality, about how to adapt ancient optics to modern bodies in the hope of recreating a particular portrait style of decades past. The proprietor of one of the best known specialist camera shops in England recently told me, 'we don't sell these cameras to photographers. Our customers are only interested in the aesthetic appeal of the artifact.' Yes, he was talking about Leica cameras. I had visions of Oskar turning in his grave at the very thought of it! But Barnack was an engineer, a designer, inventor of things, and I guess his primary interest was also in the artifact.

This fascination with superbly made instruments is no stranger to the English – not that they are a particular exception. But it strikes me, having had the good fortune to travel the world extensively, and meet with many people interested in photography, that we are perhaps more concerned with this aspect. In France for example, whenever the topic of conversation amongst friends and family turns to photography, the emphasis is on the image; discussion centres on certain photographs and photographers, not, as is invariably the case in England, on types of camera. When Robert Doisneau died in 1994, the news of his passing made the front page of *Le Monde* newspaper. Doisneau spent a lifetime documenting the French way of life; his photographs are as much a part of French culture as the culture itself. In France, youngsters who know little or nothing of photography know who Robert Doisneau was, just as they know of Henri Cartier Bresson.

In England, one is hard put to find anyone outside the doors of a camera club who recognizes the name of Bill Brandt or Tony Ray-Jones, outstanding photographers who have made significant contributions to the ethnographic study of the English. Only one name has become a part of popular photographic culture here; David Bailey. His contribution is also significant, but the main body of his work was produced thirty years ago.

In a way, I wouldn't have this situation any other way. In any case, all the information the budding photographer is intent on procuring can be obtained from a wide variety of other sources. What concerns me more than anything is the idea that the ability to create good photography can be acquired over the sales counter, and that the level of how good or great this ability may be, is linked to the depth of one's pocket.

Academics will no doubt argue that this is not the case. Perhaps. At least for a very small minority who are fortunate enough to live, study or work in the kinds of environment cognisant of the underlying problem. For the majority, the evidence that this is indeed the case is all around us, and is perpetuated by those who have a vested interest. I mentioned that I would not have this situation any other way. It would be more accurate to say that I would not have had it another way. It gave me a head start. The learning curve is long and sometimes arduous, and whatever changes are made for the better, for the concern of image making rather than for the concern of hardware, will not affect what I do today or tomorrow. Today's young photographers will have to work as long and as hard as I have to reach the same position on the curve. In an ideal world, what's needed is a shift in the direction of teaching.

Recently, I asked the librarian of my daughter's school for an indication of the size and content of the photographic section. 'Small', she said, 'and it mostly contains books about cameras'. This is a state school with a good academic record and an embryonic photographic department which struggles to cater to the needs of older students.

I was inclined to conduct a survey of other schools, until I was told by a friend who lectures in the environment that his wider experience was very similar. At a higher level, another friend who had previously spent twenty years as a professional photographer in industry, recently returned to full-time education in fine art and photography as a mature student. His assessment of what is being taught at his establishment would lead one to believe that as long as current thinking persists in academic and teaching circles, the next generation of graduate photographers will spend years swimming in a sea of refuse. Most may never find their true direction or the conviction that great photography can benefit society.

This is the way things are. And perhaps it is meant to be. There is only so much room for the good and the great.

This preamble is intended to serve as a cautionary note to photographers who have graduated to the ownership of a Leica R. If you like, it underlines my oft-stated observation that ownership does not a great photographer make. To obtain that status, many other aspects, which are totally unrelated to Leica, need to be grasped and then with luck, experience and diligence, one might, after a lifetime, be able to count on the fingers of one hand, some excellent works.

Probably the most damaging aspect of teaching camera craft revolves around the idea that simply by looking through the viewfinder, one will see pictures. For this to happen, the user is required to be blessed with a particular talent which needs no further refinement.

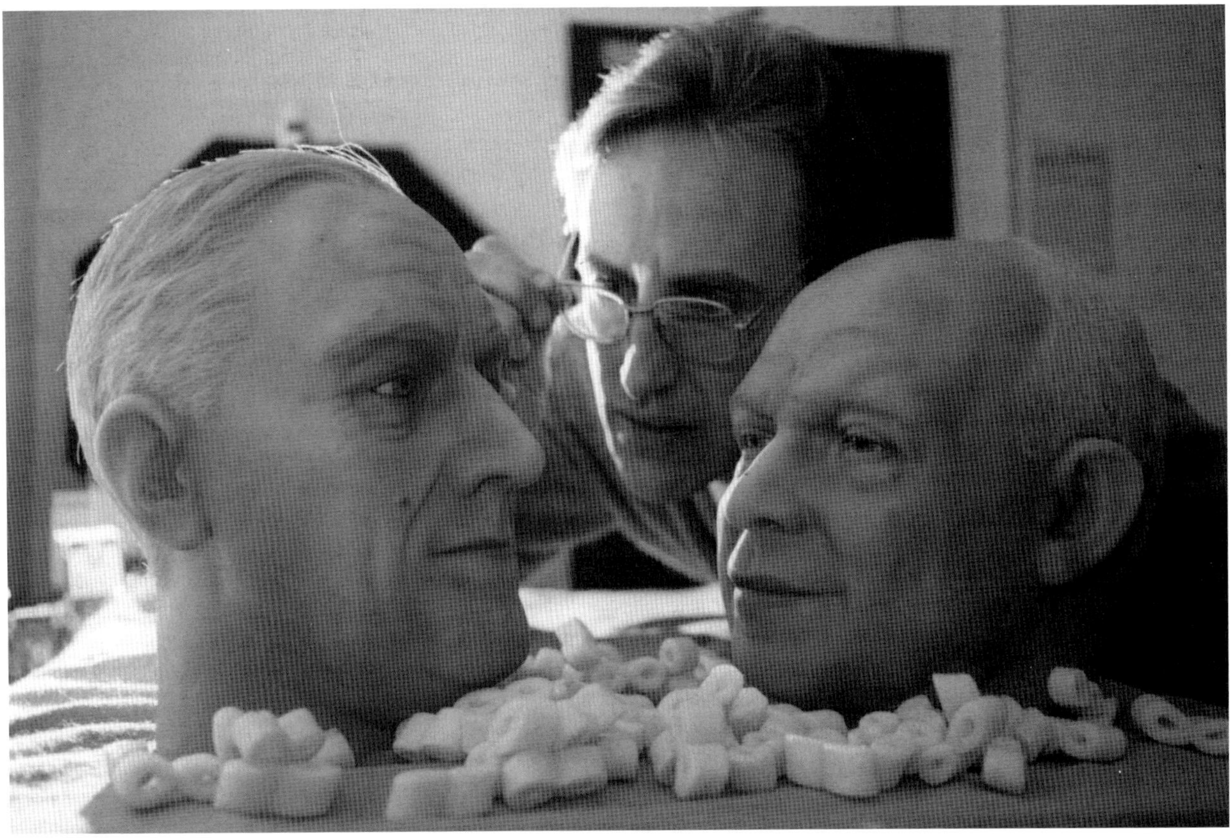

Fig. 193. I sometimes wonder if I would have approached this subject in the same way with a rangefinder camera. The wax sculpture heads of Franklin Roosevelt and Dwight Eisenhower were to be used as part of the 50th Commemoration of D-Day at the D-Day Museum in Portsmouth, England. I was invited to witness the unpacking and this was the first idea that came to mind, a face off with the museum curator forming the peak of the triangle. I lit the front with a small flash mounted on the camera and shrouded it with a special diffuser which triggered a larger slave-driven backlight.

In practice, it is rarely the case and advancing to that stage is not made any easier by proclaiming theoretical possibilities for the 24 x 36mm frame.

Photographic awareness can be easily developed. Although the Leica-R viewfinder image is near life-size, the physical dimensions of the screen are really too small for the practical purpose of learning to see pictures. Beginners and users steadfastly glued to the screen in the hope something worth framing will suddenly appear will obtain a better idea of what is possible by using a cardboard frame through which to view the world.

The aim is to develop a way of seeing whereby ordinary life is framed. This is an imaginary frame, one carried in the mind's eye, and which can, and often does, vary in size and shape. Using a piece of card measuring approximately 40 x 28cms, cut an aperture measuring 36 x 24cms. This leaves a 4cm-wide frame which should be covered with black paper or painted black. The wider you can make the frame the better, so don't hesitate to use a larger piece of card if it is available.

Holding this in front of your eyes at the normal viewing distance of about 30cms, select various objects around a room. Without moving the objects, try to arrange them into an agreeable composition. Imagine you are a camera. Move around, up and down, backwards, forwards, until light and the relationship of planes forms a balance.

Holding the frame at the recommended distance provides an angle of view which is close enough to that of a standard 50mm lens. Bringing the frame closer to the eye, or stretching it further away, has the same effect as changing the lens focal length on the camera. You will notice the immediate effect of this more readily when the frame is brought closer to the eyes. Suddenly, a much wider angle of view is possible. By aligning the frame with say, the front garden gate from a convenient window, tape the frame to the glass and then step back a few meters, always keeping your eye on the gate through the frame. The further back you retreat, the more apparent the telephoto effect. Go back far enough and you will be able to see the kind of effect, you would obtain using a very long focal length lens, such as a Telyt 400mm.

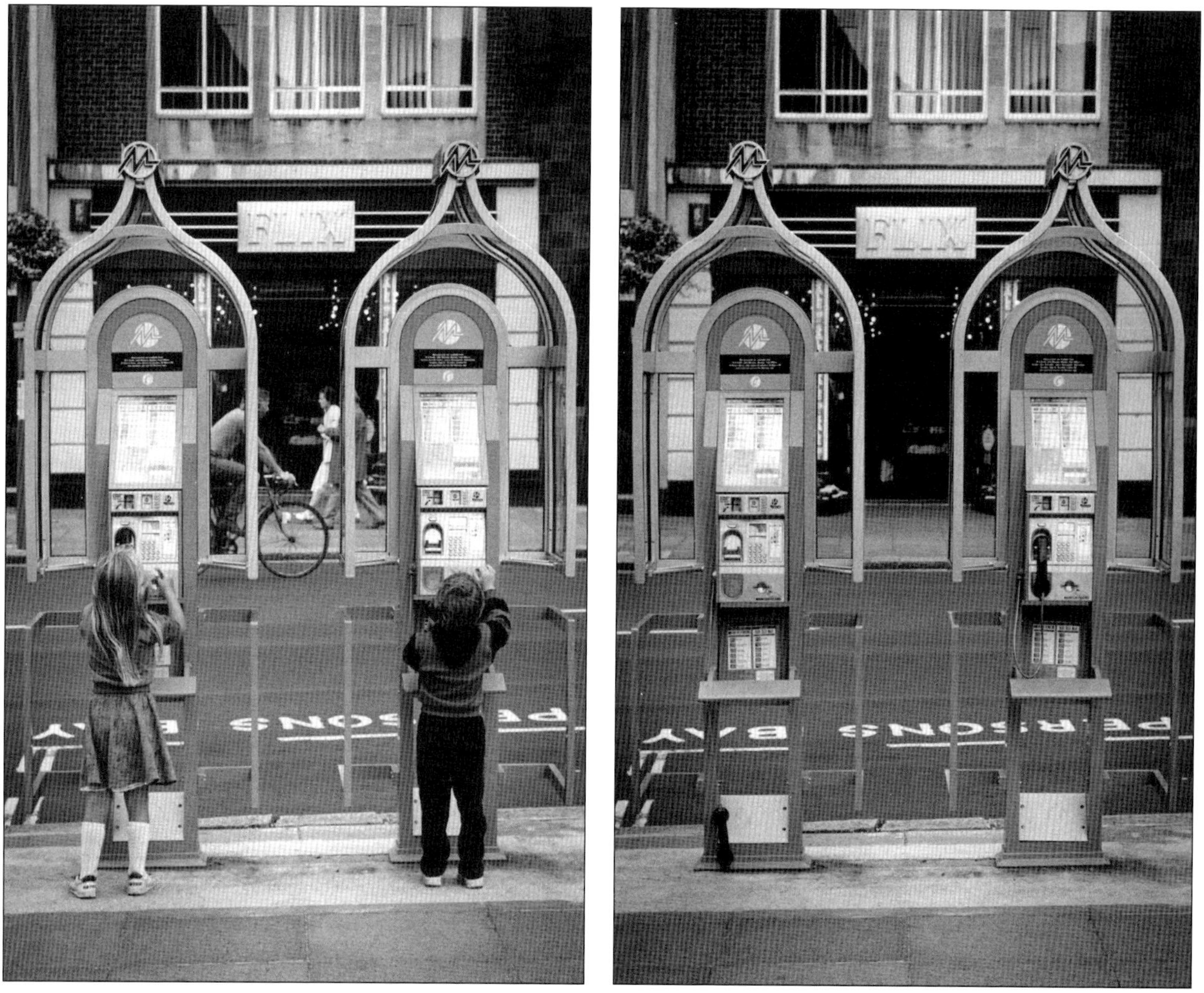

The end of an icon of contemporary British street furniture; the pictures aptly reflect the demise of a corporate dream when used as a pair. This is not a decisive moment as such; more a mere micro-dot in the huge screenplay of everyday life. It is often the dots however, which punctuate the passing of time and provide observant photographers with a plethora of subjects worth recording.
Summicron 50mm.

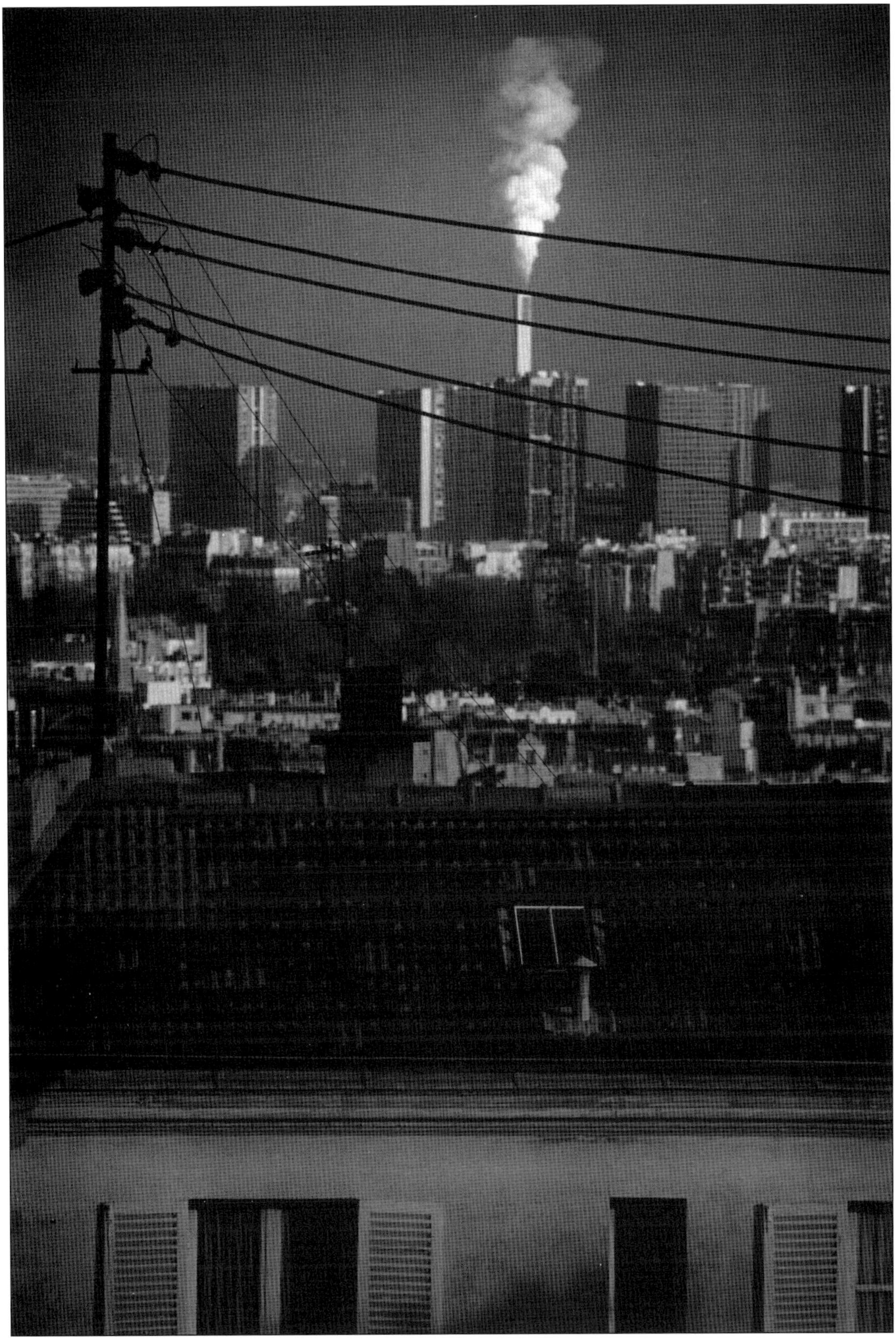

Paris suburbs. The great vistas are frequently photographed with wide angle lenses. This has the effect of diminishing scale so that when a normal print is viewed, all the 'greatness' of the original scene is lost. Used from the correct distance, telephoto lenses help the photographer retain a sense of scale and proportion in the print. The greater the focal length however, the further back the photographer must trek.

'Well,' you say, 'I can do this with the camera'. Of course. But it takes longer to change lenses than it does to move your arm. More importantly, because you are not using the camera, the mind is free to concentrate on what is being viewed. The size of the frame makes a greater impression on the mind and once you have done this several times, there is a residual subliminal effect. An imaginary frame takes over; when this is combined with the diminutive viewfinder of the camera, the order of things will begin to fall into place more rapidly.

The concerned enthusiast can take this exercise a stage further, well into the realm of pantomime. Keep the frame. Find a larger cardboard box which is roughly of similar dimensions in width and height but approximately 60 to 70 cms in depth. Pierce a circular hole in the centre of one end, no more than two to three millimetres in diameter to begin with. At the other end, remove the box flaps and tape the frame in their place. Next you will need a large sheet of translucent tracing paper. The type used by draughtsmen is best and usually only obtainable from graphic arts suppliers.

Tape a sheet of this paper over the frame aperture. Arrange the box so that it can be easily supported and aimed at a brightly lit scene. The front or back garden seen through a window will do nicely. Darken the room and then view the image formed on the tracing paper. I have used the English 'make do' approach rather than one which involves scientific calculation, but at any rate there will be an image, probably not bright and probably not very sharp.

The hole formed in the front of the box has the same effect as a single lens element in bending light rays to form an upside down, laterally inverted image. This is exactly how the camera lens forms the image at the film plane. What you see through the viewfinder of the Leica R is a right-way-up, right-way-round image.

The point of this exercise is that it enables the viewer to gain a more dramatic impression of how the photographic image is formed, while providing a sizeable screen image, albeit upside down, which can be viewed at a sensible distance.

The analogy is a little like visiting an art gallery. In many instances you will find large paintings which require the viewer to step back in order to obtain a proper view. While the miniature reflex camera viewfinder provides a clear, bright and contrasty image of a scene, it is too small to be viewed from a comfortable distance. In arranging the still life, the portrait, or scanning the landscape, one needs space to be able to see the picture clearly formed in the mind. Only then can you put the Leica R to the eye with any confidence.

Some photographers will hold different opinions, arguing perhaps that you can only be 'photographically honest' when viewing a scene with the camera. This assumes from the outset that the user is fully aware of the effect certain focal length objectives can have on the result; the way scale and proportion of the object are changed. Using large-as-life aids in the beginning helps the novice to understand more clearly the changes which take place as the camera is moved around.

I wrote in the *Leica M Compendium* of how the rangefinder camera helps to liberate visual thinking. The miniature reflex camera does exactly the opposite; it has a tendency to confine visual thinking, more so when the user is not sufficiently practised in the art of seeing without a camera. Part of this has to do with the nature of the instrument. The very fact that it requires the user to look carefully at the small viewfinder image which is in effect isolated from the rest of the scene, is part of the problem. This, of course, is the designer's intention, the argument being that image isolation helps the user to concentrate on what is viewed, to focus correctly, to ensure the graphic content _ composition – is perfect, as well as to ensure the correct exposure measurement. But what of the rangefinder concept? No such isolation exists there. One has a frame suspended in the viewfinder which for the most part gives a clear indication of what lies beyond the perimeter. The viewfinder is also so close to the corner of the camera that it actually encourages the user to look to the wider scene most of the time with the eye which is not stuck in the camera. The two systems are as different as chalk and cheese.

Oddly, this problem doesn't exist with other types of camera which employ the reflex system. Large and medium format cameras, being rather bulky, are handled in a different way. The waist-level viewing screen of a Hasselblad or Rolleiflex, for example, allows the user more visual freedom. This is because the image, except when being finely focused, can be viewed from a considerable distance from the eye, on a smaller scale than the cardboard box experiment, but nonetheless in a similar manner. The nature of the experienced photographer concerned about image making is to cast around for a better viewpoint.

This ability to see the picture without the aid of a camera is really the key to more successful photography. Once you have mastered the art of framing the world in your mind, or even with the black cardboard frame, which is to be recommended, the process needs to be continually honed. Professional photographers working day in, day out, practice this continuously, though they may not be aware of the mental mechanics. Those who make pictures for pleasure will not have the opportunity to expose as much film or attend so many varied assignments, so the mind will need some extra stimulation from time to time.

This can be gleaned from illustrated books, magazines, newspapers, television, the cinema. One of my favourite sources of inspiration is art galleries. I have no special favourites, there is always something to catch the attention. Artists have a way of seeing life which is quite different from the way photographers see, which may explain to some degree why so many of the world's great photographers produce so much outstanding work. Many of them were trained as artists before turning to the camera to make a living.

Art and photography have gone hand-in-hand for more than a century and a half, which may also account for why the photographic press of some European countries concentrates rather more on the image than on the hardware. In England art exists of course, but it thrives in a clubby environment pursued in the main by the slightly eccentric who, in the provinces anyway, seem reluctant to share what they are up to with ordinary mortals. The notion that being involved in 'art' is some kind of prissy occupation is not as strong as it once was at some levels of society, but it exists nevertheless. Determined photographers anxious to find new inspiration will ignore the barriers.

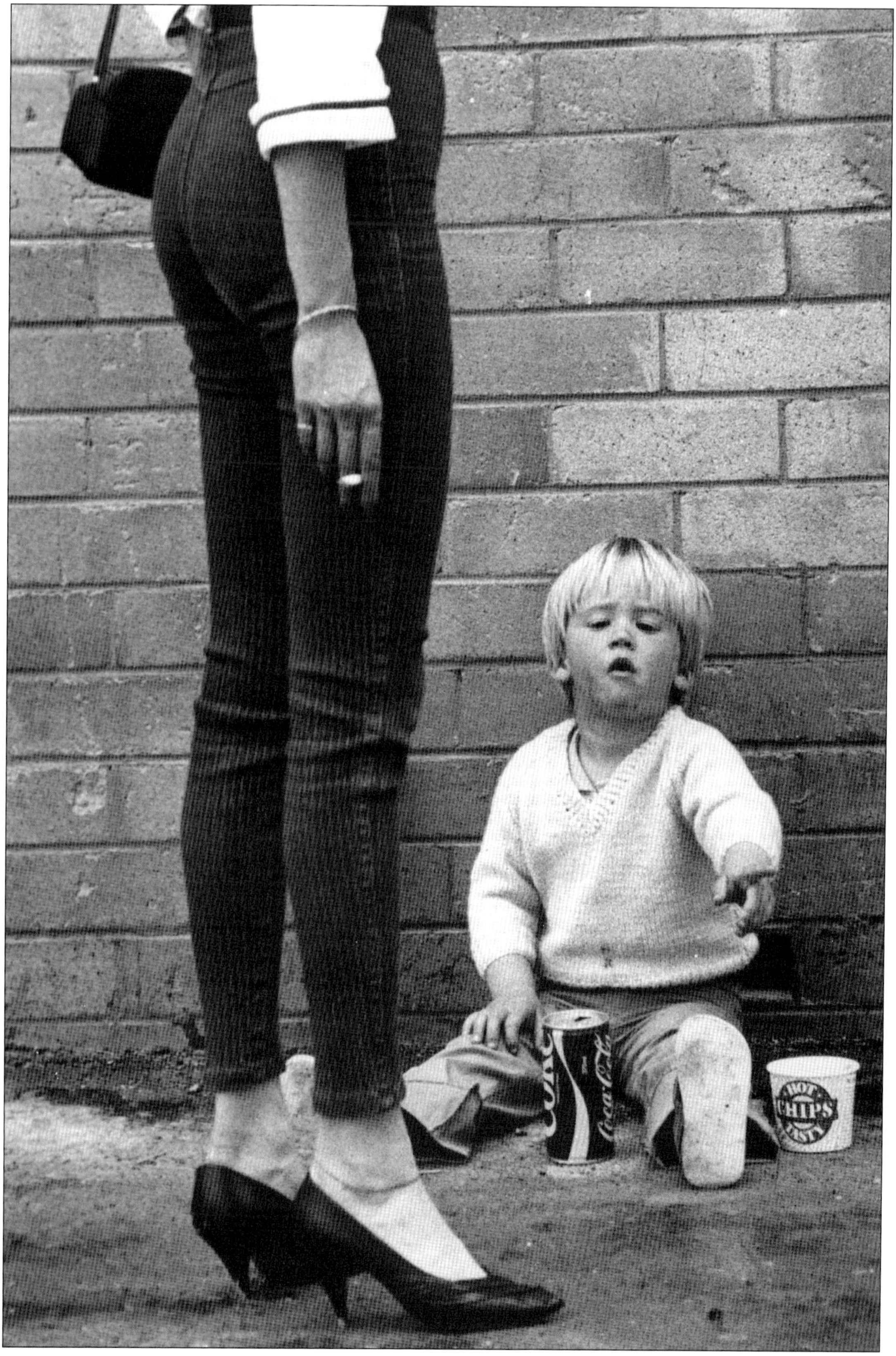

Fig. 195. A medium length telephoto zoom lens such as the Vario-Elmar-R 70-210mm can be a useful asset to the travel, press, and amateur photographer roaming the streets.

CHAPTER 8

Telephotography

The standard 50 – 60mm focal length angle of view closely approximates that of the human eye. In photographic circles, this length is frequently maligned by enthusiasts, it being neither wide nor long enough for their taste. The perception of how things look photographically should be the arbiter of choice when it comes to focal length.

These days, if we wander outside the circle of Leica R users and look at other brands, we can see that manufacturers cater for more varied precepts. The majority of single lens reflex cameras are often offered for sale in kit form; comprising a body, a short zoom lens covering focal lengths from say, 28mm to 70mm, and electronic flash unit (if not built-in to the camera).

Leica do produce a short zoom lens, but the more knowledgeable photographer understands that while the image quality obtainable from modern zoom lenses is very high, they cannot better a prime objective. The other consideration, and one which is often overlooked, is that the vast majority of zoom lenses in this short focal length are relatively slow compared to the equivalent fixed focal lengths. The Vario-Elmar-R 35-70mm has a maximum aperture of f/3.5, decreasing to f/4.5 at the long end.

The standard focal length however, whether in prime optic or zoom form, can limit the photographer's ability to expand visually, though of course, with extremely careful processing, it is possible to simulate the effects obtainable with longer focal lengths. The black-and-white practitioner may be able to obtain some satisfaction by producing effective images on a large scale, but this is really no substitute for the real thing. The colour photographer working with reversal materials is confronted with the problems of duplication, involving enlarging and cropping of the original image, a process which requires meticulous attention to

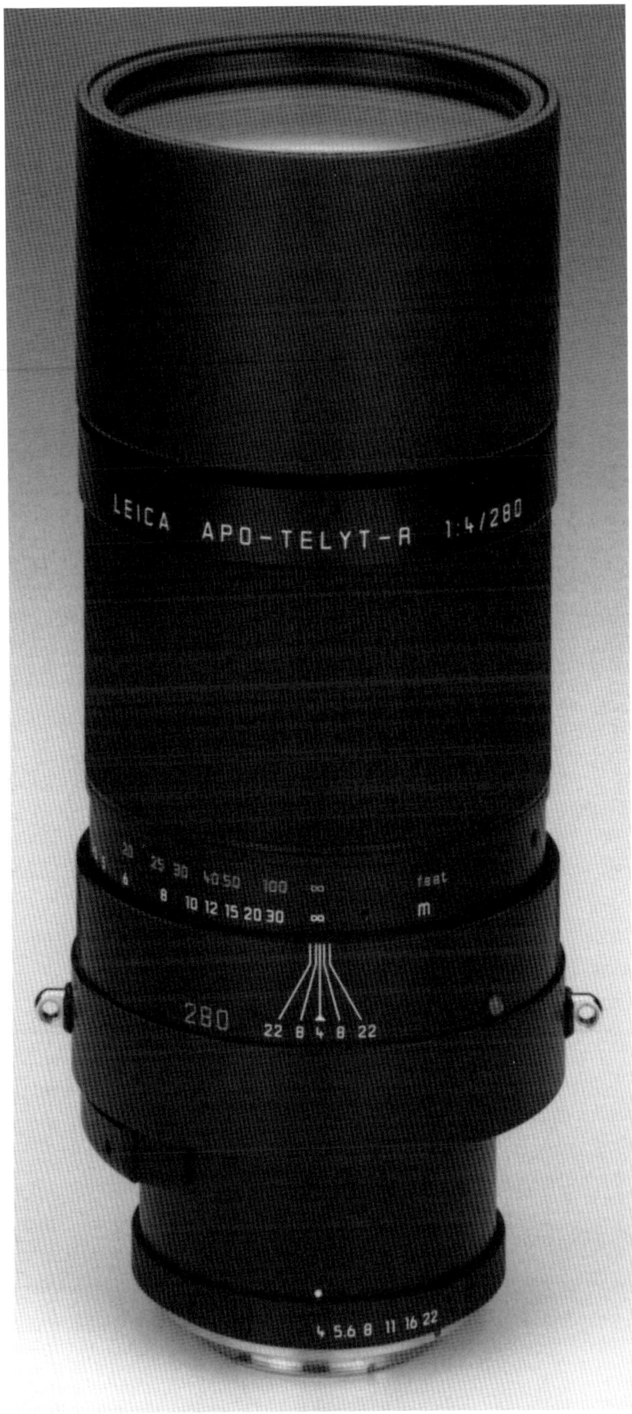

Fig. 194. Another view of the fabulous Apo-Telyt-R 280mm f/4. *Leica Camera GmbH*

detail if it is to be successful. The colour print worker will encounter problems in overcoming visible grain factors inherent in large scale enlargements with all but the very slowest speed emulsions. In the end, the desired effect and superior quality of image will be more easily obtained by using the correct focal length objective at the beginning.

For some Leica R users, it may not be a question of which focal length to go for next, but simply a more economic question of when. I know of amateur enthusiasts, even some freelance professionals, who, having obtained their first Leica R-camera, soon come face-to-face with the very real problem of justifying the considerable outlay required for the next purchase. It is beyond the scope of this work to suggest how these problems might be resolved. But I would say this: if you are the owner of a Leica R-type camera and you feel stuck and unable to progress photographically with the basic 50mm standard lens, dig deeper into your imagination.

Many of the world's best photographs have been made with the humble 50. There are photographers whose armoury is comprised only of 50mm lenses – all different; I use several myself, and each one has a character which can be exploited in different ways. The uses to which this focal length can be put are almost limitless, but so much depends on the way the individual sees the world. Stuck with this and nothing else, it is only a matter of training and self discipline and, as I have said on numerous occasions before, no matter how many lenses you have in your bag, you can only use them one at a time.

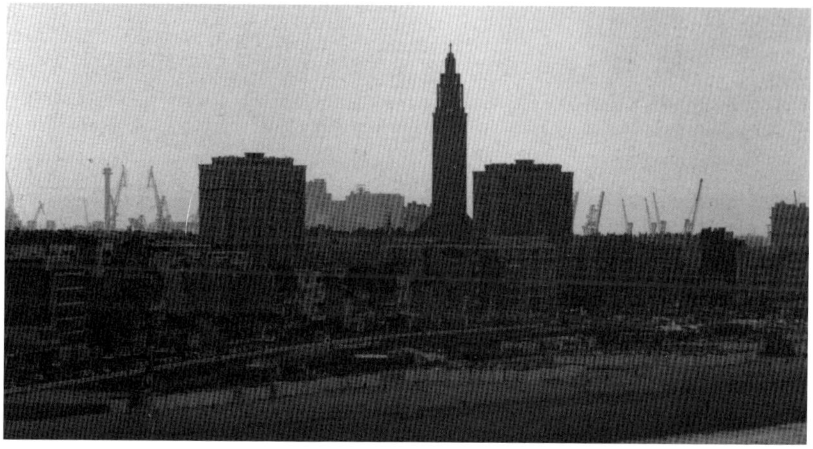

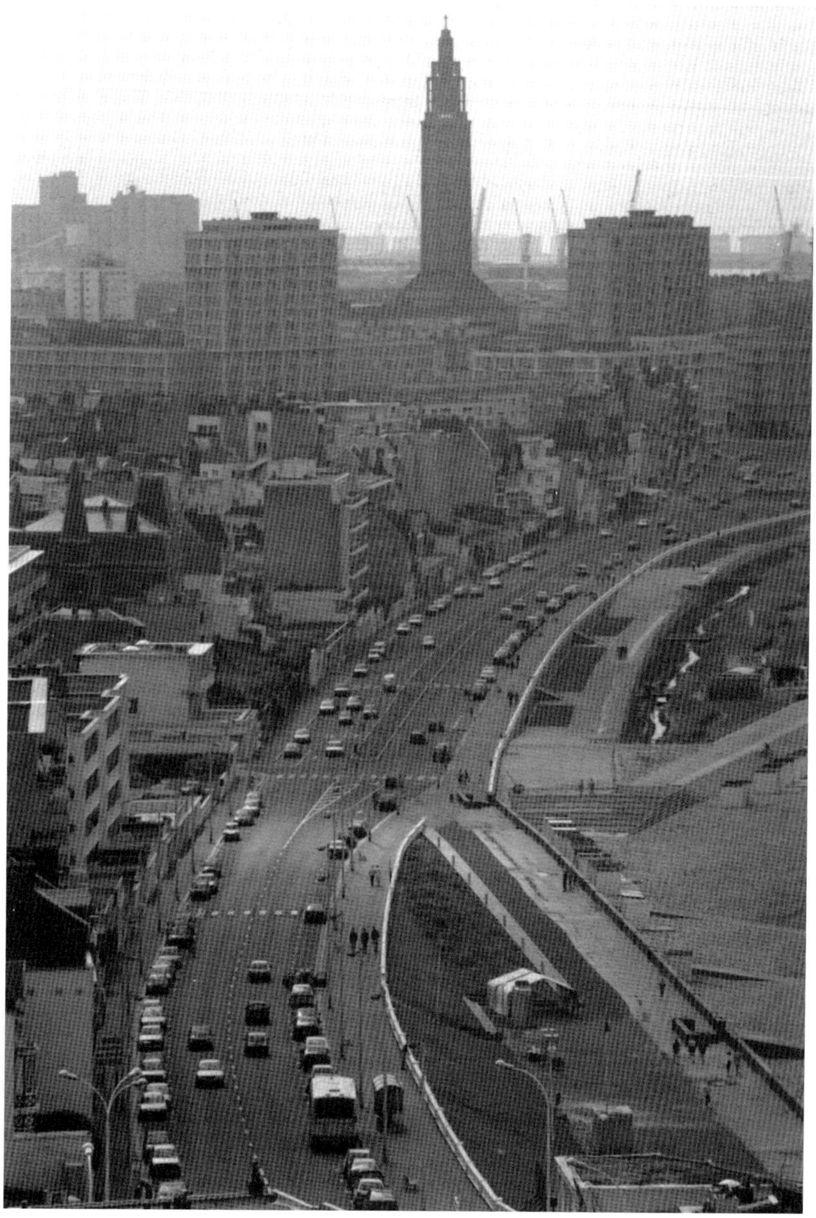

8.2 A Matter of Choice

As to the question of what is the next best and most useful size, there is no simple answer. Much will

Fig. 197. For these three views of St.Josephs Church in Le Havre, I used the lightweight Elmar-R 180mm, f/4 lens. This is a big building which dominates the city skyline. I shot it from opposite sides using the lay of the land to gain a suitable vantage point.

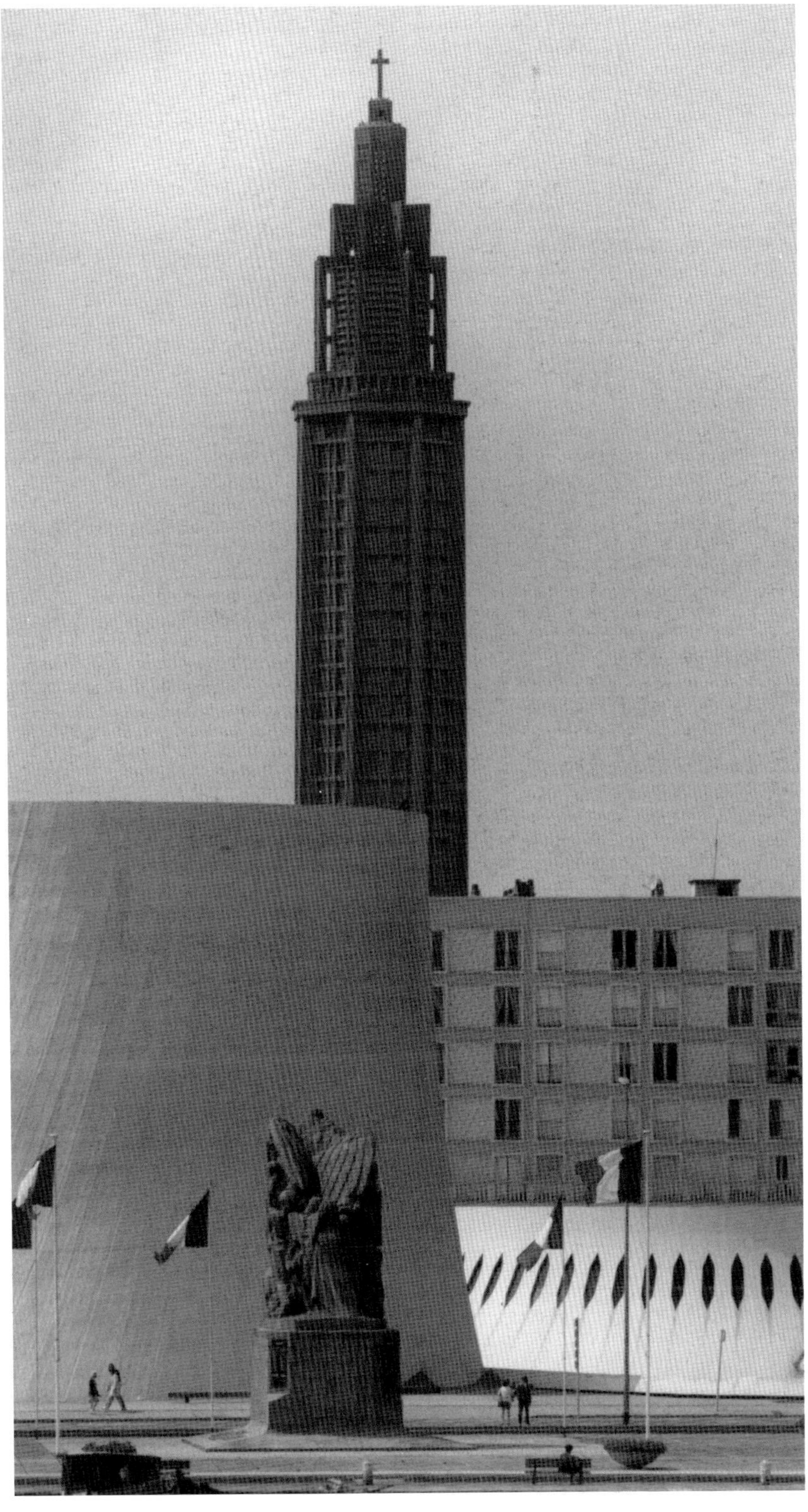

depend on the primary purpose. Wildlife specialists will have a greater need for tele-objectives at the longer focal length end than in the mid-range, because there will be more situations arising where the distance is too great to be efficiently overcome with shorter lenses (remote control situations aside).

Photographers with a need to cover a variety of sports may find these are served better by one or two telephoto lenses in the 180mm to 280mm range which can be combined with an extender. Four very different 180mm objectives are available to the Leica R user, any one of which can be matched to regularly encountered circumstances. The Elmarit-R 180mm, f/2.8, for example, is fast enough to be useful in a range of situations where the highest possible shutter speeds are essential to stop action. Combined with the use of high speed film, even a football match played under the worst winter weather in a badly lit stadium can be effectively covered. The physical dimensions of the current lens are not so great that it prohibits porterage for a wide variety of other assignments.

Photographers regularly assigned to specialist sports which mostly take place under cover, such as table tennis, fencing, weight lifting, will almost certainly find the newer Apo-Summicron-R 180mm, f/2 the answer to many of their dreams. This expensive objective has true internal focus with three of its nine elements being moved in two groups backwards and forwards thus maintaining the same overall lens length as focus is adjusted.

The Apo-Summicron-R is no lightweight at 2.5kg and the majority of users will use it in combination with a monopod. The extra large diameter of the adjustment ring permits finger-tip control of focus almost to the standards of

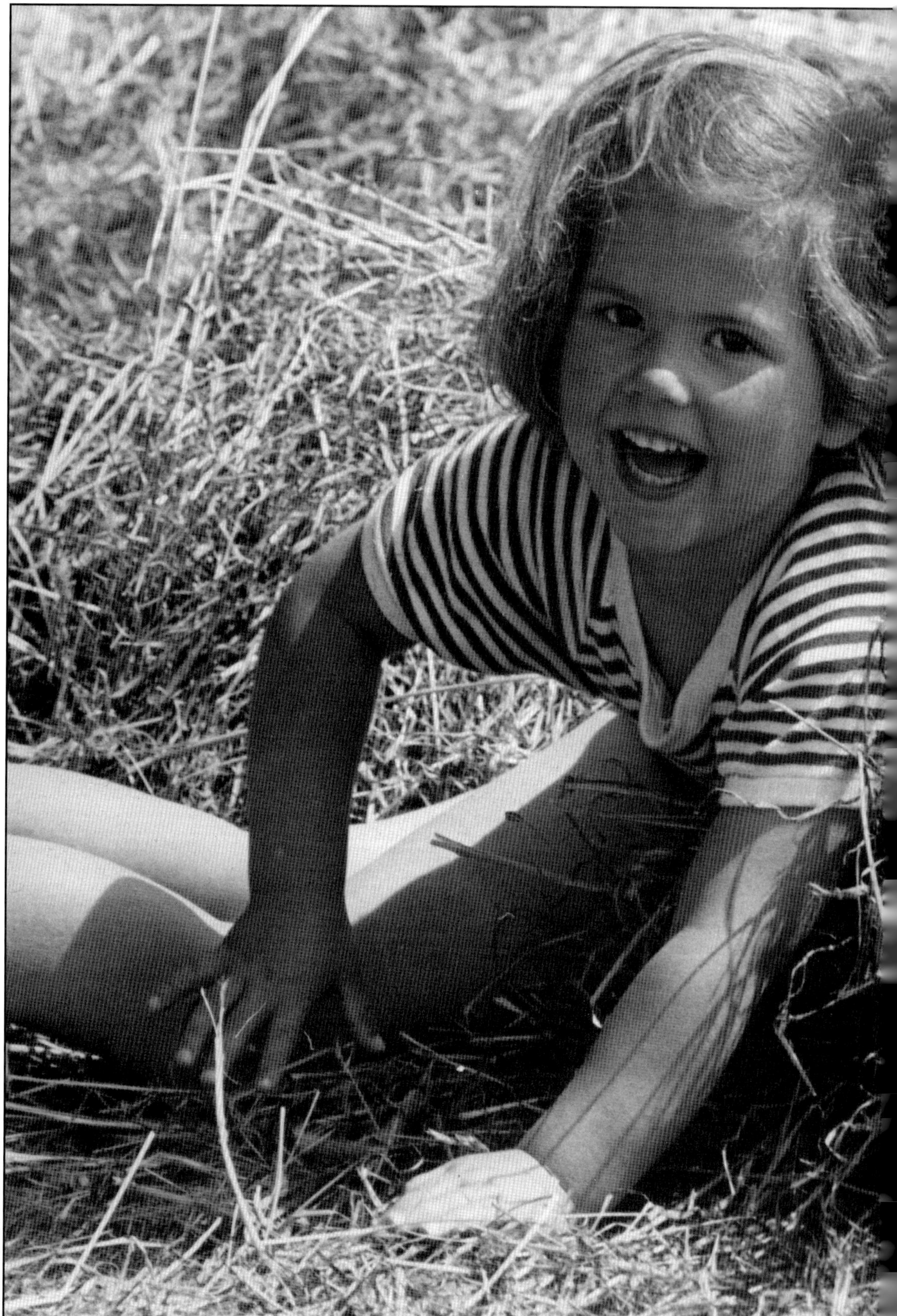

Fig. 198. The Elmarit-R 135mm, f/2.8 is one of the most useful general purpose objectives, permitting a useful working distance to be maintained between subject and photographer.

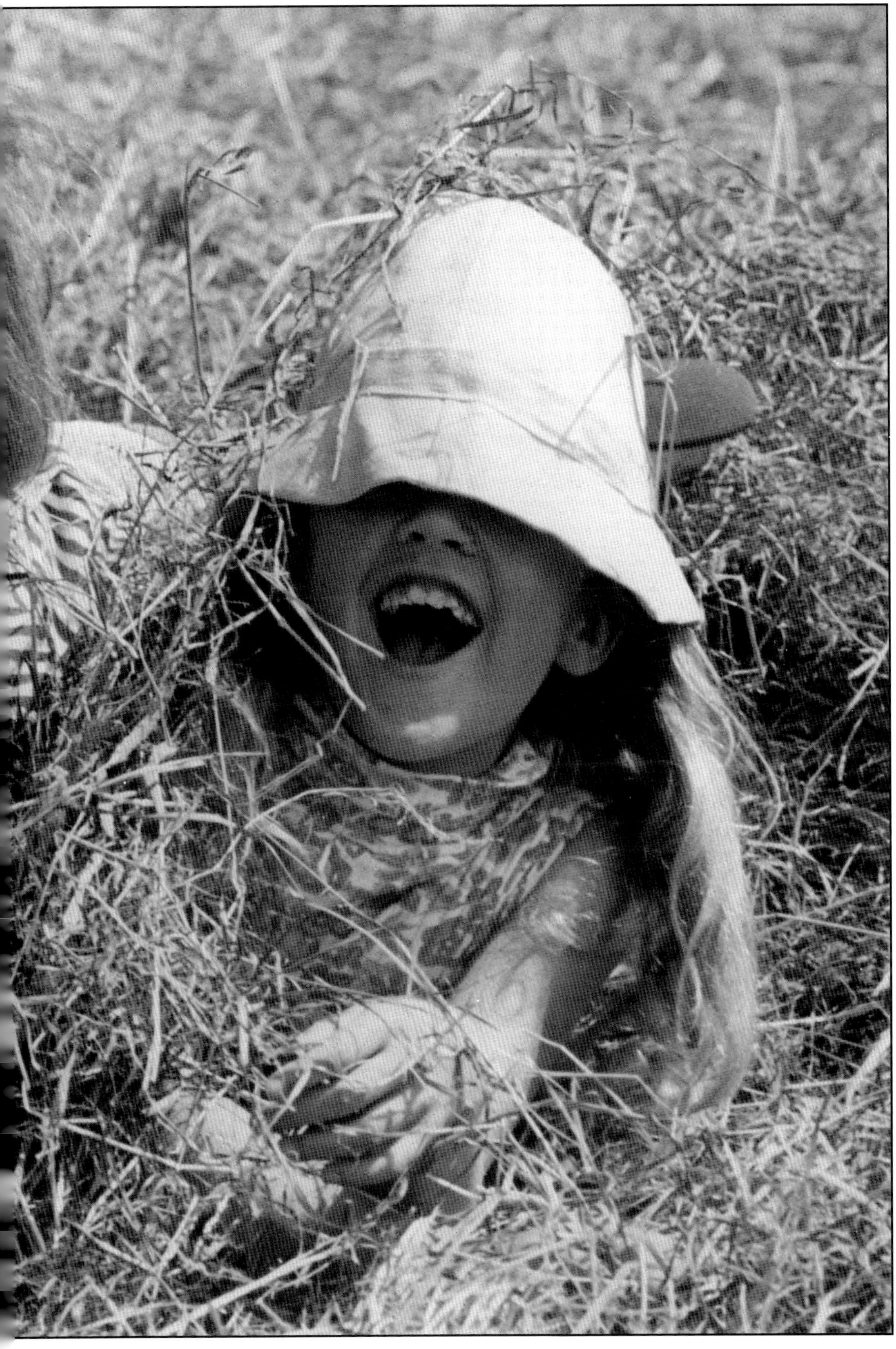

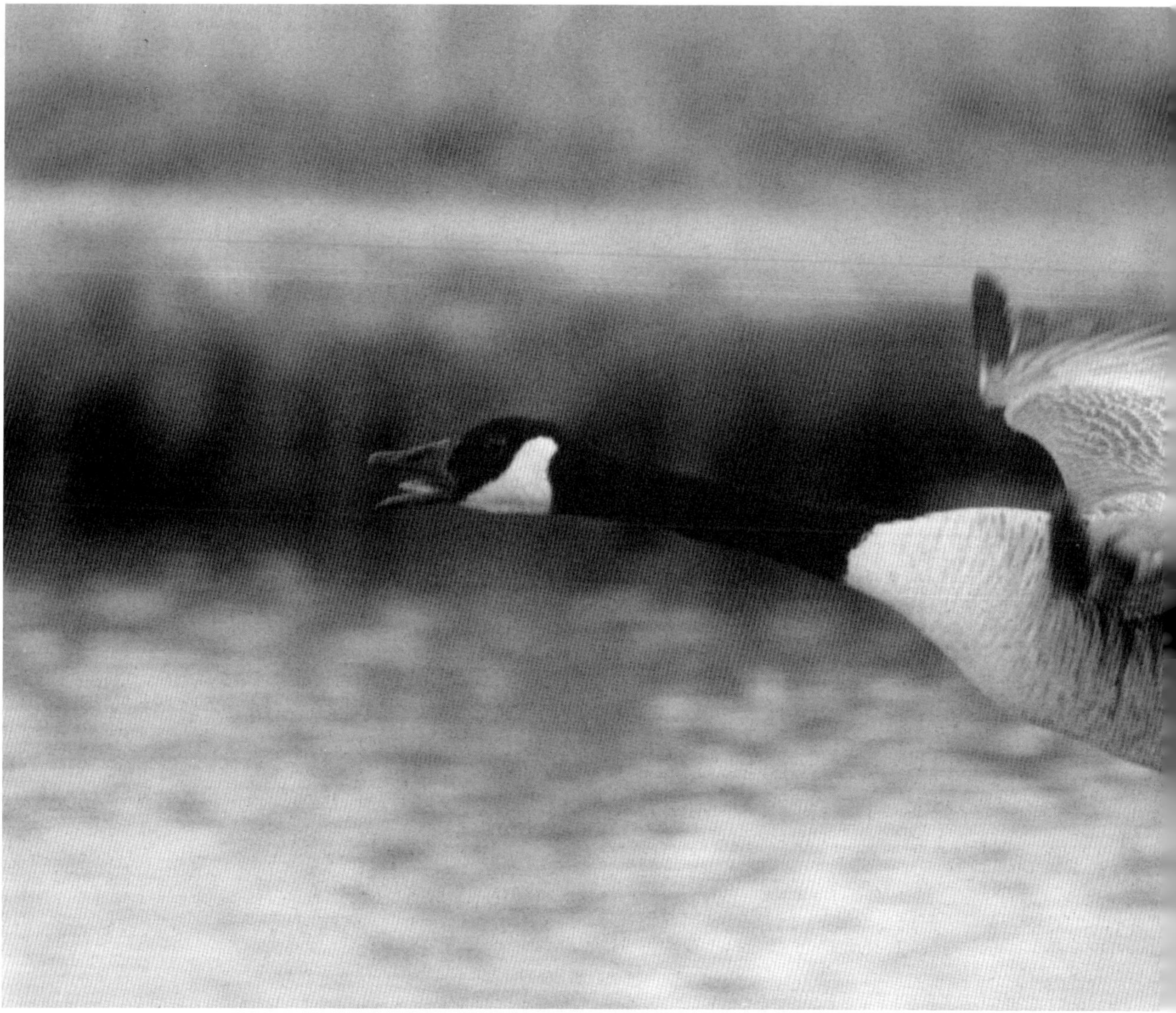

Fig. 199. Canada Goose. Angénieux 180mm DEM f/2.3 APO lens. Available in Leica-R fitting on the used market. A superb lens with internal focusing.

micrometer finesse. You will not find the kind of gravelly jerkiness inherent in some lesser brands. Combined with the Apo-Extender-R 2x, this objective can satisfy the demands of a great many distant situations likely to arise with other sports assignments, and in this context the considerable outlay required and the fact that only one large lens will have to be carried instead of two, begins to make more sense. With the extender fitted, the lens weighs about the same as the Apo-Telyt-R 280mm, f/2.8, but the bulk is significantly less and the effective focal length more useful in some respects even though a full stop in speed is lost.

In the days before wide aperture telephoto objectives were readily available – not so long ago for those not old enough to appreciate that era – a great many sports events had to be covered with equipment of lesser specification. That is to say, for example, that one of the most commonly used lenses, almost a standard for some photographers, was a 200mm, f4. This is catered for by Leica in the form of an Elmar-R 180mm f/4, a comparatively humble maximum aperture compared to the Apo-Summicron f2 just discussed.

This is the lightweight among 180's; at 540g one hardly notices it is there. Its physical dimensions are also only marginally more that the Elmarit-R 135mm, f/2.8. Obviously, this is not a lens for the table tennis photographer endeavouring to work with high quality ISO 64, or even ISO 200 Kodachrome under appalling light conditions. But it has considerable merit in other areas.

I find this focal length one of the most useful for many assignments, from travel photography through to

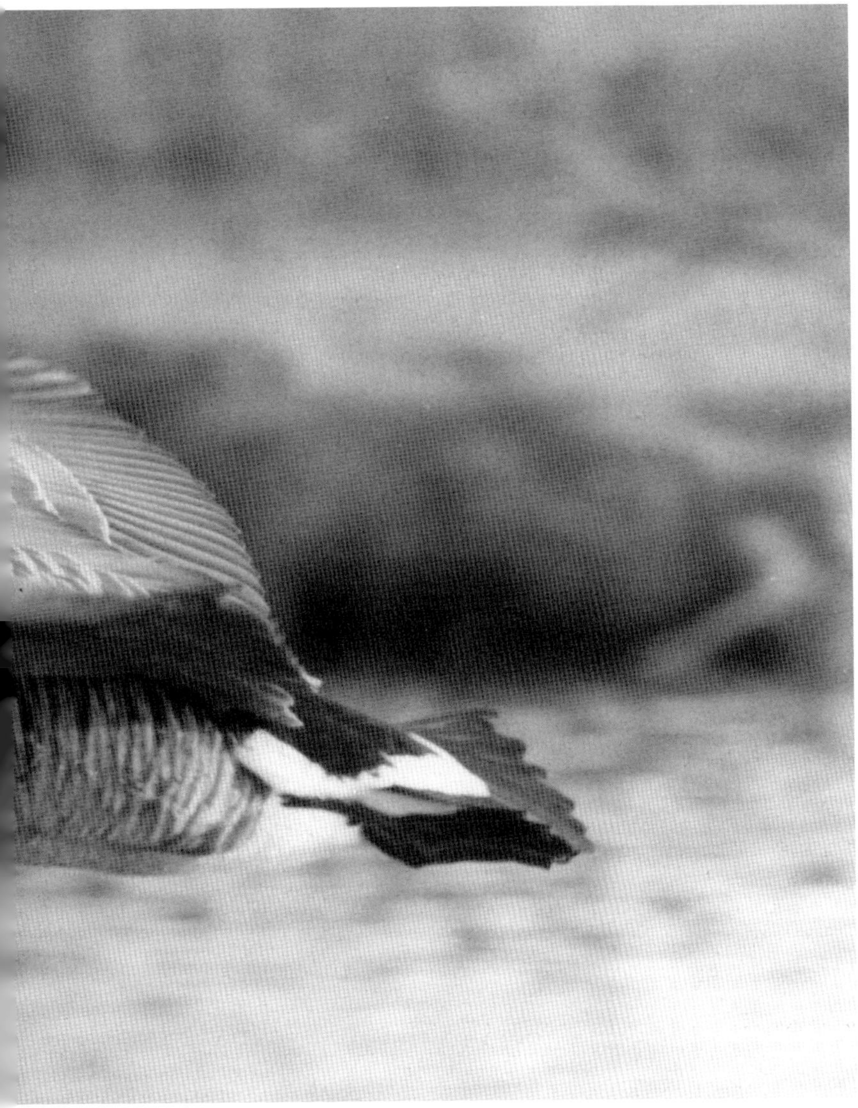

certain sports subjects. A really dull day at sea will not diminish my appreciation of its physical advantage, for even with ISO 25 film it is possible to work at fast shutter speeds with the diaphragm at maximum aperture, knowing full well that the image will not suffer because of that. On *terra firma*, this lens would run close to a first choice as a second lens in my personal line-up, mainly for its compactness, weight saving, all-round versatility and useful focal length. In cities and towns where there may be a need to isolate buildings and statues while retaining an accurate impression of scale relative to the surroundings, the 180 is hard to beat.

The final lens in this group is the Apo-Telyt-R 180mm, f/3.4. It has a slight edge in speed over the lens just discussed, and weighs just over 200 grams more. This is a beautifully balanced lens, but its main advantage for the travel photographer, photojournalist and aerial photographer is its high degree of apochromatic correction, enabling pin-sharp and highly detailed large scale enlargements to be made without difficulty. One cannot say too much about this excellent objective and if confronted with the opportunity of choice between this and the Apo-Summicron f/2, the monetary consideration would not be that high on the list. The f/3.4 version is less than one quarter the weight, so my requirements would have to centre squarely on low-light situations for the faster lens to be a priority.

During the early years of my career, my first choice of a second lens was a 135mm, f/2.8, used first on a Petriflex SLR and subsequently on a Leica M2. The Elmarit-M 135mm, f/2.8 is fitted with spectacles – 'goggles' – as they are sometimes called, which improve the rangefinder focus accuracy when using this lens. I always found this particular length provided a more natural reproduction scale for a great many subjects; it could be used effectively for portraits without the risk of flattening, or compressing the visual features too much. At sea, there were often situations which demanded its use, surprisingly so because the very nature of the environment is that things tend to happen over great distances. It therefore became one of my favourites and remained a constant companion for many years.

When I later became much more involved with sports and changed the reflex system to Nikon, the 200mm replaced the 135mm. Different subjects and different rules for photography. Yacht racing requires the photographer to work at a respectable distance from the subject – most of the time. The 200mm focal length had the edge on pulling power.

When I obtained my first Leica SLR, an R3, the choice of what to add to the lonely 50mm Summicron seemed obvious. The Elmarit-R 135mm, f/2.8 is identical in optical construction to the version used on the rangefinder camera. It's been said that once you have learned to roller skate, you never forget. I had spent so long using the 135 lenses that the impression of what an object could look like when photographed with it never left a corner of my mind. Going back to that kind of visual thinking was, as they say, a piece of cake, almost as if I had never been without it.

Using this focal length on the water again has also proved surprisingly easy. The only change in operating technique requires that my launch driver now has to approach the subject just that little bit closer. Neither of us mind about that because that is where the better pictures always are. On travel assignments, there are no end of situations where its length has proved a boon, from casual portraits and candids to landscapes and cityscapes. Its minimum focusing distance of 1.5m (5ft) leaves just enough room between subject and photographer for a respectable relationship. Once you begin to get too close, there is always that element of intimidation which can put the subject off. Armed with this, a 50mm and a 35mm Summicron, I usually feel quietly confident that not much will be missed and what I don't have, I cannot use, so not much point in looking for the pictures I cannot shoot.

However disciplined one tries to be about this subject, two criteria will play an important part in the selection of objectives. One is purpose – already mentioned. If you can be disciplined about that aspect then the answers are fairly clear cut. The other criteria is more elusive and has to do with the fact that in my experience the majority of photographers have a tendency toward fickleness. Like the weather, our ideas about how certain images look or might look, constantly change. This is a great asset in one way. It means that we never give up on the mind-searching; objects and subjects to photograph and ways to photograph to produce the best possible result. There is another side to fickleness in this context which has more to do with what certain people like to be seen wearing, around the neck or stuck on a tripod, the discussion of which ends here.

8.3. Probing the Distance Barrier

Two points of view exist with regard to the use of extreme telephoto lenses. One is the consideration of some photographers that longer telephoto lenses are best used to magnify the image. Seen from this perspective, if magnification were the only consideration, we could save ourselves a lot of back ache. The facts are right, in as much as the longer the focal length, the greater the magnifying power relative to say, a standard lens of 50mm. However, I am inclined to regard the philosophy and therefore the purpose of use, to be wrong. If tele-objectives are used simply to magnify the object to a stage where it fills the

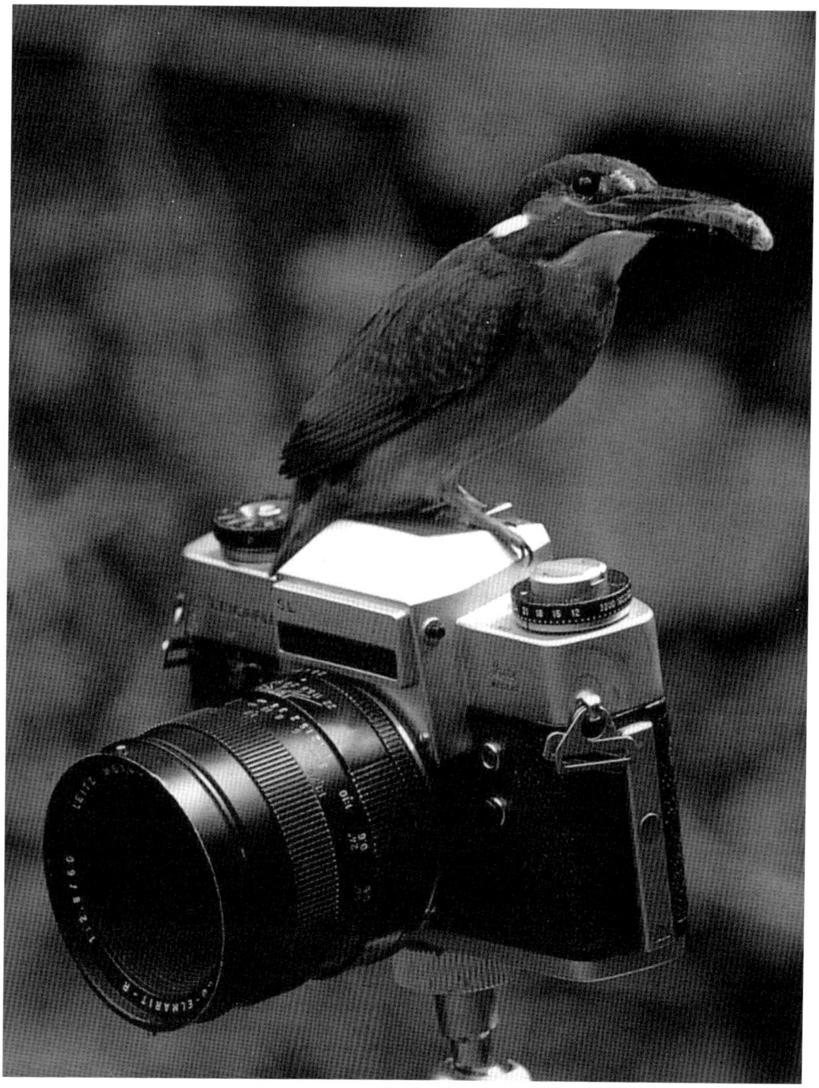

Charles W. Bruce snapped this great picture with his Leica R4 and Telyt-R 400mm f/6.8. He had been photographing a kingfisher site for some hours and, hoping for an unusual picture he rigged his tripod mounted with a Leicaflex SL near the nest. No sooner had he done so, a fishing parent landed on it.
© Charles W. Bruce.

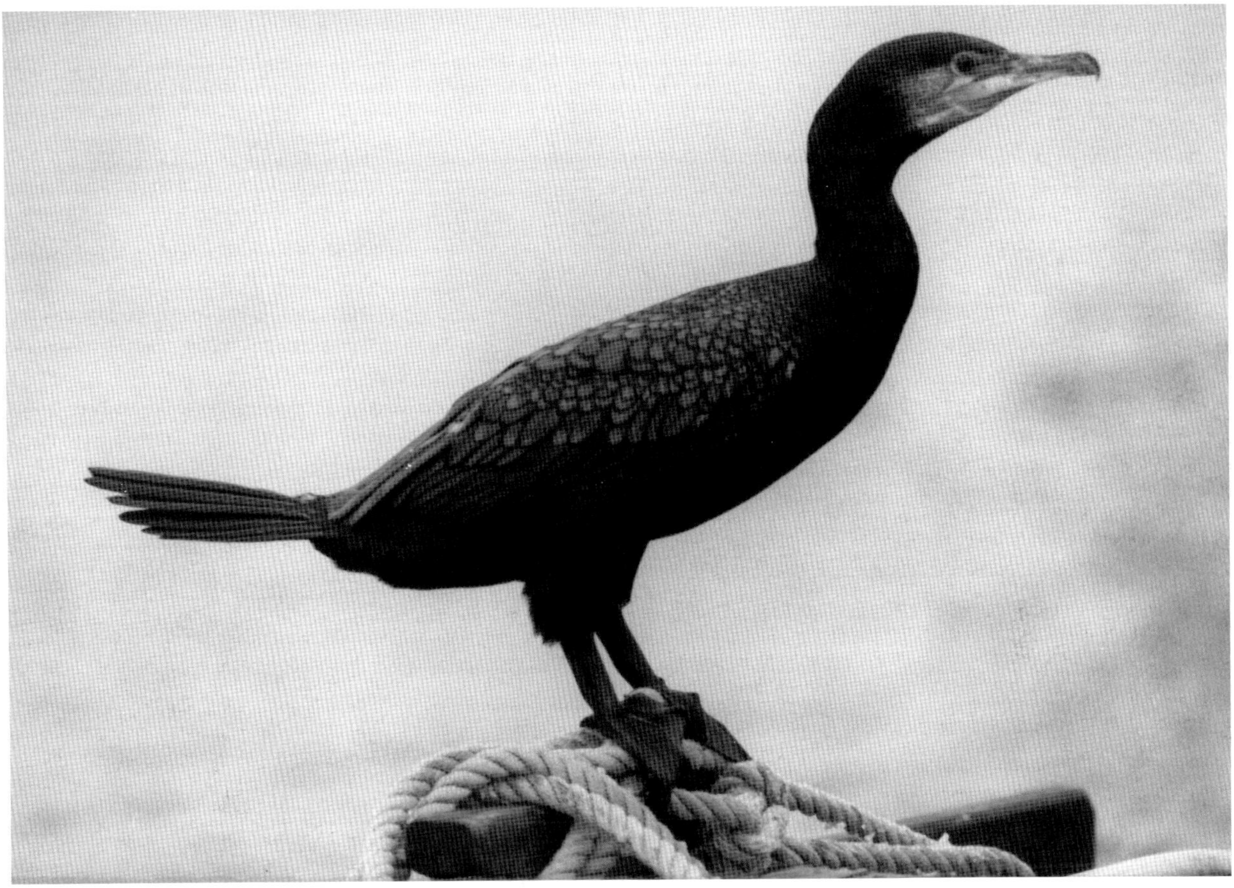

Fig. 200. Nature has given photographers a vast range of subject matter and a wonderful challenge. Tele-objectives from 180mm focal length upward are a basic requirement when the photographer intends to remain in command behind the camera.

frame, or where the viewer can clearly see the whites of a Snow Tiger's eyes, many of the optical features and the way in which these lenses can be employed by the photographer to interpret the subject are being ignored.

Obviously, there will be many occasions, in wildlife photography for example, when it is simply not possible to approach close to a subject without endangering one's own life, or frightening off the animal. In instances such as this, the longest tele objective available will be employed, but there is still no guarantee that a picture will result.

I tend to think of telephoto lenses as tools which, because of their special characteristics, can be used to obtain images of subjects which exist all around us and which in the absence of a longer focal length lens, could be photographed anyway, but perhaps not with such dramatic results. The longer the focal length, the more carefully its characteristics need to be considered in relation to the purpose to which it may be put.

If we disregard sports and wildlife subjects for a moment, which often require the use of telephoto lenses because of the way photographic access is controlled, we can turn to more ordinary matters. To take landscapes as an example, we often hear and read of experts in this field approaching the subject with short focal lengths. Sometimes a vista seen in a particular light may have a dramatic effect. The photographer turns to a wide-angle lens in order to fill the frame with as much of this vista as possible. The resulting image may be enlarged in print form, projected onto a screen or reproduced in print.

At this point it becomes a two-dimensional document, greatly diminished in size from the original and lacking its depth. While a few photographs made in this way can indeed be dramatic in their effect, they are few and far between in my opinion. Photographers who look at the scene and from it select a very small slice which can be photographed with a telephoto lens are attempting to maintain the scale of the subject as seen by the human eye. When the two-dimensional image is subsequently presented, it will be seen immediately that although the breadth of the vista is contracted, the impression of size is maintained.

This is an important feature because of the way we see things ordinarily. The mind is able to isolate very small areas of detail, even those seen over great distances. The camera cannot think, neither can the lens you fit to it, so as a photographer you must employ the most suitable tools available to maintain in the print the visual effect seen. The telephoto lens is the tool for this, but which focal length is employed will be governed largely by the distance of object to camera and how much of the object is required to fill the frame.

We can employ a simple rule of thumb here. The larger the building or monument, the bigger the landscape, the longer the lens. This brings other problems, not least of which is that in order to maintain the whole subject within the frame, the distance between subject and photographer must be increased. In many cases this may not be immediately possible because ofinterference from other objects which intrude into the frame. The determined photographer will find a way to make the picture with the longest lens possible, even if it means many hours of research to establish the best location and line of sight. Then there is the other uncontrollable factor; weather and the type of light which it produces.

Working in cities, one is frequently confronted with subjects which demand longer focal lengths. Photographers on assignments of this nature often have the added hassle of having to cover a large area in the shortest possible time. Moving around by car eliminates some of the headaches of transporting large amounts of equipment, but brings with it the major disadvantage that much of what you came to look at will be missed. The only way to ensure that you see as much as possible is to walk.

Some photographers have small baggage carts on which a large amount of equipment can be trundled around the streets. To me, this would almost be as much of an encumbrance as having to drive a car. The problem can be partially solved by selecting just one longer lens which will cover most eventualities and by adding an extender to the kit, will solve some of the remainder.

For this type of assignment, the faster Apo-Telyt-R 280mm f/2.8 would be too bulky for my liking, in spite of the fact that when fitted with the 1.4x converter, it is transformed into a useful 400mm (392mm) with a working maximum aperture of f/4. The newer Apo-Telyt-R 280mm, f/4 would be a far more desirable optic and not just because its weight is almost a kilo lighter. This lens is quite a lot bigger than one might expect, but it does not have the bulk of the f/2.8 version. It has superb balance and a beautifully smooth focus control ring covering half the overall length. It can also be used with both Apo-Extenders, though of the two, the 1.4x again gives a useful working aperture which in many situations would permit further stopping down to improve corner-to-corner sharpness.

In the realm of the less exotic, the Leica R user has a choice of older and slightly shorter lengths in the shape of a pair of 250mm, f/4 Telyt-R lenses. The earlier version is marginally heavier than the recently discontinued model, which is also fitted with a rotating tripod collar. The optical quality of both lenses is excellent, even though they have different optical designs (see Chapter 2). The Apo-Extender-R 2x and Extender-R 2x are both suitable for use with either lens, providing an effective focal length of 500mm with maximum aperture of f/8. There is no real problem in handling a lens of this focal length, but the new maximum aperture might present problems when used with slow speed emulsions in difficult lighting. The use of a monopod and/or a beanbag will be helpful.

Beyond the 300mm range, the physical length of objectives could be intimidating for some; the weight of the Telyt-S 800mm, f6.3 at almost 7 kilos would be enough to put off all but the fittest and, to be realistic, this size of lens would have limited uses in the types of environment just

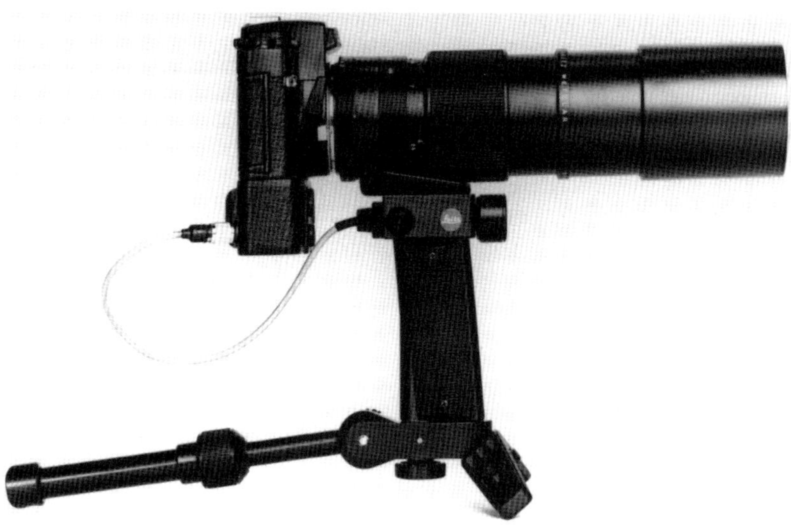

Fig. 196. A Telyt-R 350mm objective fitted with the detachable shoulder stock, motor drive and motor drive cable release to pistol grip.

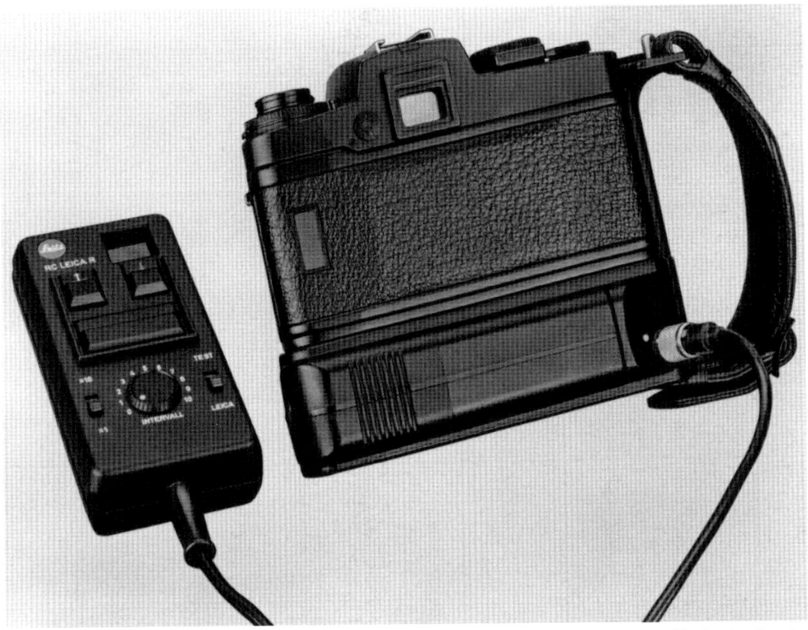

Fig. 201. A useful gadget for wildlife photographers who need to place a camera with shorter focal lengths close to a nesting site. The RC Leica R remote control switch provides a range of interval settings or manual override.

discussed. But we will return to this monster further on.

Not quite making the 'long-tom' grade is the Telyt-R 350mm f/4.8 which was first introduced in 1980 and remains in production. A similar optical design to the recently discontinued 250mm f/4, it is also fitted with a rotating tripod collar. It can just about be carried in a large gadget bag and weighs under two kilos. I'm not entirely convinced of the usefulness of the length of this lens, though I suppose 50mm doesn't make too much difference in practice.

In the 400mm league, Leica produce the substantial Apo-Telyt-R 400mm, f/2.8 which has an optical superiority unequalled in its length. This is a lens which will be seriously considered by sports photographers for two reasons. It easily converts to an effective 560mm, f/4 when used in conjunction with the Apo-Extender-R 1.4x – a length much favoured in these times for motor racing. Secondly, image quality is not impaired by adding the converter because of its full apochromatic correction. The lens features a preset focusing ring which enables the user to focus on a football goal mouth, for example, from a fixed position and lock this distance in so that the focusing ring can be easily flicked to action taking place in that area. Like its smaller 280mm counterpart, the lens has internal focusing, drop-in filters, and a large protective clip-on lens hood.

While certainly useful for many subjects, including fashion, it is not my cup of tea, being far too heavy for more general applications. My favourite at this length is the Telyt-R 400mm, f/6.8, a simple two-element achromat which is focused using a push-pull technique in a sliding tube. In this form, it is the same weight as the 350mm described above. The maximum aperture of this lens and its sibling, the Telyt-R 560mm, is f/6.8, which may be too slow for some. However, used in conjunction with the Universal Handgrip and Shoulder Stock, both objectives are surprisingly simple and quick to operate. They have the added advantage that they can both be used wide open with no loss of image quality. In fact, stopping down does not improve that aspect.

A 60mm extension tube is available for both lenses which reduces the minimum focus distance from 3.6m (12ft) with the 400mm to 2.25m (7.5ft) and from 6.4m (21ft) with the 560mm version to 3.96m (13ft). Both lens heads are also identical in optical design to the same focal length Telyts used for the Novoflex Rapid Follow Focus Grip. This device is described at some length in the Leica-M Compendium. It is comprised of a focusing tube operated by squeezing the first pistol grip. The second grip is used as an additional support as well as for firing the camera when the electrical release cable is fitted. Otherwise, the second front grip can be folded away flat and the shutter released conventionally, or by using the release of the motor drive or winder if either is attached.

Both the sliding tube push-pull method and rapid follow-focus grip are ideally suited to the physical size of these optics, but more especially to the 400mm which is superbly balanced in either configuration. Because the lens can be broken down into several parts, it is also very easy to transport in a bag. In its sliding tube, the 400mm Telyt is one of the easiest long-focus objectives to handle. An R-type camera fitted with this and a Leica Motor Drive-R becomes a powerful tool for tackling innumerable subjects from sports to wildlife and fashion to landscapes.

The Novoflex grip also separates into several parts, each component having a bayonet connection. I have used one of these objectives for many years and have nothing but praise for it. In a helicopter, on the water, at the race track or stuck in the undergrowth stalking birds, the Novoflex has never failed.

Used examples of varying age can be found on dealers' shelves, usually at moderate cost. Older versions can occasionally benefit from adjustment and you may find very early versions have damaged front element coatings. These can be replaced with new ones, but costs will vary from country to country and it is best to seek the advice of your nearest Novoflex distributor before committing funds.

The lens units produced by Novoflex are available in 400mm f/5.6 and 600mm f/8 versions, one stop faster and one stop slower than the Leica equivalents. The 400mm Novoflex is of triplet design while the 600 is an achromat. The elements are supplied by a specialist optical glass division of Agfa, based in Altenstadt.

An alternative to these longer tubed objectives exists in the form of the MR-Telyt-R 500mm, f/8, a catadioptric, or mirror lens, designed originally by Minolta. With an overall length of only 121mm, the lens is very compact for its focal length. Exposure control, in the absence of a diaphragm, is by the fitment of neutral density filters into a special mount at the rear of the lens.

This lens is small enough to be hand carried in a bag and can easily be hand-held for a wide variety of subjects. The optical construction of this type of lens gives rise to a peculiar phenomenon which is manifest in backlit photographs by bright circular highlight rings, commonly known as 'doughnuts', which are caused by the second mirror. Using the neutral density filter to control exposure does not change the working aperture of the lens; it remains at f/8, thus the depth of field also remains the same, as does the 'doughnut' size. The application of filters simply cuts down the illumination to produce effective equivalents to smaller apertures.

One optical advantage of the mirror lens is its ability to focus at near distant subjects, in the case of the MR-Telyt-R down to 4m (13.25 ft) and again, because of its optical design, will produce larger images at the close focus range than conventional lenses used without extension tubes. This feature could be useful to wildlife photographers who can take advantage of the short throw focusing ring to move from the middle to minimum distance with some rapidity.

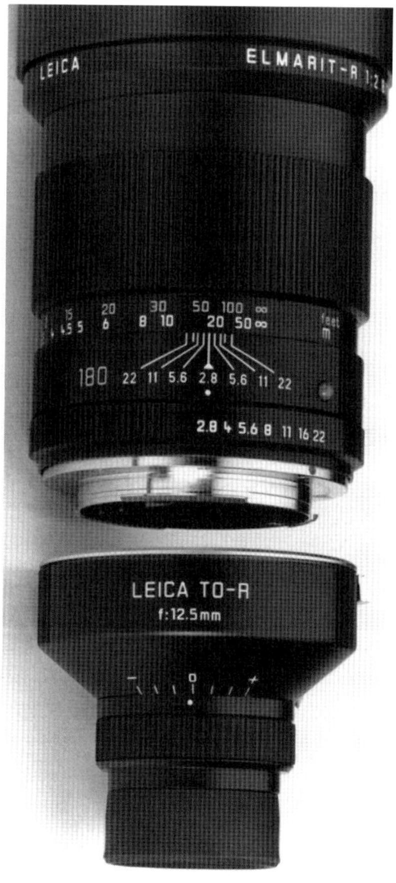

Fig. 202. And just in case you cannot quite see what is going on through the camera, Leica thoughtfully designed and manufactured this Telescope Ocular LEICA TO-R (14 234), which turns your prime lens into a powerful telescope. It has a focal length of 12.5 mm. To find the magnification factor of the objective when this is fitted, divide the focal length of the prime lens by the focal length of the telescope ocular.
Leica Camera GmbH

8.4. Longer and Further

The huge Telyt-S 800mm, f/6.3, first shown as the Telechron at Photokina in 1970, was subsequently used to cover the Olympic Games of 1972 and thereafter could be purchased to special order only. Compared with the standard 50mm lens, the 800mm has a magnification of 16x. It measures 790 mm, or almost 32 inches from one end to the other, and weighs 6.86kgs, or 15lbs. It could just about be hand held – at one end, while the other is rested on a firm support. It will be more practical, however, to use a substantial tripod, if necessary in conjunction with an additional support fixed to the front tripod socket. The simplest configuration comprises a large tripod fitted to the central mount, which permits the camera to be rotated between horizontal and vertical positions, while using a monopod with ball-and-socket head fitted to the front. Focus is by rack and pinion and the lens with camera attached can be set up and aimed by use of the sighting device on the carrying handle.

This is not an objective one plays with lightly. For a start, it is not particularly mobile, once assembled. It is the kind of equipment one uses for surveillance purposes, which could mean that it will suit the purposes of news, wildlife, sports or government departments equally well for fairly specific subjects. Its very narrow angle of view of 3° and shallow depth of field limit subject area and the zone of useful sharp focus. At an athletics meeting, the lens would be set up to focus on the finishing tape, or perhaps the long-jump pit; in the wild, probably on a nest or location likely to be frequented by the subject; news photographers might use it to obtain photographs of certain people or objects and buildings which would normally be hidden from the public gaze. I have seen it used effectively for landscapes, but atmospheric conditions will determine how successful this kind of long range photography will be.

The optical construction relies on a three-element symmetrical single group design with two identical negative elements cemented each side of the positive element. The result is a lens capable of producing images with very high contrast, excellent definition and magnificent colour differentiation. Almost all aberrations commonly associated with objectives of this type are insignificant. The lens breaks apart into several components, packing into a tough custom-made aluminium case for transportation. The retail cost of this lens would purchase several Leica-R camera bodies and a collection of shorter lenses.

For those without the wherewithal but who feel this focal length might enhance their photographic output, an alternative exists on the used market. The original Minolta 800mm, f/8 RF Rokkor-X mirror lens became available in 1972 following the Photokina show of that year. It has no diaphragm (see MR-Telyt 500mm above) but could be fitted with neutral-density filters to control exposure. I have not had the opportunity to use this lens, but from accounts written of it at the time, it maintained the very high optical specification Leicaflex users had expected and was noticeably free of chromatic aberration. This lens was discontinued from the Leitz/Leica catalogues many years ago and at the time of its listing had to be ordered directly from the Minolta distributor.

8.5. The Zoom Telephoto

The current telephoto zoom lens in the Leica-R range is the Vario-Elmar-R 70-210mm, f/4. The focal length provides a very useful range for the busy press photographer who has no need of a bag full of prime objectives to cover every eventuality. The same argument appeals to lots of photographers who simply don't want the weight and who are prepared to compromise certain demands they may have made on other objectives with the lower maximum aperture of the Vario-Elmar. Optically, this is an excellent lens, probably the top performer amongst branded and independent equivalents. Users may be hard pressed to distinguish the difference in image quality between this and prime optics in the focal length range. There is a difference however, albeit minimal, and this will become more evident as the size of reproduction in print and projection is increased.

I used a similar lens for some years for a wide variety of assignments, ranging from sports to travel, and in many different parts of the world. Looking at a cross section of the images made with that lens today, the only observation I would make is that compared to similar images made with prime lenses, the zoom products have marginally lower contrast, but it is barely detectable. Apart from the obvious weight saving, using a zoom lens often facilitates more rapid pictorial control by allowing the photographer to exclude extraneous objects from the picture without moving position. In certain situations faced by the press photographer, this might mean the difference between obtaining a splendid head shot or not.

My favourite use of the zoom lens involves the technique of exposing frames on certain subjects while zooming the lens through its focal length during the exposure. The technique is not new of course. It has been around since variable focus lenses were first introduced by the firm of Voigtländer in 1959. This technique is much more difficult to control with the more conventional two-ring control. Fortunately, the Leica Vario-Elmar-R 70-210mm has a substantial rubber covered 'one touch' focus and zoom grip, which makes the job of manipulating the lens very simple, whether zooming for effect or 'straight' pictures.

Having selected the Elmarit-R 135mm, f/2.8 as my second lens to accompany the Summicron-R 50mm, my next choice would fall squarely between this superb zoom lens and a 180mm. On balance, I think I might be inclined to opt for the zoom for the days when I want to travel really light as well as to take advantage of its great optical versatility.

CHAPTER 9

Afterword

It is only in very recent years that Leica R-type cameras have increased their popularity across the spectrum of both amateur and professional circles. In part, this has been due to Leica Camera's active international promotion of the marque as well as to their commitment to expanding the system.

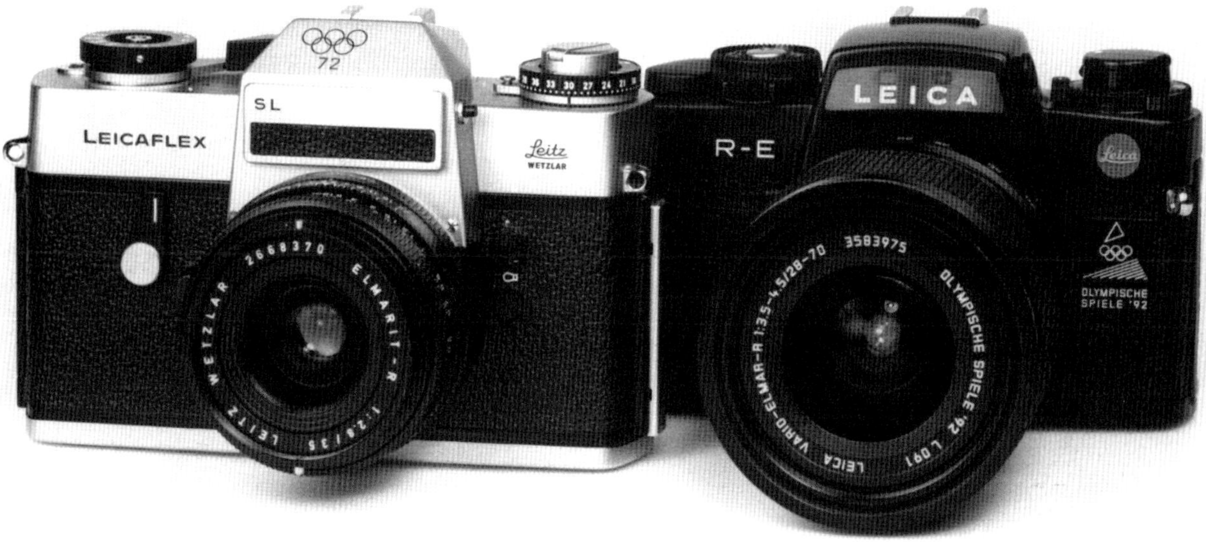

Fig. 204. A 1972 Munich Olympic Leicaflex SL and the 1992 Barcelona Olympic Leica R-E, complete with Vario-Elmar-R 28-70mm lens.
Fieldgrass & Gale/Jonathan Harris

Significant steps have been made in this direction by producing some of the accessories demanded by professionals.

In assembling the information for this volume, I have tried whenever the opportunity has arisen, to obtain some idea from Leica Camera GmbH of new products which are likely to be launched on to the market. In the Introduction for example, I raised the subject of auto-focus, two words which dedicated purists will not want to hear in relation to sophisticated Leica cameras.

For the time being at least, there is no hint coming from Solms of a single lens reflex camera of similar specification to the R7 and with auto-focus being prepared for the market. But I am sure that Leica R & D has given this type of machine a great deal of thought and has thoroughly investigated the market potential. Like a great many people in photographic circles, Leica Camera GmbH may be of the opinion that too much automation in a camera removes much of the mystery for the user; once the initial novelty has worn off, boredom sets in. Net result, sales collapse.

The level of sophistication of auto-focus in some other top ranking brands is now very high. Many photographers who were previously adamant that a/f would be of no benefit, are now reaping the rewards because of it. In its present state, it is a useful tool to be exploited like any other as a means to obtaining the best possible image. It is already good; and it will get better.

The other reason for pestering Solms on the question of new products has to do with an endeavour to see that this book is current at the time of going to press, and that it stands a reasonable chance of remaining so for some time. In the absence of better information, I believe that the Leica R6.2 and R7 will remain in the production programme for a while yet, although Solms has said that it is developing new models in the R-series which are not based on any current Minolta model. There is not much point in speculating further as to what might come next, but I would be surprised if it did not contain some sort of digital focus-confirmation feature.

In the meantime, I hope this volume will go some way to providing some of the answers sought by new members to the Leica R fraternity, and that they will enjoy using the system the more because of it.

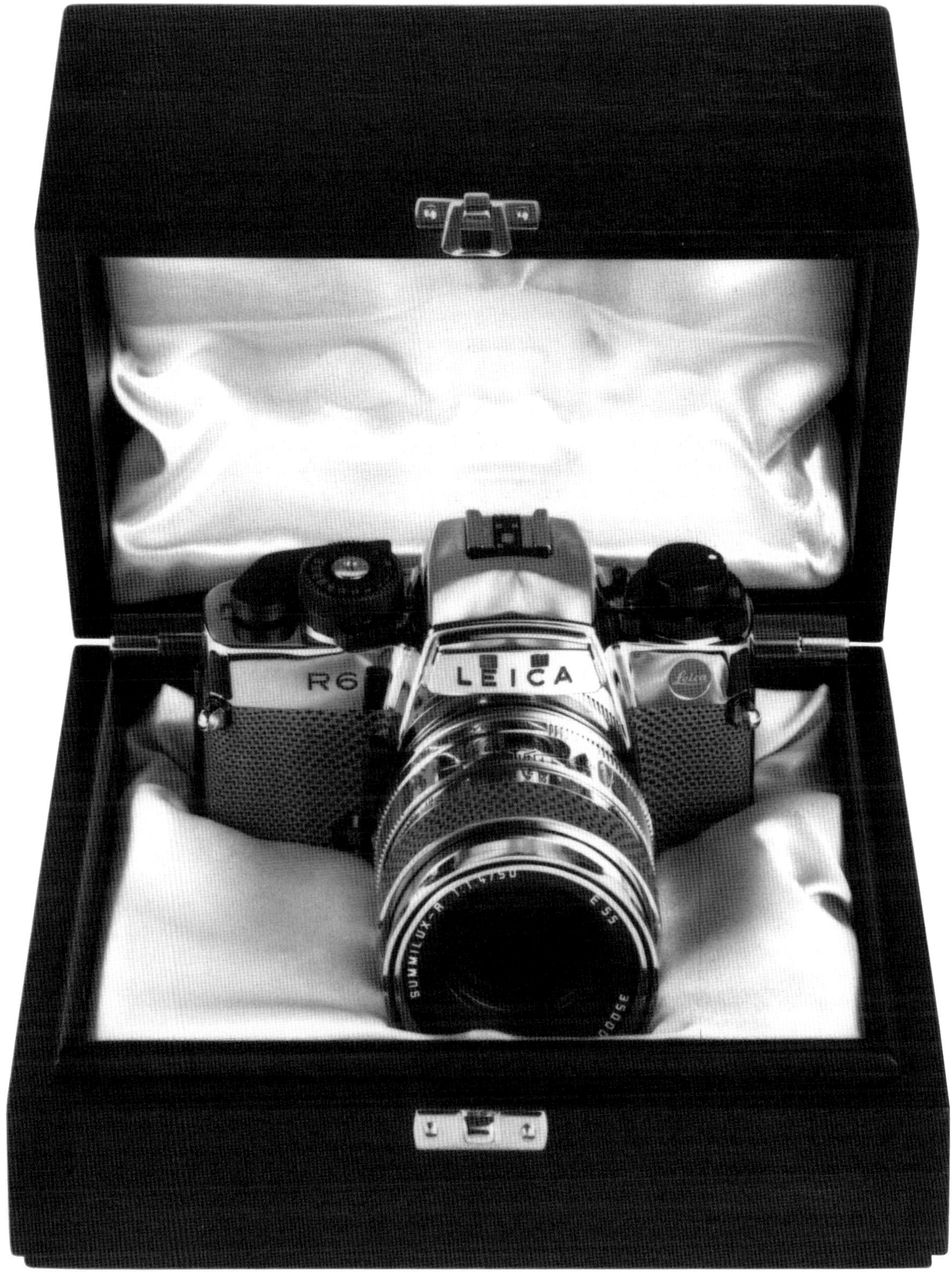

Fig. 203. A Unique Leica R6 single lens reflex – serial No. 1,750,000 – in polished platinum plate with karung leather covering the body, fitted with a Summilux-R 50mm, f/1.4 – serial No. 3,500,075 – auctioned by Christie's South Kensington in November 1989 for the record sum of £24,600. The camera was made to commemorate 150 years of photography. A platinum plate on the camera back is engraved '150 Jahre Photography 1989. 75 Jahre Leica Photographie. Leica.' The camera was enclosed in a lined mahogany box with platinum catch and a second replica plaque. The proceeds of the sale went to the World Wildlife Fund. *Christie's South Kensington, London*

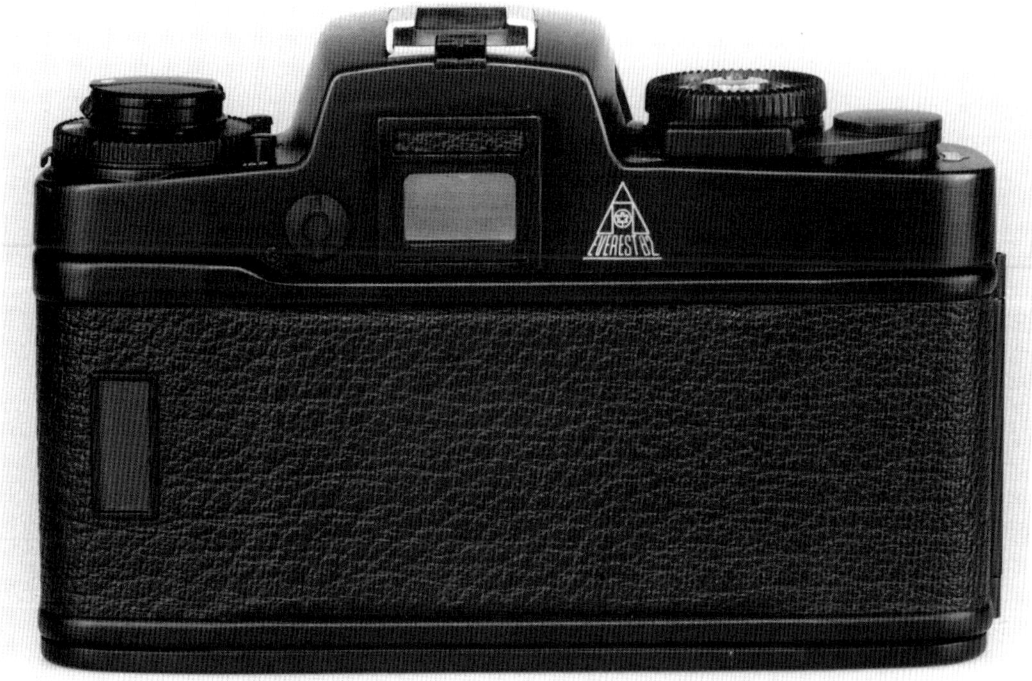

Fig. 205. The successful scaling of Mount Everest by the Canadian expedition in 1982 was marked by the issue of specially engraved Leica-R4 SLR's and rangefinder M4-Ps. 200 of each were engraved with the logo seen on the back top plate of this R4. *Fieldgrass & Gale/Jonathan Harris*

Compared with the Leica rangefinder, the volume and variety of 'collectable' pieces of the Leicaflex and Leica R-system may be lower, but no less interesting. Unusual items from the Ernst Leitz period are still brought to dealers' counters by owners who have no idea of their pedigree; occasionally they are also offered for sale in the classified advertisements of the photographic press and they can, as we have seen, be unearthed at collectors fairs.

The few prototypes and numberless pre-production models of very early cameras are already well guarded in private collections. This leaves ordinary production models, the worth of which is largely dependent on model type, cosmetic condition and special attributes, such as an interesting serial number. Many Leicaflex Standards can be found being offered by private advertisers at little more than their original cost; battered examples of a 'pie' are sometimes offered by more optimistic owners while the more usable and more plentiful SL remains moderately priced. The SL2 in all versions continues to rocket, but these too can sometimes be found more reasonably.

Part of the fun of collecting has to do with discovering the many different facets of Leica accessories and ephemera. Oddities with misspelled engravings are rare, but they do turn up. Then there is the subject of printed literature, a substantial pile of which has been published over the years. Where does it all go? When new models are launched, old literature is dumped. A few specialist dealers keep it if they can, but they are rare preservationists. What is throw-away publicity today, is collector fodder for tomorrow.

A much more difficult area and one which has interested me for several years, is the collection of Leica 'images'. Prints, negatives, transparencies, anything, so long as it is original. While researching material for this book I was lucky enough to come across a trunk full of original Leica negatives and prints made by a well known theatre photographer of the 1940's and 50's. Finds such as this are unusual and the contents of a roll of negatives are often the more fascinating because of that. One lives in the hope of finding a gem worthy of space on the wall and ultimately, as a Leica user, one has to face up to reality; it is the 'image' with which one is really concerned. As Robert E. Derecktor, the author of the foreword in my book 'Great Yachts and Their Designers' observed; 'After reading and looking at pictures, you want to get out and use, feel and see the real thing in action.'

Exactly!

Addresses for the Leica-R User

NOVOFLEX FOTOGERATEBAU
KARL MULLER
DONAUSTRASSE 78
D-8040 MEMMINGEN
GERMANY

LEICA CAMERA GmbH
OSKAR-BARNACK-STRASSE 11,
D-6336 SOLMS
GERMANY
TEL: + 49 0 64 42 208 0.
FAX: + 49 0 64 42 208 333
TELEX 4 82 610 LEICA D.

LEICA CAMERA LTD
DAVY AVENUE
KNOWHILL
MILTON KEYNES MK5 8LB
ENGLAND
TEL: 44 908 666663
FAX: 44 908 671316.

LEICA CAMERA INC.,
156 LUDLOW AVENUE
NORTHVALE
NEW JERSEY NJ 07647
USA
TEL: + 201 767 7500

MAGAZINE

LEICA FOTOGRAFIE INTERNATIONAL
8 Issues per year published in English, French and German.

Contact:

UMSCHAU VERLAG
STUTTGARTER STRASSE 18 - 24
6000 FRANKFURT/MAIN
GERMANY.

LEICA USERS PROPERTY REGISTER AND NEWSLETTER
THE LEICA REGISTER
296 CHICHESTER ROAD
COPNOR
PORTSMOUTH P02 OAS
UK.

Technical Specifications

We have included as much information as we possibly can to assist the enthusiast, and as far as we know it contains all information presently available up to the date of publication. However, as in all things, these are subject to change.

LEICA SLR Camera models

LEICA SLR MODEL	Year Introduced	Approximate Production Quantity	Shutter Type	Shutter Speed Range	Meter Type	Meter Modes: Spot	Meter Modes: Full Field	Interchangeable Screens	Exposure Compensation	Manual Exposure	Aperture Priority Selective	Aperture Priority Full Field	Shutter Priority	Auto Programme	Var. Programme	'X' Synch	Hot Shoe	P.C. 'X' & 'M'
LEICAFLEX	1964	37500	FP	B+1 sec-1/2000	Cds	●				o						1/100		o
LEICAFLEX SL	1968	70995	FP	B+1 sec-1/2000	Cds	●				o						1/100		o
LEICAFLEX SL MOT	1972	1080	FP	B+1 sec-1/2000	Cds	●				o						1/100		o
LEICAFLEX SL2	1974	24555	FP	B+1 sec-1/2000	Cds	●				o						1/100	o	o
LEICAFLEX SL2 MOT	1975	1020	FP	B+1 sec-1/2000	Cds	●				o						1/100	o	o
LEICA-R3	1976	71250	CLS	4 secs-1/1000	Cds	●	■		o	o	o	o				1/90	o	o
LEICA-R4	1980	85665(1)	VFP(3)	8 secs-1/1000	Si	●	■	o	o	o	o	o	o	o		1/100	o	o
LEICA-R4S	1983	19000	VFP(3)	8 secs-1/1000	Si	●	■	o	o	o	o	o				1/100	o	o
LEICA-R4S MOD 2	1985	6931	VFP(3)	8 secs-1/1000	Si	●	■	o	o	o	o	o				1/100	o	o
LEICA-R5	1986	13577(2)	VFP(3)	15 secs-1/2000	Si	●	■	o	o	o	o	o	o	o		1/100	o	o
LEICA-R6	1988	N/A	VFP(3)	B+1 sec-1/1000	Si	●	■	o	o	o						1/100	o	o
LEICA-RE	1990	N/A	VFP(3)	15 secs-1/2000	Si	●	■	o	o	o	o	o				1/100	o	o
LEICA-R62	1992	N/A	VFP(3)	B+1 sec-1/2000	Si	●	■	o	o	o						1/100	o	o
LEICA-R7	1992	N/A	VFP(3)	16 secs-1/2000	Si	●	■	o	o	o	o	o	o		o	1/100	o	o

(1) R4 to 1984 (2) R5 to 1988 (3) VFP=Vertical Focal Plane

TTL Flash Synch.(4)	Self Timer	Mirror-up Lock	Depth of Field Preview	Multiple Exposure	DX Film Speed Setting	Manual Film Speed Setting	Viewfinder Ancillary Light	Motor Winder Option	Motor Drive Option	Meter Battery Spec.	Dimensions LxHxD (mm)	Weight (grams)	Product Code Body Only	Year Discontinued	Availability(5)
	o	o	o			o				1.35v PX625	148x97x 57	770	10 001(c)	1968	R2
	o		o			o				1.35v PX625	148x97x 57	770	10 011(c) 10 012(b)	1974	R1 R5
						o			o	1.35v PX625	148x97x 57	770	10 013(b)	1974	R7
	o					o	o			1.35v PX625	148x97x 57	770	10 021(c) 10 022(b)	1976	R7 R3
						o	o		o	1.35v PX625	148x97x 57	770	10 023(b)	1976	R7
	o		o	o		o		o		1.55v x2	148x96.5x 64.6	780	10 031(c) 10 032(b) 10 034(s) 10 033(m)	1979	R6 R1 R6 R1
	o		o	o		o		o	o	1.55v x2	138.5x88.1x 62.2	630	10 041(c) 10 043(b)	1986	R6 R1
	o		o	o		o		o	o	1.55v x2	138.5x88.1 x62.2	630	10 045(b)	1985	R2
	o		o	o		o		o	o	1.55v x2	138.5x88.1 x62.2	630	10 046 10 047(1)	1988	R5
o	o		o	o		o		o	o	1.55v x2	138.5x88.1 x62.2	625	10 060(c) 10 061(b)	1992	R1 R1
o	o	o	o	o		o	o	o	o	1.55v x2	138.5x89.1 x63.5	625	10 070(c) 10 071(b)	1992	R6
o	o		o	o		o	o	o	o	1.55v x2	138.5x89.1 x63.5	625	10 055(b)	July '94	R1
o	o	o	o	o		o	o	o	o	1.55v x2	138.5x89.1 x63.5	625	10 073(c) 10 074(b)	current model	NEW
o	o	o	o	o	o	o	o	o	o	1.5v x4 3v x2	138.5x94.8 x62.2	670	10 068(c) 10 067(b)	current model	NEW

(4)TTL Flash Exp. only with SCA Adaptors (c) Chrome (b) Black (s) Safari (m) MOT (1) R4s MOD P - in USA (5)According to Leica International Price Guide 6th Edition, Hove Collectors Books, 1994

Current LEICA-R Objectives

LENS	Max. aperture. f/length mm	Angle of view	No. of elements/ comp.	Smallest aperture	Focus range in m	Smallest object area in mm	Recom. filter size series	Length in mm	Diam. in mm	Weight in g	Order No.
SUPER-ELMAR-R	f/3.5/15	110°	13/12(1)	22	∞-0.16	70x106	built in(2)	92.5	83.5	910	11213
FISHEYE-ELMARIT-R	f/2.8/16	180°	11/8	16	∞-0.30	401x601	built in(2)	60	71	460	11222
ELMARIT-R	f/2.8/19	96°	12/10	22	∞-0.30	264x396	built in(3)	60	71	560	11258
SUPER-ANGULON-R	f/4/21	92°	10/8	22	∞-0.20	148x221	series 8.5	43.5	78	420	11813
ELMARIT-R	f/2.8/24	84°	9/7[1]	22	∞-0.30	250x374	series 8	48.5	67	400	11257
ELMARIT-R	f/2.8/28	76°	8/8	22	∞-0.30	188x282	E55	40	63	310	11259
PC-SUPER-ANGULON-R	f/2.8/28	73/93(1)	12/10(1)	22	∞-0.28	146x219	special filter 67 EW(5)	84	75	600	11812
SUMMILUX-R	f/1.4/35	64°	10/9(1)	16	∞-0.50	266x399	E67	76	75	690	11144
SUMMICRON-R	f/2/35	64°	6/6	16	∞-0.30	140x210	E55	54	66	430	11115
ELMARIT-R	f/2.8/35	64°	7/6	22	∞-0.30	140x210	E55	41.5	66	310	11251
PA-CURTAGON-R	f/4/35	67/78(6)	7/6	22	∞-0.30	140x210	series 8	51	70	330	11202
SUMMILUX-R	f/1.4/50	45°	7/6	16	∞-0.50	180x270	E55	50.6	66.5	400	11777
SUMMICRON-R	f/2/50	45°	6/4	16	∞-0.50	180x270	E55	41	66	290	11216
MACRO-ELMARIT-R	f/2.8/60	39°	6/5	22	∞-0.27 (with adapter to 1:1)	48x72 (24x36)	E55	62.3 (92.3)	67.5	400 (530)	11253
SUMMILUX-R	f/1.4/80	30°	7/5	16	∞-0.80	192x288	E67	69	75	700	11881
SUMMICRON-R	f/2/90	27°	5/4	16	∞-0.70	140x210	E55	61	69	520	11254
ELMARIT-R	f/2.8/90	27°	4/4	22	∞-0.70	140x210	E55	57	67	450	11154
APO-MACRO-ELMARIT-R	f/2.8/100	25°	8/6	22	∞-0.45 (with ELPRO 1:2-1:1)	48x72 (22X33)	E60	104.5 (140)	73	760 (950)	11210
MACRO-ELMAR-R	f/4/100	25°	4/3	22	∞-0.60 (with adapter to 1:1.6)	72x108 (38x57)	E55	90 (120)	67.5	530 (660)	11232
MACRO-ELMAR-R	f/4/100	25°	4/3	22	Bellows only ∞-1.1:1	24x36	E55	62.5	68	290	11270
ELMARIT-R	f/2.8/135	18°	5/4	22	∞-1.50	220x330	E55	93	67	730	11211
APO-SUMMICRON-R	f/2/180	14°	9/6	16	∞-1.50	158x237	series 6	176	116	2500	11271
ELMARIT-R	f/2.8/180	14°	5/4	22	∞-1.80	193x290	E67	121	75	810	11923
APO-TELYT-R	f/3.4/180	14°	7/4	22	∞-2.50	276x414	E60	135	68	750	11242
ELMAR-R	f/4/180	14°	5/4	22	∞-1.80	175x262	E55	100	65.5	540	11922
TELYT-R	f/4/250	10°	7/6	22	∞-1.70	124x186	E67	195	75	1280	11925
APO-TELYT-R	f/2.8/280	8.5°	8/7	22	∞-2.50(7)	195x293	E112 series 5,5	261	125	2800	11263
APO-TELYT-R	f/4/280	8.8°	7/6	22	∞-1.70	120x180	E77 series 5,5	208	90/ 97.5	1875	11261
TELYT-R*	f/4.8/350	7°	7/5	22	∞-3.00	171x257	E77	286	83.5	1820	11915
APO-TELYT-R	f/2.8/400	6°	11/9	22	∞-4.70(7)	280x420	series 5,5	365	165	5500	11260
TELYT-R	f/6.8/400	6°	2/1	32	∞-3.60(8)	158x236	series 7	384	89	1830	11953
TELYT-R (System Novaflex)	f/6.8/400	6°	2/1	32	∞-2.40(8)	90x135	filter drawer	406	89	2930	11926
MR-TELYT-R	f/8/500	5°	5/5	8	∞-4.00	180x270	5 filters in delivery(9)	121	87	750	11243
TELYT-R (System Novaflex)	f/6.8/560	4.3°	2/1	32	∞-4,15(8)	124x187	filter drawer	534	98	3200	11927
TELYT-S	f/6.3/800	3°	3/1	32	∞-12,50	320x480	series 7	790	152	6860	11921
VARIO-ELMAR-R*	f/3.5-4.5/ 28-70	76-34°	11/8	22	∞-0.50	336x504 114x216	E60	84	74.8	465	11265
VARIO-ELMAR-R	f/3.5/35-70	64-34°	8/7	22	∞-1.00	632x947 338x507	E67	66.5	76.5	450	11248
VARIO-ELMAR-R	f/4/70-210	35-12°	12/9	22	∞-1.10	264x396 96x144	E60	157	73.5	720	11246

1) with floating elements
2) filter turret with UV-yellow-orange and blue conversion filter for artificial light exposures on daylight film
3) filter turret with neutral coating filter (NDx1) yellow-green-orange and blue conversion filter for artificial light on daylight film
4) horizontal or vertical offset up to 11mm, diagonal offset up to 9.5mm
5) filter for special wide-angle holder with aperture, from B&W Filterfabrik, D-6550, Bad Kreuznach
6) Offset up to 7mm
7) inner focusing
8) fast-focusing attachment by adjustable lens front component
9) special screw-in filter M32 x 05: UV neutral grey 4x, yellow, orange

APO-EXTENDER-R 2x Order No. 11 262
EXTENDER-R 2x* Order No. 11 236
APO-EXTENDER-R 1.4x Order No. 11 249

*Discontinued 1994

LEICA R-Lenses with Accessories

Product	Filter	Order No.
OBJECTIVE		
SUPER-ELMAR-R f/3.5/15mm	▪)	11 213
FISHEYE-ELMARIT-R f/2.8/16mm	▪)	11 222
ELMARIT-R f/2.8/19mm	▪)	11 258
SUPER-ANGULON-R f/4/21mm	S8,5	11 813
ELMARIT-R f/2.8/24mm	S8	11 257
ELMARIT-R f/2.8/28mm	E55	11 259
PC-SUPER-ANGULON-R 2.8/28mm	67EW	11 812
SUMMILUX-R f/1.4/35mm	E67	11 144
SUMMICRON-R f/2/35mm	E55	11 115
ELMARIT-R f/2.8/35mm	E55	11 251
PA-CURTAGON-R f/4/35mm	S8	11 202
SUMMILUX-R f/1.4/50mm	E55	11 777
SUMMICRON-R f/2/50mm	E55	11 216
ELPRO 1 Near focusing attachment		16 541
ELPRO 2 Near focusing attachment		16 542
Leather pouch for ELPRO		14 553
MACRO-ELMARIT-R f/2.8/60mm	E55	11 253
MACRO-ADAPTER-R		14 256
SUMMILUX-R f/1.4/80mm	E67	11 881
SUMMICRON-R f/2/90mm	E55	11 254
ELPRO 3 Near focusing attachment		16 543
Leather pouch for ELPRO		14 533
MACRO-ELMAR-R f/4/100mm	E55	11 232
MACRO-ADAPTER-R		14 256
APO-MACRO-ELMARIT-R f/2.8/100mm	E60	11 210
Near focusing attachment ELPRO 1:2–1:1		16 545
Tripod link STA 1		14 636
Circular flash on request		
ELMARIT-R f/2.8/135mm	E55	11 211
ELPRO 3 Near focusing attachment		16 543
ELPRO 4 Near focusing attachment		15 544
Leather pouch for ELPRO		14 553
APO-SUMMICRON-R f/2/180mm	S6	11 271
ELMARIT-R f/2.8/180mm	E67	11 923
APO-TELYT-R f/3.4/180mm	E60	11 242
ELMAR-R f/4/180mm	E55	11 922
TELYT-R f/4/250mm	E67	11 925
APO-TELYT-R f/4/280mm	▪)	11 261
APO-TELYT-R f/2.8/280mm	S5,5	11 263
APO-EXTENDER-R 1.4 x plus		11 249
Circ.-Polf. in filter turret		13 338
TELYT-R f/4.8/350mm	E77	11 915
APO-TELYT-R f/2.8/400mm	S5,5	11 260
APO-EXTENDER-R 1.4 x plus		11 249
Circ.-Polf in filter turret		13 338
TELYT-R f/6.8/400mm, complete	S7	11 953
TELYT-R f/6.8/400mm with NOVOFLEX Rapid follow-focus grip	*)	11 926
MR-TELYT-R f/8/500mm	E77	11 243
TELYT-R f/6.8/560mm with NOVOFLEX Rapid follow-focus grip	▪)	11 927
TELYT-S f/6.3/800mm	S7	11 921
APO-EXTENDER-R 2x		11 262
APO-EXTENDER-R 1.4x		11 249
ZOOM LENSES		
VARIO-ELMAR-R f/3.5-4.5/28-70	E60	11 265
VARIO-ELMAR-R f/3.5/35-70mm	E67	11 248
VARIO-ELMAR-R f/4/70-210mm	E60	11 246
CLOSE-FOCUS EQUIPMENT		
FOCUSING BELLOWS-R BR2		16 880
MACRO-ELMAR f/4/100mm for Bellows		11 270
PHOTAR-Lenses: on Focusing Bellows-R BR 2 via intermediate ring		14 259
PHOTAR f/2.4/12.5mm		54 9025
PHOTAR f/2/25mm		54 9026
PHOTAR f/4/50mm		54 9027
REPROVIT-R Repro-Tripod 220-230V/300W		16 717
RING COMBINATION for close-focus		14 159
Compatible double cable release		16 494
MACRO-ADAPTER-R		14 256

▪)=Filter built in

LEICA COMPATIBILITY

All LEICA R-Lenses, MACRO-ADAPTERS-R, APO-EXTENDER-R 2x and 1.4x, FOCUSING BELLOWS BR 2 and RING COMBINATIONS are compatible with all LEICA R-Cameras

USERS OF OLDER MODELS

Note the following cam identification (focusing index at 12 o'clock):

1. Cam 1: Tapered shape with bright edge: For LEICAFLEX
2. Cam 2: Tapered shape with bright edge: For SL and SL2.
3. Cam 3: Stepped lug with black finish: For LEICA-R.
4. Red index for lens change.
5. Auto-diaphragm coupling.

Versions and compatibility:

Single Cam Lenses: Cam 1 Only: LEICAFLEX only.
Twin Cam Lenses: Cams 1 & 2: LEICAFLEX, SL, SL2.
Triple Cam Lenses: Cams 1, 2 & 3: LEICAFLEX, SL, SL2, LEICA-R.
R Cam Lenses: Cam 3 only: LEICA-R only.

N.B.: Above is a general guide to which there are some exceptions. Please consult your dealer on using them with LEICAFLEX SL or SL2 cameras.

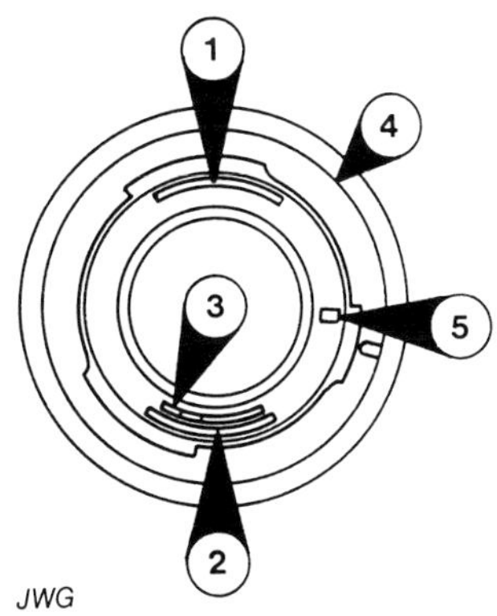

LEICAFLEX SL2 LENSES, 1974

LENS	Speed	Focal length mm	Angle of view	Number of components	Number of elements	Minimum f-stop
FISHEYE-ELMARIT-R	1:2,8	16	180°	11	8	16
SUPER ANGULON-R	1:4	21	92°	10	8	22
ELMARIT-R	1:2,8	24	84°	9	7	22
ELMARIT-R	1:2,8	28	76°	8	8	22
PA-CURTGAON-R	1:4	35	63-78°	7	6	22
ELMARIT-R	1:2,8	35	64°	7	6	22\
SUMMICRON-R	1:2	35	64°	9	7	16
SUMMICRON-R	1:2	50	45°	6	5	16
SUMMILUX-R	1:1,4	50	45°	7	6	16
MACRO-ELMARIT-R	1:2,8	80	39°	6	5	22
ANGENIEUX ZOOM	1:2,8	45-90	54/27°	15	12	22
VARIO ELMAR-R	1:4,5	80-200	12-30°	14	10	22
ELMARIT-R	1:2,8	90	27°	5	4	22
SUMMICRON-R	1:2	90	27°	5	4	16
MACRO ELMAR	1:4	100	25°	4	3	22
ELMARIT-R	1:2,8	135	18°	5	4	22
ELMARIT-R	1:2,8	180	14°	5	4	16
TELYT-R	1:4	250	10°	6	5	22
TELYT-R	1:6,8	400	6°	2	1	32
TELYT-R	1:6,8	560	4,4°	2	1	32
TELYT-S	1:6,3	800	3°	3	1	32
MINOLTA R-ROKKOR	1:8	800	3°	8	7	16 (grey filter)

Filters for LEICA-R Objectives

Size	UVa	Yellow	Yellow-green	Orange	Circular-Pol-Filter	Filter Adapter
E55	13 373	13 236	13 391	13 312	13 357*	
E60	13 381		13 392	13 383	13 376	
E67	13 386		13 993	13 388	13 377	
E77	13 337		13 333	13 332	13 334	
Series 7	13 009	13 006	13 007	13 008	13 370	14 161 (E54) & 14 225 (E55)
Series 8	13 018	13 019	13 021	13 017	13 372	14 165 (E72) 14 264 (E67)
Series VI(6)	13 012	13 013	13 014	13 011		14 160 (E44)
Series 8.5	13 024			13 023		
Series 7.5						14 222 (E59) & 14 263 (E60)
*New Type for ELMARIT-R f/2.8/28mm					13 335	

LEICA SLR Batteries

BATTERY NO.	MAKE	TYPE
D357(10L14)	Duracell	Silver Oxide
EPX 76	Ever Ready	Silver Oxide
KS 76	Kodak	Sllver Oxide
SR 44	Maxell	Silver Oxide
SR 44	National	Silver Oxide
SR 44	Panasonic	Sllver Oxide
357	Philips	Silver Oxide
357	Ray-O-Vac	Silver Oxide
SR 44	Sony	Silver Oxide
EPX 76	UCAR	Sllver Oxide
V76 PX	Varta	Silver Oxide
DL 1/3 N	Duracell	Lithium
K 58L	Kodak	Lithium
CR 1/3 N	Philips	Lithium
2 L76	UCAR	Lithium
CR 1/3 N	Varta	Lithium
PX 625	Mallory	Mercury Oxide

Focusing range m	Smallest object field mm	Viewfinder magnification	Effective measuring base	Filter size series	Length mm	Diameter mm	Weight g	Code No.
∞-0,30	401x601	0,3	0,8	–	60	71	455	11 222
∞-0,20	148x221	0,4	1,4	8/9	43,5	78	445	11 813
∞-0,30	250x374	0,4	1,8	8	46	67	375	11 221
∞-0,30	188x282	0,5	2,4	7	40	63	265	11 204
∞-0,30	140x210	0,6	3,8	8	51	70	300	11 202
∞-0,30	140x210	0,6	3,8	6	40	63	305	11 201
∞-0,30	140x210	0,6	3,8	7	61	68	510	11 227
∞0,50	180x270	0,9	8,4	6	38,5	63	330	11 228
∞-0,50	181x272	0,9	8,4	7	47	67	450	11 875
∞-0,27 with adaptor to 1:1	48x72 (24x36)	1.0	11,0	8	67 (97)	70	375 (540)	11 203
∞-1,00	485x727 216x324	0,8-1,6	8,0/24,9	8	12,2	69	774	on request
∞-1,80	173x252 415x615	1,4-3,5	19,7-123,2	E 55	157	72	710	11 224
∞-0,70	140x210	1,6	24,9	7	72	65	500	11 239
∞-0,70	144x216	1,6	24,9	7	62,5	70	720	11 219
In Foc. Bellows-R: ∞-1:1	24x36	1,7	30,4	7	62,5	66	360	11 230
∞-1,50	220x330	2,3	56,2	7	91	65	680	11 211
∞2,00	213x320	3,1	99,6	8	134	78	1325	11 919
∞-4,50	368x552	4,3	92,4	8	154	78	1380	11 920
∞-3,60	180x240	6,9	493	7	384	78	1800	11 960
∞-6,40	224x336	9,7	966	7	530	98	2300	11 865
∞-12,50	320x480	13,8	1970	7	790	152	6850	11 921
∞-8,00	205x307	13,8	1970	–	166,5	125	1800	through Minolta

Compatibility of Leica-R Lenses with Leica Extenders

Compatible LEICA R-Lenses	With APO-EXTENDER-R 2x	With EXTENDER-R 2x	With APO-EXTENDER-R 1.4x
f/2/50mm	f/4/100mm	f/4/100mm	—
f/2.8/60mm	f/5.6/120mm	f/5.6/120mm	—
f/2/90mm	f/4/180mm	f/4/180mm	—
f/2.8/90mm	f/5.6/180mm	f/5.6/180mm	f/5.6/140mm
f/2.8/100mm APO	f/5.6/200mm APO	f/5.6/200mm	—
f/2.8/135mm	f/5.6/270mm	f/5.6/270mm	—
f/2.8/180mm	f/5.6/360mm	f/5.6/360mm	f/4/250mm
f/3.4/180mm APO	f/6.8/360mm APO	f/6.8/360mm	—
f/4/180mm	f/8/360mm	f/8/360mm	—
f/4/250mm	f/8/500mm	f/8/500mm	—
f/2.8/280mm APO	f/5.6/560mm APO	f/4/400mm	f/4/400mm APO
f/4.8/350mm	f/9.6/700mm	f/9.6/700mm	—
f/2.8/400mm APO	f/5.6/800mm APO	f/5.6/800mm	f/4/560mm APO
f/8/500mm	f/16/1000mm	f/16/1000mm	—
f/6.3/800mm	f/12.6/1600mm	f/12.6/1600mm	f/8.8/1120mm
f/3.5/35-70mm	f/7/70-140mm	f/7/70-140mm	—

LEICAFLEX SL & SL2 Flash Table

<table>
<tr><th colspan="2">ELECTRONIC FLASH</th><th>B→⚡(=1/100)</th><th>⚡ Contact (upper)</th></tr>
<tr><td rowspan="4">Flash bulbs</td><td>M2</td><td>1 → 1/30</td><td></td></tr>
<tr><td>XM 1
PF 1
PF 5</td><td>1 → 1/125</td><td rowspan="3">💡 Contact (lower)</td></tr>
<tr><td>GE 5
25
M 3</td><td>1 → 1/250</td></tr>
<tr><td>AG 1</td><td>1 → 1/250</td></tr>
</table>

The upper contact marked ⚡ is for synchronizing electronic flash units at speeds of up to 1/100 sec (= ⚡ on the speed dial). The lower contact marked 💡 is for synchronizing flashbulbs. The table gives full synchronization data for the most widely used flashbulbs

LEICA R6/R6.2 Flash Table

<table>
<tr><th colspan="2">ELECTRONIC FLASH</th><th>'X'=1/100 1/60-1, B</th></tr>
<tr><td>Flash bulbs</td><td>AG 3B
Flashcubes
PF1 B
XM1 B
M3
PFC 4</td><td>1/30-1, B</td></tr>
</table>

Close-up Accessories

Macro-Adapter-R for LEICA-R lenses

LENS	Distance scale at	Distance in cm object - front lens	Reproduction scale	Object field size in mm
50mm SUMMICRON-R f/2	∞ 0,5	11.6 9,9	1:1,75 1:1,42	42x63 34x51
60mm MACRO-ELMARIT-R f/2.8	∞ 1,2	16 9,7	1:2 1:1	48x72 24x36
90mm ELMARIT-R f/2.8 90mm SUMMICRON-R f/2	∞ 0,7	32 23	1:3 1:2	72x108 90x72
100mm MACRO-ELMAR-R f/4	∞ 0,6	42 25	1:3,3 1:1,6	80x120 39x59
135mm ELMARIT-R f/2.8	∞ 1,5	75 55	1:4,5 1:3	108x162 72x108
180mm ELMARIT-R f/4	∞ 1,8	140 91	1:6 1:3,3	144x216 79x118
180mm APO-TELYT-R f/3.4	∞ 2,5	133 95,6	1:6 1:3,9	144x216 95x142
180mm ELMARIT-R f/2.8	∞ 1,8	124 78,4	1:6 1:3,4	144x216 82x123
250mm TELYT-R f/4	∞ 1,7	256 99,1	1:8,4 1:2,9	202x303 70x105
350mm TELYT-R f/4.8	∞ 3,0	477 178	1:11,6 1:4,1	278x417 97x146

ELPRO Equivalents: Old and New: Object Field: Depth of Field

LEICA-R lens	Old ELPRO	Old product code	New ELPRO	Current product code	Distance scale setting (inches) (mm)	Subject to film (inches) (mm)	Subject to ELPRO (inches) (mm)	Field covered (inches) (mm)	Reproduction ratio	Depth of Field (inches) (mm) f/8	f/11	f/16
50mm SUMMICRON-R f/2	VI a	16 531	1	16 541	∞	19 11/16" 50	16 1/16" 41	7 1/4"x10 7/16" 184x276	1:7.7	1 3/8 31	1 7/8" 43	2 3/4" 63
	VI a	16 531	1	16 541	20" 0.5	12 1/8" 31	8 1/4" 21	3 5/8"x5 7/16" 91x137	1:3.8	25/64" 9	9/16" 12	25/32" 17
	VI b	16 532	2	16 542	∞	11 7/8" 30	8 3/16" 21	3 11/64"x5 9/16" 94x141	1:3.9	13/32" 8	9/16" 11	13/16" 16
	VI b	16 532	2	16 542	20" 0.5	9 1/2" 24	5 9/16" 14	2 7/16"x3 11/16" 62x93	1:2.6	3/16" 4	9/32" 5	3/8" 8
90mm ELMARIT-R f/2.8	VII a	16 533	3	16 543	∞	29 1/16" 74	24 1/16" 61	6 5/16"x9 1/2" 161x241	1:6.7	11/16" 24	1 1/2" 33	2 1/8" 49
	VII a	16 533	3	16 543	28" 0.7	17 7/16" 44	11 13/16" 30	2 7/8"x4 5/16" 73x109	1:3.0	17/64" 6	5/8" 8	17/32" 12
135mm ELMARIT-R f/2.8	VII b	16 534	4	16 544	∞	4'11" 150	4'5 1/4" 135	9 5/16"x14" 237x355	1:9.9	2 1/4" 52	3 1/8" 71	4 1/2" 104
	VII b	16 534	4	16 544	5' 1.5	33 1/2" 84	27 3/16" 68	4 1/4"x6 3/8" 107x160	1:4.5	17/32" 12	23/32" 17	1 1/16" 25
	VII a	16 533	3	16 543	∞	29 13/16" 76	24 1/16" 61	4 1/4"x6 3/8" 107x160	1:4.5	17/32" 10	23/32" 15	1 1/16" 21
	VII a	16 533	3	16 543	5' 1.5	23 1/8" 58	16 13/16" 42	2 5/8"x3 15/16" 66x99	1:2.8	17/32" 5	5/16" 7	7/16" 10

Focusing data is given for ∞ and the shortest **engraved** distance setting of the LEICA-R lenses. Since the lenses can slightly exceed these engraved settings, somewhat higher reproduction ratios can be obtained than are shown in this table. All figures are approximate, having been rounded off for convenience.

ELPRO lenses VIa (Catalog No. 16 531) and VIb (No. 16 532) were computed **exclusively** for use with the 50mm SUMMICRON-R f/2 lens, and provide critical corner-to-corner close-up quality, even at medium lens apertures.

ELPRO lens VIIa (No. 16 533) was computed to match the correction of the 90- and 135mm ELMARIT-R f/2.8 lenses. The ELPRO VIIb (No. 16 534) is intended only for use with the 135mm ELMARIT-R f/2.8 lens.

Close-up Accessories

Three-part Ring Combination for Leica-R Lenses

LENS	Ring combination						
	2-part (length 25mm) 14158				3-part (length 50mm) 14159		
	Distance scale at	Distance in cm object - front lens	Reproduction scale	Object field size in mm	Distance in cm object front lens	Reproduction scale	Object field size in mm
50mm SUMMICRON-R f/2	∞ 0,5	13.,5 11.2	1:2.1 1:1.6	50x75 38x58	8.1 7.5	1:1.04 1.09:1	25x37 22x33
90mm ELMARIT-R f/2.8 90mm SUMMICRON-R f/2	∞ 0,7	37,6 25.2	1:3.6 1:2.2	86x130 53x79	21.4 17.6	1:1.8 1:1.4	43x65 34x50
135mm ELMARIT-R f/2.8	∞ 1,5	87.2 59.7	1:5.4 1:3.4	130x195 81x121	50.7 42.3	1:2.7 1:2.1	65x97 50x75
180mm ELMARIT-R f/4	∞ 1,8	161 97.2	1:7.2 1:3.6	172x258 87x130	96.6 75.4	1:3.6 1:2.4	86x129 58x87
180mm APO-TELYT-R f/3.4	∞ 2,5	154 104	1:7.2 1:4.4	172x258 106x159	89.4 74.0	1:3.6 1:2.7	86x129 66x99
180mm ELMARIT-R f/2.8	∞ 1,8	146 84.9	1:7.2 1:3.8	172x258 91x137	81.2 61.3	1:3.6 1:2.5	86x129 60x90
250mm TELYT-R f/4	∞ 1,7	299 104	1:10.1 1:3.2	242x363 76x114	172 85.8	1:5.0 1:2.3	121x181 55x82
350mm TELYT-R f/4.8	∞ 3,0	558 187	1:13.9 1:4.4	334x501 105x157	316 153	1:7.0 1:3.2	167x250 76x114

APPENDIX 2

Depth of Field Tables

The following depth of field tables have been included for your information and are reproduced by courtesy of Leica Camera GmbH

Depth-of-field table for 21mm lenses

f/stop \ Distance Setting, m	0.2	0.25	0.30	0.35	0.4	0.45	0.5	0.6	0.7	0.8	1	1.2	1.5	2	3	5	∞
2,8	0,196 0,204	0,243 0,258	0,29 0,31	0,33 0,37	0,38 0,43	0,41 0,49	0,46 0,55	0,54 0,67	0,62 0,80	0,70 0,94	0,84 1,24	0,98 1,57	1,16 2,14	1,43 3,36	1,87 7,91	2,46 ∞	4,74 ∞
3,4	0,20 0,21	0,24 0,26	0,29 0,32	0,33 0,37	0,37 0,43	0,42 0,49	0,46 0,55	0,54 0,68	0,61 0,82	0,69 0,96	0,82 1,28	0,95 1,63	1,13 2,26	1,38 3,69	1,78 10,00	2,31 ∞	4.24 ∞
4	0,19 0,21	0,24 0,26	0,28 0,32	0,33 0,38	0,37 0,44	0,41 0,50	0,45 0,56	0,53 0,70	0,60 0,84	0,67 1,00	0,80 1,34	0,92 1,75	1,08 2,49	1,31 4,35	1,66 17,20	2,12 ∞	3,61 ∞
5,6	0,19 0,21	0,24 0,27	0,28 0,33	0,32 0,39	0,36 0,45	0,40 0,52	0,43 0,59	0,50 0,75	0,57 0,92	0,63 1,11	0,74 1,56	0,84 2,14	0,97 3,41	1,15 8,34	1,41 ∞	1,72 ∞	2,60 ∞
8	0,19 0,21	0,23 0,27	0,27 0,34	0,31 0,41	0,34 0,48	0,38 0,56	0,41 0,65	0,47 0,84	0,53 1,07	0,58 1,34	0,67 2,07	0,75 3,26	0,85 7,70	0,98 ∞	1,16 ∞	1,35 ∞	1,84 ∞
11	0,19 0,22	0,22 0.28	0,26 0,36	0,29 0,44	0,33 0,53	0,36 0,62	0,38 0,73	0,44 1,00	0,48 1,34	0,52 1,81	0,60 3,53	0,66 9,74	0,73 ∞	0,82 ∞	0,94 ∞	1,07 ∞	1,35 ∞
16	0,18 0,23	0,21 0,30	0,25 0,39	0,28 0,50	0,30 0,62	0,33 0,76	0,35 0,94	0,39 1,45	0,43 2,36	0,46 4,49	0,51 ∞	0,55 ∞	0,60 ∞	0,66 ∞	0,73 ∞	0,80 ∞	0,95 ∞
22	0,17 0,24	0,20 0,33	0,23 0,45	0,26 0,59	0,28 0,79	0,30 1,05	0,32 1,45	0,35 3,33	0,37 45,90	0,40 ∞	0,43 ∞	0,46 ∞	0,49 ∞	0,53 ∞	0,57 ∞	0,61 ∞	0,71 ∞

Depth-of-field table for 28mm lenses

f/stop \ Distance Setting, m	0,3	0,35	0,4	0,45	0,5	0,6	0,7	0,8	0,9	1	1,2	1,5	2	3	5	10	∞
2,8	0,29 0,31	0,34 0,36	0,39 0,41	0,43 0,47	0,48 0,52	0,57 0,64	0,65 0,76	0,74 0,88	0,82 1,00	0,90 1,12	1,06 1,38	1,30 1,80	1,60 2,60	2,20 4,60	3,20 12,10	4,60 ∞	8.40 ∞
4	0,29 0,31	0,34 0,37	0,38 0,42	0,43 0,48	0,47 0,53	0,56 0,65	0,63 0,78	0,71 0,91	0,79 1,05	0,87 1,19	1,01 1,48	1,20 2,00	1,50 3,00	2,00 6,00	2,70 31,30	3,70 ∞	5,90 ∞
5,6	0,29 0,31	0,33 0,37	0,38 0,43	0,42 0,49	0,46 0,55	0,54 0,68	0,61 0,82	0,68 0,97	0,75 1,12	0,82 1,28	0,95 1,64	1,10 2,30	1,40 3,70	1,80 10,00	2,30 ∞	3,00 ∞	4,20 ∞
8	0,28 0,32	0,33 0,38	0,37 0,44	0,41 0,51	0,44 0,58	0,52 0,72	0,58 0,89	0,64 1,06	0,71 1,25	0,76 1,46	0,87 1,95	1,00 2,90	1,20 5,80	1,50 ∞	1,90 ∞	2,30 5	3.00 ∞
11	0,28 0,33	0,32 0,39	0,35 0,46	0,39 0,53	0,43 0,61	0,49 0,78	0,54 0,99	0,60 1,21	0,65 1,47	0,70 1,77	0,79 2,50	0,91 4,60	1,06 21,70	1,30 ∞	1,50 ∞	1,80 ∞	2,20 ∞
16	0,27 0,34	0,30 0,42	0,34 0,50	0,379 0,595	0,40 0,68	0,46 0,90	0,50 1,22	0,54 1,59	0,58 2,08	0,62 2,74	0,69 5,30	0,77 83,00	0,88 ∞	1,02 ∞	1,17 ∞	1,30 ∞	1,50 ∞
22	0,26 0,37	0,29 0,45	0,32 0,55	0,35 0,66	0,37 0,79	0,42 1,12	0,45 1,72	0,48 2,57	0,52 4,17	0,54 8,34	0,59 ∞	0,65 ∞	0,73 ∞	0,82 ∞	0,91 ∞	1,00 ∞	1,10 ∞

Depth-of-field table for 35mm lenses

f/stop	Distance Setting, m	0,3	0,35	0,4	0,45	0,5	0,6	0,7	0,8	0,9	1	1,2	1,5	2	3	5	10	∞
	1,4	0,298	0,347	0,396	0,444	0,493	0,59	0,68	0,78	0,87	0,97	1,15	1,42	1,87	2,70	4,20	7,30	26,30
		0,302	0,353	0,405	0,456	0,508	0,61	0,72	0,82	0,93	1,04	1,25	1,58	2,16	3,37	6,10	16,00	∞
	2	0,297	0,345	0,394	0,442	0,489	0,58	0,68	0,77	0,86	0,95	1,13	1,39	1,81	2,60	3,90	6,50	18,40
		0,303	0,355	0,407	0,459	0,511	0,62	0,72	0,83	0,94	1,05	1,28	1,62	2,23	3,60	6,80	21,70	∞
	2,8	0,295	0,343	0,391	0,438	0,485	0,58	0,67	0,76	0,85	0,94	1,11	1,36	1,75	2,50	3,60	5,70	13,20
		0,305	0,357	0,409	0,462	0,516	0,62	0,73	0,84	0,96	1,07	1,31	1,68	2,34	3,90	8,00	41,00	∞
	4	0,294	0,34	0,39	0,43	0,48	0,57	0,66	0,74	0,83	0,91	1,07	1,30	1,66	2,30	3,30	4,80	9,20
		0,307	0,36	0,41	0,47	0,52	0,64	0,75	0,87	0,99	1,11	1,36	1,77	2,52	4,40	10,70	∞	∞
	5,6	0,29	0,34	0,38	0,43	0,47	0,56	0,64	0,72	0,80	0,88	1,03	1,24	1,55	2,10	2,90	4,00	6,60
		0,31	0,36	0,42	0,48	0,53	0,65	0,77	0,90	1,03	1,16	1,44	1,91	2,82	5,40	20,00	∞	∞
	8	0,29	0,33	0,38	0,42	0,46	0,54	0,62	0,70	0,77	0,84	0,97	1,15	1,42	1,80	2,40	3,20	4,60
		0,31	0,37	0,43	0,49	0,55	0,67	0,81	0,94	1,09	1,25	1,58	2,16	3,42	8,20	∞	∞	∞
	11	0,28	0,33	0,37	0,41	0,45	0,52	0,59	0,66	0,73	0,79	0,91	1,06	1,28	1,60	2,00	2,50	3,40
		0,32	0,38	0,44	0,50	0,57	0,71	0,85	1,01	1,19	1,37	1,80	2,60	4,70	24,10	∞	∞	5
	16	0,28	0,32	0,35	0,39	0,43	0,49	0,56	0,62	0,67	0,72	0,82	0,94	1,10	1,30	1,60	1,90	2,30
		0,33	0,39	0,46	0,53	0,61	0,77	0,95	1,16	1,39	1,66	2,33	3,90	12,30	∞	∞	∞	∞
	22	0,27	0,31	0,34	0,37	0,41	0,46	0,52	0,57	0,61	0,65	0,73	0,82	0,95	1,10	1,30	1,50	1,70
		0,34	0,41	0,49	0,57	0,66	0,86	1,10	1,39	1,75	2,21	3,60	10,20	∞	∞	∞	∞	

Depth-of-field table for 50mm lenses

f/stop	Distance Setting, m	0,5	0,6	0,7	0,8	0,9	1	1,2	1,5	2	3	5	10	∞
	1	0,498	0,597	0,695	0,794	0,892	0,99	1,18	1,48	1,96	2,90	4,72	8,92	81,17
		0,502	0,603	0,705	0,807	0,908	1,01	1,22	1,53	2,05	3,11	5,32	11,38	∞
	1,2	0,497	0,596	0,694	0,79	0,89	0,99	1,18	1,47	1,95	2,88	4,67	8,70	67.70
		0,503	0,604	0,706	0,81	0,91	1,01	1,22	1,53	2,06	3,13	5,39	11,70	∞
	1,4	0,497	0,595	0,69	0,79	0,89	0,99	1,18	1,47	1,94	2,86	4,61	8,50	58,00
		0,503	0,605	0,71	0,81	0,91	1,01	1,22	1,54	2,07	3,16	5,46	12,00	∞
	2	0,496	0,593	0,69	0,79	0,88	0,98	1,17	1,45	1,91	2,80	4,47	8.00	40,60
		0,504	0,607	0,71	0,81	0,92	1,02	1,23	1,55	2,10	3,23	5,68	13,20	∞
	2,8	0,494	0,591	0,69	0,78	0,88	0,97	1,16	1,43	1,88	2,70	4,30	7,50	29.00
		0,506	0,610	0,71	0,82	0,92	1,03	1,25	1,57	2,14	3,30	6,00	15,20	∞
	4	0,491	0,587	0,68	0,78	0,87	0,96	1,14	1,41	1,83	2,60	4,00	6,70	20,30
		0,509	0,614	0,72	0,83	0,93	1,06	1,27	1,61	2,20	3,50	6,60	19,50	∞
	5,6	0,488	0,582	0,67	0,77	0,86	0,94	1,12	1,37	1,80	2,50	3,80	6,00	14,50
		0,513	0,619	0,73	0,84	0,95	1,04	1,29	1,65	2,30	3,70	7,50	31,40	∞
	8	0,483	0,574	0,66	0,75	0,84	0,92	1,09	1,32	1,70	2,30	3,40	5,10	10,10
		0,518	0,628	0,74	0,86	0,97	1,09	1,34	1,73	2,40	4,20	9,60	∞	∞
	11	0,477	0,566	0,65	0,74	0,82	0,90	1,05	1,27	1,60	2,20	3,00	4,30	7,40
		0,525	0,640	0.76	0,88	1,00	1,13	1,40	1,84	2,70	4,90	14,80	∞	∞
	16	0,468	0,551	0,63	0,71	0,78	0,86	1,00	1,19	1,50	1,90	2,60	3,40	5,10
		0,538	0,659	0,79	0,92	1,06	1,20	1,52	2,05	3,20	6,90	144,00	∞	∞
	22	0,457	0,535	0,61	0,68	0,75	0,81	0,94	1,10	1,30	1,70	2,20	2,80	3,70
		0,554	0,685	0,82	0,97	1,13	1,30	1,69	2,38	4,10	13,80	∞	∞	∞

Depth-of-field table for the 60mm MACRO-ELMARIT-R f/2.8

f-STOP		2.8	4	5,6	8	11	16
DIST. SETTING	REPRO SCALE						
0.236	**1:1**	0,236 0,237	0,236 0.237	0,236 0.237	0,236 0.237	0,236 0.237	0,235 0.237
0.239	**1:1,25**	0,239 0,240	0,239 0.240	0,239 0,240	0,239 0,240	0,238 0,240	0.238 0,241
0.246	**1:1,5**	0,246 0,247	0,246 0,247	0,245 0,247	0,246 0,248	0,245 0,248	0,245 0,249
0.258	**1:1,75**	0,256 0,257	0,256 0,257	0,255 0,257	0,255 0,257	0,254 0,258	0,254 0,259
0.267	**1:2**	0,267 0,268	0,266 0,268	0,266 0,268	0,266 0,269	0,265 0,269	0,264 0,270
0.291	**1:2,5**	0,291 0,293	0,291 0,293	0,290 0,293	0,289 0,294	0,289 0,295	0,257 0,297
0.3		0,299 0,301	0,299 0,301	0,298 0,302	0,297 0,303	0,297 0,304	0,295 0,305
0.32	**1:3**	0,317 0,319	0,316 0,320	0,316 0,320	0,315 0,321	0,314 0,323	0,312 0,325
0.35		0,349 0,352	0,348 0,352	0,347 0,353	0,346 0,354	0,344 0,356	0,342 0,359
0.38	**1:4**	0,373 0,377	0,372 0,378	0,371 0,379	0,370 0,380	0,368 0,383	0,365 0,386
0.4		0,398 0,402	0,397 0,403	0,396 0,405	0,394 0,407	0,391 0,409	0,388 0,413
0.43	**1:5**	0,430 0,436	0,429 0,437	0,428 0,439	0,425 0,441	0,422 0,444	0,418 0,450
0.5		0,496 0.504	0,494 0,506	0,492 0,508	0,489 0,512	0,485 0,517	0,476 0,525
0.6		0,594 0,607	0,591 0,609	0,588 0,613	0,582 0,619	0,576 0,626	0,566 0,639
0.73	**1:10**	0,724 0,744	0,720 0,749	0,714 0,755	0,706 0,765	0,695 0,777	0,680 0,798
1		0,98 1,02	0,97 1,03	0,96 1.04	0,94 1,06	0.93 1,09	0,90 1,13
1.2		1,17 1,23	1,16 1,25	1,14 1,26	1,12 1,29	1,09 1,33	1,05 1,41
1.5		1,45 1,55	1,43 1,57	1,41 1,61	1,37 1,66	1,33 1,72	1,26 1,85
2.0		1,91 2,09	1,88 2,14	1,83 2,20	1,77 2,30	1,70 2,44	1,59 2,70
3.0		2,80 3,23	2,73 3,33	2,63 3,49	2.50 3,75	2,36 4,14	2,15 5,02
5.0		4,47 5.68	4,27 6,03	4,04 6,57	3,73 7.60	3,41 9,45	2,98 15,96
∞		40,58 ∞	28,42 ∞	20,31 ∞	14.24 ∞	10,37 ∞	7,14 ∞

Depth-of-field table for 75mm lenses

f/stop	Distance Setting, m: 1	1,1	1,2	1,3	1,5	1,7	2	2,5	3	4	5	7	10	20	∞
1,4	0,993 1,006	1,092 0,108	1,190 1,210	1,288 1,312	1,48 1,52	1,68 1,72	1,97 2,03	2,45 2,55	2,93 3,07	3,88 4,13	4,80 5,21	6,62 7,42	9,24 10,90	17,15 23,99	119,23 ∞
2	0,990 1,010	1,088 1,112	1,186 1,214	1,283 1,317	1,47 1,52	1,67 1,73	1,96 2,04	2,43 2,57	2,90 3,10	3,83 4,19	4,73 5,30	6,48 7,62	8,96 11,32	16,20 26,16	84,32 ∞
2,8	0,987 1,014	1,084 1,117	1,180 1,221	1,276 1,325	1,47 1,53	1,66 1,74	1,94 2,06	2,41 2,60	2,87 3,15	3,76 4,27	4,63 5,44	6,28 7,90	8,59 11,97	15,01 29,97	59,64 ∞
4	0,981 1,019	1,077 1,124	1,172 1,229	1,267 1,335	1,46 1,76	1,64 1,76	1,92 2,09	2,37 2,64	2,81 3,21	3,67 4,40	4,49 5,64	6,03 8,35	8,11 13,04	13,61 37,79	42,19 ∞
5,6	0,974 1,028	1,068 1,134	1,161 1,242	1,254 1,350	1,44 1,57	1,62 1,79	1,89 2,13	2,32 2,71	2,74 3,31	3,55 4,59	4,31 5,96	5,70 9,08	7,53 14,92	12,02 59,90	29,85 ∞
8	0,964 1,040	1,055 1,149	1,146 1,260	1,236 1,372	1,41 1,60	1,59 1,83	1,84 2,19	2,25 2,81	2,65 3,46	3,39 4,88	4,07 6,48	5,29 10,35	6,83 18,75	10,32 349,60	21,13 ∞
11	0,949 1,057	1,038 1,171	1,125 1,287	1,211 1,404	1,38 1,64	1,54 1,89	1,78 2,28	2,17 2,96	2,53 3,70	3,19 5,38	3,78 7,39	4,81 12,93	6,04 29,48	8,61 ∞	15,32 ∞
16	0,930 1,083	1,014 1,204	1,096 1,327	1,178 1,453	1,34 1,71	1,49 1,98	1,71 2,42	2,05 3,20	2,37 4,10	2,94 6,28	3,44 9,24	4,26 19,98	5,19 156,53	6,97 ∞	10,59 ∞
22	0,904 1,121	0,982 1,253	1,059 1,388	1,134 1,528	1,28 1,82	1,42 2,13	1,61 2,65	1,91 3,63	2,18 4,83	2,66 8,24	3,05 14,29	3,67 88,51	4,34 ∞	5,50 ∞	7,51 ∞

Depth-of-field table for 90mm lenses

f/stop	Distance Setting, m: 0,7	0,8	0,9	1	1,1	1,2	1,3	1,5	1,7	2	2,5	3	4	5	7	10	20	∞
2	0,698 0,703	0,797 0,804	0,895 0,905	0,99 1,01	1,09 1,11	1,19 1,21	1,29 1,31	1,48 1,52	1,68 1,72	1,97 2,03	2,45 2,55	2,93 3,07	3,88 4,13	4,81 5,20	6,63 7,41	9,30 10,90	17,20 23,90	121,60 ∞
2,8	0,697 0,704	0,795 0,805	0,894 0,907	0,99 1,01	1,09 1,11	1,19 1,21	1,28 1,32	1,48 1,52	1,67 1,73	1,96 2,04	2,44 2,57	2,91 3,10	3,84 4,18	4,74 5,29	6,50 7,59	9,00 11,30	16,30 25,90	86,90 ∞
4	0,695 0,705	0,793 0,807	0,89 0,91	0,99 1,01	1,08 1,12	1,18 1,22	1,28 1,32	1,47 1,53	1,66 1,74	1,94 2,06	2,41 2,60	2,87 3,14	3,77 4,26	4,64 5,42	6,30 7,90	8.60 11,90	15,10 29,60	60,80 ∞
5,6	0,69 0,71	0,79 0,81	0,89 0,91	0,98 1,02	1,08 1,12	1,17 1,23	1,27 1,33	1,46 1,54	1,65 1,76	1,92 2,08	2,38 2,64	2,82 3,20	3,68 4,38	4,51 5,61	6,10 8,30	8,20 12,90	13,80 36,70	43.40 ∞
8	0,69 0,71	0,79 0,81	0,88 0,92	0,98 1,03	1,07 1,13	1,16 1,29	1,26 1,35	1,44 1,56	1,62 1,78	1,89 2,12	2,33 2,70	2,75 3,30	3,56 4,56	4,33 5,93	5,70 9,00	7,60 14,70	12,10 57,40	30,40 ∞
11	0,69 0,71	0,78 0,82	0,87 0,93	0,97 1,04	1,06 1,14	1,15 1,25	1,24 1,36	1,42 1,59	1,60 1,82	1,85 2,17	2,27 2,78	2,67 3,43	3,42 4,82	4,10 6,40	5,40 10,10	7,00 17,90	10,60 194,00	22,10 ∞
16	0,68 0,72	0,77 0,83	0,86 0,94	0,95 1,05	1,04 1,17	1,13 1,28	1,22 1,40	1,39 1,63	1,55 1,88	1,80 2,26	2,18 2,93	2,54 3,66	3,21 5,31	3,80 7,30	4,90 12,60	6,10 28,10	8,70 ∞	15,20 ∞
22	0,67 0,73	0,76 0,84	0,85 0,96	0,94 1,07	1,02 1,19	1,11 1,31	1,19 1,44	1,35 1,69	1,51 1,96	1,73 2,38	2,08 3,14	2,40 4,00	3,00 6,10	3,50 8,80	4,40 18,20	5,30 89,40	7,20 ∞	11,00 ∞
32	0,66 0,74	0,75 0,86	0,83 0,98	0,91 1,11	0,99 1,24	1,07 1,37	1,14 1,51	1,29 1,80	1,43 2,10	1,63 2,60	1,94 3,56	2,20 4,70	2,70 8,00	3,10 13,50	3,70 67,90	4,40 ∞	5,60 ∞	7,70 ∞

Depth-of-field table for the 100mm MACRO-ELMAR f/4

	1,0	0,9	0,8	0,7	0,6	0,5	0,4	0,3	0,2		0,1	Reproduction scale								
Dist. set	0,4	0,4	0,41	0,42	043	0,45	0,49	0,57	0,72	1	1,21	2	3	4	5	10	20	50	100	∞
f4	0,4028 0,4033	0,4038 0,4044	0,4076 0,4084	0,415 0,416	0,429 0,430	0,452 0,454	0,492 0,494	0,564 0,588	0,718 0,727	0,99 1,01	1,20 1,22	1,96 2,05	2,90 3,11	3,81 4,21	4,71 5,34	8,85 11,49	15,83 27.17	30,05 149.56	42.89 ∞	74.88 ∞
f5.6	0.4026 0,4034	0,4037 0,4046	0,4075 0,4085	0,415 0,417	0,428 0,431	0,452 0,454	0,491 0,495	0,563 0,589	0,717 0,728	0,99 1,01	1,19 1,23	1,94 2,07	2,85 3,16	3,74 4,30	4,60 5,48	8,47 12,22	14,62 31,72	25,92 740,50	34.92 ∞	53.50 ∞
f8	0,4025 0,4036	0,4035 0,4048	0,4073 0,4088	0,415 0,417	0,429 0,431	0,451 0,455	0,491 0,495	0,562 0,570	0,715 0,731	0,98 1,02	1,18 1,24	1,91 2,10	2,80 3,23	3,64 4,44	4,44 5,72	7,95 13,51	13,11 42,40	21,50 ∞	27.32 ∞	37.48 ∞
f11	0,4023 0,4038	0,4033 0,4050	0,4070 0,4090	0,415 0,417	0,428 0,431	0,451 0,455	0,490 0,496	0,561 0,571	0,712 0,734	0,98 1,02	1,17 1,25	1,88 2,13	2,73 3,33	3,52 4,63	4,27 6,05	7,38 15,57	11,62 73,32	17,72 ∞	21.49 ∞	27.29 ∞
f16	0,4020 0,4041	0,4029 0,4054	0,4065 0,4095	0,414 0,418	0,427 0,432	0,450 0,458	0,488 0,498	0,559 0,574	0,707 0,739	0,96 1,04	1,16 1,27	1,83 2,20	2,62 3,51	3,34 4,98	4,00 6,69	6,60 20,90	9,77 ∞	13,72 ∞	15.86 ∞	18.79 ∞
f22	0,4016 0,4045	0,4024 0,4059	0,4060 0,4101	0,413 0,418	0,426 0,433	0,449 0,457	0,487 0,499	0,556 0,577	0,701 0,745	0,95 1,05	1,14 1,30	1,78 2,29	2,51 3,75	3,15 5,51	3,72 7,87	5,85 35.54	8,20 ∞	10,80 ∞	12,08 ∞	13,69 ∞

Depth-of-field table for 135mm lenses

Distance Setting, m		1,5	1,7	2	2,5	3	4	5	7	10	20	50	∞
f/stop	2,8	1,49 1,51	1,69 1,71	1,98 2,02	2,47 2,53	2,96 3,04	3,93 4,08	4,88 5,12	6,77 7,25	9,50 10,50	18,20 22,20	39,90 67,00	195,40 ∞
	4	1,49 1,51	1,68 1,72	1,98 2,02	2,46 2,54	2,94 3,06	3,90 4,11	4,84 5,17	6,70 7,40	9,30 10,80	17,50 23,40	36,70 78,50	136,80 ∞
	5,6	1,48 1,52	1,68 1,72	1,97 2,03	2,45 2,56	2,92 3,08	3,86 4,15	4,78 5,25	6,60 7,50	9,10 11,10	16,70 25,00	33,20 101,80	97,60 ∞
	8	1,48 1,53	1,67 1,73	1,95 2,05	2,43 2,58	2,89 3,12	3,80 4,22	4,69 5,36	6,40 7,70	8,80 11,60	15,50 28,10	29,00 183,20	68,30 ∞
	11	1,47 1,53	1,66 1,75	1,94 2,07	2,40 2,61	2,85 3,17	3,73 4,31	4,60 5,50	6,20 8,10	8,40 12,40	14,40 33,10	25,10 ∞	49,70 ∞
	16	1,45 1,55	1,64 1,77	1,91 2,10	2,36 2,67	2,79 3,25	3,60 4,50	4,40 5,80	5,90 8,70	7,80 13,90	12,70 47,10	20,40 ∞	34,20 ∞
	22	1,44 1,57	1,61 1,80	1,88 2,14	2,31 2,73	2,70 3,40	3,50 4,70	4,20 6,10	5,50 9,50	7,20 16,30	11,20 96,50	16,80 ∞	24,90 ∞
	32	1,41 1,61	1,58 1,84	1,83 2,21	2,23 2,86	2,60 3,50	3,30 5,10	3,90 6,90	5,10 11,50	6,40 23,00	9,40 ∞	12,90 ∞	17,20 ∞

The upper figures indicate the object-to-film distance engraved on the relevant lens. The associated depth-of-field range is indicated in the groups.

Example: Distance = 3m

At f/4 Depth-of-field between 2,60 / 3,50

The tables have been calculated with a circle-of-confusion of 1/30mm, and the figures rounded off.

Bibliography

Benser, Walther; *My Life with the Leica*, Hove Books, 1990.

Bower, Brian; *Leica Reflex Photography*, David & Charles, Newton Abbot, 1991.

Bellone, Roger, and Fellot, Luc; *Histoire Mondiale de La Photographie en Couleurs*, Hachette Realities, Paris, 1981.

Daval, Jean-Luc; *Photography, History of an Art*, Editions d'Art Albert Skira S.A., Geneva, 1982.

Duncan, David Douglas; *Nomad, A Photographic Odyssey*, Paul Hamlyn Ltd, London, 1966: *Goodbye Picasso*, Times Books, London 1974, Grosset & Dunlap Inc., in the USA, 1974: *The Silent Studio*, W.W.Norton & Company, Inc, New York, 1976.

Eastland, Jonathan; *Cityscape Photography*, B.T.Batsford, London, 1985: *Leica-M Compendium*, Hove Books, Hove, England, 1994.

Eisenstaedt, Alfred; *Witness to Our Time*, The Viking Press Inc., New York, 1966, 1967.

Gernsheim, Helmut and Alison, *A Concise History of Photography*, Thames and Hudson, London 1965, 1971.

Hasbroeck, van, Paul-Henry; *Leica – A History Illustrating every Model and Accessory*, Revised edition, Sotheby Publications, London, 1993.

Keller, Emil G.: *The Source of Today's Thirty-Five Millimeter Photography, Part II The Leica Years 1945-80*. Butts Hollow Services, Millbrook, New York, 1989.

Kisselbach, Theo; *Leica-R4 Reflex Manual*, English Edition, Hove Foto Books, Hove, England, 1981.

Lager, James L.; *Leica, Illustrated Guide III. M and Leicaflex Lenses, Special Models and Accessories*, Morgan & Morgan, Dobbs Ferry, New York, 1979.

Laney, Dennis; *Leica Collectors Guide*, Hove Collectors Books, Hove, England, 1992.

Laney, Dennis; *Leica Camera and Lens Pocket Book*, 6th Edition, Hove Collectors Books, Hove, England, 1994.

Nakamura, Shin-ichi; *Leica Collection*, Asahi Sonorama Co Ltd, Tokyo, 1991.

Pfaender, Heinz G.; *Schott Guide to Glass*, Schott Glaswerke, Mainz, Germany.

Rogliatti, Gianni; *Leica, The First Sixty Years*, Hove Collectors Books, Hove, England, 1985.

Rotolini, Robert; *Nikon Rangefnder Camera*, Second edition. Hove Collectors Books, Hove, England, 1983.

Thesiger, Wilfred; *Visions of a Nomad*, Harper Collins Publishers, London, 1993.

The Best of Life, Time Inc., 1973.

MAGAZINES and TECHNICAL DOCUMENTS

ERNST LEITZ WETZLAR GMBH; Various technical documents, printed literature and General Catalogues published by that company pertaining to all products.

Leica Fotografie International; Various issues, Umschau Verlag, Frankfurt am Main.

Leica Photographic Bulletin, Various issues, published by Leica UK Ltd.

LEICA CAMERA GMBH SOLMS; Various technical documents and printed literature published by that company pertaining to all products.

Modern Photography, December 1975 issue (for Leicaflex SL2 details), ABC Leisure Magazines, New York.

Wilfred Thesiger's Photographs 'A Most Cherished Possession'; Exhibition catalogue published by Pitt Rivers Museum, University of Oxford, England, 1993.

CARL ZEISS, Oberkochen, Germany. Technical documents C10-48-41e, etc.,

Index

Page numbers in bold refer to a main entry with a full description of the camera or lens concerned.

Page numbers in italics refer to illustrations.

M